Contemporary English
in the
Elementary School

PRENTICE-HALL INTERNATIONAL, INC., *London*
PRENTICE-HALL OF AUSTRALIA, PTY. LTD., *Sydney*
PRENTICE-HALL OF CANADA, LTD., *Toronto*
PRENTICE-HALL OF INDIA PRIVATE LTD., *New Delhi*
PRENTICE-HALL OF JAPAN, INC., *Tokyo*

Contemporary English in the Elementary School

Iris M. Tiedt / *Sidney W. Tiedt*
San Jose State College

PRENTICE-HALL, INC., ENGLEWOOD CLIFFS, NEW JERSEY

We dedicate this book to the children.

To the Reader

"Thurber did not write the way a surgeon operates, he wrote the way a child skips rope, the way a mouse waltzes. . . ." Those of you who have read the whimsical writings of James Thurber can appreciate this comment made by another imaginative lover of language, E. B. White, author of *Charlotte's Web*.

It is this feeling for language, delight in words, enthusiasm for literature that we have tried to project throughout *Contemporary English in the Elementary School*, for we are concerned with projecting this love of language to elementary school children everywhere, and it is through you that we hope to achieve our purpose.

This is a methods book; it is a book of strategies and ideas. Our own experience has shown us that successful teaching is directly related to knowledge of content combined with effective teaching strategies. This book focuses on YOU in the pedagogical encounter, YOU in the classroom with sixty eyes and ears waiting to see what you will do. What these children think of English will depend on what YOU think of English, for one of the most important aspects of your style of teaching is your attitude, your enthusiasm for learning and for helping children learn.

The teacher needs methods and techniques, just as a doctor, lawyer, painter, draftsman do. They spend their life-times studying and perfecting techniques and so must the teacher. Which techniques shall we select? Only the best, the most simulating, the most effective will suffice. Therefore, let us reach out for strategies that "waltz" or even "swing." It is toward this end that we have stressed imaginative, creative approaches to English which may assist you in creating a *new image* for the study of English as exciting, provocative, and fun.

We have not written the "last word" on teaching English in the elementary school, for we continue to conceive of new approaches and we find ourselves learning from our students just as you will be doing. The study of the English language in all its rich detail is a vast, many-faceted topic to explore. It is our hope that we will expose you to some of the fascinating aspects of this study and suggest possibilities for transmitting these concepts to young students. We also hope that we will sufficiently interest you in the study of the English language and literature so that you will begin probing the outer limits and the innermost reaches of this ever growing field of knowledge.

We should like to express our sincere appreciation to those elementary school teachers and students with whom we have been learning, for their interests and their needs inspired the writing of this book. Our appreciation goes also to those authors and publishers who granted permission to reproduce illustrative materials which have assisted us in attaining our goals.

Iris M. Tiedt
Sidney W. Tiedt

Contents

> It is the supreme art of the teacher to awaken
> joy in creative expression and knowledge.
>
> *Albert Einstein*

1

English in the Curriculum

Do you remember the day when you first made sounds resembling human language? Of course, you don't, because this momentous event occurred when you were still a baby. You were struggling to talk, to imitate the human speech you heard around you. Now you speak so easily that it is difficult to imagine yourself without the ability to speak, to communicate with other human beings. Speech is so much a part of us that we tend to take this ability for granted.

In the same way we take the English language for granted, too. The words come as we need them, and when we say them, with miraculously little effort on our part, they come out in coherent sentences. It is not until we find ourselves in an English class that we stop to take a look at this language which we have been using so freely. There is much that we know about English, for we are experienced in its usage, but on the other hand, there is much we can discover, for the subject is rich and enriching.

By almost any criteria used the study of English is the most important subject included in the elementary school curriculum. Elementary schools from their humblest beginnings were basically language schools. In our early colonial days the schools developed primarily as reading and writing schools which utilized the famous Hornbook and the Blueback Spellers as texts.

Not only historically has English been prominent, however, for it continues in importance in spite of the rise of newer curricular areas such as science and mathematics. More classroom time is spent on English than on any other single subject. In California the importance of English is codified in state law which reads: "Instruction is required [in the areas of English] for a minimum of 50% of each week in grades 1 to 6." [1]

There is good reason for this emphasis on language study, for it is ability to use a language which has lifted man above all other animals. As Charlton Laird phrased it, man is a *"languagized* animal." In spite of our numerous problems of communication, language remains an amazing achievement the origin of which will probably never be known. It is impossible for us to imagine a world without language. Consider for a moment how our lives would differ if there were no human language. The fish is the last to know the sea, it is said, and this analogy may be extended to include students and their language, for although we use our language daily, we don't really know much about it.

Another factor making the study of English increasingly important to us is the tremendous growth of communication in the modern world. Communication has increased in many ways—in terms of time spent communicating, expense, volume, and economic significance. We live in a verbal world, one in which language plays an essential role.

In this book we are exploring the teaching of English in the elementary school, for we are concerned that young people know their linguistic heritage and be able to use English to the fullness of its potential according to each student's ability. As we embark on this venture, let us first determine the goals toward which we are working, for as Bertrand Russell states, "Before considering how to educate, it is well to be clear as to the sort of result which we wish to achieve." [2] What are the aims of education in twentieth-century America? What are the specific goals for teaching English? As we conduct our search for the answers to these questions, we shall examine the questions basic to all of education:

> What shall we teach in the English curriculum?
> Why do we teach English?
> Who will teach English?
> How shall we teach English most effectively?

In this chapter we shall specifically investigate the aims of English education and the role of the teacher in achieving these goals.

What Shall We Teach?

"What knowledge is of most worth?" questioned Herbert Spencer, and this is the question which must concern the elementary school teacher.

---

[1] California Education Code; California Administration Code, Title 5. Education 7604 a,b,c.

[2] Bertrand Russell, *Education and the Good Life* (New York: Avon, 1926), p. 31.

How do we determine the content of a curriculum? Theoretically, the "what" that is taught stems from general aims of education, particularly, in this case, in terms of English study. Teachers, supervisors, and specialists in the study of English and English education should be involved in determining what is to be taught.

Do elementary school teachers make curriculum decisions? One elementary school principal stated his belief that teachers are not involved in curriculum decision. This attitude places the teacher in the role of an unthinking technician who merely carries out orders, and for some persons this role would be acceptable; however, the creative teacher who explores new techniques and is aware of the possibilities for teaching English would not consider this type of operation sufficiently challenging. The classroom teacher is making curriculum decisions all the time, although it is seldom obvious. *Shall I teach about the library this term? How can I introduce experimental research in the spelling unit? I think I'll try using the tape recorder to develop listening skills. Perhaps Mrs. Bruce would like to work with me on creative dramatics.* These seemingly inconsequential thoughts determine the English curriculum as it is actually presented in a classroom. Curriculum is more than a list of topics to be covered; curriculum is what actually occurs.

More than two thousand years ago Aristotle said, "All men do not agree on what they would have children learn," and his statement is still valid today. It is enlightening to know the thinking of groups and individuals who are currently influential in the determination of contemporary aims for education. One such group, the Educational Policies Commission, stated in its report of 1961: "The purpose which runs through and strengthens all other educational purposes—the common thread of education—is the development of the ability to think. . . ." The report continues, "No particular body of knowledge will of itself develop the ability to think clearly." The Commission stresses development of the "inquiring spirit" and the ability to "grasp some of the main methods—the strategies of inquiry—by which man has sought to extend his knowledge and understanding of the world." [3]

One of the most influential individuals writing on education today is Jerome Bruner. His answer to the question of what shall be taught is Structure, and he states succinctly: "The curriculum of a subject should be determined by the most fundamental understanding that can be achieved of the underlying principles that give structure to that subject." [4]

There is a need for fresh statements of objectives which will direct

[3] Educational Policies Commission, *The Central Purpose of American Education* (Washington, D.C.: National Education Assn., 1961), pp. 12-19.
[4] Jerome Bruner, *The Process of Education* (Cambridge, Mass.: Harvard University Press, 1960), p. 31.

education and assist the development of new curricula. As has been observed, the changing nature of society demands that these objectives be in terms of subject matter that is flexible and can reflect change. It appears, therefore, that objectives must be directed toward process or performance skills. The following general curriculum aims reflect this trend:

1. Focus is placed on the process of learning as we teach, *methods* of inquiry, *techniques* of research, *procedures* for experimentation. The student must focus attention on the *finding* of knowledge rather than the *storing* of knowledge.
2. Education is molded to the individual rather than to the mass. The self-fulfillment of the individual is stressed as each individual is enriched to the extent of his capacity.
3. The curriculum is more selective as fewer areas are taught in greater depth.
4. Abstract concepts, as opposed to specific facts, are stressed as skills of thinking, inquiry, critical analysis and evaluation are taught.

Stated here are only a few guidelines to the elementary school curriculum of today and of the future. Perhaps you, as a teacher of the future, and of future children, would like to probe the developing needs of the educated person in American society. How to live seems to be the basic question. Toward what goals shall we teach in 1975? Will our aims have changed radically during the next 10 years? What about the aims of the elementary school in the twentieth century? The topic is provocative, for teachers in the uncharted future of education will have more to say about what is taught and how it is taught. Students themselves will be more directly involved in this decision.

Why teach English?

It would be easy to list many objectives for the teaching of English, but a long list that covers the academic waterfront is useless. It would be far better to have a few over-all aims for English with specific aims defined for the various areas of the English curriculum.

Why should we concern ourselves with objectives in any curricular area? Why can't we *just teach?* Objectives help clarify and guide our educational destiny and assist us in determining if, and when, we have arrived. They help us decide, too, what content to teach, what concepts to select, and what to stress. Objectives are needed more desperately in elementary school English than in other curriculum areas because of the tendency to include everything in the English program. J. N. Hook tells, for example, of a professor who made a study of the aims of teaching English 25 years ago and found a total of 1,481 aims ranging from improving character to teaching the evils of alcohol.

Toward what goals shall we teach? We would like to suggest the following general aims for the elementary school English program:

1. To understand the English language and how it works.
2. To communicate fluently and clearly in written and oral forms.
3. To decode and encode English easily.
4. To know and appreciate our literary heritage of prose and poetry.

What is English?

The elementary school English program, as it presently exists, defies definition. Graham Wilson approaches the problem of clarifying the structure of English with some doubts, as he says:

> ... Certainly something special is called for to see a concept of over-all structure in English as a discipline in schools and colleges today. To begin with: the structure of what? There is *language*, which may include grammar, philology, anthropology, semantics, and general semantics, psychology, and English as a foreign language: *literature*, which may be English, American, world, and, when the time comes, interplanetary; *composition*, which may include grammar (again), rhetoric, semantics (again), and logic. Language artists speak of reading, writing, speaking, listening. This is quite a mixture. . . .[5]

Although the job is imposing, it is not impossible, and it is necessary. Let us in the succeeding pages describe some of the attempts to define and unify the English curriculum.

Separate Subject Approach. The separate subject approach is currently prevalent in the elementary schools. The so-called "language arts" designation exists in name only, for there has been little attempt to unify the study, and each subject continues to be taught separately. The use of the term "language arts" in elementary school curriculum may, therefore, be a dangerous deception.

We commonly teach reading, language, or English (which may include grammar, usage, punctuation), spelling, and handwriting. Many teachers teach creative writing as a separate subject. Note that literature as a subject is not taught in the elementary school. Usually each class has its own specified time in the class schedule and there are often curriculum guides developed for each subject. There may also be guides for listening and oral language although these areas are seldom designated as separate subjects. Not only is each subject listed taught as a discrete subject but each has its own texts and workbooks. Reading probably receives the larger portion of class time.

[5] Graham Wilson, "The Structure of English," in *The Structure of Knowledge and the Curriculum*, G. W. Ford and L. Pugno, eds., (Chicago: Rand McNally, 1964), pp. 71-2.

Trichotomy vs. Dichotomy. Currently there is an attempt to bring some order and unity out of the chaos that is English by dividing the field into a trichotomy—literature, language, and composition. This tripartite structure in many cases fits the secondary English curriculum better than the elementary, and well it should, for the definition comes to us from college and secondary school English departments.

A modification of this trinity is the dichotomy of English into two parts—language and literature. The proponents of this position cite the fact that composition is actually part of language study and that the true content in English lies in language and literature, whereas composition is a skill. Wilson argues persuasively for this position concluding:

> . . . it might be useful to think of English as language and literature, and . . . if we do, we can discover a good deal of order. Twentieth-century study of language has given us new insights into the nature of languages and into their structures. Twentieth-century literary criticism has done the same things for literature.[6]

Communications. The communications approach to defining English attempts to focus attention as much on the processes of English as on the content. This approach dichotomizes communication into sending and receiving. Sending encompasses speaking and writing whereas receiving includes listening and reading as illustrated in the following diagram.

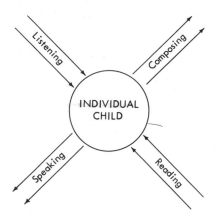

Actually the communications approach divides English into a quartet—speaking, writing, listening, and reading—the skills or processes involved in communication. To a greater extent than the two previous models this definition relates to the elementary school program.

[6] *Ibid.,* p. 86.

A Language-Centered Program. Our own inclination is to find unity and structure for English through a language-centered English program. As it now exists, English in the elementary school is highly diverse and lacks unity. This model, focused on the English language as the key component in any English program, not only centers on the language content but also brings to bear on this content the four processes of reading, writing, speaking, and listening. The diagram, "Dimensions of the English Language," illustrates graphically the diverse elements to be united in a language-focused English program which includes phonics, spelling, reading, writing, speaking, listening, and literature as well as many other concepts related to the study of the English language and the skills involved in using language. The philosophy behind this program is that, as Priscilla Tyler of the University of Illinois states: "The teaching of English is primarily the study of language."

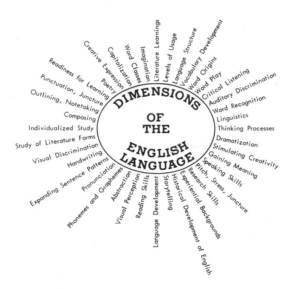

Developing a contemporary
English program

The purpose of discussing what should be taught in the English program is, of course, the development of a sound approach to elementary school English. One of the great needs in English has been the development of articulated sequences of study which provide for learning from the primary level of education through the secondary school, and indeed, beyond. New knowledge provided by linguistic studies has increased the need for reorganizing the curriculum in English.

What shall be our philosophy as we develop this program for the elementary school? Again, we shall call on some of the best thinking of students of educational curriculum from whom we derive the following guidelines:

1. The elementary school child is capable of learning more content at an earlier stage of development than was formerly thought possible. He comes to school with a more advanced experiential background and ability with language than was true 20 years ago.

2. It is possible to teach mature concepts to children at their level of comprehension. As Jerome Bruner asserts: "We begin with the hypothesis that any subject can be taught effectively in some intellectually honest forms to a child at any stage of development." Through the spiraling of the curriculum he will later learn more advanced concepts of the same subject.

3. A new conceptualization of English makes it possible to plan an exciting approach to the study of the English language in all its rich facets which will result in more effective teaching and a new image for English as a subject.

4. The study of creativity offers new approaches to instruction in the elementary school. It helps us rethink our attitudes toward evaluation, stimulus, freedom of expression, positive reinforcement, and inquiry. It leads to a new style of teaching for the teacher and focuses attention on developing each child to his fullest potential. As Nietzsche wrote:

   > Dancing in all its forms cannot be excluded from the curriculum of all noble education: dancing with the feet, with ideas, with words, and need I add that one must also be able to dance with the pen?

With these broad guidelines firmly in mind what will our English program include? It is our belief that an excellent (and why settle for less?) English program in the elementary school must reflect these basic understandings:

1. An English program must be language-centered with stress placed on composing, both oral and written.

2. Instruction in literature is part of the English program; literature must be closely coordinated with composition and reading.

3. English instruction must be made more dramatic, more stimulating, with creative, innovative methods used to present a rich body of content about the language and its development.

4. The new curriculum must have both scope and sequence with articulation between varied stages of development.

5. Authoritarian methods must be replaced by discovery and inquiry techniques which encourage student exploration and independent study.

6. Approaches to instruction in grammar and usage must reflect the findings of linguistics.

7. Instruction in oral language arts—speaking and listening—must be incorporated in the daily schedule for English.

Presented here is a language-centered English program planned for the elementary school from kindergarten through sixth grade. The adoption of this contemporary approach to English in the elementary school necessitates reorganizing programs in the junior high school, the secondary school, and the college. We might term this inverted procedure a "reversal of the pecking order."

The Role of the Teacher

The crucial component in the educational enterprise is the teacher. We can talk about what we shall teach, why we teach it, and how, but the teacher plays the paramount role in the pedagogical encounter with the student. Cheal's study demonstrates the importance of the elementary school teacher. He found, for example, that better qualified, better paid elementary school teachers led to fewer high school drop-outs. He found, furthermore, that the influence of the elementary school teacher was greater than that of the secondary school teacher in this respect.[7]

Because teachers are of such importance it behooves us to discuss their education, their attitudes toward English, and to suggest ways the prospective elementary school teacher can prepare for teaching. The chief needs of the elementary school English teacher are (1) improved training and (2) a contemporary attitude toward English.

Training in English

"Theory without practice is like a cloud without rain," states an old Japanese saying. The teacher needs well-balanced training in both content and strategy of teaching, for the modern teacher must be able to teach those who are not always willing to learn. We must take time to develop a style of teaching as well as to discover what is going on in the field of English. For this reason, we must consider teaching as an art, a craft, and an applied science.

The well-prepared elementary school teacher needs at least a minor in English, which should include work in modern grammar, children's literature, history of the English language, poetry, advanced composition, and a course in English teaching methods. We do not see any conflict between those who stress content in English and those who stress methods, for clearly both are necessary for effective teaching.

New attitudes toward English

In almost all cases teacher attitudes toward English require modification. This is particularly true of attitudes toward language and specifically toward usage. Most people tend to be conservative toward their

[7] J. E. Cheal, *Investment in Canadian Youth* (Toronto: Macmillan, 1963).

THE STUDY OF LANGUAGE
Grades Kg-6

	KINDERGARTEN	1	2	3	4	5	6
Oral Language	Linguistic fluency: games, discussion, dramatization Auditory discrimination of sounds; listening Experiential backgrounds	Linguistic fluency: many opportunities to speak Choric speaking Vocabulary development Listening experiences	Linguistic fluency: Pantomime, Creative Dramatics Vocabulary development Word play Synonyms Homonyms Discovery of words Listening experiences	Linguistic fluency: Dramatization, Ensemble speaking Vocabulary development Use of dictionary Synonyms Word play Listening experiences	Speaking: Individually, Dramatization, Ensemble Vocabulary development Listening experiences	Speaking: Individually, Dramatization, Ensemble Vocabulary development Listening experiences	Speaking: Individual, Panel, argumentation, Ensemble, Interpretation Listening: Note taking, Critical, Variation in usage
Linguistics	Discrimination: visual and auditory What language do we speak?	Correspondence of sound and letter, Single consonants, Long and short vowels Discovering regular spelling Who else speaks English? Does all English sound alike?	Correspondence of phoneme and grapheme Blends Digraphs Word Analysis, Selected affixes, Roots Discovery of graphemic families History of American English	Correspondence of phoneme and grapheme Irregular sounds: c,g,x,q Rules: c, qu Word Analysis, Affixes, Roots Discovery of graphemic families History of American English Loan words	Review all phonemes, Common graphemes, Initial grapheme combinations Dictation practice Compare British and American spelling and word usage Use of dictionary; etymology	Extend knowledge of graphemes that are less common Latin and Greek affixes, roots Loan words Levels of usage Use of dictionary; etymology History of English; Indo-European origins, map	Irregular graphemes Use of dictionary: Etymology, Loan words, Acronyms, Invention English abroad Changing nature of language Introduction to dialectology
Composition	Language experiments Storytelling Dictation, Individual Group composition Poetry: Dictated	Language experiments Dictated stories, Individual, Group Experience stories Sentence Pattern: N-V, Expansion Poetry: Free verse, Couplet Composition skills: Punctuation, Capitalization	Language experiments Group composition Individual experimentation Pattern 2: N-V-N, Expansion techniques Identification: N, V classes Poetry: Cinquain, Free verse, Triplets Figurative language: Simile Composition skills: Punctuation, Capitalization	Language experiments Individual composition Pattern 3: N-LV-N, N-LV-Adj. Expansion techniques Identification: N, V, Adj, Adv Poetry: Haiku, Limerick, Free verse Figurative language: simile, metaphor Composition skills: Punctuation, Capitalization	Language experiments Patterns: N-V, N-V-N, N-LV-Adj, N-LV-N Expansion: Modification, Compounding Identification: N, V, Adj, Adv, Det, Prep Vocabulary development, Word play, Thesaurus Composition: Paragraphs, Letters Poetry: Cinquain, Free verse, Quatrain Composition skills: Quotations	Language experiments Patterns: N-V, N-V-N, N-LV-Adj, N-LV-Adv, N-V-N-N Expansion: Modification, Compounding, Subordination Identification: 11 word classes Vocabulary development: Dictionaries, Word play Composition: Sentence, Paragraph, story, research Poetry: Imagery, Varied forms Composition skills: Abbreviations	Language experiments Pattern practice, expansion Vocabulary development, discovery, Thesaurus, Word play Composition: Stories and paragraphs, Articles and research, Poetry - all forms Composition skills: Juncture and punctuation
Reading and Literature	Readiness for learning Listening to literature Experiential background Orientation to books	Orientation to words and books Many listening opportunities Beginning reading of experience stories Independent reading of literature Poetry: Variety of form and subject	Individual and group composition for reading Independent reading of literature, Sharing reading Poetry: Variety of subject, "It doesn't have to rhyme"	Independent reading of literature Coordinated with composition Conferences and seminars, Reviewing, discussing Poetry: Relationship to music	Literature reading: Reviewing of books, Seminar and conference Coordination with composition Library skills-research Poetry: Variations in form, Work of Sandburg	Literature reading: Reviewing, Seminar and conference Coordination with composition Library skills-research Poetry: Imagery-simile, metaphor, symbolism, Work of Frost	Literature reading: Reviewing, Conference and seminar, Coordinated with composition Independent study in library Poetry: Nature of Poetry - form, subject, music, image, Work of Whitman

language, and teachers might be said to be "museums of virtue" when it comes to language. Linguists, however, have pointed out the constant change in language, noting that this change represents normal growth, not necessarily to be considered deterioration. We shall explore this aspect of language more thoroughly in Chapter 2.

Teachers also need to be more critical, more aware of the fundamental issues in English. Like an editor, they select methods, materials, and content, which should enliven the life and the professional role of the teacher, for English cannot continue to be taught in the same conventional way which teacher has passed to teacher throughout the decades. We must strive to teach with a flair and feeling for the language. English must be taught, not as a fossil subject, but as a dynamic, ever-changing force. Teachers of English have the most fascinating content to work with of all the curriculum in the elementary school. There is no reason, therefore, why English should not be the most interesting and vital subject.

Your personal growth

It is one thing to help you assess your knowledge and ability, but it is quite another to assist you in remedying any weakness and to guide you in your personal growth as a potential English teacher. The writing of this book represents our major effort at helping you become excellent teachers; however, we would like to suggest another avenue which you can begin exploring now and which you will continue to investigate as you continue to grow. What more effective method can we suggest than reading books about language? We have collected, therefore, a LANGUAGE LIBRARY, consisting of some 30 paperback titles which we recommend for your purchase and study.

A LANGUAGE LIBRARY OF PAPERBACK BOOKS

For the Teacher of English in the Elementary School

Allen, Harold B., ed. *Readings in Applied English Linguistics.* (Appleton-Century-Crofts, $4.50) Collection of articles providing background in applied linguistics.

Allen, Patricia, comp. *Best Books for Children.* (Bowker, $3.00) An excellent book selection aid.

Barnhart, Clarence L. *The Thorndike Barnhart Handy Pocket Dictionary.* (Bantam, 50¢) An indispensable aid for your desk.

Brook, G. L. *A History of the English Language.* (Norton, $1.45) The development of the English language for the general reader.

Burroughs, Alvina, *et al. They All Want to Write.* (Holt, $2.75) Discussion of children's writing and its motivation.

Carroll, John B. *Language and Thought.* (Prentice-Hall, $1.50) Presentation of language as communication, behavior, and thinking.

Ciardi, John. *How Does a Poem Mean?* (Houghton Mifflin, $4.00) The study of poetry; how a poem conveys meaning.

Cowley, Malcolm, ed. *Writers at Work.* (Viking, $1.65) Interviews with famous authors who talk about writing (two volumes available).

Crosby, Muriel, ed. *Reading Ladders for Human Relations.* (American Council on Education, $2.50) An annotated bibliography of books for all levels.

Devlin, Joseph. *A Dictionary of Synonyms and Antonyms.* (Popular Library, 75¢) Handy dictionary of synonyms and antonyms.

Fries, Charles C. *Linguistics: The Study of Language.* (Holt, $1.50) Excellent presentation of development; from *Linguistics and Reading.*

Gelb, I. J. *A Study of Writing.* (Phoenix, $2.95) Evolution of writing and relationship of writing to speech.

Hall, Robert A., Jr. *Linguistics and Your Language.* (Anchor, $1.45) Revised edition of *Leave Your Language Alone.*

Hayakawa, S. I., ed. *The Use and Misuse of Language.* (Premier, 75¢) A selection of nontechnical articles on words and their effect.

Laird, Charlton. *The Miracle of Language.* (Premier, 60¢) A popular exploration of the English language.

Larrick, Nancy. *A Teacher's Guide to Children's Books.* (Merrill, $2.75) Discussion of children's trade books; selection aid.

Malstrom, Jean and Annabel Ashley. *Dialects—U.S.A.* (National Council of Teachers of English, $1.00) Study of regional variety of American English.

Marckwardt, Albert H. *American English.* (Oxford, $1.95) Growth of American English; comparison between American and British English.

Mearns, Hughes. *Creative Power of Youth.* (Dover, $1.75) Excellent discussion of stimulating student writing.

Nicholson, Margaret. *A Dictionary of American English Usage.* (New American Library, $6.50). Based on Fowler's *Modern English Usage.*

Partridge, Eric. *A Dictionary of Clichés.* (Dutton, $1.35) A fascinating collection of curious expressions and clichés.

Pei, Mario. *The Story of Language.* (Monitor, 75¢) Popularized version of historical development of language.

Potter, Simeon. *Language in the Modern World.* (Penguin, 95¢) Presents linguistics to the lay person.

Schlauch, Margaret. *The Gift of Language.* (Dover, $1.95) Introduction to historical and comparative linguistics.

Sturtevant, Edgar H. *An Introduction to Linguistic Science.* (Yale, $1.45) Readable introduction to linguistics intended for the uninitiated.

Tiedt, Iris M., and Sidney W. Tiedt, eds. *Readings on Contemporary English in the Elementary School.* (Prentice-Hall, $3.95) New concepts in English selected for the elementary teacher.

Walter, Nina. *Let Them Write Poetry.* (Holt, $2.75) Writing poetry in the elementary school.

Weekley, Ernest. *The Romance of Words.* (Dover, $1.25) Interesting origins of English words.

Books to Investigate

Association for Supervision and Curriculum Development. *Yearbook: Learning and Mental Health in the School.* Washington, D.C.: The National Education Assn., 1966.

Bloom, Benjamin. S., ed. *Taxonomy of Educational Objectives.* New York: Longmans, Green, 1956.

Bruner, Jerome S. *The Process of Education.* Cambridge, Mass.: Harvard University Press, 1960.

—— *On Knowing.* Cambridge, Mass.: Harvard University Press, 1962.

Educational Policies Commission. *The Central Purpose of American Education.* Washington, D.C.: National Education Assn., 1961.

Ford, G. W., and Lawrence Pugno. *The Structure of Knowledge and the Curriculum.* Chicago: Rand McNally, 1964. See section by Graham Wilson: "The Structure of English."

Gardner, John W. *Excellence: Can We Be Equal and Excellent, Too?* New York: Harper, 1961

Hersey, John. *The Child Buyer.* New York: Knopf, 1960. Fiction discusses education's problems.

Peddiwell, J. Abner. *The Saber-Tooth Curriculum.* New York: McGraw-Hill, 1939.

Raths, Louis E. *et al. Values and Teaching.* Columbus, Ohio: Merrill, 1966.

Sexton, Patricia. *Education and Income.* New York: Viking, 1964. See especially chapters 1 and 2.

Warren, James., Jr. *The Teacher of English: His Materials and Opportunities.* Denver, Colorado: Swallow, 1956.

Language is not an abstract construction
of the learned.

Walt Whitman

2

Linguistics and
the Study of Language

"What is this thing called 'Language'?" Language is so much a
part of our existence that we are somewhat perplexed to attempt
its definition. It is human speech in both written and oral forms,
as a dictionary might briefly note, but it is more than that, for
language connotes complicated processes of thought for both the
speaker and the listener as well as for the writer and the reader.
In a society as complex as our own the ramifications of language
are extensive, for language is a means for social mobility, and it
has become a weapon. The advertiser depends on his persuasive
powers to convince the buyer, and mass media bombard the individual with language in varied form.

As we ponder the nature of language, we can note characteristics of language. It is human, for it requires more intelligence
and more complex vocal equipment than other animals possess,
and it is universal. All peoples have developed languages (although not always with a written form), but the languages developed have been diverse, and even those that are clearly related
are distinctly different. Language, furthermore, is learned anew
by each human child through imitation of adults. Language is
highly flexible in that the human vocal apparatus is capable of
making many more sounds than are ever used, and it is creative.
As Barnett observes, "Alone of all creatures on earth, man can
say things that have never been said before—and still be understood . . . man has the capacity to create every time he speaks." [1]

[1] Lincoln Barnett, *The Treasure of Our Tongue* (New York: Knopf, 1964),
p. 70.

14

The study of language, thus, is of direct concern to each individual, for language is a vital part of his existence. Spoken and written language, in which he is the sender, or language that is heard or read as he receives a message—all forms of language are important in the process of communication. The study of language focuses attention on:

The nature of language
Our linguistic heritage and its development
English in the world culture
Analysis of English grammar and usage concepts
Using language to communicate in varied ways

The specific purpose of this chapter is to examine new concepts of language which have been derived from developments in linguistics. We shall focus our attention on contemporary concepts of grammar and usage and methods of presenting this information in the classroom. Spelling (sounds of English and the graphemes used to represent them), composition (punctuation through study of juncture and stress), oral composing (stress and pitch), and the fascinations of word study are discussed in detail in other chapters. A well-integrated English program will have language as its center with literature, reading, spelling, composition, handwriting, speaking, and listening coordinated into a cohesive study. Literally, the discussion of this entire book focuses on the English language.

New Concepts of Language

"There is no such thing as the 'Queen's English.' The property has gone into the hands of a joint stock company and we own the bulk of the shares." So wrote Mark Twain in *Following the Equator* as he expressed a concept that for many of us today proves revolutionary.

During the decade of the sixties the study of linguistics has added to the knowledge explosion, bringing to light new concepts of our English language which bear challenging implications for teachers of English. As a result of scholarly studies of language, we now realize that English is not only a language rooted in the past, but it is a live, and lively, language which is constantly changing, developed by the very people who use it in daily speech and writing.

What is linguistics?

This important area of study has been defined as:

. . . the scientific study of language. It is inductive, objective, tentative and systematic; it is concerned with reportable facts, methods, and principles; it works by means of observations, hypotheses, experiments, postulates, and inferences; its products are descriptive verbal or algebraic statements about language.[2]

Another definition states:

> Linguistics is the study, according to rigorously defined methods or principles, *of language as a system*. The linguist is concerned, not with the listing of miscellaneous items, as in a dictionary, but with the recurrent patterns and characteristic relationships.[3]

"Linguistics," writes noted authority Mario Pei, "is the study of language, and the etymological meaning of language is 'that which pertains to the human tongue.'"[4] The term *philology*, which is also the study of language, is, by contrast, the study of language as it reveals the culture of a people; the philologist is more concerned, therefore, with the meaning of language, whereas the linguist studies the structure.

Linguistics has contributed the following new concepts of language and language study which have influenced English instruction:

1. Language constantly changes.
2. Change is normal.
3. The spoken language *is* the language.
4. Correctness rests upon usage.
5. All usage is relative.[5]

Within the broad area of linguistic science there have developed subareas which focus attention on specific aspects of language structure, for example, historical linguistics, psycholinguistics, comparative linguistics, geolinguistics, descriptive linguistics. It is within the last area of focus, descriptive linguistics, that the examination of the structure of the English language developed, bearing with it changed perspectives of our supposedly "familiar" language.

One of the prime movers of this development has been Charles C. Fries, author of *The Structure of English*, who has been both praised and blamed for his attention to English structure and the resulting questioning of traditional grammar. There are those who preceded his work—Otto Jespersen, Edward Sapir, and Leonard Bloomfield—and there are others who have followed his lead in developing this study of the structure of English, but it is Fries who is credited with establishing important basic concepts such as the well-researched fact that there exist *social levels* of

---

[2] James B. McMillan, "Modern Linguistics and the Teaching of Freshman English," *College Composition and Communication* (December, 1954), p. 140.

[3] Hans P. Guth, *English Today and Tomorrow* (Englewood Cliffs, N.J.: Prentice-Hall, 1964), p. 25.

[4] Mario Pei, *Invitation to Linguistics*, (Garden City, N.Y.: Doubleday, 1965), p. 1.

[5] Commission on the English Curriculum, National Council of Teachers of English, *The English Language Arts* (New York: Appleton, 1952), pp. 274-77.

language usage rather than "right" and "wrong" usage. His chief contribution has been to lead the way toward a more realistic approach to the study of language and a more realistic approach to the teaching of English.

Emphasis in linguistics is clearly on the scientific approach to language. Ignoring existing concepts or *mis*conceptions, the linguist sets to work to examine the language as it is in operation. Subsequent statements about language are not derived from intuitive prescriptions for what language "ought to be" but are based firmly on direct observation of the language as it is used by the people. The study of English includes, therefore, direct research of this language as it is used by widely differing socioeconomic groups within the United States as well as the English of Great Britain and that of Africa, India, and other parts of the world.

To provide some insight into the significance of linguistic study, we can cite an interesting field project undertaken by a group of international linguists in the spring of 1966 when they met to create a new alphabet for the Mandingo languages which include, for example, Bambara (spoken in Mali), Malinké (Mali, Guinea, and western Senegal), Songhay-Jerma (Mali and Niger), Tamashek (Tuareg), Hausa (Nigeria and Niger), Kanuri (Nigeria and Niger) and Fulani (scattered from Senegal to northern Cameroon). As is true of many languages, these tongues existed primarily in spoken form, for efforts to write the languages had been unorganized and conflicting.

With contemporary emphasis on education, publication, and mass communication, however, came the need for a written language. Convened by UNESCO, the assembled linguists attacked these problems:

1. Proposing for these languages a common alphabet for all the consonants they share.
2. Creating an alphabet simple enough to avoid technical and economic problems disadvantageous to educational systems and publishing ventures.

What seems an impossible task was accomplished in one busy week, for the linguistic scholars developed a practical alphabet which encompasses the sounds of these six languages and deviates only slightly from the systems of most European languages. The creation of this alphabet will enable these African peoples to work more effectively toward mass education. As the UNESCO report states, "Six linguistic groups spread over seven nations now have alphabets that should enable them to start on the more and more urgent task of transcribing an immense heritage of oral literature." [6]

[6] Adapted from *UNESCO Features* No. 477, p. 1.

Comparing grammars

The change brought about by linguistic studies which has probably caused the greatest controversy for teachers is that of modern approaches to grammar. The only grammar which teachers have been taught is the so-called "traditional" grammar which linguistics has revealed as an inaccurate representation of English sentence structure. Naturally it is disconcerting to find that this knowledge is no longer useful, and there remains resistance to change as noted by W. Nelson Francis:

> The definitive grammar of English is yet to be written, but the results so far achieved are spectacular. It is now as unrealistic to teach "traditional" grammar of English as it is to teach "traditional" (i.e., pre-Darwinian) biology or "traditional" (i.e., four-element) chemistry. Yet nearly all certified teachers of English on all levels are doing so. Here is a cultural lag of major proportions.[7]

Actually, several grammars have been developed for the English language: (1) traditional, (2) historical, (3) structural, and (4) generative or transformational.[8] It is interesting to note also that other grammars are in the process of being developed, for with new perceptive minds come new approaches to the structure of English, and too, the flexibility of our changing language may create a need for new descriptions. Each grammar has made its contribution as we will note in the following discussion.

Traditional Grammar. Traditional grammar has its roots in the eighteenth century and the work of Joseph Priestley, Robert Lowth, George Campbell, and Lindley Murray, who were prescriptive, basing their precise rules on Latin, which they viewed as a perfect language, and on their own concepts of linguistic "correctness." It is the work of these early scholars which is evident in many English texts today as we observe the emphasis on "correct usage" and definitions of parts of speech, for example, "A noun is the name of a person, place, or thing."

Historical Grammar. Historical grammar developed in the late nineteenth and early twentieth centuries and is chiefly associated with the Danish linguist, Otto Jespersen. The historical approach to grammar destroyed the concept of Latin as an "ideal" language as linguists pointed out the fact that Latin, like many other languages, was derived from the Indo-European language. The chief contribution of this study was the recognition of language relationships and origins. Historical investigation

---

[7] Francis, W. Nelson. "Revolution in Grammar." *Quarterly Journal of Speech.* October, 1954. pp. 229-312.

[8] Thomas, Owen. "Grammatici Certant." *English Journal,* May, 1963. Reprinted in: *Linguistics in the Classroom.* Champaign, Illinois: National Council of Teachers of English. p. 6.

of language also explained many peculiarities of spelling and discrepancies between spelling and pronunciation.

Structural Grammar. Structural grammar is a descriptive grammar which began with the work of Leonard Bloomfield in the first half of the twentieth century. He attempted to separate structure of language from its meaning, that is, he distinguished between study of syntax and that of semantics. The purely descriptive approach employed by the structural linguist caused panic among traditionalists who deplored the structural grammarian's failure to judge "correctness" of usage. Attempting to present language as it really exists are such linguists as Charles C. Fries, James Sledd, H. A. Gleason Jr., Archibald Hill, and many others.

Also ascribing to the theories of structural grammar was the editor of *Webster's Third International Dictionary*, Philip B. Gove, who was heavily criticized for "abdicating his responsibility." The literature is full of plaints, for example, that of *The New York Times*:

> Webster's has, it is apparent, surrendered to the permissive school that has been busily extending its beachhead on English instruction in the schools. This development is disastrous because intentionally or unintentionally, it serves to reinforce the notion that good English is whatever is popular.[9]

Philip Gove's letter in reply concluded with these words:

> Whether you or I or others who fixed our language notions several decades ago like it or not, the contemporary English language of the Nineteen Sixties—the language we have to live with, the only language we have to survive with—is not the language of the Nineteen Twenties and Thirties.[10]

Studies of the structure of English led to new concepts of (1) phonemes (the sounds of English, which number about 44), (2) morphemes (meaningful units of language), and (3) phrase structure. The structuralist also devised a new system of classifying the words in a language. Unlike the traditional grammarian, the structuralist bases definitions on syntax rather than on meaning. He has discovered, for example, that all nouns are distinctive from other words in that a noun can be made plural and possessive. This is not true of any other group of words—verbs, adjectives, adverbs, and so on. Here, then, we have a clear test for identifying nouns. Can all of the following words be classified as nouns? Might any of them also be included in other categories?

mother	winning	footstep	drive
pupil	score	telephone	parking
English	publishing	pencil	spelling

[9] *The New York Times,* October 12, 1961.
[10] *The New York Times,* November 5, 1961.

Compare this syntactic approach to classifying words with that of traditional grammar, which bases definitions on the meanings of words. Are there words in this group which could not be identified as the "name of a person, place, or thing"?

Generative Grammar. Generative grammar (sometimes called "transformational") is based chiefly on the work of Noam Chomsky and Robert Lees, whose works appeared in 1957 and 1960, respectively. Generative grammar extends the concepts of structural grammar, which was concerned with syntax devoid of meaning, to include the semantics of language. It seeks to:

1. Identify kernel sentences—simple, declarative, active sentences with no elaboration; e.g., Joe has a dog.

2. Supply rules for transforming kernel sentences.
    Judy ate a big hamburger.
    Is Judy eating a hamburger?
    Judy is not eating a hamburger.
    What is Judy eating?

3. Identify obligatory transformations and optional transformations.
    An obligatory transformation: agreement of subject and verb.
    Mary is tall. (We cannot use *are* in this sentence.)
    An optional transformation: any elaboration of a kernel.
    The teacher is working. (We may add *tired* to describe teacher or *in her room* to designate the place, but these additions are optional.)

Generative grammar has developed very exact rules for transforming sentences, and these rules are usually stated in a formula. The changing of a kernel (simple, active, declarative) sentence into the passive form is stated in this formula:

Passive = Second noun phrase (+ auxiliary) + *be* + past participle + by + first noun phrase

Thus, the kernel sentence—Mrs. Parker called Joe—is made passive by applying the formula.

Joe (NP₂) was (form of *be*) called (past participle) by Mrs. Parker (NP₁).

Questions about grammar

There has been much confusion about grammar: comparisons of traditional grammar and that of the structuralist and transformationalist, the misconceptions about grammar and usage, and the amount of assistance which knowledge of grammar provides to composition ability. To clarify important concepts, we shall explore these questions.

1. What Is Grammar? The definition of grammar is somewhat difficult, for there are many conceptions of what grammar is, and far too many of these conceptions have been proved to be *mis*conceptions. We can begin defining grammar by pointing out, therefore, what grammar *is not*.

Grammar is not "usage." For many English instructors the problems of using "shall" or "will" or distinguishing between the use of "I" and "me" means the teaching of grammar. The linguist observes, however, that knowledge of this nature pertains to the manner in which English is used, to the selection of words according to appropriateness, not to the study of the structure of the English sentence, for grammar and usage are separate studies.

Grammar is not "good English." The placing of emphasis on the "correctness" and "incorrectness" is related to the study of usage. As we will point out in the discussion of usage, these concepts are relative depending on our personal values and the situation in which speech takes place.

Grammar is not "parts of speech." Some teachers have assumed they were teaching grammar as they drilled students on the identification of eight parts of speech. In the first place, linguists quickly teach us that there are more than eight categories of words in English, and that mere identification of each word as belonging to a certain category does not take note of the structural meaning of the sentence. We soon see, too, that many words fall into more than one category, for example:

His *running* of the race was unexpected.
The *running* water was cold.
John was *running* toward the school.

Jim hit a *home* run.
They were at *home*.
The family headed *home*.

Grammar is not "the mechanics of composition." Another interpretation of grammar has been the knowledge of punctuation, capitalization, and spelling—skills of composition. Although it is true that knowledge of juncture (the pauses in spoken language) has relevance for the study of grammar as well as for the use of punctuation, the study of punctuation is not the study of grammar.

How, then, shall we define *grammar* in accordance with modern linguistic concepts? One definition is "the system of devices in the English language which signal structural meanings." [11] Other writers note that grammar is a study of the way a language works encompassing morphol-

[11] Metropolitan School Study Council. *Structural Linguistics; an Introduction for Teachers and Administrators,* (New York: Teachers College, 1961), p. 2.

ogy (meaningful forms), syntax (sentence structure), and phonology (sounds).[12]

It will be some time, however, before these definitions are assimilated by the teaching profession and even longer until the public understands, for example, that there is a distinction between grammar and usage. When critics of education cry, therefore, for a return to the teaching of grammar so that our young people will gain skill in composition, we can be certain that these representatives of the public really want the classroom teacher to stress the teaching of "correct usage." The assumption that knowledge of grammar *does* increase ability to write is the subject of the next question.

2. *Does Knowledge of Grammar Improve Ability to Speak and Write?* Research reports conclude:

> In view of the widespread agreement of research studies based upon many types of students and teachers, the conclusion can be stated in strong and unqualified terms: The teaching of formal grammar has a negligible, or, because it usually displaces some instruction and practice in actual composition, even a harmful effect on the improvement of writing.[13]

Research indicates that skills of composition are learned through composing, not through learning to identify classes of words, rules of grammar, and so forth.

Paul Roberts, who has authored a set of language books which feature transformational grammar for elementary school students,[14] asserts:

> It is not to be expected that study of the grammar, no matter how good a grammar it is or how carefully it is taught, will effect any enormous improvement in writing. Probably the improvement will be small and hard to demonstrate and for the large number of students who lack the motivation or the capacity to learn to write, it will be nonexistent.[15]

We should be cognizant also that researchers note the need for more extensive studies of composition, and this would certainly be true of the effects of instruction along the lines of structural and generative grammars which have only recently found their ways into the schools. It is our own observation that work in expanding basic sentences does increase student flexibility in writing by suggesting possibilities for more effective original sentences. Successful creation of interesting sentences stimulates student

[12] Mary E. Fowler, *Teaching Language, Composition, and Literature,* (New York: McGraw-Hill, 1965), p. 183.

[13] Richard Braddock, et al., *Research in Written Composition,* (Champaign, Ill.: National Council of Teachers of English, 1963), pp. 37-8.

[14] The Roberts English Series (New York: Harcourt, 1966).

[15] Paul Roberts, "Linguistics and the Teaching of Composition," *English Journal* (May, 1963).

desire to write and composition skills do improve. Mere knowledge of terminology or ability to classify English words does not improve composition skills, but moving beyond that basic information to manipulation of words, phrases, clauses, that is, to composing, does improve ability to write. Again, however, research is needed to investigate this aspect of composition.

3. *Why Is Traditional Grammar No Longer Considered Satisfactory?* Linguistic studies have pointed out that, as can be readily proved, traditional grammar does not describe the English language. The following criticisms of traditional grammar have been made:

1. Prescriptive rules based on Latin, a dead language, had little effect on changing usage of a living language.
2. Traditional grammar did not recognize the changing nature of language.
3. Its definitions of word classes were based on meaning which changes for a word in varied contexts, and the definitions were ambiguous.

The emphasis on learning sterile rules which had no meaning for the student made the study of English boring and distasteful to students and actually inhibited learning. As Marckwardt observes, students tended to adopt a "classroom dialect, a sapless and super-correct form of the language employed only within the hearing of the English teacher and in written work subject to her scrutiny, and for the most part, dropped like a hot-cake as soon as the hour was over." [16] It is probable, too, that an excessive amount of time was spent, furthermore, on repetitious drill in usage when time might more wisely have been allocated for writing.

4. *Does Modern Grammar Offer Something More Effective Than Traditional Grammar?* Modern grammar (based on structural linguistics and generative grammar) emphasizes learning about grammar by engaging in the work of the linguist, that is, examining the language itself. Inductively, then, the student can discover word classes, for example, through learning processes advocated by Bruner.[17] He can also discover sentence patterns and methods of expanding them as we will discuss in more detail later in this chapter. The advantages of modern grammar include the following:

a. Description of the structure of English is based on a study of this unique language as it is actually used.
b. Grammar is differentiated from usage.
c. The student acquires a more realistic attitude toward language and language study.

[16] Albert H. Marckwardt, "Grammar and Linguistics in the Teaching of English," *Illinois English Bulletin*. XLVI, 1 (October, 1956), p. 3.
[17] Ibid.

    d. Modern grammar offers a more positive approach to study of the English language which appeals to students.

    e. Emphasis on creating original sentences after study of sentence structure patterns suggests a beneficial relationship between grammar study and composition.

Questions about usage

The usage of language, as we have noted, was stressed in traditional grammar, which prescribed detailed rules for usage and taught concepts of "correctness" and "incorrectness." New concepts of language based on description of language have altered attitudes toward usage, which is now viewed as changing along with the changing language. There are many questions about concepts of usage which merit our examination.

1. What Is the Difference Between Grammar and Usage? Grammar, as has been explained, is the study of the structure of English speech, the language as it operates, the syntax. Grammar does not consider the meaning of individual words.

The study of usage, on the other hand, explores the choices we make in using words. Do we choose to say, for example, "Mary and I are going." or "Mary and me are going."? Either sentence conveys the same meaning, but one selection may be more acceptable in a specific situation. The study of usage is concerned with the appropriateness of language in context.

2. What Usage Shall We Teach? Linguists recommend that we teach the concept of varied levels of usage. Usage that is acceptable in an informal social situation may not be acceptable in a written composition and vice versa. We recognize, but don't condemn, the presence of varied social dialects among which *standard* English is only one, and even this dialect may vary regionally.

We teach, therefore, educated forms of standard English without undue stress on picayune points that really achieve little. Pooley recommends that we forget, for example, a number of specific items of usage which were formerly taught:

1. Any distinction between *shall* and *will*.
2. Any reference to the split infinitive.
3. Elimination of *like* as a conjunction.
4. Objection to the phrase "different than."
5. Objection to "He is one of those boys who *is*."
6. Objection to "the reason . . . is because. . . ."
7. Objection to *myself* as a polite substitution for *I* as in "I understand you will meet Mrs. Jones and myself at the station."
8. Insistence on the possessive case standing before a gerund.[18] [Note that there is an example in this item.]

[18] Robert C. Pooley, "Dare Schools Set a Standard in Usage?" *The English Journal* (March, 1960), p. 180.

3. *What Is "Good" English?* The definition of good English written by Robert C. Pooley in 1933 has been widely quoted and remains a valid statement today:

> Good English is that form of speech which is appropriate to the purpose of the speaker, true to the language as it is, and comfortable to speaker and listener.[19]

The reader will find that there is no mention in this definition of "correctness" or of knowledge of rules of grammar.

4. *Does Memorization of Rules Improve Usage?* Meckel reports that "Improvement of usage appears to be most effectively achieved through practice of desirable forms than through memorization of rules." [20]

The child learns language through imitation from infancy, and it is true that many of his language patterns and knowledge of English usage are formed before he comes to school. Both home and the peer group are highly influential in determining usage. Changes will be brought about only when the student discovers a reason for changing his speech, and learning of rules does not provide sufficient motivation.

5. *Is Slang "Bad"?* Here again we must rethink our concepts of correctness and usage. Slang is a vernacular of the young which has a high interest value and often provides a means for snaring the interests of students in language study. Termed in French, *"la langue verte,"* slang represents the growth, the aliveness, of our language. Have students list as many slang words as they can. The words can be defined, categorized into word classes, used in sentence patterns, and compiled by several lexicographers into a dictionary of SLANGUAGE. Entries might read thus:

BOSS—good, nice, pretty—That convertible is boss!

CAMP—so old it's *in*—His surfer outfit is really high camp!
Batman is camp.

The teacher does not teach slang, but aims students toward standard English without authoritatively condemning slang. Students are taught the concept of varied levels of usage of which slang is one as is standard English. Sometimes words which originate as slang become elevated to a higher level of acceptability, and on rare occasions a slang word becomes acceptable as standard English.

---

[19] Robert C. Pooley, *Grammar and Usage in Textbooks on English*, Bureau of Educational Research Bulletin No. 14 (Madison, Wis.: University of Wisconsin, August, 1933), p. 155.

[20] Henry C. Meckel, "Research on Teaching Composition and Literature," in N. L. Gage, ed. *Handbook of Research on Teaching*, American Educational Research Assn. (Chicago: Rand McNally, 1963), p. 981.

New terms introduced by linguistics

The study of linguistics has introduced many new terms into the vocabulary of teachers at all levels. It is imperative that we have a working knowledge of these words in order to discuss intelligently the arguments and the contributions of linguistics.

Phoneme. (fō′nēm) Unit of speech sound; e.g., /p/, /ch/, /ey/

Grapheme. The spelling of a phoneme; e.g., the spelling of the long ā or phoneme /ey/ might be thus: play, flame, fail, pain, care, break

Morpheme. The smallest meaningful unit in the language; e.g., *tigers* contains two morphemes—the word *tiger* and the plural inflection *s*, both of which give meaning.

Bound morpheme. A morpheme that cannot stand alone; e.g., *ful.*

Free morpheme. A morpheme that can stand alone; e.g., *play.*

Phonology. The study of the sounds of any language, the intonations, stress, and juncture.

Morphology. The study of changes in word form and the meanings of these changes; for instance, the *-ed* suffix to form past tense of verbs.

Grammar. Study of the way any language works, the structure of the language.

Prescriptive grammar. An analysis that chiefly tells (prescribes) how language should be used.

Descriptive grammar. An analysis of language as it is actually used.

Language Instruction

Our primary concern as teachers is the translation of our knowledge about grammar and usage into classroom experiences for the student. What are the implications of new concepts of language for English instruction? What knowledge shall we transmit to the elementary school student? How can we most effectively present information about language to the elementary school child?

"Perhaps of all the creations of man, language is the most astonishing," wrote Giles Lytton Strachey in *Words and Poetry.* As students are exposed to this astonishing language, to what J. Donald Adams has called, "the magic and mystery of words," they will, it is hoped, gain some of this feeling for the English language. They will be intrigued by their ability to manipulate the language, to achieve astonishing results, to create "beautiful arrangements." Teacher enthusiasm will serve to develop this feeling of deep involvement and interest in language which leads the student to independent investigation.

Objectives of language instruction

Toward what goals shall we direct instruction in language? We shall direct language study in the elementary school toward goals similar to those of other levels of education as we provide understandings in the following areas: (1) our literary heritage, the history and development of English, (2) the structure of the English language, its grammar, (3) the study of usage of American English, and perhaps most important, (4) composing (both oral and written) with English. Within each area we shall attempt to develop major concepts as enumerated in this. statement of objectives:

1. The history and development of the English language
   a. English is part of the Indo-European language family.
   b. Changes in spelling and pronunciation influence contemporary spelling and pronunciation; changing nature of language.
   c. Origins of English words; continuing growth of English.
   d. Comparison of American and British English.
   e. English is part of the world culture.

2. The structure of the English language, grammar
   a. Specific sounds (phonemes) can be identified for the English language; corresponding graphemes can be identified.
   b. English words can be grouped according to their function in sentences; some words may belong to more than one group.
   c. Word order helps to signal meaning.
   d. English sentences are based on distinct patterns.
   e. Basic sentence patterns can be elaborated through specific techniques.

3. Usage of American English
   a. There are varied levels of acceptable usage or varied degrees of appropriateness of usage.
   b. Usage concerns the selection of specific words to be used in any given speech situation.
   c. Usage is not labeled "right" or "wrong," for the choice of usage is an individual operation. Usage may be judged on the basis of suitability to the context, whether it be a social context or a composition context.
   d. Speech dialects differ according to region and social class. Even standard English allows for variety of acceptable speech.
   e. We should develop sensitivity to language habits which are analogous to habits of eating and dress.

4. Oral and written composition in English
   a. The purpose of using language is to communicate ideas and feelings.
   b. The success of composition is evaluated on the basis of success in communicating.
   c. Skills associated with written composition, for example, spelling, punctuation, and handwriting, facilitate communication.
   d. In order to communicate one must first have an idea, or thoughts, to communicate.

  e. An extensive vocabulary facilitates effective communication.
  f. We gain skill in effective communication through practice in composing varied types of messages.
  g. The study of other persons' attempts to communicate (literary models) can aid growth in ability to compose and to communicate.

This last section of stated objectives is so vitally important that a separate chapter has been written on speaking, and two others focus attention on written composition. In this chapter, therefore, we shall direct our study of classroom techniques to instruction in grammar and usage with some attention given to historical backgrounds of English.

Which "grammar" shall we teach?

Our approach to grammar in the elementary school must clearly be eclectic, a synthesis of elements from varied approaches to English grammar. Which elements shall we select for instruction in the classroom? The following concepts, drawn from varied grammars, appear to contribute to the young person's understanding of the English language and its use:

1. Traditional grammar: terms for classifying words (plus others from structural grammar)
2. Historical grammar: origins of English words, development of the language, changes in spelling and pronunciation
3. Structural grammar: identification of word classes, study of sentence patterns, expansion of basic patterns
4. Generative grammar: generating varied sentences from a core or basic sentence

What is the purpose of instruction in grammar? Concepts of grammar lead to a better understanding of English sentences and of "how language works." They also enable the teacher and student to communicate ideas about language as they use the vocabulary of the linguist to discuss more precisely the relationships of words. An eclectic approach to grammar leads to a greater interest in language activities as students compose sentences in paragraphs in stories. A limited amount of time should be spent on study specific to grammar or usage, for instruction time can be spent to greater advantage in actually using the language both orally and in written forms or in reading the language.

Student knowledge of grammar

An elementary school student already knows grammar before he enters school, for he has been using grammar since he began to speak. A wise approach to the study of grammar, therefore, is to impress the student with his own knowledge of grammar rather than to stress the esoteric, difficult nature of the study on which the class is embarking. Student knowledge of grammar can be brought out in many ways.

Request the students to suggest sentences orally which can be written on the board. Occasionally a student may suggest only a phrase or subordinate clause as a sentence, but all should be written, thus:

> We are in the third grade.
> That book is interesting.
> The sun is shining today.
> Tom's new red coat.

The groups of words can be read aloud by students who test them to see if they "feel" like sentences. Students will note that "Tom's new red coat" is incomplete, and they can supply an ending so that the group of words sounds like a sentence.

Notice that we have not confused the children (and ourselves) by attempting to apply a definition of a sentence, for example, "A sentence is a complete thought," for we are hard pressed to define the terms of this definition. The intuitive knowledge of the student is more reliable. As more exact knowledge is acquired concerning English sentence patterns, the child will know that this phrase is incomplete as a sentence because it lacks a verb or predicate.

A group of teachers working in an NDEA English Institute developed "A Rationale of Modern Grammar" [21] which was introduced as follows.

YOU ARE A WALKING GRAMMAR

Look at the following groups of words. Some of them are grammatical English sentences. Some are not. Which ones would you call grammatical? On your paper write E after the numbers of the grammatical English sentences, and non-E after those you consider nongrammatical.

1. John lost his report card.
2. Cats the birds stalk.
3. The story interesting to me was.
4. The story was difficult for me.
5. Mort couldn't finish the exam.
6. Lylee didn't find his pen.
7. At him she the pillow threw.
8. The apple sour tastes.
9. It was a beautiful quietly.
10. These memory stand out in my mind.

What sentences did you select as acceptable grammatical English sentences?

You were able to select these sentences because you are a speaker of English. Any native speaker of English could select them. As a matter of fact, you were able to recognize English sentences long before you

---

[21] NDEA Contemporary English Institute, 1965, San Jose State College, San Jose, California. Workshop Instructor: Iris M. Tiedt. Chairman of the Committee: William Gerald.

started to school, though you probably weren't aware of it. You certainly were able to make up and use English sentences, and you did it without even thinking about it. And today, even though you have not had any training in what makes a sentence and might have trouble trying to tell someone what a sentence is, you do make sentences whenever you talk.

We have within us something that makes it possible for us to turn out sentences in our language. We might say we have in our minds a sentence-making machine with which we can put the proper words together in the proper order so that they come out English sentences. The grammatical process which we have built into us might be thought of as a machine into which the various elements of the language go. They pass through the machine (The Grammatical Process) and come out acceptable English sentences. Because native speakers have this built-in ability, we say they have an *intuitive* knowledge of their native language, which means that they are able to use it without being taught.

To prove to yourself that you have this kind of built-in knowledge, see if you can put the following groups of words together to make English sentences.

1. around the old corner the limped man
2. the fat sat smugly toad pad on his
3. his class could the new not boy find
4. vitamins you gives spinach
5. rocket air off the in went the
6. first Oswald finished was
7. permission you gave to go she

You knew how to put these words together to make English sentences without thinking of any rules. But a person who speaks a language other than English, say a student in France, could not have produced English sentences from these groups of words nor could you make a French sentence (unless you happen to know French) out of the following groups, although your French counterpart could:

1. parlent vitement hommes les garçons aux
2. moi les livres donnez plaît s'il vous

THE GRAMMAR OF THE LANGUAGE

The knowledge we have which enables us to make the sentences of our language is called the grammar of the language, and we say a language has "grammaticality," which means it can be explained by a grammar.

Now you may have heard about something called grammar. Maybe you have even studied a subject which your teachers called grammar. Many young people have the notion that grammar is something you have to study so that you know how to speak correctly. If perhaps you feel that you don't know very much about it, the preceding exercises should have proved to you that you actually do know a great deal about the grammar of English. You use it every day!

Before beginning any formal study of grammar it is important that students have had many opportunities to use English words and sentences. It is for this reason that stress is placed on oral language experience for beginning students, particularly those from disadvantaged backgrounds (see Chapter 13). These initial experiences will, however, reflect the teachings of linguistics. Young children can participate in language experiences like the following as they develop their abilities:

Selecting a sentence from an experience chart or dictated story, the teacher might say, for example, "We saw a movie. I wonder if we could do some interesting things with that sentence?" Using the analogy technique, she might lead the group to replace *movie* with other things that might have been seen (nouns), thus:

We saw a boy.
We saw two dogs.
We saw the teacher.

Then substitutions for the pronoun, *we,* might be explored:

The class saw the movie.
Joe saw the movie.

In this way, although the children don't know the terminology of grammar or even the fact that they are studying grammar, they are being introduced to the practice of substituting words in a common sentence pattern. INVENTING SENTENCES is a worthwhile oral activity that can be repeated with infinite variety.

Beginning readers can gain practice in reading while they are reinforcing their knowledge of English word order. Given words in confused order, they can construct a sentence that is grammatical, thus:

ran school to Tim
are going you where
new I a hat want

SCRAMBLED SENTENCES may sometimes contain an unnecessary word in this way:

visited car grandmother Polly her
happy is our neat room

Classifying words

Traditional grammar identified eight parts of speech; of these eight categories, seven are still useful, but structural linguistics has identified other function words which appear in English sentences. The first four classes—noun, verb, adjective, and adverb—are open classes to which an unlimited number of words can be added. It should be noted also that words frequently appear in more than one class, for instance, the word *book.* The other categories are called *function* or *structure* words—prepositions, conjunctions, subordinators, auxiliaries, intensifiers, pronouns, and determiners— [22] which are relatively limited in number, for only infrequently is a new word added in these categories.

Noun. A noun is a word that can be made plural or possessive and may follow the words *the, a,* or *an.* A noun fits in patterns like these:

She has a _____ (book, ball, pencil, dress, headache).
He looked at the _____ (house, car, boy, dog, spot, movie).

Verb. A verb is a word that can be changed from past to present and usually (except for forms of *to be*) adds *s* when patterned after *it, she, he.* The morpheme *ing* may be added to a verb. A verb fits in patterns like these:

The boy _____. (runs, plays, speaks, shouts, ran, played).
They _____ it. (found, chased, wanted, like, have, want).
What are you _____? (saying, doing, missing, singing).

Adjective. An adjective patterns with the word *very,* as *very lovely girl, very soft music, very small boy,* and the adjective can follow a linking verb.

She is very _____. (happy, pretty, nice, healthy).
The very _____ boy arrived. (tired, tall, unhappy, first).

Adverb. Adverbs pattern like *often, up,* or *sadly.*

Mary sings _____. (well, clearly, often, sweetly).
The baby climbs _____. (up, eagerly, down, quickly).

Determiners. The determiner signals that a noun follows. Included in this class are *the, a, an, every, each, this, that, these, those, my, one, two, three, four, most, more, either, neither, our, your, their, his, her, its, no, both, some, much, all, any, several, few.*

_____ cat chased _____ dog.
_____ boys played with _____ ball.

Pronouns. Pronouns (like proper nouns) do not pattern with determiners, but they substitute for nouns or proper nouns.

The boy is tall.   *Bruce* is tall.   *He* is tall.

A special group of pronouns also function as determiners when followed by a noun, thus:

These boys are helpful.   *These* are helpful.
That man is Mr. Sutter.   *That* is Mr. Sutter.

[22] Paul Roberts, *English Sentences* (New York: Harcourt, 1962), *passim.*

Intensifiers. Intensifiers (*very, quite, somewhat, rather*) pattern with adjectives and adverbs, thus:

Jim was *very* talkative.	Jim walked *very* slowly.
He was *somewhat* uncertain.	He was *rather* uncertain.

Auxiliaries. The auxiliary signals that a verb follows. Some auxiliaries (*do, be, have, can*) may also serve as independent verbs, and only two (*be, have*) pattern with the past form of verbs.

I *can* go.	He *did* help the teacher.
He *has played.*	She *was* helping.

Subordinators. Subordinators are linking words that join subordinate subject-predicate word groups (clauses) with independent subject-predicate word groups (clauses). Included are *who, when, until, unless, that, since, if, that, what, which, whenever, while, although, as, because, whatever, whichever, whoever, how, before, whether, as if, unless, until.*

Their house is the yellow one *which* faces the park.
She is the person *who* called you.
When you return home, send me a copy of that book.

Conjunctions. Conjunctions are linking words which join equal words or groups of words. Included in this group are *and, but, for, either . . . or, neither . . . nor, not only . . . but also, or, yet.*

Either David *or* I will come.
Her name is Joanna, *but* everyone calls her Jo.

Prepositions. Prepositions signal that a noun follows, usually in a prepositional phrase which serves an adjective or adverb function. Common prepositions include *about, above, across, after, among, around, at, before, by, in, for, from, in, into, of, off, on, over, since, through, to, under, up, upon, with, within.*

The cat jumped *over* the box.
At noon we stopped working.
Walk *to* the corner *with* me.

What techniques can we use in the classroom to introduce students to these parts of speech? One of the most effective ways is the inductive approach through which students make linguistic discoveries for themselves. A class is asked, for example, to see how many words they can name in five to ten minutes as two recorders write the words on chalkboards. The students then examine the group of unsorted words to determine how these words can be sorted or classified. Varied methods may be explored—alphabetical order, length of words, meaning (animals, feelings, etc.—not all words will fit semantic groups), and so on.

Discoveries can be guided by the teacher who might ask, for example, after varied methods have been tried, whether any of the words can be made plural. After this identification of the noun class other groupings can be gradually introduced.

Additional practice in identifying words can be effected through the use of analogical patterns as words are supplied which fit given patterns, as in the first experiment:

● Nouns and Determiners:

The _____ and the _____ followed the _____.

_____ mouse is in _____ cage eating _____ cheese.

I want to buy a _____ and two _____.

● Can you unite these sentences?

Sheryl is pretty. She is popular. She studies hard.

The siren shrieked. The car pulled over. The driver got out.

This boy is the winner. He has long legs. He is in the fifth grade.

● What word would you choose?

We walked _____ the hill.

_____ the assembly we returned _____ class.

He sat _____ the table.

The child was climbing _____ the box.

● Why is the meaning of these words uncertain?

Plan moves ahead.

City shelters poor.

Ship sails today.

Exploring English sentence patterns

The sentence merits considerable attention in the study of language and in developing composition skills. The ability to write effective, varied sentences can be introduced through study of sentence structure.

Basic Patterns. Although linguists have identified numerous sentence patterns, there appears to be little reason for teaching more than five basic patterns in the elementary school.

N–V (Subject–Predicate)

The simplest pattern is a noun followed by a verb. Whitehall observes:

The subject-predicate sentence is *the* sentence of written English. Its grammatical structure accounts for almost all the English grammar that is practically useful to a writer of the language. Understand this structure, this grammar, and you will have the grammatical dynamics of the language well within your grasp.[23]

[23] Harold Whitehall, *Structural Essentials of English* (New York: Harcourt, 1956), p. 37.

Experiments:

Girls *giggle*. Girls *run*. Girls *sing*. (Analogical changes)

Boys *shout*. Boys *fight*. Boys *race*. Boys _____

Cows *moo*. Cows *eat*. Cows *walk*. Cows _____

The girls giggle. (Expansion—determiner)

Boys shout *loudly*. (Adverb)

In the morning cows moo. (Prepositional phrase)

The *amused* girls were giggling. (Adjective)

N–V–N (Subject–Predicate–Object)

Experiments:

Boys run races. *Girls* run races. *Horses* run races.

Jane eats *ice cream*. Jane eats *sandwiches*. Jane eats *everything*.

Mrs. Barker *reads* books. Mrs. Barker *buys* books. Mrs. Barker *enjoys* books.

Boys and girls run races. (Expansion—compounding)

Jane eats *ice cream and cake* (Compounding)

Mrs. Barker reads books *about Africa*. (Modification)

A world traveler, Mrs. Barker reads books about Africa. (Apposition).

N–LV–N (Subject–Linking Verb Predicate–Noun Complement)

Experiments:

This dog is a terrier, This dog is a collie.

My mother is a tall woman. My mother is a good driver.

Henry was a teacher. Henry was a barber.

This dog *which is lost* is a terrier. (subordinate clause)

Although my mother is a tall woman, she is thin. (subordination)

Henry was a teacher *in a small college*. (prepositional phrase)

N–LV–ADJ (Subject–Linking Verb Predicate–Adjective Complement)

Experiments:

Nancy is pretty. Nancy is intelligent.

Carnations are sweet. Roses are sweet.

Karl appears old. Karl appears unhappy.

Nancy and Susan are pretty. (Compounding)

Carnations and roses are sweet. (Compounding)

Although Nancy is pretty, Susan is more intelligent. (Subordination)

Carnations are sweet, *but roses are lovelier*. (Coordination)

N–V–N–N (Subject–Predicate–Direct Object–Indirect Object)

Experiments:

Daddy gave me the book. (to me)

She read Peter a story. (to Peter)
The teacher told Larry the assignment. (to Larry)
Daddy gave me the _____. (book, money, permission)
Daddy gave _____ the book. (Mother, the neighbor)
_____ gave me the book. (Milly, A friend, My teacher)

Complete the formula:

$Noun_1$	Verb	$Noun_2$	$Noun_3$

Creating original sentences

The chief purpose of examining the structure of English sentences and experimenting with methods of expansion should be, as we have previously noted, the development of student ability to create, to compose, to generate original sentences. Experiments with sentence patterns and methods of expanding basic patterns should lead, furthermore, to greater skill and confidence in creating sentences that are not only interesting and effective but are also written with style, a style that is distinctive for each individual. To achieve this end we must provide many opportunities for the student to compose sentences and to discuss sentences. How can we work toward this end?

Generative (also called "transformational") grammar suggests the technique of changing a basic sentence (kernel) into many varied forms. Students can work with one sentence to produce its many varieties (transforms) in this manner:

Basic sentence:	That book is yellow.
Negative:	That book isn't yellow.
Question:	Is that book yellow?
	Isn't that book yellow?
	Which book is yellow?
	Where is the book that is yellow?
Others:	Here is the book that is yellow.
	There is the book that is yellow.
	It is that book which is yellow.
Basic sentence:	Tom drives the car.
Negative:	Tom doesn't drive the car.
	Tom cannot drive the car.
	Tom may not drive the car.
	Tom should not drive the car.
Question:	Can Tom drive the car?
	Will Tom drive the car?
	Must Tom drive the car?
Imperative:	Tom, drive the car.
	Drive the car, Tom.

Even more helpful, however, in teaching students to compose varied sentences is the process of expanding the basic pattern. Through many experiments in developing given sentences, the student acquires great flexibility in producing interesting original sentences. Note that as each sentence pattern was introduced, the experiments encouraged students to expand the pattern. After students have explored the possibilities for expanding sentences, have them examine the methods that have been used to expand a given sentence. Inductively, they can discover certain methods of expansion which can be repeated. At this time the common terminology for these methods should be supplied to provide the vocabulary for discussing sentence development:

Modification

Basic sentence—The boy went home.

The tired, but happy, boy went home. (Development of noun cluster)
The boy went home after school. (Prepositional phrase)
The boy immediately went home. (Adverb)
Having completed his work, the boy went home. (Participial phrase)
Combination: Having completed his work, the tired, but happy, boy immediately went home after school.

Compounding

Basic sentence—Debbie lives on Oak Street.

Debbie and Karen live on Oak Street. (Subject)
Debbie lives on Oak Street and goes to Maynard School. (Predicate)
Debbie lives on Oak Street, and she attends Maynard School. (Whole sentence)

Apposition

Basic sentence—Mr. Hadmon is an interesting person.

Mr. Hadmon, *our sixth grade teacher,* is an interesting person.
Our sixth grade teacher, *Mr. Hadmon,* is an interesting person.
An interesting person is our sixth grade teacher, *Mr. Hadmon.*
Mr. Hadmon, *well-read and informed,* is an interesting person.

Subordination

Basic sentence—Joe likes to play ball.

Joe, *who is in eighth grade,* likes to play ball. (Modifying subject)
Joe likes to play ball *whenever he has a chance.* (Modifying predicate)
Although Joe likes to play ball, he also studies hard.
Because Joe likes to play ball, he practices each Saturday.

The student's linguistic library

Following is a brief bibliography of books which will provide supplementary reading in the area of language study. All are recommended for the elementary school library, for the elementary school student will find research intriguing as he studies early development of English, the work of the linguist, origins of English words, and discovers "word play."

Alexander, Arthur. *The Magic of Words*. Prentice-Hall, 1962. (Intermediate)*
Language development.

Applegate, Mauree. *The First Book of Language*. Watts, 1962. (Intermediate)
Discusses use of parts of speech in writing.

Asimov, Isaac. *Words from the Myths*. Houghton Mifflin, 1961. (Intermediate,
Advanced) Explains origins of words which appear in the Bible.

—— *Words in Genesis*. Houghton Mifflin, 1962. (Intermediate, Advanced)
Excellent book on origins of words associated with mythology.

—— *Words of Science and the History Behind Them*. Houghton Mifflin,
1959. (Intermediate, Advanced)

—— *Words on the Map*. Houghton Mifflin, 1962. (Intermediate, Advanced.)

Batchelor, Julie F. *Communication: From Cave to Television*. Harcourt, 1953.
(Intermediate) Explores the many ways of communicating.

Cahn, William, and Rhoda Cahn. *The Story of Writing from Cave Art to
Computer*. Harvey House, 1963. Development of language.

Denison, Carol. *Passwords to People*. Dodd, 1956. (Intermediate) An entertaining introduction to the history of language.

Epstein, Samuel and Beryl. *The First Book of Words*. Watts, 1954. (Intermediate) Beginning study of language.

—— *The First Book of Printing*. Watts, 1955. (Intermediate) History of
printing.

Ernst, Margaret S. *In a Word*. Knopf, 1939. (Intermediate) Word origins;
illustrated by James Thurber.

—— *Words*, Knopf, 1936, (Intermediate) Development of the English
language.

—— *Words: English Roots and How They Grew*. Knopf, 1937. (Intermediate) Origins of English words.

—— *More about Words*. Knopf, 1951. (Intermediate) An assortment of stories
about word origins.

Evans, Bergen. *Comfortable Words*. Random House, 1962. (Intermediate, Advanced) Stories of word origins.

Evans, Bergen and Cornelia Evans. *A Dictionary of Contemporary American
Usage*. Random House, 1957. (Advanced) Excellent reference and provocative information.

Fadiman, Clifton. *Wally the Wordworm*. Macmillan, 1964. (Primary, Intermediate) Wally's adventures as he eats his way through the dictionary.

* Although it is impossible to "grade" books because student abilities vary widely, we have attempted to indicate difficulty and interest, thus: Primary (Levels 1-4), Intermediate (Levels 5-8), Advanced (Levels 9-Adult).

Ferguson, Charles. *The Abecedarian Book*. Little, Brown, 1964. (Intermediate, Advanced) Clever observations about words.

Folsom, Franklin. *The Language Book*. Grosset, 1963. (Intermediate) Explores all aspects of language development.

Friend, M. Newton. *Words: Tricks and Traditions*. Scribner, 1957. (Intermediate, Advanced) Collection of facts and information about words.

Funk, Charles. *Heavens to Betsy*. Harper, 1955. (Intermediate) Humorous explanations of curious expressions.

———— *Hog on Ice and Other Curious Expressions*. Harper, 1948. (Intermediate). More about words in our language.

———— *Thereby Hangs a Tale*. Harper, 1950. (Intermediate) Exploration of clichés and idioms of English.

Funk, Charles E. and Charles E. Funk, Jr. *Horsefeathers and Other Curious Words*. Harper, 1958. (Intermediate) Word origins.

Funk, Wilfred. *Word Origins and Their Romantic Stories*. Grosset, 1950. (Intermediate, Advanced) An excellent book about word origins; presents outline of affixes derived from Greek and Latin.

Hansen, Carl F., *et al. A Handbook for Young Writers*. Prentice-Hall, 1965. (Intermediate) Paperback handbook covering grammar and usage.

Hofsinde, Robert. *Indian Sign Languages*. Morrow, 1956. (Intermediate) Presents Indian "vocabulary."

———— *Indian Picture Writing*. Morrow, 1959. (Intermediate) Symbols of Indian language.

Hogben, Lancelot T. *Wonderful World of Communication*. Garden City Books, 1959. (Intermediate, Advanced) History of communication.

Hymes, Lucia and James M. Hymes. *Oodles of Noodles*. Scott, 1964. (Primary) Introduction to word play.

Irwin, Keith G. *The Romance of Writing*. Viking, 1957. (Advanced) Early developments of writing.

Juster, Norton. *The Phantom Tollbooth*. Epstein & Carroll, dist. by Random House, 1961. (Intermediate) A fictional context presents many concepts about words and the dictionary.

Kaufman, Joel. *The Golden Happy Book of Words*. Golden, 1963. (Primary) Introduces many words.

Laird, Charlton and Helene Laird. *Tree of Language*. World, 1957. (Intermediate) Development of the English language.

Lambert, Eloise. *Our Language*. Lothrop, 1955. (Intermediate) History of our language.

Lambert, Eloise, and Mario Pei. *Our Names: Where They Came from and What They Mean*. Lothrop, 1960. (Intermediate) Exploration of names.

Mathews, Mitford M. *American Words. World*, 1959. (Intermediate, Advanced) Origins of words.

Merriam, Eve. *A Gaggle of Geese*. Knopf, 1960. (Primary) Explores unusual words for groups of things.

Moorhouse, Alfred C. *The Triumph of the Alphabet; A History of Writing*. Abelard, 1953. (Intermediate, Advanced) The story of writing.

Morris, William, and Mary Morris. *Dictionary of American Word Origins.* Harper, 1963 (Intermediate, Advanced) Up-to-date words and their origins.

Ogg, Oscar. *The Twenty-Six Letters.* Crowell, 1948. (Intermediate) History of writing.

O'Neill, Mary. *Word Words Words.* Doubleday, 1966 (Intermediate) Rhymes about words.

Osmond, Edward. *From Drumbeat to Tickertape.* Criterion, 1960. (Intermediate) Development of writing and printing techniques.

Partridge, Eric. *A Charm of Words.* Hamilton, 1960. (Intermediate) Stories about words.

Pei, Mario. *All about Language.* Lippincott, 1954. (Intermediate, Advanced) Development of language.

——— *Our National Heritage.* Houghton, 1965. (Intermediate, Advanced) Cultural and linguistic heritage of Americans.

Provensen, Alice, and Martin Provensen. *Karen's Opposites.* Golden, 1963. (Primary) Introduction to antonyms.

Radlauer, Ruth S. *Good Times with Words.* Melmont, 1963. (Intermediate) Using varied words in creative writing.

Rand, Ann, and Paul Rand. *Sparkle and Spin.* Harcourt, 1957. (Primary) Enjoying words together; excellent illustrations.

Reid, Alastair. *Ounce, Dice, Trice.* Little, Brown, 1958. (Intermediate) Introduction to word play by an imaginative collector of words.

Rogers, Frances. *Painted Rock to Printed Page.* Lippincott, 1960. (Intermediate) How writing developed from primitive efforts.

Roget, Peter M. *New Roget's Thesaurus of the English Language.* Rev. by Norman Lewis. Putnam, 1961. (Intermediate, Advanced) An excellent revised edition of the famous thesaurus.

Rossner, Judith. *What Kind of Feet Does a Bear Have?* Bobbs, 1963. (Primary) Introduction to word play.

Russell, Solveig P. *A Is for Apple and Why.* Abingdon, 1959. (Intermediate) How our alphabet developed.

Sage, Michael. *Words Inside Words.* Lippincott, 1961. (Intermediate) Stresses enjoyment of words.

Shipley, Joseph T. *Playing with Words.* Prentice-Hall, 1960. (Intermediate, Advanced) Written for adults; provocative for better students.

——— *Word Games for Play and Power.* Prentice-Hall, 1962. (Intermediate, Advanced) A second book about word play and the fascination of words.

Sparke, William. *Story of the English Language.* Abelard, Schuman, 1905. (Intermediate) Interesting stories of the development of the English language.

Waller, Leslie. *Our American Language.* Holt, 1960. (Primary) Introduction to the story of English.

White, Mary S. *Word Twins.* Abingdon, 1961. (Primary) Fun with homonyms.

Yates, Elizabeth. *Someday You'll Write.* Dutton, 1962. (Intermediate) Specific information for the young writer on plot development, and so on.

Zim, Herbert S. *Codes and Secret Writing.* Morrow, 1948. (Intermediate) Fascinating language activity especially for boys.

Books to Investigate

Allen, Harold B., ed., *Applied English Linguistics*. New York: Appleton, 1958. A book of introductory readings covering the broad area of language.

Barnett, Lincoln, *The Treasure of Our Tongue*. New York: Knopf, 1964. Popularization of language study; good historical background.

Bryant, Margaret, *Current English Usage*. New York: Funk & Wagnalls, 1962. Reliable discussion of usage problems.

Dean, Leonard, and Kenneth Wilson, eds., *Essays on Language and Usage*. New York: Oxford University Press, 1963. An excellent collection of selections by known authors.

Elliott, Fred T., *Language Is You*. San Francisco: Harr Wagner, 1964. Detailed study of modern grammar in workbook form.

Fries, Charles C., *Linguistics: The Study of Language*. New York: Holt, 1964. Reprint of a chapter from *Linguistics and Reading*.

Laird, Charlton, *The Miracle of Language*. New York: World, 1953. Excellent history of English; available in paper edition (Premier).

—————— *Thinking about Language*. New York: Holt, 1959. A short provocative book.

Metropolitan School Study Council, *Structural Linguistics; An Introduction for Teachers and Administrators*. New York: Teachers College, 1961. A pamphlet which presents an excellent resume.

Robert, Paul, *English Sentences*. New York: Harcourt, 1962. Detailed study of the sentence.

Tiedt, Iris M., and Sidney W. Tiedt, eds., *Readings on Contemporary English in the Elementary School*. Englewood Cliffs, N.J.: Prentice-Hall, 1967. See "The Study of Language."

Wetmore, Thomas H., ed., *Linguistics in the Classroom*. Champaign, Ill. National Council of Teachers of English, 1963. Eight articles reprinted from *English Journal*.

We dwell upon a word we know
Repeating till the word we know so well
Becomes a wonder.

Alfred, Lord Tennyson

3

The Wonder of Words

Creation, discovery, exploration, inquiry, serendipity, perception, magic—these are the concepts we wish to emphasize as we introduce students to the wonder of words. States the imaginative author, Alastair Reid:

> ... If you grow to love words for their own sake, you will begin to collect words for yourself, and you will be grateful, as I am, to all the people who collect odd words and edit odd dictionaries, out of sheer astonishment and affection.[1]

Words, the basic symbols which make up any language, are the tools of the writer and speaker. Spoken, written, read, or heard, they affect the lives of every person from birth. Words are so integral a part of our way of living that the early development in children of a positive attitude toward words and word study is important, for it is through this pleasurable feeling for words that the young student will learn to use them with effect.

How can we promote this feeling for words? We certainly cannot accomplish this end through the assigning of lists of words to be learned, no matter how interesting they are or how useful we know them to be. The approach to student involvement with words must be rather through discovery and inquiry techniques, for it has been found that young people tend to remember and to be interested in those discoveries which they themselves make. It is this approach to word study which we shall explore in this chapter.

[1] Alastair Reid, *Ounce, Dice, Trice* (Boston: Little, 1958), Introduction.

Words in Perspective

There are certain aspects of any word which can be studied—structure, sound, meaning, history—any one of which may provide the avenue toward reaching student interest and developing pleasure in the use of words. The presentation of varied perspectives of words will teach students to view words in different ways. As they learn to examine words from many angles, they will learn to use words with imagination.

Structure

Structure, in the case of a word, has multiple meanings. Looking at a word as a whole we note its shape, its appearance, its configuration. Examining the word further, we find that it is made up of individual letters and that longer words are composed of groupings of letters or syllables. We note, too, that many syllables appear frequently, as in the case of affixes (suffixes and prefixes) or other common groupings of letters. Examining the structure of varied words can be most enlightening and enlivening as in these suggestions:

- Word Shapes—Primary level children are easily taught to observe the shape of words. They trace the form of the letters with their fingers in an effort to familiarize themselves with the word. Each student can select a word which interests him. He then prints or writes this word in as many different ways as he can imagine to see how the word changes in appearance. Here is the word TRAIN, for example:

train TRAIN train niart

After he selects the type of print or script to use he executes the word on a half sheet of colored paper using large letters. (Words containing many ascending and descending letters provide more interesting shapes.) The word shape is outlined with a contrasting crayon to emphasize the shape before it is cut out. The shape is then examined to determine what it suggests—an animal, a human figure, a building, a plant—and a picture is drawn with the shape as the center of interest.

- Playful Words—Encourage students to relate the meaning of words to their appearance in a humorous type of word play. Each student can produce an example like those shown on p. 44, to be displayed on a bulletin board captioned WORDS WITH IMAGINATION:

Word Ways

al☼ft

♪uet

sno☃w

pi🐁e

ball⚇ns

fli͡ᴾ

rain

What is the value of this type of word play? Is time spent in this manner justified? The chief argument for presenting word play activities in the classroom is that these activities promote a feeling for words, a liking and respect for words. Words should never frighten or be considered dull, dutiful responsibilities. Rather they should intrigue and fascinate, inviting the young writer to play with them, to manipulate them. Intrigued by words met in this fashion, the child reaches out to discover other words.

● Word Architecture—The study of prefixes and suffixes which can be attached to root words can lead to the construction of magnificent edifices by young architects. Given a root word, each can see what words can be built. The root LIGHT, for instance, might be built into the following structure:

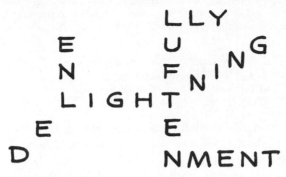

- Letter Addition—The building blocks are letters this time, with each child adding a letter at a time to produce a word. How many words can you make as you begin with the letter *O?* The answer might be:

O . . . SO . . . SON . . . NOSE . . . NOOSE . . . SNOOZE . . . SNOOZED

With I one student built these words:

I . . . IT . . . SIT . . . SITE . . . SPITE . . . SPRITE . . . PIRATES

- Repeaters—The structure of some words is particularly intriguing as in the case of words which are composed of two identical parts:

    Poohpooh   Mimi   Tata   Rahrah

More commonly these words have slight variations resulting in a rhyming effect.

    Chitchat   Hubbub   Zigzag   Tiptop   Razzledazzle

Have students conduct a search for examples of repeaters.

Sound

The sound of words—the way we say them, pronunciation, musical effects—also lends stimulus to word study. Activities focusing attention on the sound of words can be oral so that the differences can be more readily discerned by students who may miss the full significance of these differences if the words are read silently.

- Homonyms—Students are usually familiar with some examples of the words which sound alike but are not spelled alike—*to, too, two,* and *for, four, fore.* The class can conduct a Homonym Hunt, however, to discover hundreds of less familiar homonyms—*aisle, isle, I'll; council, counsel; marry, merry, Mary; carrot, carat, caret.* Each can present a set of homonyms on a poster illustrating the differences in meaning.

- Heteronyms—Introduce students to the group of words which have different pronunciations and meanings although they are spelled exactly the same. Provide a number of examples and then encourage students to discover as many other examples as possible. Each can prepare a page for a class wordbook entitled HETERONYMS, which includes examples like these:

SEPARATE—Please separate the completed pages.
SEPARATE—Each child had a separate room.
SUBJECT—Don't subject me to that experience.
SUBJECT—What is the subject of your talk?

Beginning with oral activities and developing into written activities, word study emphasizing initial sounds in words is helpful. Not only do these activities lead to the discovery of new words but they also assist in the learning of phonics skills which aid spelling and reading. Here are examples of varied approaches:

● Print a large *B* on the board. "Let's see how many words we can name in ten minutes that begin with *B*." Everybody takes a turn suggesting words which are printed on the board—*baby, bird, book, bus, Billy, Boston, ball, balloon.* . . .

● Print a large *P* on the board. "Let's see how many words we can name in ten minutes that begin with the *P sound*. Every word must contain more than four letters today." More advanced students can suggest—*princess, pleasant, plaster, paradise, pounce*. (*Pony, pheasant*, and *pea* would not be accepted according to the restrictions set.)

● "How many words can you write which begin with the first syllable RE?" Have students, without the aid of dictionaries, list as many words as possible which begin with this prefix—*refund, renew, refuse, repeat, research, reside*. Compare results after ten minutes writing examples on the board. Later, dictionaries may be explored to discover the numerous words which might have been included in this list. (*Reptile, rescue*, and *red* are not examples of this prefix.)

● "How many words can you name that begin with the sound CAT?" Students may be able to suggest *catalog, catsup, catacomb, catch, catcher, catechism, category, catfish, cattle*. After sharing any contributions have each one explore these words in the dictionary. (Would *cathedral* be acceptable this time?)

Meaning

The meaning of a word, its definition, includes both the word's denotation and its connotation. In order to communicate successfully in our complex world we must be aware not only of the meaning of a word for us, but what that same word might mean for the person to whom we are speaking. Our world would be most confusing if we were all like Humpty Dumpty in Lewis Carroll's *Through the Looking Glass*, who said:

". . . There's glory for you!"
"I don't know what you mean by 'glory,'" Alice said.

Humpty Dumpty smiled contemptuously. "Of course you don't—till I tell you. I meant, 'There's a nice knock-down argument for you!' "

"But 'glory' doesn't mean 'a nice knock-down argument,' " Alice objected.

"When I use a word," Humpty-Dumpty said in rather a scornful tone, "it means just what I choose it to mean, neither more nor less."

"The question is," said Alice, "whether you *can* make words mean so many different things."

"The question is," said Humpty-Dumpty, "which is to be Master—that's all."

The exploration of varied meanings for both common and uncommon words offers an excellent opportunity to introduce extended use of the dictionary. Vocabularies will grow as students delve deeply to discover the ideas behind the words they encounter. Your use of intriguing words in the classroom will cause students to stretch to meet your challenge, for they love new words, big words, unusual words. So speak of homonyms, clichés, palindromes, and acronyms and alert young minds will question, understand, and use these interesting words, too. There is a need to explain, but never to "water down" the English language for children of the twentieth century.

● Word Alchemy—A diverting type of extended definition which strives to demonstrate the relationship of two words. These definitions are often humorous and tend to stretch the imagination as in this example:

Can you change this pebble into a diamond?

Pebbles are rocks;
To rock is to sway;
To sway is to quake;
A quake can break glass;
Glass is like ice;
Ice sparkles like diamonds.

Presto! We have changed a pebble into a diamond!

● Confusing Words—There are many words which are frequently confused; for example, *affect* and *effect*. Displaying groups of words and encouraging a search for groups of confusing words will assist students in familiarizing themselves with the use of these words. Here are a few to initiate the search:

accent, ascent, assent (Which two are homonyms?)
dessert, desert (Can these words be homonyms?)
loose, lose, loss
accept, except
they're, there, their
you're, your
whose, who's

● Writing Definitions—Have students be *lexicographers.* Imagine their amazement when you question, "How would you like to be lexicographers today?" Each student can select several common words to define so that there is no question about its meaning, A chair, for example, may be defined as "something to sit on," but what about a bench or a stool? Definitions can be tested by a board of examiners.

● Unfamiliar Words—Present a word that is likely to be unfamiliar to almost everyone. Have each person write the definition of this word. Then use the same word in a sentence context. Each will rewrite the first definition. Then check the dictionary definition. How many had a correct definition the first time? Did context aid others in discovering the correct definition?

● Long Words—Students are fascinated by enormous words. Share some of the following impressive examples and encourage students to submit any others they find:

  sesquipedalian
  sesquicentennial
  hippopotomonstrousesquipedalian
  pneumonoultramicroscopicsilicovolcanoconiosis
  floccinancinihilipilification
  antidisestablishmentarianism
  ptertiaryoctylphenoxyethyoxyethylodimethylbenzylammoniumchloxide

> What is the longest word in the dictionary?
>
> SMILES—There is a mile between the first letter and the last.

● Jingo Lingo—Jingo Lingo consists of a two-word verse (sometimes called Terse Verse or Hinky Pinkies) plus a humorous definition. Students will delight in composing *Daffynitions* to accompany the verse which might include the following:

SPINAL FINAL:	The big examination for medical students.
VOTER QUOTER:	A public opinion poll.
STOUT SCOUT:	An overgrown cub.
TIGER GEIGER:	Necessary equipment for every big-game hunter.
FEATHER WEATHER:	It's for the birds!

● Context and Definition—Encourage the use of the context to reveal the meaning of a difficult or unfamiliar word. Present new words in sentences which provide some clue to the meaning, having students write the definition of the underlined word before checking themselves with the dictionary.

  It was a *picayune* matter, but he insisted on proving the statement.

  The *enormous* dog frightened the small girl.

  They felt it was *expedient* to hold the meeting immediately.

  The food was completely *unpalatable* although we were hungry.

  Can you trace their *itinerary* on the map?

● Reworded Proverbs—Able students will especially enjoy disguising familiar proverbs by rewording them. These proverbs are then presented to the class which can try to identify the original saying. What proverbs are being stated in these examples?

Were desires stallions, mendicants would be equestrians.

The absence of prevarication proves to be an advantageous plan of action.

History

Another aspect of word study is the origin or history of a word, its etymology. Where do words come from? How do words get into our language? The histories of words make fascinating reading, and a number of books have been written about the origins of words. Most of the following can be used by the better student in the middle grades through the adult reader. The information provided can be retold for younger students.

Ernst, Margaret, and James Thurber, *In a Word*. Knopf, 1939.
————. *More about Words*, Knopf, 1951.
Evans, Bergen, *Comfortable Words*. Random House, 1962.
————, and Cornelia Evans, *A Dictionary of Contemporary American Usage*. Random House, 1957.
Ferguson, Charles W., *The Abecedarian Book*. Little, Brown, 1964.
Funk, Charles, *Horsefeathers and Other Curious Words*. Harper, 1958.
————, *Thereby Hangs a Tale; Stories of Curious Word Origins*. Harper, 1958.
Funk, Wilfred, *Word Origins and Their Romantic Stories*. Funk, 1951.
Morris, William, and Mary Morris, *The American Dictionary of Word Origins*. Harper, 1963.
Partridge, Eric, *A Charm of Words*. Hamilton, 1960.

In examining the origins of English words, students will soon notice that there are a number of specific sources of words: (1) coined words, (2) borrowed words, (3) adapted words, (4) names of inventors or persons associated with certain objects or ideas. (5) imitations of sounds, and (6) fusions of known words. Students can make individual studies of words which originated in different ways or the class can work together in compiling collections of words which fall into the listed categories. Described here are additional activities to stimulate learning about word histories.

● Portmanteau words—Students will be intrigued by these new words which have been created from two words pressed together as in these examples:

chortle—chuckle + snort (Lewis Carroll)
slanguage—slang + language
slithy—slimy + lithe (Lewis Carroll)

● Word Inventions—Introduce students to Lewis Carroll's poem, "Jabberwocky," which is composed of invented language. Students can invent words for objects or ideas which they think need new words. What words could be invented for the following?

> A chair with a broken leg.
> A letter that has been opened by mistake.
> A book that no one enjoys reading.
> A trip to the oceanside.

● A second-grade child wrote this poem after a class discussion of words and how they are used:

WORDS [2]

by Cindy Rowland

Words are sometimes gentle and sweet;
Words are sometimes nice and neat.
Words are sometimes mean or cruel;
Some are slang, not according to rule.

Some are common words like *if* and *and;*
Some are words from a foreign land.
But words always have to mean something—
A robin's egg or a blue jay's wing.
How many words there are nobody knows.
When a word comes, it never goes.

● Acronyms—Where did words like *radar* or *snafu* originate? Many contemporary words have been derived from the words used to define a concept, but most people have long since forgotten (or never knew) the definition. Words composed of the first letters or syllables of a longer term are called *acronyms;* many organizations known by a series of letters which have become the name itself are also examples.

SNAFU = *S*ituation *N*ormal: *A*ll *F*ouled *U*p
RADAR = *Ra*dio *D*etecting *a*nd *R*anging
UNESCO = *U*nited *N*ations' *E*ducational, *S*cientific, and *C*ultural *O*rganization

● People and Places—Students can conduct a search for words in common usage which are based on place names or the names of people, as in these examples:

People	*Places*
camellia	frankfurter
Fahrenheit	hamburger
macadam	italics
pasteurize	marathon
pompadour	shanghai
victorian	waterloo

[2] Teacher: Kathy Woodbury, Second Grade, Coventry School, Campbell, California.

● Word Cartoons—Encourage the investigation of word origins which can then be shared through the drawing of illustrative posters depicting the origin of especially interesting words. Here are a number of words which have intriguing histories.

agony	gargantuan
alphabet	journey
anecdote	magazine
bombast	milliner
bonfire	pedigree
canopy	quixotic
chivalry	queue
deliberate	uranium

The Teacher and Words

What do you know about words? Have you ever read a page in the dictionary? Do you notice words as you read? Do you find yourself jotting words on slips of paper for further investigation? We hope that you share the feeling expressed by Evelyn Waugh, who wrote: "Words should be an intense pleasure just as leather should be to a shoemaker. If there isn't that pleasure for a writer, maybe he ought to be a philosopher."

Although it is true that most teachers are not writers, it is equally true that the teacher who knows little of the lore of words and has no real enthusiasm for experimenting with words and the effects they produce will never instill a love for words in the student. For this reason it is imperative that you examine your own knowledge of words and explore means to acquire additional knowledge.

Self-evaluation

One of the simplest methods for assessing your knowledge of words is through a vocabulary test intended for adults. Of the 10 common words presented below, for how many can you select the correct meaning? If you correctly identify nine or ten, you're on the right track, but less than five correctly identified would certainly indicate that you need to concentrate on becoming more aware of words.

1. ambiguous: (a) having two separate parts, (b) desiring fame, (c) uncertain in meaning, (d) talkative
2. chastise: (a) punish, (b) chase, (c) virtuous, (d) help
3. effervescent: (a) efficient, (b) bubbly, (c) hopeful, (d) quiet
4. garrulous: (a) small, (b) rapid, (c) wordy, (d) completed
5. implacable: (a) misplaced, (b) hurried, (c) insolent, (d) relentless
6. mien: (a) bearing, (b) definition, (c) rudeness, (d) place
7. petulant: (a) soothing, (b) flowerlike, (c) fretful, (d) stopping
8. sagacious: (a) wise, (b) unhappy, (c) green, (d) fastened
9. timbre: (a) lumber, (b) tone, (c) shy, (d) time
10. writhe: (a) inscribe, (b) right, (c) twist, (d) anger [3]

[3] ANSWERS: 1-c, 2-a, 3-b, 4-c, 5-d, 6-a, 7-c, 8-a, 9-b, 10-c.

As a teacher of English, it is important, too, that you know words commonly used in the study of the English language. It is surprising to find teachers who mispronounce or use incorrectly terms that should be well known to a teacher in the language arts. Can you identify the following terms? Can you pronounce them easily?

homonym	obsolete	linguistics
antonym	archaic	phonics
synonym	colloquial	phonetics
cliché	onomatopoeia	phoneme
euphemism	alliteration	etymology

Acquiring knowledge

How does one improve one's knowledge of words? Just as for the elementary school student, the answer is not the learning of long lists of words; this type of study might result only in killing any real interest in words. Rather you must develop habits of inquiry and an awareness of words, so that you notice words that sparkle, words that are peculiar, words that offer something to you personally. The steps are three: (1) desire, (2) explore, and (3) experiment.

We shall assume that the desire is present or you would not be reading this paragraph, so we can safely proceed to the exploration. A good place to begin exploring words is in books. Here are several we would recommend:

● *Playing with Words* by Joseph T. Shipley. (Prentice-Hall, 1960).

"You should enjoy words, play with them, make them familiar. Then they will respond to you, and let you command them. And the right word will come for your need." You will meet many fascinating words and ideas about words while browsing through this small book.

● *Word Origins and Their Romantic Stories* by Wilfred Funk. (Funk, 1951).

This book is particularly recommended because the histories of words are grouped in an interesting manner. Also worth careful study is the last section, which presents the many Latin and Greek affixes and common roots which compose a large percentage of the words in the English language.

● *Ounce, Dice, Trice* by Alastair Reid. (Little, Brown, 1958).

Although this book was written for children, it is equally delightful for the adult who is being introduced to word play. What is a Hamburgler? You'll know after reading this book.

Next let's turn to the dictionary. When purchasing a dictionary, try to obtain one that provides the etymology and gives synonyms. Get in the habit of using the dictionary to find the meanings of words which puzzle you. Use a file card as a bookmark when reading so that you can jot words down easily for later investigation. A special type of dictionary which is also very useful for anyone who is interested in words is the thesaurus (there's a word for investigation), which is simply a dictionary of synonyms. Several synonym dictionaries are now available in paperback editions.

To become well acquainted with words you must do more than explore—you must *experiment*. You must *use* words, for using a word makes it truly yours. The many word activities described for use in the classroom throughout this chapter will provide ideas for experimentation for you, too. Your experimenting with the activity will lead to your better understanding of the technique as well, so that you will be better able to teach students. Here are other ideas about words to assist your individual experimentation.

● List 10 common adjectives. Can you name two synonyms for each adjective?

● Open the dictionary to any page. Which words do you know on this page? Read the definitions of the words you don't know. Which of these could you add to your every day vocabulary?

● Purchase a small spiral notebook in which to jot interesting words or ideas about words. You will meet intriguing ideas in the most unusual places—billboards, magazines, conversation, a menu, the newspaper.

● Have you ever heard of an OXYMORON? This esoteric word means the use of two apparently incongruous words to produce an epigrammatic effect as in these examples:

      sweet sorrow   broadly ignorant
      cruel kindness   trained incapacity

Conduct a search for *oxymora* (plural) and you will have a rare collection, a conversation stopper.

Classroom Strategies

Planning experiences with words is a worthwhile effort, for not only are you teaching specific information about words presented, but you are also generating interest in language, its study, and its use. Word study, too, is appropriate to the entire elementary school curriculum, for words are an integral part of any subject matter taught. We shall explore in this section a wide variety of word activities which might be used in the classroom.

Concepts to be taught

What concepts are we trying to teach as we present words in the class-room? There are many concepts to be considered, and they range widely in complexity. Listed here are some ideas to teach about words which we have presented in a developmental sequence. Consider the back-ground of the group with which you are working before deciding what concepts to present, for within this sequence each concept can also be introduced at varying levels of difficulty.

1. Words may name people, places, and things.

   Begin with rather ordinary names, moving quickly to more exotic, exciting names. Maps, almanacs, and dictionaries will suggest fascinating examples.
   Do names make a difference? Shakespeare wrote: "A rose by any other name would smell as sweet." Do you agree?
   Discuss the ways we have changed names in our society as marks of status. A janitor is now a custodian; an undertaker is now a mortician; a hairdresser is now a beautician. These and other euphemisms can instigate interesting studies by able students.[4]

2. Words may tell that action is taking place.

   An excellent oral exploration of words focuses on the concerted effort of a class to compile a collection of synonyms for a verb which is overworked in common usage. Have students suggest sub-stitutes, more exact words, for WALK as these synonyms are listed on the board:

slip	trip	stride
rush	waddle	steal
stroll	skip	bounce
strut	creep	limp

   Varied types of walking can then be demonstrated. A discussion of situations which require certain kinds of walking may ensue. When would you creep? When would you rush? Who might waddle? Who might bounce?

3. Words may describe people, places, and things.

   The study of adjectives is fascinating as you begin thinking of synonyms for commonly used examples. List a variety of phrases to be explored together:

a pretty girl	*a tired man*
vivacious lass	weary worker
charming miss	exhausted fieldhand
attractive girl	exasperated father
chic mademoiselle	fatigued scholar

---

[4] Read the chapter on Euphemisms in H. L. Mencken's provocative work, *The American Language* (Knopf, 1936).

4. Words may describe actions.

Show a picture which depicts action, perhaps a boy throwing a ball. How does he throw the ball—carefully, wildly, accurately, swiftly? Introduce sentences in which adverbs may be inserted to influence the meaning of the writer.

Mildred spoke _____.

The author wrote _____.

They ran _____.

5. One word may have many meanings.

Explore *Multiple Meanings* of many common words. "Words are like those insects that take their color from their surroundings," remarked Elihu Root, and it is interesting to explore the influence of context on the meaning of even a simple word like *run:*

He can *run* fast.
The rabbit's *run* was small.
The politician will *run* for office.
It is a short *run* to the city.
She has a *run* in her stocking.

Each student can choose one word—*trunk, list, swing, plant, catch*—which has multiple meanings that can be depicted on pages for a class book of words. Students might also write verses about words to illustrate their varied meanings as in this example:

What Is a Trunk?

A trunk is sometimes
An elephant's nose.
It's part of your body
Or a large case for clothes.
A tree has a trunk,
And so does your car.
And a telephone trunk line
Carries messages far!

6. Different words may mean almost the same thing.

Explore words which describe color. How many ways can you express RED, for example? Have students conduct searches for varied examples displaying the discoveries on a large Color Wheel. Near Red would be some of the following:

Cherry, vermillion, rose, ruby, scarlet, flame, crimson.

Which word does not belong?

glisten, glitter, shine, round
aid, help, lame, assist
increment, coffers, addition, increase

7. Words are often made of distinct parts.

Discuss prefixes—*pre, ex, in, de,* etc. Select one prefix, having the class name as many words beginning with the syllable as possible (without dictionaries). For EX, words might be listed thus:

example	exercise	examine
examination	exit	excellent
explain	exclaim	exciting

Examine a variety of words to discover the parts which compose them.

entangle	respectfully
recruitment	remarkably
hopelessness	delighted
insightful	inscription

8. Two words may be put together.

An intriguing activity with compound words is a type of CHAIN REACTION in which students try to name a compound word which begins with the last half of the previous word named, in this way:

Hangman, Manhole, Wholesome (permit liberties), Somewhere, Wherever, Everlasting.

The object is to make the chain as long as possible, so students try to use words which have possibilities. EVERLASTING, above will break the chain.

9. Some words are more colorful than others.

Have students collect words which fascinate them for a variety of reasons. Have each present a favorite word telling the class about it. You can share favorites, too. Words like these are interesting to us.

Shibboleth	Potpourri	Caravansary
Scrimshaw	Quixotic	Effervescent

Why do you like certain words? Who knows? The meaning may intrigue you or just saying the word which has a certain rhythm may be pleasant.

10. Some words have unusual characteristics.

Palindromes are words which form the same word (or even a whole sentence) when read either forward or backward as:

RADAR HANNAH MADAM LEVEL TOT
Rise to vote, sir.
Able was I ere I saw Elba. (words reputedly spoken by Napoleon)

Present a group of words like these:

ABSTEMIOUS, FACETIOUS, ABSTENTIOUS, ARSENIOUS

Do you notice any peculiarity about these words? Display them for a day or two if necessary to permit students to think about them.

(They contain the five common vowels in alphabetical order.) Others contain the five vowels, but not in order—AUCTIONEER, GRACIOUSNESS, CAULIFLOWER, EQUATION, and so on.

11. Many English words have been borrowed from other languages.

    Conduct a search for words borrowed directly from Spanish, French, Italian, German, and other languages. French words might include:

boudoir	ballet	entrée
encore	souvenir	en route
fiancée	vogue	parole

12. Words develop and change in meaning.

    Have students investigate the meaning of words as they develop historically. Try some of these:

bureau	rankle	heckle	stink
garret	tawdry	magazine	patter

13. Words are often invented or coined to meet needs.

    Students can investigate the origin of words which have been coined as: BLURB, GERRYMANDER, ALPHABET, MAVERICK, OK, MACKINTOSH.

    Are there objects or ideas for which we need new names in our society? (See the section on "History" at the beginning of this chapter for more ideas about Word Inventions.)

14. Some words and phrases become worn out.

    Clichés are fascinating and humorous. Consult Eric Partridge's *Dictionary of Clichés* for explanations of the origins of many of these diverting expressions. Taken literally they provide motivation for stories and illustrations. What happens, for example, when someone interprets these expressions literally?

    > That boy is a *dog in the manger.*
    > Do you always *beat around the bush?*
    > Come, let us *bury the hatchet.*
    > They were *head over heels in love.*
    > Be careful, you're *skating on thin ice!*
    > Poor John isn't *out of the woods yet.*

Planning experiences with words

Many experiences with words develop by accident when something said in the classroom suggests a brief discussion about words or when students ask questions about words encountered which then leads to further research or study. In addition to these highly beneficial incidental experiences there is also a need for teacher-planned lessons about words.

Planned experiences with words frequently focus attention on the use of the dictionary, which is certainly a most essential tool for even the youngest student. The teacher must be cautious, however, when planning dictionary studies to ensure that these activities are not dull, drill-type lessons which may actually kill student interest in words and in using the dictionary. Too many dittoed sheets read something like this:

> Here are twenty words. Find each word in the dictionary.
> Write the definition of each word and use it in a sentence.

A little ingenuity will serve to heighten student interest while at the same time providing for teaching dictionary skills. Using a title for the activity makes it sound more enticing. A different method of indicating whether the child has found the required definition will also relieve the monotony of just "finding words in the dictionary." The following examples are taken from a duplicated sheet entitled: TAKE YOUR CHOICE, which is one way of enlivening dictionary usage.

> Which would you rather be—a SPELUNKER or a PHILATELIST? _____
> Why? _____
>
> Which would you rather have—a QUIRT or a SACHET? _____
> Why? _____
>
> Would you rather be a PRINCIPAL or ruler of a PRINCIPALITY? _____
> Why? _____

In the type of questions used in this example there is no *one* right answer. The answer to the question *Why?* is an individual response which may differ from those made by other students. We need to emphasize this kind of individuality through open-ended questions and the encouragement of more creative answers.

Individualized approaches to words

Word study can often be pursued individually. The gifted student is particularly well prepared to investigate varied aspects of words. Games and puzzles are diverting and informative as before-school activities or for the student who completes an assignment ahead of schedule.

The following word games are suggested for use in the classroom. Students should be encouraged not only to solve examples given but also to create word games to share with other members of the class. We have noted that more actual learning and enjoyment is derived from the development of the game itself than from its solution.

● Scavenger Hunt—This variety of word quiz, and others, can be prepared by students who often display real skill in writing provocative types of word activities. The students' dictionaries are needed for these discoveries:

What is the word following *murder?* _____

Find two birds. _____   _____

● Yes or No—Again dictionaries are needed to determine the right answer.

Is a bird fond of eating limericks? _____

Is a lion carnivorous? _____

Might a lady be garrulous? _____

● Introduce students to Spoonerisms, speech slips of the type made by the Reverend W. A. Spooner of Oxford University. Have students invent these slips and create situations around them for fun with words and writing. Here are two remarks supposedly made by this illustrious gentleman:

"Is the bean dizzy?"

When a parishioner complained, "Someone is occupewing my pie," he rejoined, "I'm very sorry, Madam. I'll sew you to another sheet."

● Add an A to the following words to produce a new word. Each student should try to find additional examples.

rod—road
pry—pray
red—read
fir—fair
slam—salaam (2 A's)
bird—baird
bred—bread
shred—shared

● The interest of this type of puzzle depends on its form, DIAMOND O. Definitions will usually need to accompany the unsolved example.

```
              c  O  t
           s  n  O  w  y
        u  n  d  O  i  n  g
     r  e  s  t  O  r  i  n  g
  s  u  b  t  l  O  o  r  i  n  g
     d  e  p  l  O  r  i  n  g
        s  p  r  O  u  t  s
           p  r  O  u  d
              t  O  n
```

A student teacher [5] in a third-grade classroom used a number of word activities with the children. Then she encouraged each child to construct an activity. Geoff produced a group of scrambled words:

MAKE WORDS OF THESE

1. sdnuo—noise   s_____
2. npduo—hit   p_____
3. inur—to wreck r_____
4. urn—flee   r_____
5. lsraya—fee   s_____
6. yco—shy   c_____
7. mjup—pep   j_____
8. stsasi—help   a_____

Michelle developed a group of antonyms with the instructions: "Draw lines to their antonyms."

dog	glad
white	sea
mad	south
happy	cat
land	girl
north	sad
west	stand
boy	black
sit	east
father	work
sister	out
in	brother
play	mother

● Word Brackets [6]—For this game print a word vertically on the chalkboard. Choose a holiday word, one connected with a subject being studied, or an interesting new word you wish to introduce. To the right print the same word with its letters reversed in order as shown. The object is to insert letters between those given to make new words, the longer the better, for every letter inserted gives the player a point. Students will enjoy challenging each other.

G	n	a	T		G	i	a	n	T
H	i	s	S		H	e	a	r	S
O	h	i	O		O	l	e	O
S	m	a	s	H		S	p	e	e	c	H
T	a	G		T	e	a	c	h	i	n	G

Score: 10   Score: 18

[5] Mrs. Bonnie Manley teaching with Mrs. Young, Booksin School, San Jose, California.

[6] Tiedt, Sidney and Iris. *The Elementary Teacher's Complete Ideas Handbook.* Prentice-Hall, 1965, p. 76.

● DOUBLE TACTICS—Two students can play a word-forming game on a frame as in the illustration. As the players alternate turns, each tries to form a word by adding only one letter at a time. Each word formed scores one point.

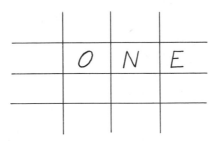

In this example Jill started with the letter O, Mary added N to score with ON. Then Jill added E to form ONE. We readily see that Mary can place a letter before ONE to form BONE, TONE or CONE.

● TOM SWIFTIES—The Tom Swifty was a twentieth-century contribution to word play. Small books quickly appeared illustrating the use of adverbs especially appropriate to the quotation in a sentence as in these examples:

"I'll have seafood salad," she muttered crabbily.

"What a beautiful piece of wood," he remarked craftily.

"My, I'm terribly hoarse today," she whinnied.

"That song is too long," he announced curtly.

Students can invent Tom Swifties and portray a situation in which someone is making this remark. The humorous illustrations can be displayed for enjoyment by all and later compiled in an entertaining book.

● WORDBOOKS—Encourage individuals or groups of students to conduct searches for interesting categories of words. The types of words collected may reflect an individual interest—SPACE WORDS, WORDS AND NUMBERS, HORSES AND WORDS, WORDS ABOUT DOGS—or a collection may be focused on WORD ODDITIES, SPANIARDS IN OUR LANGUAGE, ANTONYMS, WORD PLAY, MY FAVORITE WORDS, etc.

● WORD PUZZLES—Here is another variety of word puzzle which can be developed by students. What is the secret word?

S	a	f	e	t	y
s	C	o	l	d	s
s	a	H	a	r	a
t	h	r	O	a	t
h	o	l	l	O	w
s	p	r	a	w	L

Word study in all subject areas

Word study is of particular importance in that it permeates the entire elementary school curriculum. A student who has developed an inquisitive attitude toward words will reach out to the words of science, the words of history; he will be constantly aware of the intrigue of words. The alert teacher will utilize opportunities that arise to further word interests whether they occur during the language period or in the middle of a mathematics lesson. Included in this section are suggested activities which relate interest in words to subjects other than English itself.

SCIENCE is a subject which offers many fascinating new words. Begin a study of words that are related to space, medicine, birds, cats, insects, and so on. Display a group of words with related pictures.

● *Words of Science* by Isaac Asimov (Houghton Mifflin) is an excellent collection of words in this field. The story behind each word is explained in readable fashion by a reputable scientist whom some will recognize as a writer of science fiction.

● CATEGORIES is an interesting word game that can feature knowledge in science, thus:

	Space	*Biology*
A	*astronaut*	*ant*
T		
O		
M		
I		
C		

● Word Quizzes can focus attention on scientific knowledge. Have students compose questions like these:

With what word does the name of this animal rhyme? GNU _____

Where would you expect to find an egret? _____

What is the origin of our word HELICOPTER? _____

What does the prefix TELE mean? _____

MATHEMATICS can be helpful in furthering interest in word study as we begin thinking about the words which denote number and the processes used in computing. The study of numerology also provides fascinating words which are intriguing to the young student.

- THE ORIGIN OF NUMBER WORDS can be the title of an interesting collection of words related to numbers. Have a page for each numeral, on which are presented words related to that numeral. The page on which a large 1 is printed would bear some of these words with information about their origin:

one	primary	prime
first	unison	unicorn
solo	unity	primer
sole	unanimous	lone

- The magic powers with which numbers were supposed to be endowed can provide material for challenging research. Information gathered might be presented on a bulletin board, for example, bearing a large cut-paper 3, around which is mounted information about the magic properties of this number and its influence.

    It is related to the Holy Trinity.
    Three strikes in baseball.
    Three magic wishes.
    I'll give you three guesses.
    Third time's a lucky charm.

SOCIAL STUDIES provides a wealth of word-centered activities as we discuss words in history, the history of words, words related to travel and the map, words we have borrowed from other lands and languages, words in propaganda, and so on.

- WORD CROSSINGS are provocative ways of showing relationships between words. The main word is supplied while definitions are given for the other words to be identified as in this example:

```
                    F
1.  N   O   R   M   A   N   D   Y
2.      P   A   R   I   S
                    N
                    C
3.          S   E   I   N   E
```

The word FRANCE would be printed in place with spaces for the other letters. Definitions might be: (1) section, (2) city, (3) river. Students can construct Word Crossings for names of people, regions, countries, etc.

- ACROSTICS also lend themselves to words in social studies. An acrostic can be developed for a person's name, a country, river, city, and so on. Here is an Acrostic for FRANCE:

F	R	A	N	C		
R	H	O	N	E		
A	L	P	S			
N	A	P	O	L	E	O	N
C	A	L	A	I	S	
E	I	F	F	E	L	

What is the secret of this puzzle? (The first letter of each word read vertically spells a word.) Definitions are written to assist the solution of the puzzle.

- *Words on the Map* and *Words from the Myths* (Houghton Mifflin) are two titles by Isaac Asimov which explore words related to areas in the social sciences.

ART offers not only an interesting vocabulary of its own but also techniques and media for enhancing the study of words related to other subjects.

- WORD CUTTINGS are made by writing a word on the fold of a sheet of paper as indicated. The word is then cut out without disturbing the fold. Opened flat, the word cutting forms an attractive design, thus:

- WORD COLLAGES provide an unusual method for displaying words which interest students. Each student clips words from magazines selecting words on one particular theme—FRENCH WORDS, SPRING WORDS, PROVOCATIVE WORDS, R WORDS—or a potpourri of words can be included. The collection of words is then arranged over a poster with pieces of colored paper used to unite the clipped words and to add color and interest to the collage.

- WORD INTERPRETATIONS can be made by each individual. Each person selects a word—FREEDOM, MUSIC, COLOR, BLUE, TRADE, LANGUAGE, SCIENCE, HEAT, and so on. He then develops a poster on which the word appears as well as drawings which interpret the meaning of this word for the individual.

- WORD BOOKS can be tastefully enhanced by the addition of an attractive cover prepared through simple art techniques—stenciling, crayon resist, dribbling of paint in patterns, etc. The form of a booklet can also add interest to the project—the long, slim form; paper cut in an unusual shape; varied types of ties. Attention to printing and the arrangement of a title on the page will assist students in preparing a more effective booklet, a work in which they can take pride.

Books to Investigate

Some of the books listed here are more adult than others. All will, however, suggest ideas for use in the classroom. All are books you will want to know.

Alexander, Arthur, *The Magic of Words*. Englewood Cliffs, N.J.: Prentice-Hall, 1962. "In man's kind of language sounds, markings, and gestures stand for feelings, things, and ideas. Let's take our friend the dog again. "Dog" stands for a certain family of animals. But we could just as well use *Hund*, as the Germans do; or *chien* if we prefer French; or *perro* if we like to speak Spanish. *Dog, Hund, chien, perro;* each of these word are symbols for the barking creature we call 'man's best friend.' " (p. 19)

Epstein, Sam, and Beryl Epstein, *The First Book of Words*. New York: Watts, 1954. An introductory treatment of the development of our language written with a simple vocabulary that enables the young reader to discover facts about language independently.

Fadiman, Clifton, *Wally the Wordworm*. New York: Macmillan, 1964. A clever story of a whimsical worm's adventures as he eats his way through the dictionary.

Ferguson, Charles, *The Abecedarian Book*. Boston: Little, Brown, 1964. The chief interest of this book lies in its clever commentary about the pronunciation, spelling, origin, and meaning of each word presented.

Funk, Wilfred, *Word Origins and Their Romantic Stories*. New York: Grosset and Dunlap, 1950. One of the best books about word origins, this book presents intriguing stories about English words. It also contains an invaluable section on Latin and Greek affixes and roots and the words we have made from these components.

Lambert, Eloise, *Our Language; The Story of the Words We Use*. New York: Lothrop, 1955. Here is a well-written presentation of understandings about the English language, its history, geography, and usage.

Merriam, Eve, *A Gaggle of Geese*. New York: Knopf, 1960. This "picture book" explores a more advanced study of words for varied groups—*pride* of lions, *kindle* of kittens, etc.

Morris, William, and Mary Morris, *Dictionary of American Word Origins*. New York: Harper, 1963. An excellent collection of up-to-date words with stories about their origins.

Rand, Ann, and Paul Rand, *Sparkle and Spin*. New York: Harcourt, 1957. This colorfully illustrated book presents beginning concepts about words for the younger student.

Reid, Alastair, *Ounce, Dice, Trice*. Boston: Little, Brown, 1958. Here is a fascinating book by an author who is fascinated by words—an excellent introduction to word play.

Shipley, Joseph, *Playing with Words*. Englewood Cliffs, N.J.: Prentice-Hall, 1960. A reliable resource for the person interested in words and varied word-centered activities, this book was written for adults, but will supply much useful information for the classroom.

Waller, Leslie, *Our American Language*. New York: Holt, 1960. Here is another book for primary grades as they study the growth of the American language and the creation of new words for new things.

> The world of reality has its limits; the world of
> imagination is boundless.
>
> *Jean Jacques Rousseau*

4

Stimulating Creativity

What is creativity? Why is creativity significant? Who is the
creative individual? How can we encourage creativity in the
classroom? Creativity is an elusive, and at times all-inclusive,
term which many have found difficult to define. Writers in this
field offer varied interpretations which will help us determine a
working definition for the word *creativity*.

J. P. Guilford of the University of Southern California, author
of *Personality* and considered one of the leading authorities in
this field of research, was the first to use the term "divergent
thinking" as a necessary component of creativity. He states further: "Creative thinking is distinguished by the fact that there is
something novel about it." [1]

Donald W. MacKinnon, Director of the Institute of Personality
Assessment and Research at Berkeley, Calif., a pioneer in the
study of creativity who conducted extensive studies of creative
adults, defines creativity as "the ability to make original significant responses to a problem." [2]

E. Paul Torrance, former professor of educational psychology
at the University of Minnesota and Director of its Bureau of Educational Research, has studied many aspects of creativity, providing particular insight into the problems of the creative child at
the elementary school level. His book, *Guiding Creative Talent*,

---

[1] Joy P. Guilford, *Personality* (New York: McGraw-Hill, 1959).
[2] Donald W. MacKinnon, ed., *The Creative Person* (Berkeley, Calif.:
University of California, General Extension, 1962).

defines creativity as "the process of sensing problems or gaps in information, forming ideas or hypotheses, testing and modifying these hypotheses and communicating the results." [3]

It is interesting to note that each of the men quoted defines creativity in terms of the process rather than the product produced. This is an important distinction, for many misundertsandings arise between those who conceive of creativity in terms of a painting or a novel and those who view it as an ability, a way of thinking or perceiving. For purposes of our discussion we shall define creativity as "the ability to produce something original, to see new relationships, and to use imagination and inventiveness." In this chapter the term *creativity* is used synonymously with *originality, perceptive thinking,* and *inventiveness.*

"Creativity at its highest level has probably been as important as any human quality in changing history and in reshaping the world," writes Calvin W. Taylor, editor of *Creativity: Progress and Potential.* "As few as three or four highly creative minds can make a crucial difference." [4] Historian Arnold Toynbee states, in the same vein: "To give a fair chance to potential creativity is a matter of life and death for any society." [5]

To illustrate the contemporary nature of this concern for creativity we note that in the *Reader's Guide to Periodical Literature* during the period 1953-1963, for example, more than 60 articles were listed under the topic "Creativity." Torrance reports, furthermore, that in a collection of summaries of literature in psychology and psychiatry relating to creativity half of the selections were dated from 1950 to 1959 in a volume covering a period of one hundred years. [6]

Creativity has something to offer all persons as an area of study. It is important to stress the point that *every* person is creative; it is the *degree* of creativity which varies. We are concerned here not only with the highly creative individual but also with the *least creative child.* Our aim is to stimulate creativity in all children, and this aim will influence our methods and even the content we teach. As Torrance notes:

> One of the most revolutionary changes I foresee is a revision of the objectives of education. Today we proclaim that our schools exist for learning. We say that we must get tougher and make pupils learn more.

[3] E. Paul Torrance, *Education and the Creative Potential* (Minneapolis, Minn.: University of Minnesota Press, 1963), and *Guiding Creative Talent* (Englewood Cliffs, N.J.: Prentice-Hall, 1962).

[4] Calvin W. Taylor, ed., *Creativity: Progress and Potential* (New York: McGraw-Hill, 1964).

[5] Arnold Toynbee, "Has America Neglected Its Creative Minority?" *California Monthly* (February, 1962).

[6] E. Paul Torrance, *What Research Says to the Teacher: Creativity,* AERA-DCT Research Pamphlet Series, No. 28 (Washington, D.C.,: National Education Assn., 1963).

Schools of the future will be designed not only for *learning* but for *thinking*. More and more insistently, today's schools and colleges are being asked to produce men and women who can think, who can make new scientific discoveries, who can find more adequate solutions to impelling world problems, who cannot be brainwashed—men and women who can adapt to change and maintain sanity in this age of acceleration. This is the creative challenge to education.[7]

Identifying the Creative Child

One of the problems related to creativity which holds great significance for the school is that of identifying creative students. How can the teacher in the classroom recognize the creative individual? What characteristics are typical of the creative person? Can we test for creativity?

Research in creativity

Identifying creativity in the child is not easy, which may account for our failure to recognize this type of giftedness. The commonly used IQ test, it has been found, does not indicate creativeness. Although most researchers find a positive correlation between intelligence and creativity, the high scorer on the intelligence test may not score high on tests of creativity. Nor is the student who receives the highest grades necessarily the most creative child.

MacKinnon studied more than 500 famous people—writers, architects, composers, and so on—who were judged by their peers to be creative. In studying these famous artists MacKinnon found that in general they (1) had disliked school, (2) did not identify with teachers, and (3) had in many cases dropped out of school. These findings have great implications for teacher education.[8]

This study and others which followed resulted in a body of generalizations about the creative person which may prove helpful as we attempt to identify and to understand the creative student. The creative person has been found to possess the following traits:

1. Nonconformity of ideas, but not necessarily of dress and behavior
2. Egotism and feelings of destiny
3. Great curiosity, desire to discover the answer
4. Sense of humor and playfulness, lack of rigidity
5. Perseverance on self-started projects
6. Intense emotions, sincerity
7. Tendency to be shy, hide ideas, daydream, isolate self

[7] E. Paul Torrance, *Education and the Creative Potential* (Minneapolis, Minn.: University of Minnesota Press, 1963).

[8] Donald W. MacKinnon, ed., *The Creative Person* (Berkeley, Calif.: University of California Press, 1962).

Victor Goertzel and his wife, Mildred Goertzel, studied the childhoods of 400 of this century's best-known men and women. Their book, *Cradles of Eminence,* describes findings relevant to the study of the creative: (1) most of those people studied did not like school, (2) most of the parents had a love for learning and determination to reach goals, and (3) the creative child was not a contented child.

The latter finding has particular relevance for the classroom, for studies show that the teacher may find the creative student is not always the well-liked child, the agreeable, conforming child; he may impress the teacher as a disagreeable, uncooperative child who is mischievous, who daydreams when supposed to be completing assigned work. The suppression of creativity, it is believed, may lead to learning disabilities, behavior problems, and even serious neurotic conflicts, or psychoses.[9]

The Minnesota study of elementary school youngsters identified three characteristics which differentiated the highly creative child from the less creative but equally intelligent children:

1. Reputation for having wild or silly ideas
2. Work characterized by the production of ideas off the beaten path
3. Work characterized by humor, playfulness, relative lack of rigidity and relaxation.[10]

Many researchers have observed a decline in imagination as the student advances through the grade levels. Further research indicates an increase in creativity in the primary grades followed by a gradual slump at the fourth-grade level with another at the seventh grade. This finding has significance for those who are designing elementary school curricula.

Guilford, in his research at the University of Southern California, found the creative individual to be:

1. Sensitive to problems
2. Fluent in ideas
3. Mentally flexible
4. Divergent in his thinking.[11]

Testing for creativity

Although a variety of tests have been devised for testing creativity, they are largely in experimental stages requiring further development and use to increase reliability and validity. It is interesting, however, to note the types of tests which are being developed.

[9] Victor Goertzel and Mildred Goertzel, *Cradles of Eminence* (Boston: Little, Brown, 1962).

[10] E. Paul Torrance, *What Research Says to the Teacher: Creativity* (Washington, D.C. National Education Assn., 1963).

[11] Joy P. Guilford. *Personality* (New York: McGraw-Hill, 1959).

Barron utilized incomplete drawings as well as interpretation of ink blots as a basis for determining creativity. He found the creative person to be especially observant, with greater independence of cognition.[12]

Guilford developed a variety of tests including word associations, for which the subject is given 25 pairs of words which have only remote associations. The task is to provide a third word which relates the pair. Given cat and fish, for example, a person might supply words like animal, food, or pets. The test score is determined by the number of associations made in four minutes. He also used tests for flexible thinking such as listing many uses for a common object (a brick, a tin can) or supplying plot titles for given stories.[13]

A number of tests have also been developed at the University of Minnesota by Torrance and others. These tests consist of both verbal and nonverbal forms. One verbal form (B), for example, is entitled:

"Just Suppose—" which consists of six tasks for the student to perform, each of which is a written composition based on a picture and an improbable situation as in this example:

> JUST SUPPOSE: Our shadows were to become *real* . . .
> WHAT WOULD BE THE CONSEQUENCES?

The directions which accompany this test form appear on the front cover, reading as follows:

> INSTRUCTIONS: On the pages which follow are six improbable situations or conditions—at least they don't exist now. This will give you a chance to use your imagination about all of the other exciting things which might happen IF these improbable conditions might come to pass.
>
> In your imagination JUST SUPPOSE that each of the situations described were to happen. THEN think of all of the other things that would happen because of it. What would be the consequences? Make as many guesses as you can.
>
> Write your guesses as rapidly as you can in the blank spaces on the page opposite the picture. You will be given five minutes for each of the improbable situations. As soon as time is called, turn the page and proceed immediately to the next situation. Do not worry too much about spelling, grammar, and the like, but try to write so that your ideas can be read.

This type of test is scored on three points: (1) fluency, or the number of responses; (2) originality, or uniqueness; and (3) flexibility, or variety.

---

[12] Calvin W. Taylor and Frank Barron, *Scientific Creativity: Its Recognition and Development* (New York: Wiley, 1963), pp. 227-37.

[13] Joy P. Guilford, "Creativity: Its Measurement and Development," in *A Source Book for Creative Thinking,* Sidney J. Parnes and Harold H. Harding, eds., (New York: Scribner, 1962), pp. 151-68.

In addition to the Consequences Test there are other verbal varieties which include:

Unusual Use: Name all the possible uses for (a tin can).
Improvement: How would you improve (this toy pictured)?
Impossibilities: Name all the impossibilities you can.

It is enlightening to observe the differences between the test of creativity and tests which are more commonly constructed. The student is instructed in the creativity test to (1) write as many different answers as possible and (2) think of answers which no one else will include. The test of creativity gives the high score to the person who can think of answers which are different (divergent thinking); the student is never required to guess the *one right answer* which the instructor has in mind. There is no one right answer, for these open-ended questions require the student to think, to invent, to imagine. Getzels and Jackson found, on the other hand, that the IQ test stresses "convergent, retentive, conservative" cognitive processes.[14]

Observing creativity in the classroom

It is admittedly difficult to score tests of creativity when such scoring requires the skill of an expert. This fact does not, however, exclude the classroom teacher from identifying creative characteristics in the children with whom she works nor does it eliminate the teacher from teaching *for* creativity.

Through observation the teacher can discern signs of creativity. Awareness of the many facets of creativity will lead to watchfulness and recognition of creative characteristics. A child's possession of one or two of these characteristics may or may not signal creativity. Robert's asking many questions may merely indicate that he needs more training in listening skills or that he wants attention. There are always a multitude of factors to be considered. The asking of probing, discerning questions, on the other hand, is an excellent indication of the creative thinker. Here is a list of characteristics which can be readily observed by the classroom teacher:

1. Probing, discerning questions
2. Avid interest in a specific topic or project
3. Unusual ideas and ways of expressing ideas
4. Great curiosity and a need to explore the answers
5. Playfulness in behavior and in use of words

[14] Jacob W. Getzels and Philip W. Jackson, *Creativity and Intelligence* (New York: Wiley, 1962).

Encouraging Creativity

It is our belief that everyone is creative to a certain degree. Although some question the teachability of creativity, the atmosphere of the classroom can stimulate, encourage, and make every effort to avoid stifling whatever creativity may exist in any child. The development of a classroom environment which is conducive to creativity, then, is the first step toward promoting creativity in the classroom. There are a number of specific attitudes which the teacher can develop both in herself and in students to encourage the growth of creativity.

Respect unusual questions and ideas

Too often we are busy and hesitate to take time for questions which to us appear nonsensical, poorly timed, or not pertinent to the subject under discussion. How do we develop the necessary respect for the questioning attitude both in ourselves and in our students?

1. Make it plain to the class that good questions have value. A large box can be covered with question marks in which a child can at any time insert a card or sheet of paper on which a question which puzzles him is written. Each week a time can be allocated for answering these questions or for discussing them with the class. Those questions which do not produce a ready answer can be researched by volunteers who report their findings at the next question period.

2. Students can write questions which they might ask about any unknown object, person, or place. About an unknown object, for example, students might ask:

   Is it large or small?
   What color is it?
   Is it a useful object?
   Would it be found in a kitchen?

A sense of worth for each individual and his contributions

In a sense the teacher must often act as a buffer between the highly creative child and his peer group, for these peers may represent his severest critics. They can stifle creativity through ridicule, rigid insistence on the exact truth, and on conformity to group standards. The attitude of the students toward imaginative ideas and divergent ways of thinking reflects the attitudes of adults who influence their thinking; the teacher's own attitude is reflected here, too. How can we promote this sense of the worth of each individual?

1. Accent the positive in evaluating student work. There is some small aspect of any student effort which can be praised, and it is for that

praiseworthy bit, no matter how small, that we should search. Circle it, underline it, draw attention to it in some way; under the light of praise it will grow.
2. When displaying student work, display something by everyone. Must only "perfect" papers be given the limelight? Extract unusual uses of words, effective phrases, new words from student writing to display with the caption, WORD WIZARDRY. When featuring poetry, select a line or poem by every student.

Stimulation of creative thinking

The teacher needs to aim at stimulating creative thinking rather than mere memorization of miscellaneous facts. We sometimes have a tendency to "stuff" students like sausages rather than to concentrate on developing their abilities to think. It has been said that "we never step in the same stream twice." The facts and figures which we teach students today may prove virtually useless, outdated in our fast-moving society. Margaret Mead states this idea thus: "No one will live all his life in the world into which he was born and no one will die in the world in which he worked in his maturity." The ability to think creatively, however, will prove worthwhile no matter what the developments of the future. How can the teacher stimulate creative thinking?

1. Provide the student with many opportunities for problem solving. The problem may actually exist, as, "How can we decrease the noise in our lunchroom?" or it may be purely hypothetical, "If you were eight feet tall, what problems would you face; how would you solve them?" These problems can be attacked by the group orally in discussion or by the individual through writing.
2. An interesting and rewarding technique for stimulating the imagination of young people is Brainstorming (designed by Alex Osborn), which produces a multitude of ideas within a short time. The entire group works on the solution of a problem, the improvement of an object, or the exploration of a topic in a joint effort to suggest solutions, changes, ideas. The rules for Brainstorming include: [15]
   a. No criticism or ridicule is allowed.
   b. Any idea is acceptable, no matter how fantastic.
   c. New ideas can be based on previous suggestions.
   Students must be introduced to this technique with the teacher acting as the leader. Later, however, when the technique is more familiar, small groups can brainstorm ideas on specific problems. In beginning a brainstorming session the teacher may have to suggest a few ideas to get the group started. It is best to begin with a problem or topic that is familiar to the entire group. An interesting topic for an elementary classroom is the improvement of the student desk, something which is familiar and of concern to each individual. Suggestions might include: a personal pencil sharpener, a padded seat, a built-in television set.

[15] Osborn, Alex F. *Applied Imagination.* New York: Scribner, 1957.

A positive attitude toward failure

When a student makes a mistake or a project fails to produce the expected results, the student should not experience a sense of personal failure. Mistakes should be viewed as stepping stones toward success much in the manner of Thomas A. Edison's often quoted remark as he continued to discover methods that did not achieve the desired electric light bulb. How can the teacher develop positive attitudes toward failure?

1. Assist the student by not overburdening him with corrections. A composition which is returned to the student blushing with red pencil marks may prove an insurmountable obstacle to his ever writing anything of worth. Praising wholeheartedly that which is of value in his work has been proved to result in more effective development of writing skills. If a correction needs to be made, concentrate on one or two items which can be readily assimilated at one time by the young writer.
2. Encourage experimentation with the clear understanding that the results are never guaranteed successful. Students should be encouraged to play with words, to invent new forms for poetry, to attempt new effects in their writing without any fear of so-called "failing." These experiments add to the feeling for discovering, exploring, trying the wings of originality.
3. Assume the role of a guide and consultant rather than of one who knows all the answers and stands ready to point out punctuation errors, faulty construction, or misspelling. Teachers need to become admirers of student ideas, accepting them and enjoying them. We should celebrate the achievements of these young people rather than make much of their mistakes.

Acceptance of the nonconformist

As studies have pointed out, the highly creative child has problems functioning as part of a group. For this reason he may cause disturbance or refuse to conform to our standards of behavior. It is difficult for the teacher of 35 children to condone or understand this type of behavior, and the first inclination has been to chastise the child with the entire class listening. The teacher must make a conscious effort to investigate the child's reasons for causing disturbance or for failing to conform. If he is a creative child, some understanding on the part of the teacher may lead to rewarding solutions of this problem.

Although we grant the relative ease of writing about the classroom situation as opposed to actual operation in the classroom, a better approach to this type of problem involves talking to the child privately. Questioning him about his behavior and discussing the reasons for some measure of conformity in any group situation has proved beneficial. But above all, provision must be made for some outlet for his creative abilities and an opportunity for him to become part of the group. The teacher can assist him in reducing his isolation from his peers by letting him share results of individual experimentation. He might "teach the class" for 15 minutes as he explains the project which he is developing.

The class must be helped to understand the creative child. As Plato wrote: "What is honored in a country will be cultivated there." The teacher's obvious approval and interest in the activities of the child will make his work take on interest and value for his peers. Introducing creative activities for the entire class will lead them to understand the need for divergent thinking and the challenge of producing original ideas. Students can read and discuss creative people of the past, pointing up the fact that their ideas were not always acceptable to people of their times. These approaches may lead to a measure of admiration for the child who formerly was tagged with having "wild ideas."

Parents who understand the concern for creativity

Parents, like teachers, have trouble understanding the nonconforming child. What we adults value is not always manifested by the child and therein lies a conflict which may well be disastrous for the germ of creativity which struggles to exist. Studies show that the home influence has great effect on the development of creativity; whether creativity is stifled or nurtured, therefore, is not the sole responsibility of the school. It is the concern of the school, however, to promote understanding of the creative child and it is to this end that the teacher and the school work as they assist the parent in understanding the need for concern about creativity.

A communique from the school to the home can feature Creativity, briefly outlining the significance of this element of human intelligence and stating the concern of the school for encouraging creativity in children. This informational sheet can draw attention to articles in general magazines or books which parents may be interested in reading such as these examples:

Mackinnon, Donald W., "What Makes a Person Creative?" *Saturday Review* (February 10, 1962).
Torrance, E. Paul. *Guiding Creative Talent*. Englewood Cliffs, N.J.: Prentice-Hall, 1962.

Ways can also be suggested for parents to encourage creativity in their own children in much the same manner that the school does:

1. Respect questions and ideas of the child.
2. Encourage experimentation and exploration.
3. Give the child time to think and to express himself.
4. Accept the child for what he is.

5. Avoid giving the child a sense of personal failure.
6. Help the child understand himself.
7. Recognize and value the talents of the creative child.

Discussion or study groups can also be helpful in promoting understanding of creativity. Science Research Associates has produced a unit of study for this approach to creativity.[16] Speakers can be obtained to present this topic to the group. Parents of unusually creative children should be invited to come to school to discuss the problems of the individual child.

Teaching English Creatively

English as an area of the elementary school curriculum lends itself to creative approaches. The teaching of English creatively, however, requires the teacher to develop new perspectives of English and of the objectives we are trying to achieve. It is important, observes Kneller, "to recognize that if a person is to make full use of his talents, he should learn to think creatively in a range of situations and on a variety of subjects. The mind, in other words, should be trained to think creatively at the same time that it is trained to think logically." [17]

Criteria for a creative English program

In order to determine the degree of creativity of any English program we must first establish some type of criteria. These criteria will reflect what we know about creativity in general as applied to the various areas included in the English curriculum. Let us examine some of these criteria:

1. Is the program different in some way from that of the past year?
2. Do the children enjoy English activities?
3. Is stress placed on use of the imagination, playing with words, inventiveness?
4. Is the child praised for that which he *does* accomplish rather than criticized for the mistakes he has made?
5. Are many opportunities provided for writing, speaking, and listening creatively?
6. Does the teacher function as a guide rather than a judge?
7. Is there evidence in the room that children are writing?

We can apply the concepts of creativity to all areas included in the broad term of English. Particularly adaptable to creative approaches

[16] June S. Heinrich, *Creativity in the Classroom* (Chicago: Science Research Associates, 1964).

[17] George F. Kneller, *The Art and Science of Creativity* (New York: Holt, 1965), p. 78.

are writing and dramatics, but we can also apply these stimulating concepts to listening, speaking, and even to spelling and the mechanics of writing.

In many respects English has pioneered specific aspects of creativity through creative writing and creative dramatics. Hughes Mearns, writing in 1929, for instance, stated: "Good teaching is not solely the business of instructing; it is also the art of influencing another. Primarily, it is the job of uncovering and enlarging native gifts of insight, feeling, and thinking." The revised edition of his challenging exploration of the creative potential of youth, *Creative Power,* is being widely heralded by contemporary writers who are now cognizant of the import of the methods used by Mearns in stimulating creativity. Mearns admonished his young writers in these words:

> You have something to say. Find out what it is. That is the beginning. Once really started, it will carry you through life; for you will be doing for yourself all that education can ever do for anybody, encouraging that deeper and powerful self to rise within you and take possession.[18]

Methods to promote creativity

The English program can become more creative as the methods used tend to encourage creativity. Again, methods should aim at encouraging creativity rather than stifling it. In the past, instruction in English relied chiefly on the authoritarian approach to learning—memorization, rote learning, drill—deductive techniques. Research is indicating that students can learn more effectively by creative methods—questioning, experimenting, exploring, discovering—inductive methods. Studies in science and mathematics have led the way toward the use of inquiry and discovery methods.

The following approaches allow for individual development, and, therefore, permit the creative child to operate in a freer environment:

1. Use of open-ended topics which encourage thinking
2. Independent study and research
3. Free selection of topics for speaking and writing
4. Less emphasis on form, more on ideas expressed
5. Reward of diverse contributions
6. Guidance through individual conference or consultation
7. Tests which emphasize divergent thinking

Materials that stimulate creativity

There is a dearth of materials now available which truly exemplify the concepts embodied in the study of creativity, for instructional ma-

[18] Hughes Mearns, *Creative Power: The Education of Youth in the Creative Arts,* rev. ed. (New York: Dover, 1958).

terials still chiefly reflect authoritarian methods of teaching and convergent thinking. What is needed now are books, films, records, and other teaching aids which will assist the teacher in emphasizing diverse contributions, encouraging questions, stimulating new ideas, providing opportunities for problem solving.

Creative approaches to spelling, listening, and speaking need to be developed. There is a need, too, for material which permits the individual to advance according to his ability, flexible material which meets the needs of the child and the teacher. A wide variety of instructional aids must be designed specifically to promote creativity. A few booklets have appeared which will stimulate the thinking of the teacher and suggest creative approaches in English:

Darrow, Helen F. and R. Van Allen, *Independent Activities for Creative Learning*. New York: Teachers College, 1961.

Myers, R. E. and E. Paul Torrance, *Invitation to Thinking and Doing* ... Boston: Ginn & Co., 1964.

Tiedt, Sidney and Iris M. Tiedt, *Creative Writing Ideas*. San Jose, Calif.: Contemporary Press, 1965.

Teachers can also experiment with their own materials as they develop devices for motivating creative writing, adapting materials which are presently available. Students, too, can be motivated to create materials which can be used by the class.

Curriculum revision in English

Not only is there a great need for new methods and materials in English, but the curriculum itself needs re-examination. If we accept the concepts offered by researchers of creativity, then courses of study will require revision. Activities which stress creative thinking and allow for originality must be incorporated in the entire program.

We hear primary teachers say securely, "That's fine for the upper grades, but our children don't write well enough." We object wholeheartedly, for first-grade children *do write*, as will be discussed in more detail in Chapter 10. These children discuss, they dictate, and they print their own stories as their ability progresses through the year. Young children, begin developing many creative abilities through speaking, listening, and dramatics. This problem is only one of those which must be considered by curriculum revisers. We must begin stimulating creativity in children as early as possible, for there are those who remind us that the school has already missed the most crucial early years.

Curriculum revision is not easily effected, but it must come if we are to reach our goal of developing each child to the fullest extent of his abilities. What are the blocks to revision? In most cases they are rigid thinking, refusal to accept change, and even actual fear of the new approaches entailed in changes proposed. One hears remarks such as these which represent the immovable force:

"We tried that years ago and it didn't work."
"Why, that would cost the district too much money."
"Those ideas would never work with my class."
"That's another one of those *progressive* ideas."

In order to overcome these inhibiting factors to curriculum revision one must first understand these opposing viewpoints. Fixed ideas and values represent the direct opposite of open-mindedness and divergent thinking, the very things the creative teacher would promote in children. It is difficult to change these ways of thinking which have developed over long periods of time.

Many people feel threatened by the thought of doing something different. They fear being wrong or making a mistake. Conformity has been so much a part of them that they wouldn't think of making a change unless it was already nationally accepted. Others actually feel threatened by the creative child himself; they need to dominate the child they teach. These teachers fear that which remains mysterious and incomprehensible to them.

Changes will not be made overnight, but those which are considered advantageous to the student are coming and will continue to gain acceptance with time. We can already find evidence of the tendency in this direction as more and more school systems include creative activities in their English programs. Creative teachers are leading the way.

Developing Your Own Creativity

It is generally conceded that a teacher who is creative will be better able to teach creatively and to establish empathy with the child who is creative. Creative teaching promotes creative behavior in students. How can the teacher evaluate his own creativity? How can the teacher stimulate his personal creative development?

Get acquainted with yourself

The first step in developing personal creativity is the acceptance of ourselves as we exist, for as individuals we often fail to become acquainted with our own personality. We never think about ourselves. What are our strengths? What are our weaknesses? We need to make an honest appraisal of our behavior patterns. Why do we do the things we do? Why do some things irritate us? We need to gain some understanding of ourselves and to accept ourselves as we really exist.

We can prepare for the further expansion of creative abilities by view-ing ourselves in the role of the learner, of one who is ready to make discoveries, to explore. Are we truly interested in exploring new terri-tory? Isn't life too short to waste on boredom? Being creative does not mean that every person should immediately write a poem or short story and send it off to *Harper's*. Creative abilities and interests may lie in diverse areas—landscaping a garden, flower arranging, designing a book-case, solving a problem, organizing a work area, preparing new teaching materials, *ad infinitum.*

Many persons are stymied when creativity is mentioned, for they im-mediately reject the possibility that they can create, saying helplessly, "I am just not creative." One of the requisites for creativity is the "open mind," the willingness to explore possibilities. We shall operate, there-fore, on the premise that every individual has some elements of creativity.

Explore creative activities

Creativity can be expressed in widely varied ways—experimenting, planning, organizing, writing, speaking, constructing, thinking. We wish to dispel the narrow view that immediately associates creativity with a product of the acknowledged arts—a painting, a novel, a symphony.

Begin thinking about events, objects, ways of doing things, in new ways. Examine your own school or room. Can you explore the possibilities for organizing, decorating, or arranging it for more efficient and enjoyable living?

Consider the time that lies before you each day. Can you discover ways of planning your activities more effectively? Are there periods of time which can be used creatively? You can think, plan, and organize while doing rather mundane tasks such as walking, ironing, or cutting grass. Keep a notebook handy for jotting down ideas which originate during these periods.

The teacher can look at teaching creatively. Examine the problems of the classroom with a new eye toward solving them, for problems were made to solve. Take another look at Phil who is causing disturbance; think of the causes and possible solutions for this problem. Explore a variety of possibilities, keeping the mind open for varied answers to prob-lems which arise.

The teacher can create a finger play story to tell to students, introducing this story by saying, "Here is a story which I made for *you*." They will take special interest in this gift, perhaps responding by making a story themselves.

The teacher can also participate in creative activities which are intro-duced to the students. This is one of the most effective methods of inter-esting students in creative activities, for it immediately demonstrates the teacher's value for these activities. If composing poetry is fun, enriching, and worthwhile for students, might it not also prove rewarding for the teacher? What could be more inspiring to the class, as the teacher tells them about Haiku, than the presentation of a Haiku written by the teacher? It immediately involves the class far more than would the Haiku of Buson or Shiki, who are only names to the child.

Invent creative ways to teach. New and different methods lend a sparkle to teaching for both the teacher and the students. If the teacher is bored with the method used in teaching spelling, think how bored are the students. Experiment with different approaches, exploring possibilities for effective teaching without dull routine. Don't be afraid to be different. There are too many conformists and not enough nonconformists in the teaching ranks.

Creativity has much to offer the elementary school classroom; it has much to offer the teacher of English. The findings of researchers in this area should lead to the re-examination of the objectives and aims of the elementary school English program. These objectives should encompass efforts not only to avoid the stifling of creativity which exists in each child but also to stimulate the growth of that creativity in varying degrees.

Taking into consideration the findings of research in creativity and that knowledge which we now possess about teaching and learning processes, the classroom teacher can best stimulate creativity through:

1. Rewarding diverse contributions; encouraging questions and new ideas
2. Accepting the creative child for what he is, a child with all the usual problems of childhood plus an active thinking brain
3. Reducing the overemphasis on sex roles. Boys can enjoy poetry, art, music; girls can enjoy science and things mechanical
4. Helping the creative child adjust to the group situation, reducing his isolation and helping him participate
5. Helping the child solve personal problems; helping parents understand the creative child and the significance of creativity
6. Recognizing the talents of the creative child, making obvious the value of the contributions of each child by praising sincerely
7. Using a variety of stimuli in form of methods and materials and developing an atmosphere conducive to creativity
8. Assuming the role of a guide, not a chastiser-corrector; avoiding rigid thinking and evaluating
9. Developing a positive attitude toward failure
10. Encouraging experimentation and divergent thinking

Books to Investigate

Anderson, Harold H., ed., *Creativity and Its Cultivation.* New York: Harper, 1959.

Darrow, Helen F., and R. Van Allen, *Independent Activities for Creative Learning.* New York: Teachers College, 1961.

Getzels, Jacob W., and Philip W. Jackson, *Creativity and Intelligence.* New York: Wiley, 1962.

Goertzel, Victor, and Mildred Goertzel, *Cradles of Eminence.* Boston: Little, Brown, 1962. An interesting study of creativity in known persons.

Heinrich, June S., *Creativity in the Classroom.* Unit Two: SRA Teacher Extension Service. Chicago: Science Research Associates, 1964. A unit of study for use in in-service programs.

Kneller, George F., *The Art and Science of Creativity.* New York: Holt, 1965. An excellent overview of creativity.

Lowenfeld, Viktor. *Creative and Mental Growth.* New York: Macmillan, 1957.

Mearns, Hughes, *Creative Power: The Education of Youth in the Creative Arts.* New York: Dover, 1958.

Myers, R. E., and E. Paul Torrance, *Invitation to Thinking and Doing.* Boston: Ginn, 1961. Various titles of workbooks to stimulate creative thinking.

Shumsky, Abraham. *Creative Teaching in the Elementary School.* New York: Appleton, 1965.

Taylor, Calvin W., ed., *Creativity: Progress and Potential.* New York: McGraw-Hill, 1964.

Torrance, E. Paul, *Guiding Creative Talent.* Englewood Cliffs, N.J.: Prentice-Hall, 1962.

The hearing ear is always close to the speaking tongue.

Ralph Waldo Emerson

5

Perceptive Listening

Chattering, whispering, shouting, and calling; requesting, commanding, instructing, and teaching—we hear, we listen to language all day, every day. It has been estimated that we listen a book each day, talk a book each week, read a book each month, and write a book each year. The elementary school course of study, however, usually shows little evidence of the significance of this comparison, for in actual practice more time is allotted to the teaching of reading and writing than is specified for teaching speaking and listening skills.

The twentieth century's contribution of radio, televison, and recording devices has resulted in the literal bombardment of the human ear with messages of varied content as well as varied intent. Witty's study [1] of the television viewing of Chicago children revealed that in 1962 elementary school children averaged 21 viewing hours per week. It is probable that this number has increased over the past years.

A study in 1950 [2] found that elementary school students listened 158 minutes (about 2½ hours) each school day, which means that more than half the school day was spent in listening

[1] Paul Witty and Paul Kinsella, "Televiewing: Some Observations from Studies 1949-1962," *Elementary English*, Vol. XXXIX, No. 8. (December, 1962), 772-779.

[2] Miriam E. Wilt, "A Study of Teacher Awareness of Listening as a Factor in Elementary Education," *Journal of Educational Research* (April, 1950), pp. 626-36.

while the remainder was shared by reading, speaking, and writing. This study further pointed up the fact that teachers were largely unaware of the importance of listening in daily classroom activities.

Listening as a Receptive Skill

Listening is to speaking as reading is to writing, for both listening and reading are receptive skills. The listener receives the spoken word. The skills of listening and speaking are, therefore, interdependent; the success of one depends on the success of the other. The speaker is usually trying to reach a listener, who may present blocks to reception which the speaker must overcome if he is to convince the listener of an argument, share an idea, or raise a question. The listener, on the other hand, is dependent on the speaker for the content of what he is to hear, the rate of speaking, and the clarity of enunciation and pronunciation.

Listening has been defined as a:

> . . . learned receptive skill. It is a personal, often private absorption of ideas and attitudes expressed through oral language. To listen implies attention and responsive thinking, sometimes only casual, often quite intent and indeed critical. Listening differs from hearing, which is a physiological process and does not involve interpretation.[3]

Primacy of the listening skill

Of the four facets of language ability—reading, writing, speaking, and listening—listening is the primary skill, for it is as a listener that the baby is first aware of speech. Through imitation of the sounds heard he learns to form words, and through listening he continues into adult life learning new ways with pronunciation, inflection, sentence patterns, and the many complexities of adult speech.

It is perhaps this primary nature of listening which has made us consider it a natural skill, one that is known by everyone, one that does not require teaching. It has been only in the last 20 years that researchers have investigated the nature of listening and the success with which we as individuals are able to listen. Russell questions this attitude toward listening instruction when he writes: "Can we assume that listening will take care of itself? Few deny the importance of listening, but it is not incorporated in curricula. Studies have consistently proved that instruction in listening improves listening abilities."[4] Research should make a difference in the classroom, yet Anderson notes:

[3] Ralph C. Staiger, "Defining the Terms, "*Children and Oral Language* (Washington, D.C.: Joint Committee of the ACEI, ASCD, IRA, NCTE, 1964), p. 3.
[4] David H. Russell, "A Conspectus of Recent Research on Listening Abilities," *Elementary English* (March, 1964), p. 263.

Except in isolated instances, virtually the only instruction in listening that children and young people receive in the schools is the quite useless admonition of "pay attention" and to "listen carefully." Listening, at all educational levels, has been the forgotten language art for generations.[5]

Objectives of teaching listening

What is the purpose of the classroom teacher in teaching listening? Toward what objectives are listening activities directed? The general goal is the improved efficiency of the teaching-learning experience in the elementary school. More specifically, however, listening instruction is directed toward:

1. More efficient use of classroom time through increased effectiveness of reception
2. Awareness of the significance of listening as a skill and the value of increasing effectiveness
3. Provision of extensive practice in listening for varied purposes

Levels of listening

"To listen is an effort, and just to hear is no merit. A duck also hears." Thus Igor Stravinsky expressed the importance of moving beyond the mere hearing of sounds. Listening is vital for the musician, but it is also a skill needed by every person every day.

Many sounds are in the air at any one time. Some of these sounds are heard. Others never reach the individual's level of awareness; he is "tuned out"; he is not listening. There are sounds which he may hear, but does not listen to. Still other sounds will cause him to listen, but with little attempt to understand or respond. The highest level of listening is reached when the individual listens with purpose and comprehension. The latter level of listening has been termed "auding" to distinguish the process described from mere hearing or listening without perception.

Levels of listening can be considered, therefore, as consisting of these degrees of advancement and effectiveness: (1) hearing, (2) listening without specific response, and (3) auding, or listening with intent and comprehension. It is auding that we are endeavoring to teach in the classroom as children learn to take notes from spoken recordings, to listen to the imagery of poetry, or to evaluate positions presented in a debate.

> Listening is what a woman does when she's not supposed to hear.
> WILL ROGERS

[5] Harold A. Anderson, "Needed Research in Listening," *Elementary English* (April, 1954), pp. 215-24.

Difficulties of listening efficiently

Listening is not a facile skill, for there are many factors which impede listening efficiency. The listener, for example, has no control over the rate of speed of the speaker. In *vis-à-vis* conversation it is perfectly permissible to request a friend to speak more slowly, but the lecturer addressing a group of 400 has his audience literally at his mercy. He not only may speak rapidly but he may also possess speech characteristics which prevent effective listening. As is pointed out in the chapter on Speaking, the speaker has a responsibility to those who are listening, but this responsibility is not always recognized and assumed.

The speaker may mispronounce words or he may place words in odd contexts (we hesitate to say that he may not always know the meanings of words he uses), which cause confusion in the listener's mind. While floundering to grasp one point, the listener is no doubt missing the next. He is forced to skip ahead mentally with the speaker and hope that the points missed were not vital to understanding the total message.

The organization of the speaker also influences listening efficiency. The well-organized speech is followed with relative ease, whereas the discussion which flits from topic to topic with no obvious framework may lose many listeners en route to the main point.

Usually the listener has no written guide to assist his task of listening. The provision of a script or type of libretto for material to be heard will aid listening efficiency. Reading a play or story which is to be presented on record will greatly aid comprehension when the recording is played for the first time. An outline of the material to be heard enables the listener to follow the report of detailed information.

Another factor which impedes comprehension is that there is seldom an opportunity for repetition in the speaking-listening situation. A line that is not "caught" in a play, a television program, or a speech is not likely to be repeated. If time and circumstance permit, a record may be replayed to permit listeners to hear portions of a selection again. The tape recorder has the further advantage of permitting the listener to stop the recording immediately in order to replay lines which he would like to hear again.

The group listening experience contains hindrances to effective listening which are not present in an individual listening situation. As a member of a group, John may hesitate to request that the speaker repeat a statement or that a portion of the tape be replayed. He may hesitate to expose his failure to understand or he may fear disapproval of his request for repetition. Listening abilities vary as do other abilities, and it is for this reason that we would not expect all students to listen with the same efficiency. Individualized approaches, as in any other area of the curriculum, will also prove effective in teaching listening skills as each child develops his abilities according to his individual capacity. Listening stations in individual classrooms or in a central library will assist individual development of listening abilities.

Successful listening also depends on the maturation of the listener. A child of five will usually be unable to listen with comprehension to a lecture intended for an adult audience. No doubt the child will quickly "tune out," as he attempts to listen but discovers that he cannot understand. Children who become bored with adult conversations often attempt to gain attention by creating distractions clearly meant to annoy the adult until he pays attention to the child.

The experiential background and the knowledge of the listener also influence his ability to listen with comprehension. This is one of the basic problems of the disadvantaged child whose background has not prepared him to understand ideas presented with a middle class white child in mind. The urban child who has never seen a cow or pig may be totally unconcerned by a discussion of the farm.

Background or previous knowledge may also distort meanings if they cause the listener to conceive of something entirely different from that intended by the speaker. When Father queries "Where is that new pipe?" Terry may begin searching for a pipe his father might smoke, whereas his dad is preparing to repair the kitchen sink.

Insecurity may also prevent a student's listening. His need for attention may be so great that he is concentrating on waving his hand for permission to say something. His own needs and desires disable him as a listener, for he is actually unable to sit quietly listening while someone else talks. Unless he is talking, he is not interested. He would dominate a conversation or discussion if permitted to do so.

Listening tasks

We are impressed by the large percentage of our time spent directly or indirectly in listening, but just what skills are involved in this complex subject or ability? Incorporated in the broad term of *listening* are the following categories of specific skills: (1) Reception, (2) Comprehension, and (3) Assimilation.

Reception:
　　Hear sounds made externally
　　Distinguish variety in sounds (auditory discrimination)
　　Decide to listen or not to listen

Comprehension:
　　Follow words used
　　Understand ideas expressed
　　Recognize purpose for listening

　　　　Note details
　　　　Receive new ideas and information

Assimilation:
  React to ideas expressed
    Disagree
    Ask questions
    Make additions
    Evaluate

  Reinforce learning through use
    Follow directions
    Repeat information to another
    Develop given information
    Adapt ideas presented

Each stage of listening development is important to the total listening experience. Receiving sounds is essential, for lack of reception clearly eliminates any possibility for comprehension and assimilation of what is heard. The three tasks of the listener are interdependent and self-generating, for reception leads to comprehension, which in turn leads to assimilation and reaction, and the cycle begins again as the question or commentary is in turn received, comprehended, and reacted to.

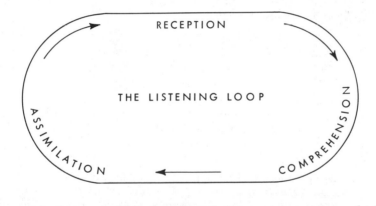

We can examine specific techniques of classroom instruction which will tend to increase listening efficiency. Although each focuses on only one aspect of the complex of listening skills, increased efficiency in one task increases over-all efficiency.

1. Auditory discrimination between sounds
   Which of these words does *not* begin like BIRD?
     balloon brother castle

2. Appreciation or oral interpretation of others
   Play recordings, for example, *Alice in Wonderland* (Caedmon, TC 1097) for enjoyment.

3. Location of central theme or idea
   Read or play recorded passages to provide practice. The student may

be asked to state the main idea or several possible themes may be suggested from which a selection is made.

4. Discovery of new word meanings from context

   Talk about words after reading aloud, for example, "Armies in the Fire" by Robert Louis Stevenson.

5. Awareness of the power of words

   Tape passages which propagandize; have students identify examples of slanting, loaded words, glittering generalities, etc.

6. Discovery of specific details

   In what state did Philip live?
   Where was Linda going?
   How did Mr. Pepper obtain a penguin?

7. Recognition of imagery in writing

   Discuss types of figurative language—simile, metaphor, etc. Try to remember several images or figures of speech while listening to "The Daffodils" by William Wordsworth.

8. Comparison of two or more examples

   Have all students write descriptions of a single item or event. These passages can be recorded or several may be read by one person (it is best for this purpose if the writer does not read his own passage). Discuss the variety of treatment.

9. Recognition of fact and opinion

   After student talks on assigned topics, discuss the presence of both fact and opinion in the speech. Was fact substantiated? Was opinion qualified?

10. Learning needed information

    Provide many opportunities for students to take notes on taped or read passages which explain how to do something. Ability to follow directions may fall in this category.

11. Selection of pertinent data

    Provide experience with passages which include directions for doing something as well as a number of bits of extraneous information. Students record the information necessary to perform a specific operation.

12. Repetition of what has been heard

    Read short stories such as *The Mean Mouse and Other Mean Stories* by Janice Udry (Harper, 1962). After each story ask someone to see if they can retell the story as the class listens to determine which details are omitted.

Developing Skills of Listening

"Now listen carefully," says the teacher, almost automatically as she begins a classroom presentation. Do students obey this perfunctory admonition? How can we tell? When we ask children to write or to speak, we can immediately ascertain the degree to which the direction is being followed, but a child may appear to be listening intently when in reality his mind is relishing thoughts of a promised trip to the zoo or reliving the mad adventures of Batman. The teacher has competition, and in many cases it is "stiff" competition.

Examining present practices

Studies by Ralph B. Nichols and others point out that without training in listening most of us operate at only 25% efficiency.[6] Research also indicates that direct instruction in listening does increase listening effectiveness.[7] It is obvious that training in this essential skill should be included at all levels of education.

We find, according to Wilt's study, that children actually spend half their school time listening, but at what level of efficiency? Is this a wise use of student time? How might their time be better used? Does the teacher spend too much time talking when students should be more directly involved? Does the fact that only one child usually speaks while more than thirty listen indicate a low level of direct participation? Does it indicate a need for varied grouping techniques or individualized approaches to learning?

Is listening as practiced a guided, purposeful experience? We say the class is listening, but are the children really auding or are they merely waiting their turn to participate? Are they literally wasting their time? Could teaching techniques be more exciting, more stimulating, if greater use were made of visual aids—films, filmstrips, pictures, direct observation, experimentation, field excursions? Perhaps some periods of "listening" should be eliminated from the daily schedule.

Let us turn to listening experiences that are better planned, more purposeful, and, therefore, more stimulating and more effective. Children need specific practice, for example, in critical listening. They need to listen to each other and to combine speaking and listening skills. We need positive approaches to listening instruction based on provocative material, new ideas, something the child can become excited about; otherwise slovenly listening habits will be encouraged along with justifiable disinterest, apathy, and boredom with school.

Preparing for effective listening

What conditions will assist the teacher in promoting effective skills of listening? How can we overcome factors which impede listening effi-

[6] Ralph B. Nichols, "What Can Be Done About Listening?" *The Supervisor's Notebook*, Vol. XXII, No. 1 (1960).

[7] Sister Mary Kevin Hollow, "Listening Comprehension at the Intermediate Grade Level," *Elementary School Journal*, December, 1955, 158-61.

ciency? We can begin by checking the physical condition of the classroom and of the children themselves. We can also consider the material to be presented and the methods to be used.

1. Check the physical conditions of the classroom, for little attentive listening will be done in a room that is poorly ventilated, overheated, or unusually cold. Are some children overdressed for the type of work in which they are engaged? Have excess clothing—sweaters, sweatshirts, jackets—removed immediately on entering the classroom.
2. Recommend physical examinations for children who appear to have unusual difficulty hearing. Some children feign hearing difficulties as an excuse for inattentiveness. A report from the doctor will clarify the child's ability so that the teacher is more certain in approaches used with each individual child.
3. Vary the routines of teaching so that children do not become overly fatigued or bored. The attention span or the listening attentiveness of the younger child in particular is relatively short. Long periods of uninterrupted listening are less efficient than are short experiences interspersed with more active learning activities.
4. Plan learning activities to include more speaking by children and less by the teacher. The observer in the typical elementary school classroom quickly notes that the majority of the speaking is by the teacher, with relatively infrequent opportunities for students to speak. Children who are involved in an activity listen more readily, more attentively, for there is a reason to listen.
5. Avoid distractions which prevent effective listening. Noises from the street or the activities of other children in the classroom may be so distracting as to make listening literally impossible. Listening Centers which provide earphones for each child have the advantage of closing out other sounds. Room dividers can prevent visual distraction of the child who is listening.
6. Set the style in listening. How the teacher listens to children may influence their habits of listening. The teacher who obviously is not sufficiently interested in a child's presentation before the class to listen to it attentively cannot expect the class to listen. If the teacher is busy grading papers or preparing art materials at the back of the room, what chance has the young speaker of holding the attention of his peers?
7. Discuss the purpose of the listening experience. Are we listening to get the main idea of a story or are we trying to compare two ways of presenting information? Are we listening especially to notice interesting ways of using words or are we trying to gain information about a Greek myth?

Characteristics of good listening habits

The identification of desirable habits of listening should lend direction to classroom activities. Student-compiled lists of AIDS TO GOOD LISTENING have been found helpful in motivating individuals to work on specific skills. Nichols published a list of "Eight Significant Listening Habits" which identifies the good listener as one who:

I. Maintains an awareness of his own motives in listening

    A. Develops speedily in each situation his own motives for effective listening

    B. Analyzes the speech and adjusts himself to his own motives

II. Shares with the conveyor responsibility for communication

    A. Applies himself to the different techniques of the speaker

    B. Assumes his half of the responsibility for communication

III. Arranges favorable conditions for listening

    A. Adjusts himself for any personal hearing disability or for poor room ventilation or temperature

    B. Ignores any outside or unnecessary distractions

IV. Exercises emotional control during listening

    A. Postpones personal worries

    B. Does not permit an immediate dislike for a speech or speaker

V. Structuralizes the presentation

    A. Recognizes conventional compositional techniques

    B. Adjusts his system of note taking to the organizational plan of the speech

VI. Strives always to grasp the central ideas in the presentation

    A. Focuses on central ideas and tends to recognize the characteristic language in which they are stated

    B. Has the ability to discriminate between fact and principle, idea and example, evidence and argument

VII. Exploits fully the rate differential between thought and speech

    A. Demands continuous attention—staying on the track with the speaker

    B. Does these: mental anticipation of each of the speaker's points; identification of the techniques used in the development of each point; and mental recapitulation of points already developed

VIII. Seeks frequent experience in listening to difficult expository material

    A. Is acquainted with such radio programs as: "Invitation to Learning," "America's Town Meeting of the Air," and "Meet the Press"

    B. Has experience in listening to difficult material [8]

[8] Ralph G. Nichols, "The Teaching of Listening," *Chicago Schools Journal*, Vol. XXX (June, 1949), pp. 273-78.

The listener must assume an active role in developing listening skills, for no other person can listen for him, and no one can force him to listen. The task of listening, therefore, must be approached with a positive attitude which assumes that the listener wants to hear, to find out something; he wants "to listen." We are all aware of the ease with which the mind can slip to thoughts of an unrelated subject as a well-meaning soul chats on and on about a movie she just saw. What's more, she will never be aware that we have ceased listening, for our outward appearance remains the same (with a little care about yawning).

The listener, too, must assume responsibility for the success of the speaking-listening encounter; he must be prepared to hear with an open mind what this speaker has to impart. The listener does everything he can to promote understanding. He keeps his eyes on the speaker, makes certain that he can both see and hear, and takes appropriate notes. Following the speaking-listening experience, the listener may ask questions, comment on the information discussed, and utilize the acquired information.

Studying listening with students

Present listening as an active process. The students can discuss their roles as listeners, for analysis of the responsibilities of the listener will lead to more active participation in the listening act. Training clearly directed toward increasing listening efficiency can be interesting to the group as they use themselves as guinea pigs in a scientific bit of research to determine whether their practicing will better their listening abilities.

Why is listening important? This queston may lead to a study of time spent each day in listening as each child keeps a LISTENING DIARY. One fourth-grade boy recorded his daily listening activities, thus:

7:00 When I awoke, birds were singing.

7:15 I watched a TV show.

7:30 Mother called me for breakfast; we talked together.

7:45 My dog barked outside the door for his food.

8:00 Music was playing on the radio.

8:30 The telephone rang.

8:40 On the way to school I heard—
    a horn blowing
    children talking
    cars moving
    the traffic lady's whistle

8:55 The school bell rang.

9:00 Miss Dell called the roll.
   We talked about spring.
   We read aloud in reading class.

10:10 We played "Flying Dutchman."
   Miss Dell read a chapter of *Chitty–Chitty–Bang–Bang*.
   She explained division and we did mental arithmetic.

12:00 At lunch we whispered; music was playing.
   We played "Dodge Ball."

12:45 Joe read about the mission at Santa Barbara.
   Then we answered questions about the missions.
   We located missions on the map.
   We saw a film about Father Serra.
   Miss Dell asked if we would like to make dioramas.

1:30 We played ball.
   We sang songs and played a new record.
   Sandra reported on her science experiment.
   We talked about a picture and wrote a story about it.
   Some people read their stories.

3:00 Lots of noise on the way home.
   A fire engine passed.
   Mom told me she had two jobs for me.
   Then Jim and I played astronauts.

6:30 We had dinner. Dad talked a lot, mostly to Mom.

7:15 I watched TV until Mom called me.

8:30 Dad talked to me after I was in bed.
   Golly, there's listening in everything!

It is also helpful if students develop simple guides to good listening which are specific, thus:

LOOK at the speaker.
CONCENTRATE on what he is saying.
THINK about what he has said.
TALK about what he has said.
   Ask questions.
   Add information.

Relationship of listening to thinking

Listening is a vital part of the complex thinking process. As the elementary school student participates in listening activities in the classroom, he hears words which symbolize meanings. Through practice he learns to abstract meaning from these words and the order in which they are arranged. Through listening he learns to:

Make generalizations
Sort ideas, reject or accept
Group into categories
Observe similarities and differences
Make comparisons
Develop or adapt concepts

Children should be exposed to varied types of thinking processes which will require careful listening and reaction. After hearing two poems about the same general topic, for example, "P's the Proud Policeman" by Phyllis McGinley and "Bobby Blue" by John Drinkwater, children can compare the treatment of the subject. In the second poem, for instance, the name *policeman* is never mentioned. How do we know that the poet is describing a policeman?

The child's listening vocabulary is the largest of all his vocabularies. He will understand many words which he would hesitate to use in speech or be unable to read or write. What factors account for the greater size of the listening vocabulary?

1. Meaning can be deduced from the general context provided by the speaker.

   The situation was so *ridiculous* that the whole family began laughing.

   (The word *ridiculous* obviously is associated with laughter.)

2. The exact meaning is not necessary to understanding.

   The *cheetah* is the fastest runner in the animal world.

   (The child may not know exactly what the cheetah looks like, but he gathers enough meaning to permit discussion.)

3. The burden for introducing the new word lies with the speaker, not the listener; it is the speaker who must be more familiar with the meaning in order to use a word coherently.

4. The speaker's tone of voice implies certain connotations of approval or disapproval.

   The boys were just too *unruly*.

Because the listening vocabulary is so much more extensive than those of speaking, reading, and writing, we must be careful to provide stimulating discussion material for the primary-level classroom as well as for intermediate and upper grade levels. Discussion must not be limited to the content of controlled vocabulary readers, for instance, for these young minds are feasting on more exotic fare via television. We have a tendency to underestimate the abilities of children to understand broad concepts if couched in understandable terms, demonstrated visually, and presented in a stimulating context. This is one strong argument for the teacher's oral reading of books that are too difficult for children to read to themselves, for children can handle ideas orally and visually which may be too difficult for them to read about. First graders will enjoy listening to *Charlotte's Web* although few would be able to read it enjoyably.

Research indicates that there is a high correlation between reading and ability to listen with comprehension, and there is a corresponding increase in reading ability with increased ability to listen. A strong reading program therefore, should provide much listening experience, for the child requires time to develop aural-oral skills which in the long run will add to improved reading abilities. We will find this need recognized more clearly in working with the disadvantaged child and in the teaching of foreign languages which have long advocated the aural-oral approach to language before composition and reading are taught.

Listening to what?

Students need direct instruction in becoming aware of the listening act, for they are habituated to listening in an unstructured fashion. We as listeners can be likened to the television set with which they are so familiar. We receive sounds which are changed into thoughts, but if our listening mechanism is not properly tuned in, we fail to receive the proper message or we receive no message at all. Carrying the analogy further, the message may be severely distorted if the framing knob has been turned too far.

Listening is not an isolated skill to be practiced for 15 minutes a day and then forgotten. We never know when a message will be directed toward us, for listening is an integral part of all of life. Because this skill, or complex of skills, permeates all areas of the curriculum, effective methods of listening will be better taught in the context of varied subject matters—social science, literature, science, language study, music, art.

Can we establish a sequence of listening abilities to be followed from primary grades through junior high school? It is only through sequential development of these abilities that true listening efficiency will be attained. Young children who have learned to identify similar sounds and to follow simple directions will attack progressively more difficult skills and eventually will learn to listen critically to recorded presentations of literary works or to the commentary of news analysts. Described briefly here are varied suggestions for teaching listening to elementary school students.

1. Hide several items under the teacher's desk. As a noise is made with each item, let children identify the different sounds and discuss the differences.

2. Take children for a walk and have them list all the things they heard after they return. Repeat the technique after several days to see if they improve in perception.

3. Play notes on the piano to see if students can tell half steps from whole steps.

4. Play I TOOK A TRIP TO ZANZIBAR in which the first child may say, "I took a trip to Zanzibar and took along a toothbrush." A second child may say, "I took a trip to Zanzibar and took along a toothbrush and a poodle." A third may say, "I took a trip to Zanzibar and took along a toothbrush, a poodle, and a baseball bat." And so it goes.

5. Give a series of short directions with the children following them exactly. NOW HEAR THIS: Walk to the chalkboard, write your last name, and place the chalk on the reading table. Increase the number of directions as abilities grow.

6. Tape common sounds, for example, those from the kitchen—mixer, refrigerator running, slamming oven door, opening a can—and identify the sounds.

7. Have one child start a story with each child adding something in turn—a Traveling Tale. Each must listen to be able to add to the story.

8. Recite five less familiar proverbs, having students write each one after it has been said once, as "Learning is like rowing upstream; not to advance is to drop back."

9. Have students listen next to a wall or the floor to see if they can distinguish what's going on.

10. Listen to SILENCE! Everyone is as quiet as possible. Is this Silence? Are there noises still to be heard?

11. Read a portion of a story that is unknown to the students and let them complete the story after listening to the beginning.

12. List words that express sounds. LOUD SOUNDS: shouts, honking, crash, scream, clamor. SOFT SOUNDS: whisper, singing, cooing, scrape, hum, buzzing. Have children listen for SOUND LANGUAGE as stories are read aloud. Let them describe SOUND SITUATIONS which can then become part of a story.

13. Write a question on the board: "What language is spoken in Brazil?" Then read a paragraph which contains the answer as well as other information. Then read a paragraph asking the question after the listening experience. Compare the number of right answers; discuss the reasons for any differences in the number of right answers.

14. Practice taking notes from teacher-taped passages read from a textbook. Discuss the first set of notes taken. Project examples with the overhead projector to compare differences. Play the same material again as a new set of notes is produced. Repeat this procedure with other taped material.

15. Develop skill in remembering sequence of events by playing a short taped story (fairy tale, myth) or a poem. List the events that happened in order; then replay the selection to check accuracy. For variety provide a list of events in scrambled order with each child numbering the items in order of happening; then compare results.

Critical listening

What is the function of the critic? Students must first develop concepts which lead to constructive criticism before serving as critics of fellow students' oral presentations. A discussion can lead to the following generalizations:

Criticism should help a student improve.
Criticism should assist the class in understanding the qualities of good speaking.
If criticism is totally negative, it is more discouraging than helpful.

Students can be given listening assignments in which they must make a Listening Report to evaluate what was heard. Listening assignments may be for speeches made on radio or television, taped talks available in the classroom Listening Center, or student speeches. A form for reporting might be something like this:

General Evaluation:

10   9   8   7   6   5   4   3   2   1   0
Excellent   Could be better   Not satisfactory

Report:
Who spoke? _____
What topic? _____
Where? _____
When? _____
Main idea? _____
_____
Reactions: _____
_____

Materials to Investigate

Borten, Helen, *Do You Hear What I Hear?* New York: Abelard-Schuman, 1960. An imaginative book about sounds for children.

Duker, Sam, *Listening Bibliography.* New York: Scarecrow Press, 1964. Annotated bibliography of articles and books.

Elkin, Benjamin, *The Loudest Noise in the World.* New York: Viking, 1954. A small boy investigates the loudest noise.

Nichols, Ralph G., and Leonard Stevens, *Are You Listening?* New York: Mc-Graw-Hill, 1954. Provides background reading about the listening process.

Russell, David H., and Elizabeth Russell, *Listening Aids through the Grades.* New York: Teachers College, Columbia University, 1959. An excellent collection of listening activities.

Schreiber, Morris, *An Annotated List of Recordings in the Language Arts.* Champaign, Ill.: National Council of Teachers of English, 1964. An aid in selecting spoken records for classroom use.

Tiedt, Sidney W., and Iris M. Tiedt, *The Elementary Teacher's Complete Ideas Handbook.* Englewood Cliffs, N.J.: Prentice-Hall, 1965. Chapter 4 contains practical ideas for instruction, "Listening to Learn."

Wagner, Guy, *et al., Listening Games.* Darien, Conn.: Teachers Publishing Corporation, 1962. Activities to develop listening skills.

6

Living in a Verbal Society

"Remember that you are a human being with a soul and the divine gift of articulate speech; that your native language is the language of Shakespeare and Milton and the *Bible:* and don't sit there crooning like a bilious pigeon"—so wrote the inimitable Shaw in *Pygmalion*.

We could scarcely overemphasize the importance of speech as a means of communication in our verbal society, for we speak far more frequently than we write or read. Ability to speak effectively can mean the difference between success in life and the lack of success; indeed, verbal facility can actually mask an individual's deficiencies. Through the spoken word we transact business, express feelings, and communicate ideas; speech is a direct form of communication, a person-to-person relationship. Our purpose in this chapter is to explore the needs of the child in developing speech abilities and to examine strategies for providing varied experiences in speaking in the classroom.

Language Development

The child learns to speak his language long before he begins to read or write it, and the process of learning to speak is a much more natural act. The child lives with the language, constantly experimenting in its use. For the most part learning to speak is an enjoyable experience, for the child is encouraged through praise and attention. Throughout infancy his efforts at imitating adult speech are positively reinforced by adult approval and assistance.

Before entering school the child has been practicing spoken language for four to five years and has usually developed an extensive speaking vocabulary before he has any reading or writing vocabulary at all. The extent to which this spoken vocabulary is developed determines success in beginning reading experiences, for the child must know words in order to read them with meaning or to use them in composing sentences. This preschool background in speaking not only provides the child with knowledge of words but also familiarizes him with the grammar of the English language. Thus, the child in kindergarten can tell a teacher which of these spoken groups of words is a sentence.

Mark goes to school.

Dog the street down runs the.

The child knows his language "by ear," and as he begins to compose sentences we rely more on this intuitive sense of rightness than we do on rules. It is linguistically valid to ask the child, "Does that sound right?" The disadvantaged child lacks such intuitive knowledge of language, for his language experience has been meager compared to that of the child in a typical middle class home; he therefore has no wealth of practice to provide him with knowledge of grammar, sentence patterns, and word order. His problem is of such acuity and such national impact that we have devoted a chapter specifically to "Language for the Disadvantaged Child."

An extensive study of children's language is being conducted by Walter Loban at the University of California. This longitudinal study is investigating language used by selected students throughout their school experience from kindergarten through high school. The report of the findings at the conclusion of the first seven years has been published under the title, *The Language of Elementary School Children*.[1] Dr. Loban's findings relevant to oral language development lead him to this conclusion:

> ... In this study the superiority of the high group in handling oral signals effectively—their skill at using pitch, stress, and pause—combined with their relative freedom from using partial structural patterns is impressive. It would be difficult not to conclude that instruction can yet do more than it has *with oral language*. Many pupils who lack skill in using speech will have difficulty in mastering written tradition. Competence in the spoken language appears to be a necessary base for competence in writing and reading. Modern equipment for recording and studying the spoken word makes possible marked advances in such instruction.[2]

[1] Walter D. Loban, *The Language of Elementary School Children* (Champaign, Ill.: National Council of Teachers of English, 1963).

[2] *Ibid.*, p. 88.

"The scraps of lore which children learn from each other are at once more real, more immediately serviceable, and more vastly entertaining to them than anything which they learn from grown-ups." [3] So begins the fascinating study, *The Lore and Language of Schoolchildren*, by Iona and Peter Opie, which explores the widely varied lore of children which has been transmitted orally. This extensive study reveals that the same rhymes and riddles appear in variant forms not only throughout Great Britain, the locale of the study, but also in the United States and even in non–English-speaking countries. At times it is noted also that a particular bit of lore has been discovered in early literature, indicating that children's lore transcends time as well as geographic boundaries.

These verses of childhood, it is observed also, are not intended for adult ears, for "part of their fun is the thought, usually correct, that adults know nothing about them." Here is what the Opies term an "unselfconscious culture . . . unnoticed by the sophisticated world, and quite as little affected by it. . . ." [4]

Studying children's language in the United States is Dr. Ruth Strickland at Indiana University, who conducted a study of 575 children in the six grades of the elementary school. Taping the informal language of children, those assisting Dr. Strickland analyzed children's speech, comparing the content of the child's speech with that used in textbooks. These findings were significant in that children's language was found to be "far more advanced than the language of the books in which they are taught to read." Strickland found, furthermore, that the quantity and quality of children's language is largely determined by environment and experiential background rather than by native intelligence. [5]

These findings are substantiated by Noel's study of children and their language background at home. She found that the quality of a child's language is determined by the language of his parents and noted also that improvement in use of standard English is dependent on the cooperation of the home in exposing the child to standard English. [6]

These studies indicate that we tend to underestimate the child's ability to comprehend oral language. The extent of his listening and speaking vocabularies enables him to understand concepts that adults formerly thought too difficult to be introduced at early levels. Also emphasized is the important relationship between oral language development and ability to read.

[3] Iona and Peter Opie, *The Lore and Language of Schoolchildren* (London: Oxford University Press, 1959), p. 1.

[4] *Ibid.*, p. 2.

[5] Ruth Strickland, "Interrelationships between Language and Reading," *Volta Review.* (September, 1958), pp. 334-36.

[6] Doris E. Noel, "A Comparative Study of the Relationship between the Quality of the Child's Language Usage and the Quality and Types of Language Used in the Home," *Journal of Educational Research* (1953), pp. 161-67.

*Objectives of oral language
    instruction*

What are our obectives in oral language instruction? We certainly would not list "preparation of each student to be a public speaker" as an aim of the elementary school oral language program. Recognizing the basic nature of oral language and the importance of effective speech, however, we direct instruction toward these ends:

1. Linguistic fluency

    Ability to speak without hesitation
    Information about which to talk (experiential background)
    Vocabulary with which to speak
    Gradual movement toward use of standard English
    Familiarity with speech patterns

2. An extensive speaking vocabulary

    Pronunciation
    Meaning
    Variety
    Knowledge of usage levels

3. Effectiveness of speaking

    Elements of successful speaking
        Delivery
        Voice
        Content
        Bearing

    Specific parts of the speech
        Introduction
        Conclusion
        Choice of topic
        Use of words

    Variety in style presentation
        Humor
        Audience participation

The Contributions of Linguistics

Linguistics has pointed up the primacy of the spoken language and has gone directly to the oral language to observe the characteristics of language in action. It is noted that written language is actually a derived form cf language, a kind of speech dialect.

As is discussed in a preceding chapter, the linguist clarifies certain concepts which are reflected in the teacher's attitude toward language in the classroom. Relevant to the growth of ability in speaking effectively are the following concepts:

1. The spoken language is the primary form of language.
2. Children learn language naturally through an aural-oral method.
3. The child knows the grammar of his language before entering school.
4. Patterns of sentences typical to a language can be identified.
5. We gain meaning from word order.
6. Juncture, stress, and pitch (pauses, accents, tone) convey meaning.

We shall explore some of these concepts pertinent to spoken language as it is used in the elementary school classroom.

Techniques for practicing oral patterns

We can borrow techniques from instruction in foreign language to help children alleviate deficiencies in the easy use of patterns of oral English. Grammatical constructions can best be taught through aural-oral methods which include some of the following approaches.[7]

> *Repetition:* Listen and repeat exactly as heard.
>
> Teacher: I see a dog.
>
> Child: I see a dog.

Analogy: Repeat exactly with one change.

Teacher: I see a dog.
Ann: I see a horse.
Fred: I see a cat.
Sue: I see an elephant.

> Begin a PROGRESSIVE CONVERSATION so that all members of the group participate in this type of analogical replacement, thus:
>
> Teacher: I see a dog. What do you see, Jim?
> Jim: I see a horse. What do you see, Phyllis?
> Phyllis: I see a cat. What do you see, Joan?

Inflection: Change the form of a word.

Teacher: There is one girl.
Sue: There are two girls.

Teacher: There is one house.
Fred: There are two houses.

[7] Nelson Brooks, *Language and Language Learning* (Harcourt, 1964), pp. 156-61.

Completion: Finish the statement.

Teacher:	Susan is tall, but . . .
Joan:	Mary is taller.
Teacher:	John is big, but . . .
Carol:	Phil is bigger.

Expansion:

(See page 37 for more information on expanding sentences.)

Teacher:	Steve is happy.
Chuck:	Steve is happy because he finished his work.
Teacher:	Milly is happy.
Ann:	Milly is happy because she has a new dress.

Transformation: Change a given sentence to negative or interrogative form.

Teacher:	Judy is here today.
Carol:	Judy is not here today.
Teacher:	Judy is here today.
Fred:	Is Judy here today?

Restoration: Student makes sentence from a group of words.

Teacher:	picture, wall, hanging
Chuck:	The picture is hanging on the wall.
Phyllis:	Is the picture hanging on that wall?

Response: Answer or make a rejoinder.

Teacher:	It is chilly in this room.
Mary:	It feels fine to me.
Jim:	I think you are right.
Joan:	Shall I close the door?

Pitch, stress, and juncture

Linguists point out the varied shades of meaning possible through the spoken language which are not possible in written composition. Gestures and facial expression add meaning, as does the individual's use of intonation patterns, that is, stress, pitch, and juncture. What do we mean by these terms?

Stress: accent or loudness

Which word would you stress in the following sentences? Try stressing each word in turn.

What are you planning to do?
I'm not ready to go.
Who does he think he is!

Pitch: highness or lowness of tones

Which part of this sentence has the highest tone?

My name is Irene. (Can the pitch vary?)

Juncture: pauses (clues to punctuation in composition)

Can juncture change meaning? Explore the pauses in these sentences.

That lady is a queer bird.
Where did they find Joe's will?
Help somebody please.

Actually, to be more precise, the linguist notes four degrees of stress which can be marked in all speech, four degrees or levels of pitch, and four types of juncture according to the length of the pause. For our present purposes, however, it is sufficient to note the effect that each of these features of intonation has on meaning of the spoken language. We quickly notice the variation in meaning which is obtained by stressing different words in a sentence. There is truth in the statement: It isn't *what* you say, but *how* you say it, that matters. Students will enjoy experimenting with spoken language as they explore these concepts.

- Tape several samples of student speech in the classroom. Analyze these samples sentence by sentence to note pitch which is recorded, thus:

  2   1   1   4   3   3
  What are you doing here, Jim? (4 is high; 1 is low)

- Work with several sentences on the board first so that disagreements can be discussed and the tape replayed to check points made. Then students can experiment with analyzing other sentences.

- Compare the different variations of pitch and stress possible in a simple interjection or phrase.

  All right. (Say it with anger, annoyance, agreement, reluctance)
  Please.
  Go ahead and take it!
  Yes.
  No.

- Compare the manner of speaking the same word in two different contexts. Is it exactly the same?

  What present did you give her?
  Were you present when they arrived?

- Heteronyms provide provocative material for comparison of stress or accent as in these examples:

  Did you present Mrs. Smithson with a present?
  Should a rebel rebel?
  Are you content with the content of his remark?
  That magician standing in the entrance may entrance you.

● How does changing juncture change meaning? The results are often amusing. In what situation might the following have been appropriate?

"I will not hit any, Mother," she said sweetly.
"I will not hit any mother," she said sweetly.
"How will you help me?" he asked.
"How! Will you help me?" he asked.

Strategies for Speech Instruction

How can we teach students to speak effectively? Classroom instruction in oral language skills must be directed toward (1) providing many opportunities for speaking, (2) stimulating the child to want to speak, and (3) providing for constructive evaluation. In this section we shall explore varied strategies to be used in the elementary school classroom to achieve these goals.

Promising practices in oral language

As we observe in classrooms and talk to teachers throughout the nation, we note the use of specific techniques in promoting oral language, whether the person involved be a teacher working with primary or preschool boys and girls or an instructor of adults who are learning English as a foreign language. It is worthwhile to note a few of these general practices.

Small Group Work. It is imperative that children work individually or in small groups (5-6) as they engage in activities designed specifically to develop speech abilities. The advantages of the small group include:

1. A sense of security for the child who is uncertain about his language abilities
2. Greater opportunity for each individual to speak
3. A better diagnostic situation as the teacher strives to guide individual development

Unless a child is particularly agressive (and the child who needs help with language is far from agressive), he can be lost even in a group of 25. It is interesting to analyze the amount of speaking that children actually do in the typical classroom. As noted in the preceding chapter, more than half of student time is spent in listening activities.[8] Speaking is more often done by the teacher than by class members.

Increased Focus on Oral Language. Linguistics has pointed the way toward an emphasis on oral language in the elementary school. It has become evident that success in school depends on linguistic fluency and

---

[8] Miriam Wilt, "A Study of Teacher Awareness of Listening as a Factor in Elementary Education." *Journal of Educational Research* (April, 1950), pp. 626-36.

the development of an extensive vocabulary, and we note that speech development is related to later development in reading. For these reasons we see a tendency to allot more class time for activities which encourage speaking by the child.

Why have teachers not stressed oral activities previously? A major deterrent is the unstructured nature of oral instruction and the fact that the teacher has had few materials to assist her in developing oral abilities. There has been confusion about the aims of instruction in oral language with emphasis being placed largely on "correct usage." We have failed also, as in other aspects of elementary school English, to develop a sequential program for speech development. With linguistic emphasis on speech as the primary form of language will come assistance for the teacher who is working with elementary school students.

Use of the Tape Recorder. The tape recorder is invaluable in speech development. Although all classrooms will not be equipped with language laboratory facilities, each can and should have a Listening and Speaking Center which is planned around a tape recorder fitted with earphones and microphones for listening and recording. In this way language development can be accomplished individually as children work with teacher-prepared tapes or those available commercially. Specific ideas for using the tape recorder are described on page 124.

Variety in classroom speaking experiences

Although children need many opportunities to engage in informal speaking situations, they also need a growing number of experiences in speaking with and before a group. There are various ways of providing speaking experiences in the classroom.

Discussion. The most familiar form of speaking in the classroom is a discussion of a common topic which often arises from studies or activities undertaken by the class. These discussions may focus on:

● Answering questions to which there is no specific answer.

  Why did people move westward in the United States?

● Giving opinions about current issues.

  Should we continue spending money on space exploration?

● Solving a problem.

  How can our class raise enough money to go to Science Camp?

● Talking about ideas and feelings.

  What makes you happy?
  Would you like to live the life of Pippi Longstocking?

Ability to participate successfully in discussions is a significant skill for an adult to acquire. Students can discuss what specific skills each should develop as a way of improving skill in discussion, for example:

- A feeling of responsibility for contributing to a group discussion.
- Ability to ask intelligent, pertinent questions.
- Willingness to listen to contributions of others.

Assigned Speaking. Assigned speeches in the elementary school should never be long, and the topics assigned should allow for individual interests so that students are talking about topics which are interesting to them. Schedule delivery of speeches so there are never too many delivered at one time, for the whole class will lose enthusiasm if forced to listen to other students speaking for more than 20 minutes. Vary assigned speaking experiences, thus:

Explanation: How to do something.
  How to make scrambled eggs
  How to make money
  How to make an impression
  How to write a news story

Argument: Why I hold this opinion.
  Girls are awful. (Boys are terrible.)
  A woman should never be President of the United States.
  We should reform our spelling system.
  Everyone should know how to type.
  No one should have to attend school unless he wants to.

Humor: How these words came to be spoken.
  "George, You are the cat's meow!"
  "I got that story straight from the horse's mouth."
  "Cross my heart and hope to die."

The art of asking questions

The inquiry method has drawn attention to the significance of question asking as a part of the thinking act. What kinds of questions are students asking? Are they sensible according to known information? Do they penetrate to the core of the problem? Students need experience in asking penetrating questions. They can be encouraged to compose more effective questions through some of the following methods:

Students write questions as they review a subject being studied. These questions can be asked during class to assist student review. From the questions submitted to the teacher a number are selected to appear on the examination.

TWENTY QUESTIONS and ANIMAL, VEGETABLE, OR MINERAL? are games which encourage question asking. Students quickly learn the types of questions which best serve to narrow the field.

WHAT QUESTION WOULD YOU ASK? Given a specific situation, the student is requested to decide what question should be asked. Suggested questions are compared and discussed as to their merits, for example:

> You are walking down the street when you notice a six-year-old boy you know on the roof of a house. WHAT QUESTION WOULD YOU ASK.

> You are downtown alone when suddenly you find that you have lost your money. WHAT QUESTION WOULD YOU ASK?

Oral Book Reviews. The oral book review provides a welcome relief from the overworked written book report form. Encourage students to explore novel ways of sharing books orally:

● Interview a character in the book. Two members of the class may share this review with one serving as the character to be interviewed.

● Give a first-person account of an event in the book read:

> Wilbur speaks, for example: "I tell you I was so lonesome I thought I'd die when suddenly I heard Charlotte's sweet voice . . ."

● Tape a portion of the story after having practiced reading that part of the book aloud in order to achieve the best interpretation.

● Describe a book from the eyes of its author:

> Mrs. Beverly Cleary, for instance, describes the creation of Henry Huggins (imaginary information, of course): "I decided to write about a boy because they usually have more interesting adventures than do girls, and I chose the name, Henry, because it seemed to fit an adventuresome boy. . . ."

● Present an award to the author of a prize-winning book (either for illustrations or for story content) explaining why this book was selected for the award.

● Prepare pictures of important incidents in a book. Then tell the story briefly as the pictures are shown. (This could be a scroll theater presentation prepared by several students who have read the same book.)

Impromptu Speaking. The extemporaneous speech is presented without time for extensive planning and should be regarded as a "speech experiment." Certainly evaluation will take the form of praising any aspect of the experiment which turns out well. Sets of cards (3″ x 5″ file cards) can be developed with student assistance to provide stimulating topics for the short unrehearsed speech.

● *Quotations by famous people*—Why I agree or disagree.

> You must look *into* people as well as at them.[1]
>> *Lord Chesterfield*

> Behavior is a mirror, in which everyone shows his image.
>> *Johann von Goethe*

---

[1] For additional quotations see *Quotes for Teaching* by Sidney W. Tiedt (San Jose, Calif.: Contemporary Press, 1964).

No man is an Island, entire of itself.

John Donne

To be of use in the world is the only way to be happy.

Hans Christian Andersen

● *Small pictures*—how this illustration fits in a story.

●*Two words*—how these two words are related.

●*Questions*—answer the question.

Have you ever been afraid?
What is the funniest thing you have ever seen?
What was the most exciting moment in your life?

● *Introductions*—pretend you are asked to introduce a famous speaker. What would you say as you introduce—

Mark Twain
Jacqueline Kennedy
Lyndon B. Johnson
Theodore Geisel (Dr. Seuss)

● *What do you do now?*—Card presents an improbable situation which the speaker reads aloud, concluding with his action. Motivate this speaking experience by reading from Sesyle Joslin's *What Do You Say, Dear?* (Harcourt). Cards can be written as a writing experiment after reading this book.

● *It's A Joke*—Read the joke on the card and then tell it to the group without aid of the card.

●*Extra! Extra!*—Cut unusual headlines from old newspapers. Students may create "enchanting examples" by cutting out single words from the paper as needed. The speaker uses the headline as the topic for his speech.

Literature motivates oral language experiences

Literature serves as an excellent stimulus to oral language while at the same time aiding speech development through expansion of ideas and vocabulary. Reading a title from children's literature provides a common body of knowledge about which the group can talk immediately without need to build up a background of information, for everyone can have an opinion about the book read. We can bring literature into the classroom as part of the oral language program, thus:

Sharing Books. Let's talk about books, use books, enjoy books together, for explorations in children's literature add to growth in reading, writing, general information, thinking, as well as speaking and listening. The following suggestions contribute literature learning as well as oral language development.

Reading Together. Small groups of students can form READING CIR-
CLES which meet at a specified time to read a book together. Each child
takes a turn reading aloud, passing the book on when he is tired of reading. Emphasis is on enjoyment of the book in a group situation which
brings readers together according to interests rather than abilities, for there
is a need to learn to work with persons of mixed abilities. Time is spent
on talking about points of interest as the story progresses.

WORDLESS BOOKS. In the Wordless Book the child creates literature
himself, usually in an impromptu approach. A teacher can prepare a
paperback booklet which may bear the title THE WORDLESS BOOK,
or other titles may be used each of which suggests a story on a specific
theme:

> *Tom's Adventures at the Beach*
> *Camping in the Deep Woods*

At least one commercially prepared wordless book is now available which
has certain advantages in that it contains the illustrations for a story without words. *What Whiskers Did* by Ruth Carroll (Walck, 1965) is the
story of a small dog.

Storytelling. "Everyone is a potential storyteller," writes Ruth Sawyer,
and she notes also that whether conscious of it or not "everyone has
been telling stories since he learned to talk." [9] We can encourage students
to tell stories with enthusiasm and effect by providing opportunities for
telling stories and assisting students in finding good material for storytelling. Experiences in storytelling can be exciting and rewarding.

RIDDLES AND JOKES: A first step in beginning storytelling might be
the telling of riddles which have some story element. The joke contains a
little more story content and requires much the same skill as the telling of
a longer story. In each case practice is required and close attention must
be paid to the conclusion, in this case the "punch line."

FAMILIAR STORIES: Young children will develop skill in following
the sequence of a story as they tell stories cooperatively. "The Little
Red Hen found a grain of wheat. What did she say then, Neil?" Each
child contributes to the telling of this story, which may then be retold
as the contributors stand in order before the class, each telling his line
or two at the appropriate time. Legends, folktales, stories of mythology,
fairy tales—all provide excellent storytelling material for the elementary
school.

THE STORYTELLERS: A club can be formed of students who have
special interest and ability in storytelling. This group can use varied approaches to storytelling, both individual and group, depending on the
material. At times they can present samplings of their repertoire to an
appreciative audience.

[9] Ruth Sawyer, *"How To Tell a Story"* (New York: Compton's, n.d.), pp. 3-4. Reprint from *Compton's Pictured Encyclopedia*.

For students in the elementary school, storytelling is wisely directed toward short stories, verses, myths, folklore. Humor, surprise endings, and audience participation add to the effectiveness and the enjoyment of both performer and audience. The values of storytelling experiences include:

1. Attention to voice quality—pitch, tempo, enunciation.
2. Investigation of literature suitable for presentation, an interesting research project for able students.
3. A pleasurable combination of literature and language experiences, delight in words and their use.
4. Appreciation of literature—What makes a good story?

Almost all children's books can be used as storytelling material. Those which contain many illustrations can be used in storytelling before the child learns to read, for after hearing the story he can retell it by following the illustrations. Bruno Munari's enchanting book, *Who's There? Open the Door* (World) is a favorite as is Albert Lamorisse's *The Red Balloon* (Doubleday). Children of all ages will enjoy retelling stories they have read and enjoyed. In addition we have listed here a selected few collections of short stories which proved excellent sources of storytelling material:

Andersen, Hans C., *Fairy Tales* (Walck).
Arbuthnot, May H., *The Arbuthnot Anthology* (Scott, Foresman).
Bacmeister, Rhoda, *Stories to Begin On* (Dutton).
De la Mare, Walter, *Tales Told Again* (Knopf).
Fenner, Phyllis, ed., *Giants and Witches and a Dragon or Two* (Knopf).
Hamilton, Edith, *Mythology* (Little, Brown).
Huber, Miriam B., *Story and Verse for Children* (Macmillan).
Kipling, Rudyard, *Just So Stories* (Doubleday).
Lang, Andrew, ed., *The Blue Fairy Book* (Longmans).
Leodhas, Sorchie, *Gaelic Ghosts* (Holt).
Sandburg, Carl, *Rootabaga Stories* (Harcourt).
Thorne-Thomsen, Gudren, ed., *East o' the Sun and West o' the Moon* (Harper).

Choric Speaking. Group recital of selections from literature, both poetry and prose, is an excellent technique for enriching the oral language program and for encouraging all children to speak. A wealth of material is appropriate for this purpose.

Poems are made for saying or reading aloud, for only through an oral approach to poetry do we truly get the full effect of the rhythm, the music of this phenomenon of language. Oral presentation of poems and verses, furthermore, permits a group to share the appreciation of the poet's work. In the chapter devoted to poetry we explore the use of a Poetry Chorus, but there is such a wide range of poetry available that we can add a few suggestions here without risk of duplicating our efforts.

- Short humorous verse appeals to young children as well as to students in the intermediate grades. Stress clarity of enunciation, and a long questioning pause at the comma, when speaking this anonymous poem:

A SLEEPER FROM THE AMAZON

A sleeper from the Amazon
Put nighties of his gra'mason—
The reason, that
He was too fat
To get his own pajamason.

- An occasional Tongue Twister adds spice to speaking and adds to the child's awareness of wordplay:

I saw Esau sawing wood [pause]
And Esau saw I saw him; [quickly]
Though Esau saw I saw him saw [pause]
Still Esau went on sawing.

A tutor who tooted the flute
Tried to tutor two tooters to toot.
Said the two to the tutor,
"Is it harder to toot, or
To tutor two tooters to toot?"

- Verses known to children, for example, rope-jumping songs, provide good rhythmical chants:

Not last night but the night before,
Twenty-four burglars at my door.
I went downstairs to let them in;
They hit me over the head
With a rolling pin!

- Combine actions with speaking a poem as in this selection from *Mother Goose:*

The noble Duke of York [majestically]
    He had ten thousand men.
He marched them up a very high hill; [last words quickly]
    Then he marched them down again.
And when he was up, he was up; [quickly]
    And when he was down, he was down; [quickly]
And when he was only halfway up
    He was neither *up nor down!* [distinctly]

- A poem that tells a story lends itself to clear enunciation and varied intonation:

THE SECRET

Unknown

We have a secret, just we three,
The robin, and I, and the sweet cherry-tree;
The bird told the tree, and the tree told me,
And nobody knows it but just we three.

But of course the robin knows it best,
Because she built the—I shan't tell the rest;
And laid the four little—something in it—
I'm afraid I shall tell it every minute.

But if the tree and the robin don't peep,
I'll try my best the secret to keep;
Though I know when the little birds fly about
Then the whole secret will be out.

● Repetition adds interest to a poem for younger children, and also makes it easier to learn.

SING OUT!

Iris M. Tiedt

Sing, sing, sing;
    Racing to the swing.
Hum, hum, hum;
    Spring at last has come!
Call, call, call;
    The grass is growing tall.
Shout, shout, shout;
    School will soon be out!

● Older children will enjoy the humor and the actions of this delightful poem by William Makepeace Thackeray:

A TRAGIC STORY

There lived a sage in days of yore,
And he a handsome pigtail wore;
But wondered much and sorrowed more,
    Because it hung behind him.

He mused upon this curious case,
And swore he'd change the pigtail's place,
And have it hanging at his face,
    Not dangling there behind him.

Said he, "The mystery I've found—
I'll turn me round"—and he turned him round,
    But still it hung behind him.

Then round and round, and out and in,
All day the puzzled sage did spin;
In vain—it mattered not a pin—
    The pigtail hung behind him.

And right and left, and roundabout,
And up and down and in and out
He turned; but still the pigtail stout
  Hung steadily behind him.

And though his efforts never slack,
And though he twist, and twirl, and tack,
Alas! still faithful to his back,
  The pigtail hangs behind him.

Prose should not be ignored as a source of excellent material for speaking together. Explore the literature of the social sciences or combine storytelling techniques with choric speaking.

Enrich a social studies experience by teaching children the Gettysburg Address, for there is no more beautiful piece of American literature than this famous speech:

Four score and seven years ago our fathers brought forth on this continent, a new nation, conceived in liberty, and dedicated to the proposition that all men are created equal.

Now we are engaged in a great civil war, testing whether that nation, or any nation so conceived and so dedicated, can long endure. We are met on a great battlefield of that war. We have come to dedicate a portion of that field, as a final resting place for those who here gave their lives that that nation might live. It is altogether fitting and proper that we should do this.

But, in a larger sense, we can not dedicate—we can not consecrate—we can not hallow—this ground. The brave men, living and dead, who struggled here have consecrated it, far above our poor power to add or detract. The world will little note, nor long remember, what we say here, but it can never forget what they did here. It is for us the living, rather, to be dedicated here to the unfinished work which they who fought here have thus far so nobly advanced. It is rather for us to be here dedicated to the great task remaining before us—that from these honored dead we take increased devotion to that cause for which they gave the last full measure of devotion—that we here highly resolve that these dead shall not have died in vain—that this nation, under God, shall have a new birth of freedom—and that government of the people, by the people, and for the people, shall not perish from the earth.

Combine the arts of storytelling and choric speaking as several individual speakers, for example, tell the story of Wanda Gág's *Millions of Cats* with a chorus coming in on the repeated words which add so much to the story:

Hundreds of Cats, thousands of Cats, millions and billions and trillions of cats . . .

Creative dramatization

A way of stimulating speaking is through many forms of dramatization. The source of ideas for dramatization is endless, and variation in the form of dramatization is sufficiently wide to provide for all interests and abilities. As Winifred Ward explains:

> The term "creative dramatics" includes all forms of *improvised* drama— drama created by the children themselves and played with spontaneous dialogue and action. It begins with imaginative play of the young child, which mirrors life as the child sees and feels it, and is followed by simple story dramatizations. It also includes: creative plays based on ideas and on literature, dramatizations of incidents from the social studies, original dance, pantomimes, creative work in puppets and shadow plays, and integrated projects in which many of the subjects in the school program contribute to an adventurous play which the children create from a book or a story. . . .[10]

A major advantage of creative dramatics is that participants do not learn set parts or lines. For this reason they literally cannot "make a mistake." Varying from simple actions and dialogue to the dramatization of a lengthy story, this form of dramatics permits children to interpret roles freely. As Geraldine Siks observes:

> This freedom of imagination that characterizes child-thought is both the envy and terror of the adult. . . . Children in their own way are highly creative because of their innate freedom of imagination. . . . Creative dramatics utilizes and challenges the imagination of the child.[11]

Emphasis in creative dramatics is not on preparation of a drama to be presented before an audience, but on providing opportunity for the child to express himself freely. All children will participate in the acting at one time when space and the type of dramatization permit, for there need be no audience at all. At other times one portion of the class, perhaps a third or a half, will participate while the others observe and await their own turns. An effective classroom arrangement for creative drama is the THEATER IN THE ROUND, with chairs forming a circle from which observers can readily view the action.

What are the advantages of dramatization as a way of developing language abilities? They include the following:

1. Pleasure is combined with learning.
2. Physical and social abilities are developed.
3. Freedom of action encourages the child's expression.
4. Preparatory discussion extends vocabulary and interests.

Specifically, we may choose to encourage language development through these enjoyable creative activities.

Pantomime. A good dramatic activity to begin with; we include it here although the mime in performance uses no language.

---

[10] Winifred Ward, *Creative Dramatics* (Washington, D.C.: Association for Childhood Education, 1961), p. 3.

[11] Geraldine B. Siks, *Children's Literature for Dramatization* (New York: Harper, 1964), pp. 1-3.

Pantomime does include language, of course, as the children plan, talk about the mime's role, or try to guess what act is being mimed. Activities like these introduce children to creative dramatics.

GUESS WHAT I'M DOING: An interesting way to initiate experiments in pantomime is to ask students to mime an activity as others try to identify the activity depicted. Favorites are:

Peeling a banana and eating it
Unwrapping gum and chewing it, blowing bubbles
Opening an umbrella as it suddenly begins to rain
Person being bothered by a mosquito or fly
Petting a cat
Making a sandwich
Combing hair before a mirror

Interpreting Situations: Briefly sketch a situation in pantomime. Have several groups try the same topic to see how the interpretation develops. Students enjoy suggesting *interesting* situations, for example:

Showing a bad report card to Mother and Dad
Teenage girls talking on the telephone
Father giving son first driving lesson
Two children watching puppies in a pet store window
Boy finds money, runs to store, buys candy
Child breaks vase, runs to hide

Finger Play Activities. An oral activity that is particularly suitable for work with primary children is the finger play story which may aim at teaching some concept such as the difference between *left* and *right* or the order of the numerals in addition to encouraging young children to speak. "Ten Little Indians," usually sung, is an example of finger play that teaches children to count to ten while they are developing language abilities.

A favorite finger play is "Eency Weency Spider" which again is a song that has appeal for children. Children can also invent finger plays to accompany familiar songs, for example, "Three Blind Mice."

A wonderful story to motivate finger play activities after children have developed some familiarity with this technique is *A Handful of Surprises* by Anne Heather and Esteban Francés (Harcourt) which presents five puppets, named Mac, Marc, Tink, Tarc, and O'Tooley, who fight constantly but always stay together because each is a finger on the hand of Fleek, the clown. The story tells of their troubles and how they finally learned to get along together. (See illustration, page 120.)

Puppetry. A form of dramatization which delights young people of all ages (up to 95) is puppetry. Puppetry as a means of encouraging students to speak has many advantages, one of which is the hiding of the individual person who can then feel free to play his role with enthusiasm.

they are all hitched to the same hand!

Even the shyest third-grade boy can call out Maurice Sendak's wonderful line, "And now, let the wild rumpus start!" [12]

Puppets should be kept simple so that emphasis remains on the use rather than the construction, for our concern here is with language development. Simple, but effective, puppet heads can be made from:

Faces cut from magazines mounted on cardboard for stiffness
Styrofoam balls with features and hair pinned on
Toe of a sock stuffed with cotton or small rags
Layers of paper glued and dried over an orange or ball
Plasticine covered by white cloth

Encourage children to invent different kinds of original puppets. Clever puppets can be fashioned from almost any kind of scrap material:

Bottle caps (bugs with legs)
Walnut shells (wrinkled Indian faces)

[12] Maurice Sendak, *Where the Wild Things Are* (New York: Harper 1963).

Peanuts in shells (animals with tails, ears, legs added)
Potatoes and other vegetables (animals suggested by shapes)
Wooden spoons (faces painted on back of spoon)
Paper bags (stuffed with newspaper; add features)
Paper plates (glued to sticks; add hair, features)
Squares of cloth (tie knots for head and two hands) [13]

Dramatization of Poetry. Many poems have a great deal of narrative value which can be the basis for a skit, pantomime, or creative dramatization. For younger students the dramatic activity can take place after the teacher has read a poem to the class. "Jonathan Bing" is a good example which contains humor and a story which children can take turns portraying. Some teachers have several children be Jonathan at the same time while another group acts the part of the narrator who reminds Jonathan, "You can't go to court in pajamas, you know," sadly shaking their heads at the very thought.

Robert Louis Stevenson's "My Shadow" is another delightful poem when combined with dramatic play as a few children move according to the poem followed by "shadows" who imitate their behavior until the final verse when the shadow is left at home in bed.

MY SHADOW

I have a little shadow that goes in and out with me,
And what can be the use of him is more than I can see.
He is very, very like me from the heels up to the head;
And I see him jump before me, when I jump into my bed.

The funniest thing about him is the way he likes to grow—
Not at all like proper children, which is always very slow:
For he sometimes shoots up taller like an India-rubber ball,
And he sometimes gets so little that there's none of him at all.

He hasn't got a notion of how children ought to play,
And can only make a fool of me in every sort of way.
He stays so close beside me, he's a coward you can see;
I'd think shame to stick to nursie as that shadow sticks to me!

One morning, very early, before the sun was up,
I rose and found the shining dew on every buttercup;
But my lazy little shadow, like an arrant sleepyhead,
Had stayed at home behind me and was fast asleep in bed.

Multimedia to motivate speech

The use of multimedia is helpful in motivating children's speech. Records, tapes, films, filmstrips, slides, transparencies, the flannel board, pictures, bulletin board displays, and exhibits—all add variety and stimulus to the elementary school speech program. These media can be used in many ways as suggested in the following discussion.

[13] Sidney W. Tiedt and Iris M. Tiedt, *The Elementary Teacher's Complete Ideas Handbook* (Englewood Cliffs, N.J.: Prentice-Hall, 1965), p. 228.

Films. Many fine films are being developed. Some present a title from children's literature visually, which extends the child's vocabulary and provides a source of discussion topics after the viewing. A variety of films of excellent books and stories are available from Weston Woods, Weston, Conn., among them *The Sorcerer's Apprentice, A Snowy Day,* and *The Doughnut Machine* (from *Homer Price*).

Another type of film which presents interesting possibilities to motivate both speech and writing is the "wordless" film. A beautiful example is *Rainshower* (Churchill Films, 662 N. Robertson Blvd., Los Angeles, Calif., 90069), a 15-minute film in color. The expert photography focuses on the effects of rain in the country compared to the effects in the city— the mother runs to get washing from the line, the geese move ponderously toward the poultry yard, the parched ground soaks up the first drops— and only natural sounds are heard.

A short filmed story without sound is *The Hunter in the Forest* (Encyclopaedia Britannica Film Company, Wilmette, Ill.) which portrays the story of a hunter. Again, fine photography depicts the hunter's experiences as he bags a game bird and finally sights a family of deer. Does he shoot? Some teachers find this moment an effective stopping place for writing or discussion, after which the remainder of the film is shown.

Flannel Board. An effective device for assisting language development is the flannel board, a device much used by primary teachers but less commonly employed in intermediate grades. It has distinct advantages for instruction at all levels, for the flannel board:

1. Provides the shy speaker with a "prop"
2. Guides students through a sequence
3. Motivates student interest
4. Combines visual and oral activities.

Figures prepared by students will guide the class in retelling stories, finger play activities, choric speaking of poetry, and singing songs which have many verses. These figures can be cut from flannel, felt, or construction paper backed with sandpaper, but perhaps most satisfactory is *pellon,* a synthetic innerlining material that is sold in any fabric store.

Children in the primary grades will benefit from a guided recitation of "This Is the House That Jack Built."

THE HOUSE THAT JACK BUILT

This is the house that Jack built.

This is the malt
That lay in the house that Jack built.

This is the rat,
That ate the malt
That lay in the house that Jack built.

This is the cat,
That killed the rat,
That ate the malt
That lay in the house that Jack built.

This is the dog,
That worried the cat,
That killed the rat,
That ate the malt
That lay in the house that Jack built.

Other songs and stories for this purpose are: "Old MacDonald Had a Farm," "The Farmer in the Dell," "The Mulberry Bush," *Goldilocks and the Three Bears, Three Little Pigs,* and *The Little Red Hen.*

Suitable for presentation via the flannel board in the intermediate grades are poems, for example, "Poor Old Woman," "Jonathan Bing," as well as songs, "I Gave My Love a Cherry," "The Frog Went A-Courtin'," and other folk songs. Students enjoy the repetitive song, "Green Grass Grows All Around," for which we have provided the words and music.

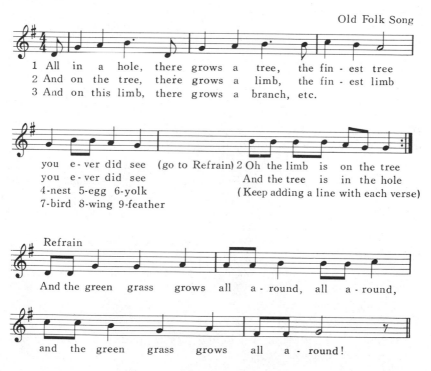

As each addition is made, all others are repeated in reverse order, with the last verse sung thus:

And on the wing there is a feather, The finest feather you ever did see, The feather is on the wing, The wing is on the bird, The bird is in the yolk, The yolk is in the egg, The egg is in the nest, The nest is on the branch, The branch is on the limb, The limb is on the tree, The tree is in the hole, And the green grass grows all around, all around, And the green grass grows all around.

Records. Again, recorded stories supply stimulating materials for discussion and for developing vocabulary. A fairy tale is featured, for example, in *Emperor's Nightingale* (Folkways/Scholastic Records, 906 Sylvan Ave., Englewood Cliffs, N.J. 07632).

We highly recommend the recording of *Ruth Sawyer, Storyteller,* who captures the listener from the moment she says, in the traditional Spanish manner, "Once there was and was not..." Two records by this author and storyteller are available from Weston Woods, Weston, Conn.

Tapes. The use of the tape recorder has a fascination of its own whether individuals are recording or the teacher is recording the whole group. Once children become accustomed to the recorder through frequent use, they lose any fear of recording or being recorded. The flexibility of recording devices and the availability of inexpensive tape make this medium invaluable in working with speech development. The following uses of the tape recorder are recommended:

- Older children can tape stories for use in Listening Centers in primary grades. Primary teachers can request specific titles for which upper-grade students volunteer, for practice is required to produce a well-read recording.

- In the same way, record materials for blind students. This would be an excellent project for a student SPEAKER'S CLUB.

- Tape speeches made by students so each can hear his own speech for purposes of evaluation. Tape a discussion to determine ways of improving discussion techniques.

- Record poetry to accompany a group of illustrative slides from parent or teacher collections. Advanced students who have access to a camera might develop a series of slides specifically for use with certain titles which they enjoy.

- Use a teacher-prepared recording which assists the child in developing sentence patterns. The child repeats patterned sentences spoken first by the teacher, thus:

  Jimmy has a dog.
  Jimmy has _____. (Child supplies "a dog.")
  Jimmy has a black dog.
  Jimmy has _____.
  Jimmy has a big black dog.

Jimmy has _____.
Jimmy has a big black dog. Can you say the whole sentence?

● Patterns can be developed to focus student learning on any aspect of language development—phonology, vocabulary development, sentence structure.

Evaluating speaking

As in all language experience, evaluation should be the responsibility of both student and teacher, and it should always be constructive in nature. Speaking should never become a traumatic experience. Evaluation should be directed toward helping the student improve, a goal which will most readily be achieved with the elementary school student through positive reinforcement rather than the shocked, "No, no" equivalent of the red pencil. Evaluation of speaking must take place immediately, for the effectiveness of the evaluation diminishes considerably with passage of time unless the speech is recorded. We shall explore techniques of evaluation which have been helpful in working with young students.

Note from Teacher to Speaker. After hearing the student deliver his "speech" the teacher writes a short note to the individual who spoke, saying perhaps:

> Dear Brian,
> You spoke clearly, and the class enjoyed your story.
> I liked your description of Onion John.
>
> Mrs. K.

Taped Replay. The teacher (or a student) tapes the several speeches given at one time. Later each student has an opportunity to "hear himself as others hear him." He is asked to make *one* specific suggestion which will help him improve his next speech.

Student Evaluation. This technique must be used with care, for students can be brutal. The whole class should, therefore, be taught the purposes of "criticism" and they should be encouraged to use positive criticism when evaluating a fellow student's speaking. The following suggestions may serve to guide student evaluation in a more positive direction:

Have only three students (rotate positions) evaluate any speaker. These three serve as the critics, and the remainder of the class is observant not only of the speaker's abilities but also of the abilities of the critics.

Have one group of five students complete evaluation forms for the speech delivered. An evaluation form similar to that illustrated can be developed by the class.

ORAL PRESENTATION

	Possible	Achievement	Comments
Interest			
Enthusiasm of speaker	5		
Audience response	5		
Expression of voice	5		
Gesture, movement of hands	5		
Friendly attitude	5		
Total	25		
Voice			
Enunciation, clearness	5		
Pronouncing words	5		
Volume	5		
Use of words (meaning)	5		
Tempo	5		
Total	25		
Organization			
Introduction, effect	5		
Organized points	5		
Knowledge of material	5		
Conclusion	5		
Total	20		
Bearing			
Rising to speak	5		
Eye contact	5		
Posture	5		
Movement of body	5		
Total	20		

Focus on One Aspect of Speech. As in the evaluation of writing, speaking is more accurately evaluated if students are told in advance that they are to focus attention on the introduction, the use of gestures, the use of humor, or another specific component of the speech. All other aspects of the delivery except that specified are then ignored in evaluation.

Test the Results. For specific types of speeches the effectiveness of the speaking can be tested by noting the results. In telling a joke, for example, the effectiveness can be judged by the audience response, laughter. When the student is assigned to explain how to do something, the success may be based on the ability of the group in general to follow the directions given.

Books to Investigate

Association for Childhood Education Internation, *Creative Dramatics*, Bulletin 2A. Washington, D.C.: The Association, 1961.

Batchelder, Marjorie, and Virginia Lee, *Puppets and Plays; A Creative Approach*. New York: Harper, 1956.

Davis, Jed H., and Mary J. Watkins, *Children's Theater*. New York: Harper, 1960.

Loban, Walter, *The Language of Elementary School Children*. Champaign, Ill.: National Council of Teachers of English, 1963. A highly readable 92-page report of an influential study.

Mackintosh, Helen K., ed., *Children and Oral Language*. Champaign, Ill.: National Council of Teachers of English, 1965. A report by a joint committee from ACEI, ASCD, IRA, and NCTE.

Malstrom, Jean, *Language in Society*. New York: Hayden, 1965. Provocative information about language to be presented to able students.

Opie, Iona, and Peter Opie, *The Lore and Language of School Children*. London: Oxford University Press, 1959.

Pronovost, Wilbert, *The Teaching of Speaking and Listening in the Elementary School*. New York: McKay, 1959.

Rasmussen, Carrie, *Speech Methods in the Elementary School*. New York, Ronald, 1962.

Sawyer, Ruth, *The Way of the Storyteller*. New York: Viking, 1955.

Siks, Geraldine B., *Children's Literature for Dramatization*. New York: Harper, 1964.

――――, *Creative Dramatics: An Art for Children*. New York: Harper, 1958.

Van Riper, Charles, and Katherine G. Butler, *Speech in the Elementary Classroom*. New York: Harper, 1955.

Ward, Winifred, *Drama With and For Children*. Washington, D.C.: U.S. Government Printing Office, 1960.

Wisconsin English Language Arts Curriculum Committee, *Teaching Speaking and Writing in Wisconsin*. Madison, Wis.: English Curriculum Center of the Department of Public Instruction of the State of Wisconsin, 1966. Instruction in speaking and writing from kindergarten through grade twelve.

It is not the hand, but the understanding of a man, that may be said to write.

Cervantes

7

Communicating through Writing

"Pencil, pad and purpose" are the necessary ingredients for writing, according to prolific author Edna Ferber. Her statement points up the fact that writing requires no elaborate accumulation of equipment; it is chiefly a matter between the individual and his pencil.

Composition has the distinct advantage of representing a totally individualized approach to learning, for each child produces to the extent of his individual abilities. The teacher prepares the class to write through discussion, explanation, and suggestion, but after that it becomes an individual matter, with some children requiring supportive encouragement as they move toward security in composing while others move ahead independently with confidence.

At the same time we must remember that there is much for any child to learn about writing, for writing is not an easy task even for the most accomplished. As Patrick Dennis observes semi-facetiously: "Writing isn't hard; no harder than ditch-digging." There is no denying that *writing is work*, and that the teacher has a responsibility for introducing the child to skills which will make his writing more effective and will help him achieve the desired end—COMMUNICATION.

Problems of Composition Instruction

There has long been criticism of instruction in composition as college instructors decry the inability of college entrants to write coherently, and of course, the high school instructor is blamed. In the usual pecking order fashion the high school blames the elementary school teacher.

Let us turn from this fruitless attempt to place blame and concentrate instead on studying the problems of teaching composition which may lead us toward more effective methods. Why have we been relatively unsuccessful in teaching writing? Might not some of the reasons be these?

1. The need for a developmental sequence in writing so that children really do write at all levels
2. Failure of *all* teachers to assume responsibility for the teaching of writing skills
3. Lack of teacher knowledge about English grammar and usage and their relationship to teaching writing
4. The feeling that primary grade children cannot write
5. The lack of clearly defined aims for teaching composition
6. Rigid approaches to evaluation which overwork the teacher and discourage the student

Sequential development in writing

One of the problems which continue to be present in the English curriculum is the need for established sequences of learning based on both the needs and the abilities of children as well as on the nature of the content to be introduced. Following Bruner's spiral curriculum concept with advanced ideas being taught in the primary grades and later studied at a more advanced level, what experiences shall we include in a developmental sequence in composition?

Primary (Kg, 1-2)

Storytelling and dramatization
Dictation of stories—individually and as group
Development of linguistic fluency
Extension of vocabulary, experiential backgrounds
Writing of sentences and phrases, paragraph stories
Introduction to four basic sentence patterns and noun and verb classes
Experiments in expanding patterns through compounding and modification
Composing poetry—free verse, couplet, triplet, cinquain
Increased awareness of words through word play, discovery, experimenting
Skills of punctuation—period, question mark

Intermediate (3,4,5)

Many experiments in writing creatively
Poetry—free verse, haiku, limerick, quatrain
Review and extension of basic sentence patterns
Expanding through compounding, modification, and subordination

Identification of word classes—noun, verb, adjective, adverb
Introduction to the function words and their uses
Vocabulary development through analogical substitution in patterns, use of dictionary, exploration
Use of literary models in writing
Focus on writing the sentence and paragraph
Developing concepts of imagery—simile, metaphor
Word study—homonyms, synonyms, antonyms, heteronyms, affixes
Word play to extend interest in vocabulary development and in use
Writing skills emphasized in all subject areas
Beginning research techniques—outlining, note taking, library tools

Advanced (6,7,8,)

Increased coordination of composition and literature study
Development of abilities of composing sentences and paragraphs
Writing the short story—beginnings, settings, dialogue, characterization
Writing of nonfiction—articles, reviews, reports
Continued use of expansion techniques with basic sentence patterns—compounding, subordination, modification, apposition
Review of word classes and function words
Poetry appreciation and composition—free verse, quatrain, ballad, triolet, invented forms
Study of imagery in writing—simile, metaphor, symbolism
Use of irony, satire, personification, alliteration, onomatopoeia
Experiments with words—word play, use of thesaurus, discovery
Advanced research techniques—library tools, bibliography, conducting a research study

Aims of the composition program

What are the aims of instruction in composition? According to Guth:

A writing course cannot miraculously widen and enrich the student's experience but neither can it teach skill in a vacuum. What it can at least start to do is to teach disciplined self-expression, responsible interpretation of experience, articulate participation in the public dialogue.[1]

Writing is more than knowledge of sentence structure, parts of speech, punctuation, and spelling. It requires involvement of the author as he expresses himself; he is revealed through his writing. He must have something to say, a conviction, and be able to focus his sentences toward that end. As LaBrant states:

Writing, put down—word by word—selected ideas to a selected audience is a labor, often painful, an ability to be improved by repetition, an act carrying both privilege and responsibility. It is neither learned nor taught without effort . . . But writing . . . is the culmination of language

[1] Hans Guth, "Rhetoric and the Quest of Certainty," *College English*. November, 1962, p. 136.

skills. There is great satisfaction in controlling writing and in producing a story, statement, poem, descriptive unit.[2]

Specific goals for the elementary school teacher of writing will be the development of student attitudes and abilities:

To enjoy expressing ideas freely in an original way

To write with clarity on a selected topic

To organize ideas for a coherent presentation of information

To distinguish between fact and opinion and to avoid sweeping generalization

To use mechanical skills in composition to aid communication

To evaluate and edit individual work, and to rewrite when desirable

To appreciate the writing abilities of others, including classmates as well as published authors

To develop confidence in ability to write through many successful writing experiences

To develop ability to write to the fullest potential

Writing—a shared responsibility

Composition is not a skill, or composite of skills, to be strictly limited to a period designated as "English," for composition is an integral part of all areas of the elementary school curriculum. No teacher and no subject is unconcerned with composition, for we use written language in many contexts and in varied ways, for example:

announcements
directions
reporting research
notes
answers to questions
book reviews
letters
news articles
speeches
evaluations
minutes of a meeting
results of experiments
words to music

Each teacher, therefore, should have some background in modern concepts of language if for no other reason than to be familiar with the vocabulary of English. He should also understand the aims of teaching composition to ensure that his "teaching of composition" is in keeping with the goals toward which other teachers are also directing their efforts.

[2] LaBrant, Lou, "Writing Is More Than Structure," *English Journal*. May, 1957, p. 256.

Primary grade children can write [3]

Often teachers of the primary grades, particularly the first grade, feel that writing has little to offer them. It is surprising, however, how much can be accomplished by these enthusiastic young students who are capable of doing almost anything.

During kindergarten and the beginning months of first grade, writing activities can be oral, for oral language leads directly to written language. The same activities described in this chapter for motivating writing can be adapted to oral approaches as children learn to think, and we develop *writing readiness.* A good atmosphere for writing is created naturally as the children learn language skills.

Dictation. An activity which lends itself to this period of language development is the dictated sentence, story, or poem which can be handled in a number of different ways. One way to begin is to encourage students to share personal experiences. One morning, for instance, children may contribute ideas like these which the teacher prints directly on the chalkboard or on a large sheet of tagboard mounted on an easel:

Today is Thursday, November 10 . . .
John has a new baby brother, David.
Steve lost a tooth this morning.
Jill is wearing her birthday dress today.

What are the advantages of this type of group dictation? The children are learning to use words to express ideas. They are learning to make simple sentences, and they are becoming oriented to words in print reading from left to right. As the teacher prints their sentences, they soon notice, too, the use of capital letters and marks of punctuation.

Later children learn to copy and to read this type of group dictation. After the class has taken a field trip to the fire station the experience story dictated might read like this:

Yesterday we went to the fire station.
The fire station is close to our school.
We saw the hook and ladder wagon.
We saw the firemen's dog, Spot.
We heard the fire bell ring.

Another variety of group dictation is the short story or poem which the group composes together orally. The teacher records this story as it develops sentence by sentence. She might begin by asking the class what animal they would like to write about, and someone might suggest a cat or dog or sometimes there is a more adventurous suggestion of a tiger,

[3] Adapted from the article by the authors: "Can Primary Children Write Creatively?" *Instructor* (November, 1965).

an elephant, or a bear. The teacher's conversation with the class, as they prepare to "write," might proceed thus:

> All right, we will write a story about a dog. I'll need your help. Are you all ready to write with me? (They will nod enthusiastically or answer aloud.) Now what shall we name this dog? (Jock) Good, Jock's a fine name for a dog. Let's imagine what Jock looks like, so we all have a picture in our minds of the dog in our story. What color is Jock? (black) How big is he? (About two feet high and a yard long demonstrated by a volunteer.)

> Can you all picture Jock now—a black dog, about so big . . . ? What is Jock doing today? (Jock is playing with a little girl, Susan.) Fine, that's a good place to begin our story. Who would like to make the first sentence? (One day Jock was playing with Susan.) What might happen next?

So the story grows with the help and encouragement of the teacher who sees that each student gets a chance to participate in some way. The story is then typed for inclusion in the class Storybook or it may be printed with a felt pen on a large sheet for use in reading activities.

A variation of group dictation is individual dictation, which is an excellent device but requires more teacher time or the assistance of a clerk, a parent, or an older child. Each student is given an opportunity to sit on the STORY CHAIR beside a primary typewriter. He tells his story while the typist records it. Individually dictated stories can be duplicated for use as reading material or they may be stapled in book form with an attractive cover decorated by the author. Each child is eager to read his story to his parents, and because he *wrote* the story himself, he reads it easily. This activity aids in developing orientation to the format of the book, left-to-right movement of reading and writing, and adds to the individual's feeling of personal potency. *He* can tell a story which is important enough to be typed, to be recorded, so that all can read it.

Writing Independently. As soon as first-grade students learn the rudiments of printing, they are intrigued by printing words, many of which they soon learn to spell. Very quickly they can compose a sentence or two expressing the ideas which they have depicted in a painting. They can also compose several sentences based on a topic introduced on the chalkboard by the teacher such as these:

● What do you do *on Saturday?*

> Students are directed to begin the first sentence thus:

> On Saturday I . . .
>> go to the park.
>> visit my grandmother.
>> go shopping.
>> play ball.

● What do you *like* best *to eat?* (I like to eat . . .)

● What *is* your *favorite toy?* (My favorite toy is . . .)

Help can be given with spelling by printing requested words on the chalkboard or on the student's paper although many teachers prefer to encourage spelling by sound so that writing is not inhibited by the need to make every word letter-perfect. There is little doubt that concern with spelling slows the child in recording his ideas; spelling will improve as he adds to his knowledge of words.

Once students have learned a simple writing vocabulary they are ready to write creatively, for writing is an area that allows each child to progress and to produce at his own level of ability. The more able child may write six good sentences while a slow child writes only one simple idea. Each is progressing, however, and can continue to progress from the stage of writing development through adulthood.

Teaching grammar and usage in relationship to composition

As was noted in Chapter 2, Linguistics and the Study of Language, many educators have mistakenly conceived of the teaching of grammar as consisting of drill along these lines:

Choose the right word:

Mary has (gone–went) to school.
Where have Billy and Joe (gone–went)?
They (gone–went) home already.

Work with sentences of this nature emphasizes specific points of usage (not grammar). There remains, however, much doubt about the transfer of the supposedly acquired knowledge to writing or to speaking, for the child is just as likely to say, "The girls have went to the movie," after having completed the above exercise as he would if he had never been exposed to the drill.

How do we learn usage? We learn it through our ears and it may be that certain usage patterns which "sound right" to us may not "sound right" to others because of exposure to different language backgrounds; This is an example of levels of usage and the acceptability of specific usage in varied situations.

As outlined in Chapter 2, we will also teach children grammar, the structure of English sentences. They will learn basic sentence patterns and the identification of word classes. This information, however interesting, does little to increase the child's writing fluency, his ability in composition. In fact, if the study of sentence structure is substituted for composing, that is, experience in writing, then the study of grammar will actually have a detrimental effect on composition, for the child is being denied valuable opportunities to write.

We must move beyond mere exercises in noting structure and classifying words, as in the case with usage, in order to develop ability to write.

You learn to write by writing, by using words to communicate ideas. It is in the expansion of basic sentence patterns through (1) modification, (2) compounding, (3) subordination, and (4) apposition that the young writer may reach out toward more mature, varied ways of expressing his ideas as with the following basic sentence which represents the simplest of patterns and contains only a noun and a verb:

Nan swam. (Pattern I, N–V)
Nan *swam and sunbathed.* (Compounding)
Nan swam and sunbathed *at the beach.* (Modification)
Nan, *the tall blonde girl,* swam and sunbathed at the beach. (Apposition)
When she was on vacation, Nan the tall blonde girl, swam and sunbathed at the beach. (Subordination)

The development of ability in writing which can be assisted through practice of this nature has little to do with identification of word classes. It is not necessary, for instance, that the child know that he is *compounding the predicate* when he uses two verbs, "swam and sunbathed," instead of just "swam." We can just as effectively extend an idea being expressed by asking pertinent questions, thus:

What else did Nan do besides *swim?*
Where did she swim and sunbathe?
How can we describe Nan?
When did she swim?

This experiment in expansion of a very simple stentence would, of course, be followed by numerous other experiments each of which suggests variations. The student learns to extend ideas, not just add *a prepositional phrase, a clause,* or *an apposition,* for we are concerned with communicating ideas rather than with the terminology of these structural features. We might find Rudyard Kipling's short verse useful in extending ideas:

I keep six honest serving men
(They taught me all I know);
Their names are WHAT, and WHY, and WHEN
and HOW and WHERE and WHO.

We must be careful, therefore, that we do not become so enamored with instruction in usage and grammar, as we follow the trend toward teaching linguistics, that we spend an undue amount of time on drill, a teaching technique that is familiar to us, but that has been proved to be less than effective. We must be jealous in our allocation of student time, for time is limited, and it must be used for the greatest good of the student. We must constantly question ourselves concerning the degree to which we are achieving the goals for English instruction.

The evaluation process

As a teacher, Dusel noted, "Teaching English composition is very much like giving a party: first there is the excitement of making all the preparations; next, the satisfaction of seeing the whole group busy expressing themselves; then the clock strikes and they leave you alone with a sink full of dirty dishes." [4] Unfortunately, this "sink full of dirty dishes" overwhelms many teachers and even leads them to the conclusion that composition is too much trouble, with the result that their students seldom write. It is important, therefore, that we tackle the problem of evaluation realistically.

What has been the typical approach to evaluation of student writing? In general, teachers have diligently read every paper the child wrote, marking spelling, punctuation, paragraphing, fragments of sentences. The red pencil has been wielded precisely, dogmatically, authoritatively. Is it possible that the teacher of today needs to rethink her approaches to evaluation? Have we established too rigid a pattern of evaluating composition, following the lead of teachers who evaluated our own composition?

Methods of guiding and evaluating writing must reflect the philosophy stated in our objectives of teaching children to write. To achieve these objectives we must avoid discouraging student writing endeavors by authoritarian approaches to evaluation. This is not to say that student writing is never to be reworked; we simply advocate a different emphasis in evaluation. The teacher cannot, for example, tear a story to shreds and still retain the student's sense of personal worth or an atmosphere conducive to free expression. Strickland [5] emphasizes the importance of security, interest, and constructive attitudes for the young writer. She terms the grading of papers and assigning marks inappropriate for beginning stages of language development. It is for these reasons that we recommend the following general rules for guiding student development in writing without discouraging the student:

Praise sincerely in public.
Make corrections and suggestions privately.
Appreciate the efforts of the student writer.

There are a number of methods for evaluating student work and making criticism which will assist the growth of writing ability without injuring an individual student's development as a person. Described here

[4] William Dusel, "How Should Student Writing Be Judged?" *English Journal* (May, 1957), p. 263.

[5] Ruth Strickland, "The Language of Elementary School Children" *Bulletin of the School of Education*, Indiana University. 38, No. 4, July, 1962, pp. 1-131.

are examples of evaluation and guidance techniques which have been found successful in the elementary school classroom.

Individual Conferences. While students are writing independently, individuals are called to a table where the teacher reviews their writing with them. The work is examined together and the teacher suggests areas for improvement verbally, simply underlining words which require a change. This method is effective for at least two reasons. First, it is much easier to explain orally the suggestions the teacher wishes to make about sentence structure or the development of a character than it is to write the comments on the paper. Too, the teacher is able to determine whether the student understands the suggestions by questioning him or having him make the changes orally before returning to work.

Another vital attribute of the individual conference bears on the personal relationship with the student, for the individual attention given the student and his work is uplifting and rewarding to that student. Even the less verbal student, the student who receives less attention during regular class sessions, has his moment for talking to the teacher about his work. For that brief period the teacher's attention is reserved for him. The conference offers the teacher a way for getting better acquainted with more reticent students.

One or two conferences can be scheduled each day so that each student has about one individual conference per month. Since writing is such an individualized approach, students may be working on different projects as they complete specific writing experiments. Each student should be permitted to select the writing he will discuss with the teacher during his conference. If each week, the conference schedule for the coming week is announced, students will have time to complete or prepare a selection for examination.

Teacher Correction. Many teachers (and some school districts enforce this approach) feel that they must read everything that a student writes; they would not send home any written work without a grade on it. These teachers feel it is mandatory for them to mark every error in spelling, grammar, usage, and punctuation. If students write every day both in school and at home, it is literally impossible for the teacher to accomplish this enormous task. It is perhaps this task alone which has accounted for the failure to encourage students to write daily. What is the answer to this problem?

The answer is obvious although not always acceptable to teachers who resist changes in philosophy. The teacher should *make no attempt to read everything the students write.* Maize's study [6] of remedial students points up the validity of this approach. The control group in this study was

6 Maize, Ray C., "A Study of Two Methods of Teaching English Composition to Retarded College Freshmen" (Doctoral dissertation, Purdue University, 1952).

taught punctuation, grammar, and spelling and wrote 14 different compositions which were carefully corrected by the teacher. The experimental group, in contrast, wrote 40 different compositions and did not receive formal instruction in punctuation, grammar, and spelling. Their writing was corrected and discussed during class time and was not personally read or graded by the instructor. The experimental group showed greater improvement in usage and writing ability.

Other approaches to evaluation of student writing need to be explored. Reading only representative selections each week has proved just as effective in guiding development. If all writing is placed in the student's writing folder, then one day each week can be designated for reviewing the writing that has been done and the selection by each student of one piece of writing to be completed, corrected, and copied to turn in for evaluation.

In making corrections on any piece of writing there are varied ways of handling the task. Detailed corrections made with the formidable red pencil in many cases serve only to discourage and to confuse. It is considered wiser, therefore, to focus the types of corrections made, thus:

> The red pencil can be used to underline interesting imagery or the use of unusual words, in other words, to indicate teacher approval. When returning papers, the teacher must explain this novel approach or the students will immediately assume the underlined material is in error.

> Marking for only one type of error on a set of papers is another way of focusing attention and perhaps teaching more effectively. One set of papers, for example, can be examined for punctuation ability. Upon the return of these papers comments are made about common errors in punctuation.

> The use of proofreading marks assists the teacher in noting common errors without undue effort and with less student confusion. Students will be interested in learning marks actually used by editors or the class can develop a set of marks which have meaning for them:

> ¶   Begin a paragraph here.

> ⌃   Insert comma (or other mark).

> *sp*   Spelling error.

> *U*   Usage.

> *S*   Not a sentence.

> ✳   Excellent choice of words!

Types of Assignments Made. The task of evaluation is facilitated if both teacher and student have a clear idea of the focus of the assignment. A short, focused assignment is more effective than a vague, lengthy project, for sheer length of effort seldom produces quality writing. It is far better that a student be able to write one or two polished sentences or a well-organized paragraph which expounds one idea than that he produce a theme of 500 words (counted to the last *a*).

Who is Michael Phant?

> Who might this man be? Where does he live?
> What is he doing? What does he look like?
> Compare the character sketches of this imaginary person.

Create a mood.

> Imagine that you are in a specific place.
> Is it light or dark? How do you feel?
> Use words that convey the mood of the place.

Publicizing Student Writing. One of the most effective methods for guiding and evaluating student writing in a concrete fashion is through the publicizing of that work which is considered well done. Care must, of course, be taken that each student receives some measure of publicity for his endeavors. The publicizing of good writing can be accomplished in a number of ways:

> Displays on the classroom bulletin board can feature writing. A display might, for example, focus on a large picture mounted in the center of the board around which are pinned paragraphs by each student based on this picture. Collections of writings can be made containing a selection by each child. If the class is writing tall tales, have each student submit his best one for a book entitled WHOPPERS!
>
> A student publication can be produced periodically bearing an appropriate title such as REFLECTIONS, IMPRESSIONS, SHOWCASE, SPICE, VENTURE. Different types of writing can be featured, from interesting phrases to short stories, so that all have a chance to contribute. The entire group can take part in the tasks of publishing.[7]

Writing with Clarity and Effect

One of the goals of instruction in composition is clarity, the ability to make a point, to communicate ideas effectively. As Guth asserts:

> A writer must be able to express himself—if possible aptly and precisely and vigorously. He needs a feeling for words. He must be in control of the resources of language and take pleasure in their richness and variety. Such a love and respect for language is the result neither of following arbitrary rules nor of studying usage statistics. By alerting the student to distinctions and implications and overtones, the instructor can attempt to train the student's eye and ear ... No one can be a forceful writer unless language means something more to him than a prosaic vehicle for communication.[8]

[7] The foregoing was adapted from an article by the authors: "Guiding Creative Writing," *Clearing House* (March, 1964).

[8] Hans P. Guth, "Rhetoric and the Quest for Certainty," *College English*, November, 1962, p. 134.

The teacher must be active to be effective in teaching composition. Many teachers see composition as an easy subject to teach—just assign a topic and let the students write. To be truly effective, however, the teacher must assume responsibility for (1) motivating, (2) providing many opportunities for writing, (3) developing rapport with the group, (4) extending experiential backgrounds to supply content for writing, and perhaps most important, (5) appreciating the results of student efforts.

The teacher can guide students to the development of a statement of aspects of writing which should be avoided and those toward which each should constantly be striving, thus:

> What are we trying to achieve?
>
>> Writing that indicates thought
>> Use of exciting words which create effects
>> Completeness, conciseness, and clarity
>> Variety of content, words, sentence patterns
>
> What are we trying to avoid?
>
>> Passive, inactive verbs
>> Overworked phrases, clichés
>> Misplaced modifiers
>> Wordiness, tautology
>> Vague references
>> Sweeping generalizations

Introduction of the terminology of composition assists the young writer in developing a vocabulary with which to discuss writing. Note, too, that the skills and concepts of composition discussed here represent ways of thinking as well as of writing, for writing reflects thought. It is a way of expressing thought. Students can be exposed to these concepts at their levels of ability.

Punctuation

Punctuation, like spelling, has been overemphasized as an aspect of composition. Again, we stress the importance of placing primary emphasis in composition on the ideas expressed rather than the mechanics of recording the ideas. On the other hand, knowledge and use of punctuation does facilitate communication as Charlton Laird illustrates:

icertainlyshallnotkeepthisuplongitevenlooksrepulsive

if you made anything of that you have the key to make something of this too but i shall not keep this one going very long either

These samples represent an attempt/ to write modern english in ways that suggest writing in earlier days/ when there was no punctuation/ or when punctuation was not standardized as it is now/ this particular style is one used by the first english printer William Caxton/ who used a period to mark a paragraph.

th's 's ' st'll "rl"r 'n' 's'd d'r'ng ' t'm' wh'n 'v'n v'w'ls w'r' 'nd'c't'd b' p'nct"t"n [9]

We can also observe humorous, and sometimes disastrous, effects of punctuation either misused or omitted as in these examples:

No help is coming.
No, help is coming.

Seventy-nine and thirty are the winning numbers.
Seventy, nine, and thirty are the winning numbers.

"Shift!" he cried.
"Shift?" he cried.

How might we punctuate these words?

What are you giving him dope
She bought a car coat and riding boots
Mary Jane Sally and Kathy were absent

Skill in using punctuation can be greatly assisted by knowledge of the intonation patterns of our speech. As we listen to a sentence, we can usually hear the pauses, the *juncture,* which may require punctuation to aid the reader in correctly interpreting what has been written. The falling pitch and full pause, for example, tell us clearly that a period is needed, whereas a slight pause may indicate a comma. Speak these sentences, noting the type of punctuation indicated by the juncture.

John will go with us
Is John going with us
My friend John Brownton will go with us
Although he doesn't like to ride John will go
John Brownton although he doesn't like to ride will go with us

Punctuation taught to students in the elementary school should be functional, that is, it should be punctuation needed by the student as he writes. It is easy to become so entangled in minute points of punctuation that we lose sight of the aims of teaching composition. Beginning from the first stages of writing, therefore, let us teach these skills as they are needed:

    1. Period:

            At the end of a declarative sentence. *He went home.*

            After abbreviations. *Mr. Joseph B. White*

[9] Charlton Laird, *A Writer's Handbook* (Boston: Ginn, 1964), p. 358.

2. Comma:

>To separate parts of a series. *We ate corn, peas, and hot dogs.*
>
>With an apposition. *Molly, my best friend, is here.*
>
>After an introductory clause. *When I get there, I'll tell you.*
>
>To separate a quotation from the speaker. *He said, "How are you?"*
>
>After Yes or No. *Yes, I will be here.*
>
>With direct address. *Jimmy, do you know?*

3. Question Mark:

>At the end of an interrogative sentence. *Who is it?*

4. Quotation Marks:

>Around quoted speech. *Mark called, "I can go!"*
>
>Around a title of a short work—poem, article, short story. *We read "The Doughnut Machine."*

5. Exclamation Mark:

>After a word or words showing excitement. *Help me!*

6. Apostrophe:

>To show possession. *This is Sid's pencil.*
>
>In contractions. *Don't you know better?*

An occasional touch of humor helps the teaching of almost any content. Here, for example, are several ways of providing practice in using punctuation.

Cartoon figures can be used to assist students in learning to identify the portion of a sentence to be set off by quotation marks:

Jane said, "I'm delighted to see you."

Provide a paragraph or two which contain no punctuation at all. Have students compare their punctuation of the given paragraph with one you prepare on a transparency. Use a joke, thus:

>miserly Sam went to the dentist because he had a terrible toothache as dr yankum reached into sams mouth to pull out the aching tooth sam cried out doctor if it costs $4.00 to pull the tooth how much will it cost to loosen it a little

Spelling and handwriting

Although it is true that ideas expressed are more important than the mechanics of composition, frequent misspellings and illegible handwriting do prejudice the reader. The written words replace the winsome personality of the writer; there is nothing to plead for him except his writing, which stands exposed to the rude view of the critic. How far, for example, will the student advance who writes this sentence in sixth grade?

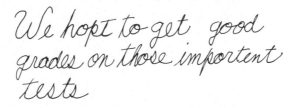

We hopt to get good grades on those importent tests

There is admittedly a certain snobbery inherent in correct spelling, and those who spell English easily do "look down their noses" at those who never learned or were never taught the intricacies of English spelling. Spelling, in this case, becomes an outward sign of education or intelligence in the eyes of the public, although only low correlation has been found between spelling ability and the intelligence quotient.

In many cases, too, it becomes apparent that spelling and handwriting do directly affect the success of written communication. Compare these sentences as you note the possibilities for misunderstanding; it is not always possible to question the person who wrote the sentence to ascertain just what he meant.

1. He could not be *hear*.   (Does the writer mean *here or heard*, perhaps?)

2. Mary Jane was hopping. (Was she? It could be that she was hoping.)

3. *You owe me $ 5 4.*   (He may get cheated.)

4. *They brought in the cot.*   (Does it meow?)

Degrees of specificity

It is important that students be introduced to concepts of concreteness and abstraction, for as Hayakawa notes:

> The reason we must concern ourselves with the process of abstracting is that the study of language is all too often regarded as being a matter of examining such things as pronunciation, spelling, vocabulary, grammar,

and sentence structure. . . . But as we know from everyday experience, learning language is not simply a matter of learning words; it is a matter of correctly relating our words to the things and happenings for which they stand.[10]

In presenting the concept of abstraction Hayakawa uses the illustration of Bessie, the cow, a familiar animal that can be touched and easily identified. As we move up the *Abstraction Ladder,* however, we find that *Bessie* can also be referred to as a member of the *cow* family and as part of the classification *livestock.* She is a *"farm asset"* and therefore, a general *"asset"* and still more abstractly, she is *"wealth."*

Trips *up and down the Abstraction Ladder* will serve to acquaint young people with these degrees of specificity as they move from the concrete to the abstract or *vice versa.*

> Make a ladder of construction paper or bamboo strips to serve as the Abstraction Ladder on which students can place cards bearing words which represent varied levels of abstraction, for example:
>
> rose climber flower plant foliage landscaping
> turkey poultry meat food farm products
> penny coin money wages income wealth
>
> In defining words we find that we must narrow the category to include only that which is defined or the definition has little meaning. How can we define a "bed"?
>
> bed = a piece of furniture (How about a chair?)
> bed = furniture in a bedroom (How about a dresser?)
> bed = a large flat piece of furniture on which we usually sleep at night (Getting closer.)

In writing we stress the importance of dealing in specific cases rather than high levels of abstraction, for the skilled author holds our interest with the rich detail with which he enlivens his writing. We often are impressed by the effective use of detail as in this passage from *John Henry and His Hammer* by Howard W. Felton:

> "You're a fine, big boy, John Henry. Mos' a man now. You're as black as the night was that saw you come into this here world. You're as strong as the wind that blowed the trees down low. Your blood is as red as the moon that grew big an' red, an' stopped an' ran backwards. An' the eyes you got sparkle an' shine like the white of a angel's wing, an' your muscles is as powerful an' easy, an' moves strong an' quiet as the river that turned right 'round in its tracks an' ran uphill." [11]

---

10 S. I. Hayakawa, *Language and Thought in Action* (New York: Harcourt, 1949).
11 Felton, Howard W. *John Henry and His Hammer.* Knopf, 1950. p. 11.

As we move down the Abstraction Ladder, we come to the least abstract term, for instance, *rose, turkey,* or *penny,* in the examples just cited.
As we write, however, we find that we don't mean just any rose, but the
red rose in Mrs. Kirk's garden, the one which always blooms in the
month of May and perfumes the yards of all her neighbors. We want to
become even more specific as we place characters in a setting and describe events. Experiments in language can lead children to become
aware of degrees of specificity in this way:

Which of these terms is most specific?

_____a lady _____that lady _____Mrs. Wilma Jones
_____a Dolly Varden trout _____a gray fish _____a speckled trout
_____the dog _____the collie in the street _____the dog in the street

We can develop a chart of specificity something like this:

1	2	3	4
girl	a girl in my class	the girl who sits in front of me	Mary Jane Nelson
pet			
house			

Ways of thinking revealed in writing

Writing is thought transferred to paper; our writing reveals us and
discloses our ways of thinking. The student needs to become aware of
fallacious thinking not only to avoid being influenced by the writing of
others but also to avoid falling into dangerous ways of thinking which
will leave him vulnerable to the critic.

A common error made by young people, and by far too many adults
also, is the *sweeping generalization.* How often do you hear the un-
qualified generalization in ordinary conversation? "Oh, everyone knows
how to dance!" "Teachers are mean!" "Those seniors are so conceited!"
We often find ourselves falling into the habit of making unsubstantiated
statements which, like those quoted, fail to allow for individual cases.
True, some seniors are probably conceited, it is likely that some teachers

are mean, and many people do know how to dance, but we know as we think more rationally that the statements made would not include the whole category described.

> Display a variety of pictures on the bulletin board. With each picture supply a generalization which students can attack to demonstrate the fallacy of making unsubstantiated generalizations. The generalization, "Every boy should have a dog," for example, might elicit the following arguments:
>
>> My cousin, Tom, is allergic to fur, so a dog is not for him.
>> A family that lives in an apartment can't always have a dog.
>> I know a boy who is so mean to his dog that he shouldn't have one.
>
> Search the newspaper for examples of generalizations which can be refuted in the same way. Students can also deliberately write generalizations, perhaps ones they have heard, which can be discussed in class. Advertising often supplies good examples of the "glittering generality" which strives to sway opinion or to sell a product.

Another type of thinking which merits attention is the *two-valued attitude* in which matters are decided as either "right" or "wrong" with no thought for the gradations of rightness or wrongness. Is a person *bad* or *good* or is it possible that a person might have one vice mixed with some desirable traits? We have encouraged this type of thinking in students by concocting tests which demand "one right answer" and make no provision for variation. Research in creativity has led to encouragement of divergent thinking through the use of open-ended questions which stimulate thought. How can we assist students in developing more flexible modes of thinking, in breaking the rigid two-valued attitude toward life?

> Analyze a character about whom the group is reading. What are his good traits? What traits are less desirable? Can we apply a simple adjective "good" or "bad" to a complex human being? Guide students to write character sketches which describe a person, real or imaginary, and show that people are both *good* and *bad* at the same time.
>
> The study of antonyms emphasizes this "either-or" thinking. Examine sets of antonyms as you discuss the gradations which are involved in any pair of *opposite* words. Introduce students to the concept of a *continuum* as you draw a long line on the board with antonyms at each end, thus:

HOT	warm	cool	COLD

> What are the many gradations which lie between HOTNESS and COLDNESS? Fill in all the terms which can be thought of—cool, chilly, warm, sweltering, and so forth. Then try other opposite concepts which represent values—HAPPY-SAD, RIGHT-WRONG. Encourage students to discover examples of two-valued thinking which can be discussed in class.

Of particular importance in writing is the avoidance of *stereotyped thinking,* which is also an example of rigidity of thought. Is every woman over 70 a "sweet little old lady?" Does every Texan wear a ten-gallon hat and ride the range each day? Do Eskimo families live in igloos? An exciting study of language could focus class attention on ferreting out stereotypes.

> Write a description which exemplifies a stereotype. Then rewrite the description eliminating the stereotyped thinking. Draw two pictures to illustrate the difference in thought.

An important distinction to be made in writing is that between *fact and opinion. Facts* are statements which can be proved, for example, the fact that a room is 30 feet long can be proved by measurement, and we would all have to agree that the statement is factual. We must recognize the changing quality of factual knowledge, however, for, as we are becoming increasingly aware, the facts of today are not always the facts of tomorrow. Facts, therefore, require constant verification.

Opinions or *judgments* are personal evaluations which reflect attitudes and values; they cannot be verified as facts can. We frequently hear opinions stated authoritatively as though they were facts, and therein lies the fallacy. Opinion has a place in thoughtful writing, but it should be identified as such by introductory words which qualify the statements as a personal judgment—"I think," "It seems to me," "According to the author," and so on. Opinion can be given a measure of validity through substantiation by quoting the opinions of others and by presenting cogent arguments which serve to support the personal judgment. We can provide many classroom experiences in working with fact and opinion.

> Debates provide opportunity to support an opinion, with students taking both sides of an issue. It is particularly interesting for a student to support the side with which he really does not agree, for he will need to think carefully to support his argument.
>
> Even primary-level children can identify fact as distinguished from opinion. Let them decide which of these statements are fact and which are not by trying to prove each statement.
>
> > John's book is red. (We need to clarify our statement—Which boy named John? Which particular book?)
> > The reading table is in the northeast corner of the room. (This statement can be verified.)
> > *Mr. Popper's Penguins* is the best book Miss Benton ever read to us. (Does everybody agree?)

Another important aspect of thought is the *drawing of inferences,* which we do continually without being conscious of the process. Again, however, we must be careful that the inferences we make are valid according to the facts known, for example:

> May is often absent from school. Can we correctly infer that she dislikes school?
>
> Chuck broke a window in the auditorium. Do we infer that he is an incorrigible troublemaker?
>
> We see a little girl on the sidewalk. Can we infer that she is lost?

Use of words

The careful selection of words to be used in any writing experiment influences the clarity and effectiveness of the finished product. One aspect of using words which determines the effect of the author's writing is *wordiness*—verbosity, repetition, tautology—which is associated with boring writing. Wordiness is an indication that the writer has refused to accept responsibility to *select* the best wording. Once acquainted with this concept, the student will begin noticing writing which requires editing to weed out excessive words. Students should be encouraged to collect illustrative samples of this type of writing, for awareness of wordiness will lead to greater clarity in student writing as each strives to produce "tighter" writing.

> Often sentences should be combined:
>
> One day Jim was going home. He saw a tiny puppy.
>
> One day on the way home Jim saw a tiny puppy.

> Sometimes words are excessive and should be cut.
>
> Henry said he would like to go along, too.
>
> Henry would like to go along.

We also strive to call forth *varied words* to create effects. We endeavor to vary our vocabulary to maintain the reader's interest and to create exciting stories. One of the purposes of rewriting is to change words which are prosaic; why waste space on dull words when there are so many scintillating choices we might make? Experiments with rewriting sentences will aid students in making better selections of effective words, thus:

> Mike called, "Wait for me!"
> Mike shouted excitedly, "Wait for me!"
>
> Bert walked out the door and walked down the street.
> Bert ran out the door and hurried down the street.

Another method of adding variety to writing is to change the types of sentence patterns and word order used. The person who continually relies on the same sentence structure places a limit on the possibilities of his writing. Experiments like these can increase student flexibility in constructing varied sentence patterns.

Madge is in third grade. She lives on Miller Street. She is eight.
Madge, who lives on Miller Street, is eight and is in third grade.
Brad was sick, but he was able to play the game.
Although Brad was sick, he was able to play the game.

Another aim of the student writer should be to avoid *triteness* of expression. As we have mentioned elsewhere, the cliché can be the subject of discussion, with experiments leading children to use more interesting comparisons of speed, heat, sound, and so on.

As hot as . . .

        a pancake ready to flip
        a rabbit in his fur coat in July

As quiet as . . .

        a feather falling on snow
        butterflies floating through the air

It is important also that students recognize the need for *clear references* in the sentences they write, for we often find ourselves puzzling over sentences which contain uncertain references or misplaced modifiers. Usually the reference can be clarified by changing a word or two or by rearranging the phrases or clauses as in these examples:

Mrs. Muskopf told Mildred she might go. (Who is going?)
Hanging in the closet he found his coat. (Who or what was hanging?)
They are always saying things like that. (Who are *they?*)

Writing Nonfiction

When we think of writing, we often forget the importance of ability to write nonfiction—articles, research reports, letters. Writing of this nature, however, can prove as exciting as any imaginative tale, and it serves to stimulate the inquiring mind of the elementary school student. How can we encourage students to write nonfiction?

The article

Informative articles constitute some of the best writing which appears each year. The article may be on any topic—world affairs, preparing for college entrance, the enrollment of a six-year-old Negro girl in an all-white school, profile of a well-known person, review of a writer's work, and on and on. Introduce young people to the writers of nonfiction for elementary school students by examining several of the excellent magazines written for this age level.

American Forests, 919 17th St., N.W., Washington 6, D.C.
American Girl, 830 Third Ave., New York 22, N.Y.
Boy's Life, New Brunswick, N.J.
Junior Natural History, 79th and Central Park West, New York 24, N.Y.
National Geographic, 16th and M Sts., N.W., Washington 6, D.C.
Science Newsletter, 1719 N Street, N.W., Washington 6, D.C.
Sky and Telescope, Harvard College Observatory, Cambridge, Mass.
Young Miss, 52 Vanderbilt Ave., New York 17, N.Y.

Students can also benefit from studying articles from general magazines: *Life, Saturday Evening Post, Reader's Digest,* and others which represent specialized interests. As they examine articles, students can be guided to observe:

● How the author began his article
   Telling an anecdote
   Flashback
   Dialogue
   Asking a question
● The steps in developing the article's content
● Any devices the author used to add interest to this writing
   Humor—Joke, play on words
   Imagery—simile, metaphor
   Illustrations (verbal)
● The summary or conclusion

An effective launching pad for the writing of nonfiction is provided by Holling C. Holling, author and illustrator of *Pagoo* (Houghton Mifflin, 1957), in a beautiful film entitled *Story of a Book.* This tall, genial man (a good image for boys) explains the way he and his wife became interested in writing about a hermit crab whose Latin name *pagurus* suggested the name of Pagoo. He describes their beginning study of the crab in the tidepool habitat, research in the library, his writing of Pagoo's life, and the preparation of the illustrations. The finished product is not technically nonfiction, for the author has added interest to the reading of detailed factual information by imagining the adventures his main character might have as he grows up in Tide-Pool Town. The effect of the film is to give the elementary school student insight into the origin of an idea, the gathering of material to write about, and the actual writing process.

Another source that supplies good background information on writing the article, which may prove helpful to the teacher as well as to the advanced student, is *How to Write Articles* by Berniece Roer (St. Louis, Missouri: The Bethany Press, 1963), a 64-page explanation of composing an article from the idea to the completed work. Written in specific terms, this book suggests ways of selecting topics for writing, the various types of articles that may be written, organization of the article, writing skills, and the important task of rewriting.

Beginning with short experiments in writing nonfiction, the elementary school student can later progress to longer articles. Emphasis at this level should, however, remain on the ideas to be expressed and on the ability to communicate with clarity and effect; sheer length is never a valid criterion for success in writing. What kinds of writing experiments shall we explore?

Explanation (How-to-do-it):

After having completed a class project, each student can write an explanation of the process. Accuracy and clarity are stressed and can be checked by passing the "articles" around the room having each person read several and write a brief comment on the back of each. Comments are aimed at helping the student achieve the assignment.

Holiday:

Short articles can explain how specific customs originated. In December, for instance, each student might tell about one symbol of Christmas— the tree, candles, bells, the star—explaining its origin, how it is associated with Christmas, and perhaps varied usages in different countries.

If a special celebration or program is held during the year, students can write about this event from any perspective they choose—as a participant in the program, as a teacher, as a member of the audience.

News:

Cut out intriguing headlines from newspapers. Each student receives one about which to write. An interesting variation of this experiment is to provide the original newspaper article so the student can compare his version with the original and realize the varied ways of thinking about any idea. Students can help collect short articles for this purpose.

Literature:

Books can provide the stimulus for writing news articles. The class can prepare, for example, the CENTERBURG GAZETTE, which contains articles about the happenings in Centerburg based, of course, on McCloskey's *Homer Price* and *Centerburg Tales.*

Experience:

After returning from a field trip each "reporter" can write about the trip as a way of summarizing the experience. Discussion will suggest various aspects of the trip to be reported, for instance, a visit to the library may elicit these headlines:

MRS. BROWN LIBRARIAN TEN YEARS
CARD CATALOG SHOWS THE WAY
WHO IS DR. SEUSS?
TRAVELING THROUGH THE STACKS

Personal experiences also provide excellent topics for articles. Here the student has an opportunity to tell about his feelings, his ideas, things he is doing outside of school. We must avoid some of the stereotyped topics that have been overworked through the years and provide a new slant to encourage students to look at familiar events and objects in new ways.

What were you doing between 4 and 8 o'clock on Friday, October 13th?

I turned the knob, flipped the channel button, and settled down to watch. It's my favorite show. Maybe it's yours, too.

Opinion:

"What is your opinion?" (Substantiate it.)
Should sixth-grade girls wear lipstick?
Should we have an hour for lunch or only thirty-five minutes?
Should boys let girls get ahead of them in line?
What is the nicest time of day?
What is your favorite food?

Research

What is *research?* One dictionary definition of this term is "studious inquiry, usually critical, and exhaustive investigaton or experimentation having for its aim the revision of accepted conclusions, in the light of newly discovered facts." Coming to English from the French word *recherche*, which means *search, quest, investigation,* just as in our English meaning, the term has the positive connotations associated with scientific study. The researcher may, however, be studying problems in widely varied fields, for example, in agriculture the researcher might study which seeds will produce the most corn per acre whereas the producer of sailboats might research the problem of which hull shape produces the greatest speed. Research takes place in all areas of endeavor, even in our schools.

For most teachers, *research* is synonymous with writing a report after reading several sources for information. Such library research is usually part of any research project, and involves special skills of taking notes, collecting information (data), developing a bibliography, and preparing a final report. Research is yet another aspect of English which is properly the concern of all teachers and is related to all subjects. The interest and the benefits of library research depend on several factors:

Library resources available
Nature of the topic under study
Guidance of the teacher
Involvement of the student

As Samuel Johnson wrote: "Knowledge is of two kinds. We know a subject ourselves, or we know where we can find information on it." It is important, therefore, that students know the tools of the library, and how to use them to gather needed information. We cannot overemphasize the necessity for having a well-equipped central library in every elementary school, with a librarian who is able to aid our young researchers. Many authorities consider it more important to teach children the skills of discovering, searching, and drawing conclusions than to teach them specific facts, for the facts will change and become useless, whereas the skills prepare the student to continue inquiring and discovering throughout his life. What library tools should the elementary school student know?

The card catalog is a basic tool which children can learn to use very early as they search for books by title or author. As they develop interests, they will want to look for Subject Entries, which will suggest titles on specific subjects—FRANCE, MYTHOLOGY, SOUTH AMERICA, TREES. We must move beyond the card catalog, however, to use more specialized indexes and reference books. Here are a number of titles which are useful in the elementary school.

Dictionaries of varied difficulty; foreign language dictionaries
Unabridged dictionary
Roget's *Thesaurus*
Encyclopedias (Several of varying difficulty)
Biographical dictionaries

Who's Who
Who's Who in America
20th Century Authors
Current Biography
Junior Book of Authors

Books of quotations

Bartlett's *Familiar Quotations*
Hoyt's *New Cyclopedia of Practical Quotations*
Simpson's *Contemporary Quotations*

Statistical references

World Almanac (available in paperback)
Statesman's Yearbook
Information Please Almanac, Atlas, and Yearbook

Geographic references
Varied atlases
Maps

Specialized references
Bullfinch's *Mythology*

Abridged Reader's Guide to Periodical Literature

Many of the magazines indexed by this tool should be available or the index is worthless. Usually an elementary school library will hold these titles for a five-year period only.

Pascal stated: *"Connaître—c'est chercher"* ("To know is to search"). This is the attitude which we are trying to instill in students from their first learning experiences, for it is only when the student feels the challenge, the excitement of discovering, that he will really begin to learn on his own initiative.

After students are acquainted with a number of the basic reference tools in the library, conduct a TREASURE HUNT. Prepare a list of reference questions to provide practice in using those tools available. The answer to the question is the reference book and page on which the answer is found. No one cares at this time to record the specific answer although students find themselves browsing as they search. Use questions like these (which can be constructed by the class itself):

What is the population of Kansas?
Who was the twelfth president of the United States?
Who said, "Give me Liberty or give me Death!"?

Let each student select one specific topic: George Washington Carver, The Vikings, Diamond Mining, Queen Elizabeth II. The object of this SEARCH is to discover *how many sources* of information can be found. Again, only the sources are listed, with no attempt being made at this time to record notes. Encourage students to investigate lesser-known references in other libraries.

To facilitate the collection of data it is important also that each student acquire skill in taking notes. According to the ability of the students involved, students can be taught to note information that will be needed in an efficient way. Certain guidelines can be established, thus:

Never copy long passages word for word.
Any sentences that are copied must be quoted. (Note the page number.)
Always refer to several sources; use sources other than encyclopedias.
Note information that fits the outline for your paper.

Few students develop expert skill in note taking without specific instruction. Instruction might be of this nature:

Provide each student with a copy of a duplicated article. After discussing the purpose for which notes are being taken, e.g., preparation of a hypothetical paper, each student takes notes. The notes can be compared (make transparencies of several for instructional purposes) and discussed as to the organization of the notes taken, the importance of items noted, any omissions, and so on.

Tape informational material—an article read by you, a radio or television presentation, a lecture—to provide practice in listening and taking notes. Again, all hear the same material so comparisons can be made to point out both valuable practices and those to be avoided. After working with the first attempts at note taking, the same tape can be replayed to permit students (particularly those who need additional aid) to take a better set of notes.

Frequently have students take notes as they search for information from varied sources. These notes are then used in class discussion to substantiate arguments or to add information.

In conjunction with note taking students should also learn to collect bibliographic information. There is nothing more frustrating than to try to locate a source after you've forgotten the author or someone else has taken the book. The development of the habit of noting all necessary bibliographic information before beginning to take notes is an invaluable practice which can be taught with the very first attempts at library research. Bibliographic forms used should be simple, but exact and sufficiently inclusive. Contrary to popular opinion, there is no *one* "right" bibliographic form; different publishers or universities often have their own stylebook or follow a specific guide. The chief aim of any guide is consistency, and it is for this reason that we establish a pattern which will be followed by the class in its work. The forms you select might be something like these:

Books:

Polgreen, John, and Cathy Polgreen. *A Look at the Moon.* Doubleday, 1962. Unpaged.

The first author's name is inverted only to assist alphabetical arrangement. We choose to omit the location of the publisher as it is usually well known; any librarian will supply these addresses if they are needed and 90 percent of them are in New York. In this entry the book is not paged, as is true of many books for primary grades, but usually the *pages read* will be indicated, which may be the total book.

Article:

Marchalleck, John D. "The Jamaica I Remember." *National Geographic School Bulletin.* May 9, 1966. Pp. 458-461.

Encyclopedia:

Encyclopaedia Britannica. "Bolsheviks." Volume 3. Pp. 889-890.

Another type of research which should not be ignored by the elementary school teacher is *descriptive research,* which involves the gathering of data in a different way. Some of the same skills are involved as in library research, for the experimenter must explore the *literature* of the field to acquire sufficient background information to conduct the research. One distinction should be noted, however, for in this research the student will be producing original material; he will be contributing to the store of information we have about any particular subject. As John Dewey observed, "Every great advance in science has issued from a new audacity of imagination."

Research can be cooperative, that is, worked on by several people, or it can be an individual project, and the research problem may be derived from any field. Descriptive research is not limited to science but may explore aspects of the social sciences, language study, mathematics, art, music, and so on. The first step in conducting research is to identify a problem. What problems might be researched in English?

> Given a free choice, what subjects do students write about?
> Do boys or girls score higher on a vocabulary test?
> Which spelling words are most frequently missed on a review test? What kinds of errors are made? Do boys or girls miss more words?

Students who acquire the research frame of reference early will be better equipped to function in a society which is rapidly becoming research-oriented. Too often we fear research because it is unfamiliar to us; we don't feel at ease with its methodology. The words of Charles Kettering may serve to reassure those who approach research with uncertainty:

> *Research* is a high-hat word that scares a lot of people. It needn't. . . . It is nothing but a state of mind—a friendly, welcoming attitude toward change. . . . It is the problem-solving mind contrasted with the let-well-enough-alone mind. It is the composer mind instead of the fiddler mind. It is the "tomorrow" mind instead of the "yesterday" mind.

We must constantly remember that we are teaching children who will live tomorrow. Research is sure to be a part of this tomorrow, and for this reason we have a responsibility for encouraging these "apprentice scholars" as they engage in bona fide research. We are not aiming at producing a roomful of research scientists but rather a class of alert, critical thinkers.

Students should be introduced to the terminology and the procedures followed by adult researchers. Most research consists, for example, of a sequence of systematic steps:

1. Selection of the problem
2. Formulation of a hypothesis
3. Choice of a method or procedure
4. Collection of data
5. Interpretation of the data
6. Report of the findings

The crucial task is the identification of the problem, which must be specific and researchable. Which of the following is a practicable research question? Which involves opinion only?

Should we use our school buildings all year long?

Do more girls study foreign languages than do boys?

Should the United States President be allowed to hold office for three terms?

Is the number of women earning doctorates increasing?

Students can suggest many problems in this fashion as they discuss the researchability of the suggested problems. Once a problem has been identified, we are ready to proceed with the study. Suppose, for instance, we select the following problem: To determine whether boys or girls score higher on a given vocabulary test. The next step is to formulate a hypothesis (an educated guess) which in this case might be: Girls will score higher on a given vocabulary test than will boys.

What method or procedure will assist us in proving or disproving the *hypothesis* (pl. *hypotheses*)? We shall construct a test of 20 items which will be administered to a group of boys and girls. We might decide to limit our N (the total group tested) to sixth-grade students; this limitation would then be added to the statement of the problem: To determine whether sixth-grade boys or sixth-grade girls will score higher on a given vocabulary test. After administering the test, the *data* (usually used in the plural; singuar form is *datum*) are collected; that is, the tests are graded and the scores tallied. The results may be placed on a graph or compiled in a table. The findings are then summarized. This particular study might later be *replicated* (repeated to check the results) or might be extended to include other grades.

Another aspect of research which adds excitement to student learning is *experimental research*, which differs from descriptive research in the manner of collecting data. As the name indicates, experimental research involves the setting up of an experiment with an X group (the group on which the experiment is tried) and a Control group (a group on which the experiment is not tried). The two groups are tested before and after the experiment and the results are compared to note the effects of the experiment. Boys will find experimental research particularly exciting as *a way of learning.*

Experiments can vary widely in topic, and they can be surprisingly simple in nature. Suggested here are a number of researchable questions which will result in challenging classroom studies:

Does careful following of the Spelling Study Steps improve spelling grades? (Half the class uses these steps for a month; the other half studies without direction.)

Does discussion of a film directly following viewing improve understanding and observation of details? (Half the class discusses the film while the others go outdoors; then comes the test!)

Will practice in listening improve ability to note details? (The X group has several planned lessons in listening; Control has none. Both groups are given a listening test.)

Once students are introduced to research, they will generate many exciting ideas for study. Studies like those involving study skills will have more effect on student behavior than any words a teacher can speak, for the students are involved.

Corresponding

"I have made this letter longer than usual because I lack the time to make it shorter," wrote Pascal. Relatively few people earn their living by writing, but everyone needs to be able to write letters. We write letters for many purposes—requesting information, keeping in touch with a friend, thanking someone for a gift. It is important that we learn forms for writing business letters as well as the art of writing interesting social letters.

An effective way to teach the writing of a friendly letter is through the stimulus of writing to someone in another city or in a foreign country. This activity can be carried out in lower grades as a group or individually by children in the upper grades. Here are several addresses which supply names of children who wish to exchange letters:

School Affiliation Service
American Friends Service Committee
160 North Fifteenth St.
Philadelphia 2, Pa.

Childrens Plea for Peace
World Affairs Center
University of Minnesota
Minneapolis, Minn.

International Friendship League
40 Mount Vernon St.
Boston, Mass.

People-to-People Letter Exchange
Box 1201
Kansas City 41, Mo.

The Canadian Education Assn.
151 Bloor St. W.
Toronto 5, Ontario
Canada

A book which we enjoy introducing to students to enliven instruction in letter writing is Sesyle Joslin's *Dear Dragon*. First an interesting situation is described which leads to the writing of a letter, for example, one illustration shows a smiling native queen welcoming the rider of an ostrich and the text reads:

> You are having a holiday traveling on ostrich-back up the Amazon and through the Rain Forest until finally you stop in a small village because there is a friendly native Queen who insists on having you for dinner.

On the next page appears the Social Letter which follows: [12]

Urucurituba, Brazil
January 14, 1967

Dear Friends:

I am having rather an exciting trip. This part of the world is beautiful and quite interesting as well.

I wish you were here.

Yours as ever,

[12] From *Dear Dragon*, text © 1962, by Sesyle Joslin; illustration © 1962, by Irene Haas. Reproduced by permission of Harcourt, Brace & World, Inc.

The illustration opposite the letter shows the ostrich rider now thoroughly tied and in a stewpot over a blazing fire writing the letter while the friendly native Queen looks on. The letter forms are meticulously correct, and the understatement used by the author lends a delicious humor to what could be a dull study.

The business letter is a useful form which students can learn. As we have noted in other cases, there is no single correct form; the main object is to supply the needed information with clarity so that the purpose of the letter is achieved without misunderstanding. Collect a variety of examples which students can examine to determine a suitable form for the business letter. Here is an excellent opportunity for class research. What forms are currently being used for business letters? An attempt might also be made to collect old business letters to note any differences from modern style. How can differences be explained? One commonly used form of business letter is the following:

> 9100 Senter Ave
> Peoria, Illinois 61600
> November 10, 19——

Prentice-Hall, Inc.
Englewood Cliffs, New Jersey 07632

Dear Sirs:

Please send me 1 copy of *A Handbook for Young Writers* by Carl Hansen and others.

You may bill me at the above address.

> Very truly yours,
>
> Mrs. Irene Markam

A popular variation of this standard form is the following:

9100 Senter Avenue
Peoria, Illinois 61600
November 10, 19——

Prentice-Hall, Inc.
Englewood Cliffs, New Jersey 07632

Dear Sirs:

Please send me 1 copy of *Readings on Contemporary English in the Elementary School* by Iris and Sidney Tiedt.

You may bill me at the above address.

Very truly yours,

Mrs. Irene Markham

It is wiser to write letters which have real purpose rather than those which are purely invented. Students can often assist the teacher in writing for free materials or in placing orders for materials, as in the samples. They can also write for information from real people or organizations— Congressmen, state legislators, state departments, travel bureau, publishers, chambers of commerce, firms, and so on. After a field trip, letters of appreciation can be sent those who assisted the class. Other activities related to letter writing include the following.

- To provide practice in writing addresses, have each child cut several slips of paper the size of a postal card. Use tagboard if the cards are to be mailed. On one side of the card is a picture, perhaps associated with social studies or depicting your local area. On the other side is the address and a brief message.

- Each child may bring one postal card to prepare to send to a friend or relative.

- Telegram techniques provide an interesting experiment in writing brief but complete information. The date, address, and signature are included without charge. No punctuation is used, and every word and figure (324 is three words) is counted. Supply fictitious information which is to be conveyed via telegram. At other times students can write the messages inventing a story to go with the message given them. Official telegram forms can be obtained from the local office.

- Write friendly greetings to patients in local hospitals or convalescent homes. Discuss the types of information which might be shared with an older person. An original poem or story might, for example, be much appreciated by these older men and women who enjoy the activities of children. Art work might also be shared.

Books to Investigate

Braddock, Richard, *et al.*, *Research in Written Composition*, Champaign, Ill.: National Council of Teachers of English, 1963 Summaries of selected research.

Brown, Don P., *et al.*, *Writing: Unit-Lessons in Composition I A*. Boston: Ginn, 1964. Composition experiences based on literature.

Good, Carter V., *Essentials of Educational Research*. New York: Appleton, 1966. An up-to-date approach to research.

Laird, Charlton, *A Writer's Handbook*. Boston: Ginn, 1964. A well-written guide for the teacher who can adapt material presented on composition.

Postman, Neil, and Howard C. Damon, *The Language of Discovery*. New York: Holt, 1965. One of a series of secondary texts which suggests ideas for work with younger students.

Tiedt, Iris, and Sidney W. Tiedt, *Readings on Contemporary English in the Elementary School*. Englewood Cliffs, N.J.: Prentice-Hall, 1967. Includes a section on composition in the elementary school.

Yates, Elizabeth, *Someday You'll Write*. New York: Dutton, 1962. Directed toward the young writer.

"Correct" spelling, that is, obedience to the rules of English spelling as grammarians and dictionary-makers set them up, has come to be a major shibboleth in our society.

Robert A. Hall, Jr.

8

Rethinking Spelling

Spelling is probably one of the most regularly taught areas in the elementary school English curriculum. Literature may be discussed only spasmodically by the teacher, creative writing may be totally ignored, but a daily spelling period is rigorously included in the classroom schedule by most teachers.

It is not too difficult to point out reasons for this attention to spelling instruction. The most obvious is that the subject matter to be taught is familiar to every teacher. It is also relatively easy to present to students, and it is easily evaluated. The teacher feels secure with the content as it is usually taught. The routine nature typical of spelling instruction provides a comfortable niche in the curriculum, for on Monday we always introduce the words, on Tuesday we test. . . .

There are few uncertainties involved in spelling instruction, but there are few excitements, and there is actually an example here of ineffective teaching. In many cases the routine becomes a "rut" which makes spelling a dull subject with little real learning taking place and much valuable school time wasted. As Horn reports, "Weekly time allotments are still much larger than can be justified either by the relative value and difficulty of spelling as compared with other subjects or by the results obtained." [1]

The task at hand, therefore, is to investigate the objectives for teaching spelling and to determine efficient and effective ways of

[1] Ernest Horn, "Spelling," *Encyclopedia of Educational Research*, 3rd ed., Chester Harris, ed. (New York: Macmillan, 1960), p. 1346.

reaching these objectives. Spelling is a tool, a skill that is closely allied with composition, or the writing of words. The prime objective in teaching spelling is, therefore, to teach children to spell words which they now need in order to write. Another phase of this objective is the teaching of words which these children will need as adults. We find that these two needs overlap and that many of the words needed by the adult are also needed by the elementary school child.

Analyzing the Task

As we strive to determine more effective means for teaching spelling, we would do well to analyze the task at hand. What is it that we are trying to teach? What are the obstacles that we will encounter? What is the role of the teacher in spelling instruction? Who is the teacher of spelling?

Selecting the basic wordlist

What words shall we teach? On what basis should they be selected? How many words should be taught each week? Published wordlists, that is, series of spelling books each of which contains a portion of the total list, are most commonly based on the above criteria although the lists vary widely. Betts found, for example, when studying 25 spelling series, that the total number of different words included was about 10,000.[2] Since each series usually presents about 4,000 words, the variation was obviously great.

All lists include a nucleus of words which are used repeatedly in everyone's individual writing, for it has been estimated that approximately 50 per cent of our writing consists of only 100 words used in varied combinations. Three thousand words comprise approximately 98 per cent of those words most commonly used.

> Students could conduct an enlightening and rewarding study of papers written over a period of time to determine what group of words is most commonly used. Their study would motivate student interest in learning these needed words, for the list would be composed of words which they themselves have discovered that *they* need to know.

How do we decide which words shall be taught at any grade level? Although it was once thought that the difficulty of spelling a word was a superior method of placing it for study by grade level, more recent studies find that, though a word may be difficult, the child's early need

[2] E. A. Betts, *Spelling Vocabulary Study: Grade Placement in Seventeen Spellers* (New York: American, 1940). p. 143. *Grade Placement of Words in Eight Recent Spellers* (American, 1949).

of the word may warrant its inclusion at a lower grade level. Horn cites the word *receive* as one which is consistently difficult for adults to spell, but which is presented in the elementary school because young children use the word widely. Words are selected for placement at specific grade levels usually on a basis of:

1. Permanent value
2. Difficulty of spelling
3. Use by children
4. Type of logical grouping [3]

Causes of spelling difficulty

In order to teach spelling effectively it is helpful to examine the causes of deficiency in spelling. Why do some students require little teaching of spelling, while other children have repeated difficulty in mastering spelling skills? Following is a list of deficiencies compiled from several sources: [4, 5]

Lack of Interest. Noted frequently as the most influential factor in learning spelling skills, the interest factor can provide a point of attack for the teacher. See the discussion of motivation of student interest.

Physical Defects. Disability of the eye or ear can cause a child to be unable to perceive the word visually or aurally. Either handicap results in misconceptions about the spelling of a word.

Intelligence. Although a high intelligence quotient does not guarantee ability to spell, the child with a low IQ is handicapped in learning any skill, including spelling. He brings less ability to the task at hand, and therefore cannot be expected to achieve at the same level as the more able child.

Poor Memory Ability. We need to focus attention on memory abilities as the child learns to perceive the word in varied ways. Memory will be assisted by the development of other skills: listening, speaking, knowledge of phonology, and so on.

Speaking and Listening Skills. How do we hear a word? How do we speak a word? Both skills are essential to correct spelling. Improved speaking and listening abilities will aid auditory discrimination, which is an essential aspect of correct spelling.

Poor Study Habits. How is spelling presented? How is the child directed to study? Is he assisted in any way with the study of spelling? A

[3] James A. Fitzgerald, *A Basic Life Spelling Vocabulary* (Milwaukee, Wis.: Bruce, 1951).

[4] James A. Fitzgerald, *The Teaching of Spelling* (Milwaukee, Wis.: Bruce, 1951), p. 193.

[5] Ernest Horn, "Spelling," in *Encyclopedia of Educational Research,* (3rd ed.), Chester W. Harris, ed. (New York: Macmillan, 1960), pp. 1347-49.

large percentage of the time spent on studying spelling by any child is in the classroom and therefore study habits can be directed by the teacher. The poor speller needs special attention to this aspect of learning spelling. He may work better in a small group situation.

Other factors characteristic of the poor speller include: lack of knowledge of word meanings, lapses, transfer of habits, individual idiosyncrasies, temperamental traits, lack of sufficient reading background, slow or illegible writing. The teacher can note physical injuries, report them to the nurse, and encourage correction of defects, but beyond that the classroom teacher must "work around" a child's disabilities. Intelligence, too, is largely a given factor over which the teacher has no control.

Other factors contributing to ineffective spelling, however, can be at least partially alleviated by the able teacher. Specific instruction can improve both speaking and listening abilities (see chapters dealing with these areas of instruction). The interest of the child in learning how to spell can usually be tempted by varied techniques which will be discussed later in this chapter. Spelling study habits can be explored individually and as a class, and the individual child's ability to remember can be improved through special attention to this skill.

The teacher's role

The chief responsibility of the teacher, as we see it, is that of establishing positive attitudes toward spelling. Presented as a problem for investigation about which the teacher is obviously knowledgeable and enthusiastic, spelling can be incorporated in a rewarding study of the English language.

Research indicates that the classroom teacher frequently dislikes teaching spelling, an attitude which would inevitably be projected to the student. If the techniques used in teaching spelling become so routinized as to be dull and uninteresting to the teacher, it is unlikely that children will display any genuine liking for this study. The individual teacher must analyze the methods employed to determine their effectiveness. The following questions should be explored:

1. Are the words studied of interest to the students?
2. Are able spellers being held down to a low level of achievement?
3. Are we spending too much time on spelling activities?
4. Are poor spellers receiving help as needed?
5. Are we reinforcing spelling learning through use of composition?
6. Do I vary techniques of teaching spelling? Is spelling "dull"? Are student attitudes positive?
7. Am I really "teaching" spelling?
8. Do I permit spelling to inhibit creative writing?
9. Are techniques of teaching spelling based on the findings of research?

The teacher has a responsibility for knowing about English spelling and about the English language in general. Knowledge of the development of the English language, and American English in particular, will enable the teacher to include information about changes in spelling, the origins of words, variations in British and American spellings, and so on. This information adds "spice" to the learning situation, and will aid in motivating student interest.

Teacher concepts of correctness should be examined, too, for a rigid, uninformed concept of correct spelling can cause confusion, and at times, embarrassment. We must be prepared to allow for differences in spelling as in these examples:

1. Which spelling is correct: *Viet Nam* or *Vietnam?* Both are seen in reputable newspapers and journals. Does one spelling *have* to be wrong?

2. Which spelling is correct: *labor* or *labour?* The first spelling is more common in the United States whereas the latter is the common British spelling. British spellings often occur in children's literature, for example, *Children of Green Knowe* by Lucy Boston (Harcourt, 1954).

3. Which is correct: *ax* or *axe, fulfill* or *fulfil?* For these and many other words two equally acceptable spellings are listed in reliable dictionaries.

4. Which is correct: *catalog* or *catalogue?* Both are acceptable; one is obviously a shortened, simplified form of the other.

Caution must always be exercised to avoid teaching which permits *only one right answer.* The discovery of such differences in spelling should be utilized by the skillful (or is it skilful?) teacher to add interest to the spelling lesson, and the child who discovers variations in spelling should be highly praised. The teacher who is aware of spelling variations will not be disconcerted by the child's questioning attitude nor will the questions be regarded as threatening teacher authority.

If you feel guilty about permitting a child to use the shorter spelling of such words as *dialog*, perhaps an examination of your attitude is in order. Why do you object? Is it that you had to learn the longer, older (and therefore, more respectable) spelling? Are these modern students "getting by with" something? Is there something inherently better in one of the two variations? Don't they both communicate? Discussions of this nature can prove highly stimulating for a class of alert elementary school students.

Spelling's place in the curriculum

Can spelling be treated only as an isolated subject matter? It is obvious that the teaching of spelling, indeed, the teaching of all composition skills, has relevance for other subject areas, for the writing of words is not the province of the spelling class alone or even of the English composition class. As we study history, for example, the names of places, persons, words specific to the study underway (*electoral college, confederacy, presidential, civilization*) are learned. Words that are not specifically subject-oriented are also needed as written work is completed in history (*there, consideration, his, avenue, your*) so that basic wordlists concern history instruction as well as English instruction.

Spelling is taught, therefore, by the elementary school teacher all day long. It is taught by all teachers in departmentalized organization. Even a teacher of art or music will have occasion to speak of spelling as children make posters or study the vocabulary of music. Some of the most effective teaching of spelling may occur at these moments when the student has a specific reason for learning to spell.

The curricular area which is most closely related to spelling is reading. The correlation between reading and spelling abilities is very high [6] (almost as high as that reported for intelligence and spelling). Words which children meet frequently in reading situations, therefore, are found to be spelled with greater accuracy than are those seen infrequently.[7] The reading experience reinforces spelling learning. The teacher can assist this reinforcement by commenting on spelling words which appear in different contexts, saying perhaps: "Now that word looks familiar."

The teaching of phonic skills which is usually included in the reading program has much to offer in reinforcing the spelling program, for these skills are helpful in both areas of study. Although the procedure is reversed in the two processes (Reading: written word to sound; Spelling: sound to written word), many understandings of phonemes and graphemes will prove mutually reinforcing. Knowledge of regular sounds, for example, BL as in blanket, will be helpful to both speller and reader.

Investigating English Spelling

Is the spelling of English a completely hopeless task? Can it be taught? Many critics have pointed with ridicule to the peculiarities of English spelling and to the fact that spelling and pronunciation are not consistent. George Bernard Shaw, one of the more literate of the critics, gibed: "How do you pronounce GHOTI, if the letters are pronounced as follows: *gh* as in *rough, o* as in *women,* and *ti* as in *nation?*" [8]

Since the days of Chaucer, spelling and pronunciation have grown ever farther apart, with pronunciation tending to change more than does spelling. This tendency continues today. An anonymous poet records many

---

[6] Nellie W. Peake, "Relation between Spelling Ability and Reading Ability," *Journal of Experimental Education.* 9: 192-3, 1940.

[7] Gertrude Hildreth, *Teaching Spelling* (New York: Holt, 1955), p. 29.

[8] The answer is FISH!

oddities of English spelling ending with the conclusion that "sounds and letters disagree."

OUR QUEER LANGUAGE

When the English tongue we speak,
Why is "break" not rhymed with "freak"?
Will you tell me why it's true
We say "sew" but likewise "few";
And the maker of a verse
Cannot cap his "horse" with "worse"?
"Beard" sounds not the same as "heard";
"Cord" is different from "word";
Cow is "cow", but low is "low";
"Shoe" is never rhymed with "foe".
Think of "hose" and "dose" and "lose";
And think of "goose" and yet of "choose".
Think of "comb" and "tomb" and "bomb";
"Doll" and "roll" and "home" and "some".
And since "pay" is rhymed with "say",
Why not "paid" with "said", I pray?
We have "blood" and "food" and "good";
"Mould" is not pronounced like "could".
Wherefore "done" but "gone" and "lone"?
Is there any reason known?

And, in short, it seems to me,
Sounds and letters disagree.

Although it is undeniably true that English contains many unusual and often inexplicable oddities, today's researchers are focusing attention on the fact that approximately 85 per cent of English words have been found to follow regular patterns of spelling.[9] Few linguists claim that English spelling is easy, but it is not entirely without reason. There are many relatively consistent rules which bear teaching and many concepts in phonics will assist the student in attacking the large body of consistent spellings.

Linguistics and spelling

What relationship does linguistics have to spelling? The basic concepts of the linguist, that is, the primacy of speech and the changing nature of any language, have a bearing on approaches to spelling instruction. Greater emphasis is placed, for example, on the teaching of oral language skills as a firm basis for beginning writing and spelling activities, for without knowledge of English words and of the sounds of English little progress can be made with spelling English words. Success with spelling is predicated on the ability to hear and distinguish English sounds.

[9] Don H. Parker, *et al.*, "Are We Teaching Creative Spelling?" *Elementary English* (May, 1963), p. 523.

The linguistic approach to spelling instruction groups words to be studied according to specific phoneme-grapheme occurrence. Beginning spellers would, for example, learn words that are highly regular in phonemic structure with a group to be studied consisting perhaps of:

bat cat fat hat mat pat sat rat

Later the blended initial consonants and digraphs would be added to increase the family of words learned with little effort:

chat flat scat that

The aim of this system is to avoid teaching every individual word as a separate learning act. The spelling task is thus much reduced and simplified.

The sounds of English

The study of sounds made in our English language (phonology) is important in developing ability to spell, pronounce, or read a word. Although researchers have pointed out that (1) regional pronunciations differ, (2) English sounds are frequently spelled in several ways, and (3) more than half of our words contain silent letters, others have found that a large percentage of English words are highly regular. It is for the latter group of words that phonics will prove particularly helpful.

Few teachers have received formal college training or study in phonics, for its teaching had not until recently been assumed as the responsibility of any college course. It is small wonder, therefore, that there has been much uncertainty and many misconceptions about this aspect of language. An encouraging trend is the requirement of a course in modern English for all students which includes an analysis of English phonemes (sounds) and graphemes (letters which represent sounds).

From the first day of kindergarten (and usually earlier) children will notice differences and similarities of sounds. Initial consonant sounds are generally recognized first—*b* as in *box*, *t* as in *Tom*, and so on. Here is a list of these common phonemes and graphemes:

Consonant Phonemes	*Graphemes*
/b/	bat
/d/	down
/f/	fairy, off, laugh, phase (Gr.), Chekhov
/g/	go, ghost, guest
/h/	help, who, Jose
/j/	Jim, hedge, imagine, soldier grandeur
/k/	cape, kitten, pick, chorus (Gr.), box, quit, khaki, plaque
/l/	like, roll, fatal, llama

Consonant Phonemes	Graphemes
/m/	man, ram, hymn, lamb
/n/	not, fan, gnat, knife, pneumonia
/p/	pit, sip
/r/	race, write (Old Eng.), Rhodes (Gr.), for
/s/	sit, cent, scent (Gr.), class, fox, psalm
/t/	ton, licked, ptomaine, Thomas
/v/	very, love
/w/	will, while, one, suite, ouija
/y/	yellow, onion, hallelujah, bouillon
/z/	zoo, is, ooze, czar, Missouri, xylophone
/c/	cheer, witch, nature, cello, Czech
/š/	ship, wish, sure, champagne, mission schwa, patient, ocean, anxious, special, fuchsia
/ž/	garage, treasure, azure, Asian, adagio
/θ/	thin, path
/ð/	this, loath
/η/	ring, rang, tongue, think

Vowel Phonemes	Graphemes
/i/	trip, been, rhythm
/e/	red, tread, said
/æ/	sad, laugh
/ə/	was, double, flood, nut, rough (the schwa occurs in many unstressed syllables: nation, elephant, pages.)
/a/	halt, job
/u/	put, would, good
/ɔ/	fall, cause, tossed, caw, bought, log
/ɨ/	her, bird, nurse, grammar, word

Diphthongs	Graphemes
/iy/ (long E)	we, bead, seen, return, niece, receive, lady, carbine, Aesop, people, suite
/ey/ (long A)	day, fade, break, neigh, lain, care
/ay/ (long I)	tiger, right, cry, lie, buy, guise, aisle bite, find, lyre
/ow/ (long O)	throw, load, hoe, cove, solo, roll, soul, beau
/yuw/ (long U)	refuse, few, beauty, queue, view
/oy/	boy, toil
/aw/	house, how
/o͞ow/	zoo, suit, do, glue, two, tomb

In teaching the vowel sounds many teachers find it practical to emphasize three sounds for each vowel, always carefully noting that these sounds are not the *only* sounds made by each vowel. A chart like this one is helpful in clarifying what may otherwise be a most confusing subject of study for those who are just beginning to use phonic skills in spelling:

		LONG		SHORT	FOLLOWED BY R	
A	make	/ey/ *	at	/æ/	car	/ar/
E	eat	/iy/	let	/e/	her	/i/
I	ice	/ay/	hit	/i/	sir	/i/
O	no	/ow/	got	/a/	for	/or/
U	use	/yuw/	nut	/ə/	purr	/i/

* When presenting to a class, do not use the phonemes provided for your use.

Instructors often teach rather odd concepts about letter sounds. One can only assume that these misconceptions were taught them as children and continue to remain as part of their store of "knowledge," which points up the need to rethink or re-evaluate our thinking periodically or, more precisely, *constantly*.

One teacher, when using the illustrated vowel chart, for example, cited the word YOU as an example of the long U sound. Why is this example incorrect? A well-known linguist equates the vowel sounds in WHO and PUT although the sounds are made in different parts of the mouth and throat.* It is plain that one needs an attentive ear to distinguish differences in sounds.

Another letter which causes much confusion is Y, which has both consonant and vowel sounds. The consonant sound is clearly identified in words like YELLOW, YACHT, YONDER. It is Y as a vowel, however, which bears clarification.

Y has no vowel sounds of its own, but serves as a substitute for I and E sounds. It would be inaccurate, therefore, to designate long and short sounds for Y, for it actually appears as both long I /ay/ and long E /iy/ as well as short I /i/. We know of no cases in which Y takes the short E /e/ sound; perhaps you will find one. Note the following examples:

* We designate the sound in WHO as /ŏŏw/ rather than /uw/ to avoid this confusion.

Long I	Long E	Short I
dye	sadly **	crypt
my	playfully **	analysis
cry	happy **	tryst
lyre	baby	cygnet
lying	theology	nymph
hyphen	identity	lyric
cypress	sticky	lynx
scythe	St. Cyr (Fr.)	rhythm
why	Ypres (Belg.)	oxygen
modify	Yperite (a gas)	Ypsilanti (Michigan city)
hygiene	Elysian	lynch
type	Lyons (Fr.)	catalyst
thyme	embryo	gypsy (the first Y)
gyrate		gymnasium
hyacinth		hymn

** The Y in the suffixes *ly* and *y* has long been designated in dictionaries as a *short i* /i/. Usage, however, denies this pronunciation, for do we not use a *long E* to end such words? It is interesting to note that Webster's *Third New International Dictionary* (1961) lists for the first time the long E as the first pronunciation, thus: 'sadlē or 'hapē. Teaching this Y as a short I is confusing to students and should be avoided when the /iy/ pronunciation is used.

As we scan the list of the sounds used in speaking English, we can readily note that some sounds are less confusing in that only one grapheme is usually used to denote this sound—/p/, /t/, /b/, /d/, /m/, /n/, /l/, /v/. These consonant sounds are among the first to be identified, and they cause little difficulty in spelling. For this reason we can safely teach words combining these consonants with the simpler vowel sounds—/i/, /e/, /æ/—in early spelling lessons.

> Display pictures of objects with the word printed below. Omit the beginning consonant so that children can determine which grapheme should be placed at the beginning of each word. Provide a variety—*vase, table, pony, baby, dog, Mother, number, picture, log, dancer.*
>
> Practice locating letter blends which occur in different positions in a word as: *sk* in *skip, risk,* and *whiskers.* Other sounds may also be located as: *sh* in *shape, overshoe,* and *brush,* and *ch* in *chatter, branch,* and *unchain.*

As students advance in ability to identify sounds, they can explore the diphthongs and those consonant phonemes which are made by varied graphemes. Often the inductive method can be used to encourage student discovery.

The sound SH /š/ is made by a wide variety of graphemes. Students can pursue a search for as many different examples as they can find. Discoveries may include: *shell, ocean, racial, sugar, delicious, vacation, fission, schwa, champagne, tissue, omniscient.*

Write 20 to 30 words containing the letter *C* on the board; for example, *coal, accident, block, accuse, scale, sick, crime, custom, concave, circumstance, circle, circus, cell, cactus, cane, cigar, ace, accept.* Have the words pronounced as the class examines the list. Ask them what they notice about the group of words. They can make generalizations which will lead to the observation that *C* has no sound of its own and might be considered to be a useless letter.

Write a few words from one extensive family; for example, *lack, back, pack, rack, sack, Jack.* After observing the similarity, have the students expand this family as much as possible, adding: *track, clack, knack,* etc. (If the word *plaque* is suggested, send someone to the dictionary.) Examine the list when completed; have children pronounce the words. Then experiment with changing the vowel to *I* or *O*. How many of these words will make words with the new vowel? Will spelling change at times?

Historical development of spelling

Ralph Waldo Emerson's description of English as "the great metropolitan English speech, the sea which receives tributaries from every region under heaven" serves to introduce students to the many languages which have contributed to the development of English. Reference books for the teacher include:

Barnett, Lincoln, *The Treasure of Our Tongue.* Knopf, 1964. An excellent introduction to the evolution of English with a section on how American English came to differ from British English.

Laird, Charlton, *The Miracle of Language,* Fawcett, 1953. A popular paperback edition by a well-known scholar which should be added to the teacher's library.

Pei, Mario, *The Story of Language.* Lippincott, 1949; paperbound, Monitor Books. Essential background of the history of English with explanations of changes in spelling.

The study of changes in the English language will add much to students' interest in the subject of spelling and will aid their understanding of some of the peculiarities of English spelling. Topics of study focusing on the English language relate to many areas of the curriculum as in these examples:

Develop a mural depicting the ENGLISH RIVER, into which flow many tributaries—French Creek, Italian Stream, Greek Riverlet, and so on. Rocks in the tributaries can be labeled with appropriate LOAN words; for example, French Creek would contain rocks bearing the words *ballet, étude, nom de plume, sobriquet, cliché, briquet,* etc.

Make a collage focusing on BORROWED WORDS from one specific country. A collage of WORDS BORROWED FROM SPAIN would feature *pinto, adiós, San Francisco, Colorado,* pictures of *toreadors,* a *corral,* scenes depicting Spain and the Spanish people, and so forth.

Encourage student research in the area of language with particular emphasis on spelling changes by including books on language in the class library. Recommended titles include:

Epstein, Sam, and Beryl Epstein, *The First Book of Words*. Watts, 1951.

Ernst, Margaret S., *Words: English Roots and How They Grew*. Knopf, 1937.

Pei, Mario, *All about Language*. Lippincott, 1954.

Spelling has long received close scrutiny by scholars, many of whom, perplexed by the incongruities of English spelling, advocated, nay, fought for, spelling reform. Their reasoning, and in many cases the changes suggested, made a great deal of sense; yet their efforts have had only slight influence and there remains little likelihood that major spelling reform will ever take place. Why not? The answer lies in the human resistance to change, especially changes in something so deep-rooted as our national language. Perhaps many would agree with Mark Twain, who remarked facetiously: "Simplified spelling is all right; but, like chastity, you can carry it too far."

One of the most influential of the scholars who advocated language reforms was lexicographer Samuel Johnson, who saw the dictionary as the means for correcting the "improprieties and absurdities" which exist in any language. He did influence spelling by the selection of that spelling to be included in his historic dictionary.

Benjamin Franklin in the United States suggested many changes for spelling in his 1768 work entitled *A Scheme for a New Alphabet and Reformed Mode of Spelling*. He recommended the dropping of superfluous letters and the use of a phonetic alphabet more nearly in keeping with pronunciation.

Noah Webster was particularly concerned with separating American and British English. He is credited with the American practice of eliminating the *u* from *honour, favour,* and other similar words. Perhaps his greatest influence, however, came through his dictionary (1828) and spelling books, which tended to standardize spelling throughout the nation.

The National Education Association became involved in spelling reform as it worked with the Spelling Reform Association. Certain spellings were actually adopted in 1898 for use in NEA publications: *program, tho, altho, thoro, thorofare, thru, thruout, catalog, prolog, decalog, demagog,* and *pedagog*.[10] It is interesting to note that several of these spellings

---

[10] Richard E. Hodges, "A Short History of Spelling Reform in the United States," *Phi Delta Kappan* (April, 1964), p. 331.

are now in general use although the percentage is small compared to the effort expended.

President Theodore Roosevelt was persuaded by the same association to introduce spelling reforms into federal publications. Public resentment and outcry was so vehement, however, as to cause the withdrawal of this decision, which resulted in the demise of that spelling reform group.

Andrew Carnegie financed a new organization in the early years of the twentieth century. The Simplified Spelling Board advocated the making of gradual changes in spelling, but only a few of its recommendations have remained in common usage; for example, *judgment* for *judgement,* which is currently a commonly misspelled word as many persons continue to include the questionable *e.*

One of the more colorful figures in spelling reform was George Bernard Shaw, who was concerned by the waste of time and effort in writing caused by inefficient English spelling. He himself used the Pitman Shorthand Alphabet, which considerably shortened the time required to produce manuscripts. In 1941, he examined an article in the London *Times* in which he noted 2671 letters used to denote only 2311 sounds. In a letter to the editor, he explained:

> The same rate of waste on the 465,000,000 letters printed annually by the *Times* gives us 94,136,952 superfluous letters, every one of which has to be legibly written or typed, read, and set up by the monotypist, cast in metal and machined on paper, which has to be manufactured, transported, and handled. Translate all that into hours of labor. Translate the labor into wages and salaries. I leave the task to the *Times'* auditors, who after staggering the proprietors with it, should pass it on to the Auditor-General to be elaborated into an estimate of the waste in the whole printing industry of the nation.

Although Shaw never achieved any spelling reforms, he did not resign himself to the lack of insight of his peers. In his will was included a fund for continuing his efforts which resulted in the publishing of his play, *Androcles and the Lion* in the Shaw Alphabet.[11] This edition includes regular spelling facing the Shavian spelling, and it is obvious that Shaw's version requires about two-thirds the space required by regular English spelling. The student interested in learning more about Shaw might refer to *George Bernard Shaw on Language,* edited by Abraham Tauber (Philosophical Library, 1964).

A more recent development in spelling innovation is the use of an augmented alphabet consisting of 44 symbols which more nearly coincide with the sounds of English. ITA, or the Initial Teaching Alphabet,[12] was

---

[11] Free copies of this book were made available to all public libraries in English-speaking countries.

[12] The Initial Teaching Alphabet is reproduced on p. 251 of this book.

developed by the grandson of Sir James Pitman in England in an attempt to simplify the teaching of reading. This alphabet, which is gaining some following, is also used in writing by the students who have learned it as in this example:

wɛɛ ar gœɛɛŋ tω ŧhe fær

The study of spelling reform is fascinating to students who are intrigued by the possibilities. The topic can be the subject of research as a class searches for books and articles (see *Reader's Guide to Periodical Literature,* or the teacher could refer to *Education Index*) which will provide more information. Follow this study with some of these ideas to engender interest in spelling as well as knowledge of phonics:

> Encourage interested students to develop an alphabet which would simplify English spelling. They can also suggest changes in English spelling which could be adopted without the use of a new alphabet.

> Discuss the topic: Will our spelling system ever be completely overhauled?

> Suggest that students write letters to scholars who are experts in specific areas related to this study:
>> Shaw's Alphabet: Kingsley Mead, Abbots Morton, Worcester, England.
>> Professor Warren S. Smith, University of Pennsylvania, Lemont, Penn.
>> ITA: Sir James Pitman, House of Commons, London, England.

Approaches to Teaching Spelling

Is there one magic method of teaching spelling? If there were, spelling instruction would not have caused concern these many years. Until one appears, the teacher's wisest choice lies in an eclectic method composed of the best ideas derived from any and all sources.

A wordlist selected chiefly from those words needed by children will form the basis of a strong spelling program, but it should not limit the content. In addition the teacher will use individualized approaches to spelling and will teach auxiliary skills in phonics and the use of the dictionary. Perhaps most important will be the attitude of the teacher, for an enthusiastic, knowledgeable teacher will add a touch of humor when appropriate, will spice teaching with interesting spelling facts, and will encourage student inquiry as she teaches spelling with vigorous, efficient competence. Incidental learning of spelling words will be facilitated as spelling growth is stimulated in all subject areas.

Perhaps most important of all, the instructional methods selected will reflect knowledge of research in spelling. An examination of the writing vocabularies of children and the words most frequently misspelled reveals many generalizations which should guide the teacher, for example, the following:

1. Spelling needs of children at varying grade levels can be determined, but each individual has specific needs also.
2. The child's writing vocabulary is larger than has been assumed and much larger than indicated by spelling curricula.
3. The upper limits of the number of words that could be used by students is not measured by spelling tests.
4. The specific words used by children depend on the topic being discussed.
5. Spelling readiness is related to reading readiness.
6. Much spelling learning is incidental which suggests that pretesting should always precede the study of a new group of words.[13]

The scope of spelling instruction

In addition to the learning of specific spellings, the period designated for spelling will focus attention on other understandings. Auxiliary skills of phonics and dictionary usage appear as part of spelling instruction although they may appear in other areas of the curriculum also. Capitalization, pluralization, and possession will also be taught as part of the spelling lesson. Let us examine these areas of study as we explore methods of presenting the knowledge involved.

Phonics. Earlier in the chapter we discussed the phonemes and graphemes of English which will be gradually introduced to the elementary school student in reading and spelling activities. Another facet of learning the sounds of English is syllabication, which assists the child in identifying sounds and in attacking the complexity of the polysyllabic word. Skills of syllabication will also assist the child in knowing how to break a long word at the end of a written line. The following rules are commonly taught:

If a word has only one syllable, *it cannot be divided.*

should   goat   book   have   light

A word which contains a double consonant should be divided between the double consonants.

mut/ter   wig/gle   lap/ping   ad/dition

Compound words should be divided between the two smaller words.

high/way   side/walk   fire/side

[13] Adapted from Ernest Horn, "Spelling," *Encyclopedia of Educational Research.*

When a word contains a prefix or suffix, divide after the prefix or before the suffix.

un/til   re/turn   sad/ness   play/ful

If two unlike consonants are between two vowels, divide between the consonants.

mon/key   ser/vant   ig/nite

If a single consonant falls between two vowels, divide after the first vowel.

ca/mel   ti/ger   li/ly   bro/ken   py/thon

If the final syllable ends in *le*, the consonant before the *le* is included in the final syllable.

cra/dle   sta/ble   bri/dle   ea/gle [14]

Dictionary Usage. Although this skill has direct relevance for spelling, it is also vital to other subject area studies. The use of the dictionary throughout the curriculum tends to reinforce learning and also increases the value of construction. Dictionary skills range from the most elementary to advanced skills involving specialized dictionaries with a sequence of abilities developing something like this:

1. Ability to say the alphabet letters in order
2. Use of alphabetical order in arranging words
3. Examination of the dictionary and its parts
4. Opening the dictionary to a specified letter
5. Finding a specified word
6. Using the dictionary to find acceptable spelling, pronunciation, and meaning
7. Using the dictionary to increase vocabulary (synonyms)
8. Making discoveries about words; studying etymology

Many kindergarten children come to school already able to recite the alphabet in order. Practice should be given in the use of this skill during kindergarten and first grade as the children become increasingly aware of the letters through phonics studies and beginning writing skills.

- Display the alphabet in the room in varied ways. An alphabet chart is helpful because all can see it, and the chart is available for reference as needed. Display letters in connection with appropriate pictures as knowledge of the alphabet is integrated with increasing vocabulary. A,B,C,D might be featured on a bulletin board with large pictures of an apron, baby, cat, and dog.
- Having children line up for recess in alphabetical order is a way of introducing alphabetical order. (Specify either first or last names.) As you

[14] Sidney Tiedt and Iris Tiedt, *Elementary Teacher's Complete Ideas Handbook* (Englewood Cliffs, N.J.: Prentice-Hall, 1965), pp. 45-6.

call out, "A," all those with names beginning with A may get in line, then B, and so on. Later introduce the concept of alphabetizing the group of A names by the second letter.

● WHO CAN FOLLOW ME? is a simple game for stimulating use of alphabetical order. As the teacher (or leader) says one letter, she points to a student who must name the following one or two letters of the alphabet. If D is named, for example, the player must name E and F.

The use of a dictionary can be started in first grade as children become accustomed to refer to a picture dictionary. Gradually the coverage of the dictionary used expands until students are introduced to the library's copy of an unabridged volume. The teacher should again beware of employing monotonous study techniques which decrease student interest.

● Opening the dictionary to a specific letter can be an enjoyable game as well as a learning experience. Which letters are in the middle of the alphabet? Which are close to the beginning? Which are near the end? Discussions of these ideas will aid the child in opening the dictionary to approximately the right place as any letter is called.

● Encourage interest in word study by encouraging student discovery. Are there words which have two pronunciations? Does the meaning change with the pronunciation? (As in the heteronyms, for example, en*trance* and *entrance*.) What words have two acceptable spellings? Do some words have many meanings? Make illustrated charts of some words which have many diverse meanings—*run, horn, hand, fly, field, beat, stock*.

● Explore synonyms for familiar words by referring to the short list of words included in many dictionary entries or by using the specialized synonym dictionary (Roget's *Thesaurus* and others). Prepare a synonym dictionary for use by class members including pages for overworked words: *walk, say, look, big, little*.

● Prepare a class book of WORD DISCOVERIES in which is included an assortment of interesting facts about words—the longest word found, words which read the same backwards and forwards (palindromes), less common homonyms (*right, wright, write, rite*), and creative uses of words in advertising.

Other Related Skills. In conjunction with spelling we can teach capitalization, pluralization, contractions, and possessive forms. Again, if we approach these skills through the inquiry or discovery approach, rather than "deadly drill," we will find that there is greater interest and, consequently, greater learning.

● Invent names to be used in stories. Write two or three letters on the board —B L R or C W. Each student is to invent a name which uses these initials—*Betty Lou Risenour* or *Carlota Wilberforce*. Have many written on the board to demonstrate the wide variety which results from a group's working on the same problem.

● To give practice in using capital letters with names of cities and states conduct an Alphabet Search as each person tries to find a city beginning with *A* (Akron, Ohio), then *B* (Baltimore, Maryland), and so on.

● This humorous poem by an unknown poet may serve to interest students in discovering examples of plurals which follow a similar pattern and those which deviate.

AN ENGLISH TEST

We'll begin with box, the plural is boxes,
But the plural of ox should be oxen, not oxes.
One fowl is a goose, but two are called geese,
Yet the plural of mouse is never meese.
You may find a lone mouse, or a whole nest of mice,
But the plural of house is houses, not hice.
If the plural of man is always men,
Why shouldn't the plural of pan be called pen?
The cow in the plural may be called cows or kine,
But a bow, if repeated, is never called bine;
And the plural of vow is vows, not vine.
If I speak of a foot and you show me two feet,
And I give you a boot, would a pair be called beet?
If one is a tooth and a whole set are teeth,
Why shouldn't the plural of booth be called beeth?
If the singular's this, and the plural these,
Should the plural of kiss ever be written keese?
We speak of a brother, and also of brethren,
But though we say mother, we never say mothren.
Then the masculine pronouns are he, his, and him,
But imagine the feminine, she, shis, and shim!
So the English, I think you all will agree,
Is the funniest language you ever did see.

● Teach any of these skills and spelling itself through the technique of dictation. Compose (or have students compose) sentences which illustrate the use of capitalization, plurals, contractions, and possessive forms, thus:

Mary's mother said, "Please, Mary, set the table."
Your three cats won't stay out of Mr. Handy's garden.
Harry's coming home for his grandfather's birthday.

Present these sentences without previous study to see how many students can write them correctly. Have students write them on the board as class members point out any errors, and each corrects his own sentences. Repeat the testing procedure.

Methods of study·

Most of the words which are included in a spelling list are words which are already present in the child's speaking or reading vocabulary. Only occasionally, therefore, is it necessary to present detailed information about the meanings of words presented. When presenting a new list of words, on the other hand, it is motivating to note with the class the interesting characteristics of the words being presented. What aspects of this list might the teacher use to add interest to spelling?

coal	goal	foal	hole	whole	mole
bowl	pole	role	roll	soul	toll

An inductive approach to this lesson will lead the children to identify several spellings for the sound ōl: *oal, ole, owl, oll, oul.* This list has been grouped according to a common sound with only the initial sound changing in each word. Extend learning by having children experiment with changing the vowel or the ending sound; for example, "If you know how to spell *coal*, what other word might you spell?" (coat, cool) What will be noticed about the pairs of words: *hole* and *whole, roll* and *role?*

An assorted group of words might be presented to a group of fourth graders.

huge	rather	spoken	hopeful	crimson
bicycle	control	present	examine	complete

We might begin with the the first word by asking, "Who recognizes this word?" "Who knows what it means?" There would follow a discusssion of other synonyms for *big.* What sound does the *g* make in this word? If we removed the *e*, what word would we have? Why is the *e* there? (To keep the *g* soft; to make the *u* long.) The word *bicycle* might initiate a discussion of the prefix *bi*, and *control* would warrant a comment on the prefix *con*. The word *present* is a heteronym which can lead to an interesting discussion (Who will·present the present?).

Pretesting. As noted previously, many spellings are learned incidentally, therefore before any study takes place the teacher should dictate each word to the group as a test, having each student attempt to spell the words correctly. The purpose of this pretesting technique is simply to determine which words are already known by each individual student. This test is marked (not graded) by the teacher, who may circle the part of each word which has been incorrectly spelled. The student can then compare the incorrect spellings with the list in the spelling book or on the board. This test-study-test method has been found more effective than study followed by testing without a pretest.[15]

The student who already knows the spellings of the words presented should spend his time with some other profitable activity rather than wasting time pretending to study. Students who need help, on the other hand, can be assisted in learning the spellings not known.

> When marking student papers, accent the positive by noting the number right rather than always marking those wrong.

[15] Gerald C. Eichholz, "Spelling Improvement through a Self-Check Device," *Elementary School Journal* (April, 1964), p. 376.

Individualizing Spelling. What is individualized spelling? No single approach has been determined although most authorities agree that the practice of teaching for individual needs which allows for individual differences is desirable. The use of a pretest is one way of allowing for individual differences, as some individual needs are immediately determined by the test. Another method is the use of programmed material, although a student might be required to study words already known. A completely individualized approach would consist of each child's developing a list of words misspelled from his compositions. Perhaps the most commonly used technique combines the use of the standard wordlist with the pretest to which are added a number of words which the child as an individual needs to learn. These words may be dictated by pairs of children who work together to check the individual portion of the spelling lists.

Inductive or Discovery Methods. An effective technique of teaching understanding about spelling is through the inductive method in which the student is led to make the discovery. Have students name, for example, words which end with the common suffix, *tion* (šən). As the words are named, write them on the board: *nation, convention, impression, examination, vacation, fission, confession, relation, aggravation, completion.* After 20 or more words have been named, ask the class what they notice about these words (that is about the spellings of this sound in English). Have them form generalizations about the spelling of this suffix. One might expect a class to suggest statements similar to these:

1. The suffix which sounds like SHUN is spelled SION or TION.
2. -TION occurs after A.
3. -SION occurs after the letter S which is then double.

Record the findings of this particular study on a chart to which additional findings can be added. The generalizations may be revised as new findings are noted; for example, someone may discover the group of deceptive words which terminate in *SION* which sounds /žən/ as in DECISION and REVISION. Also watch for the word COERCION.

Generalizations may also be made after exploring the spelling of other commonly used affixes or phoneme groups. Have students examine these examples in the manner described:

1. boner, honor, sulfur, grammar, recorder, splendor (How about martyr?)
2. ease, marry, teens, piece, detour, sardine, pique, rainy, wee, fear
3. mended, scored, shocked, crooked, hoped, spelled

Study Steps. Almost every set of spelling texts includes a list of steps for learning to spell a word. The steps usually are something like these:

1. Look at the word.
2. Say the word.
3. Say the parts of the word.
4. Try to write the word without looking at it.
5. Compare your spelling with that in the book.

These steps would undoubtedly be helpful if they were applied, but it has been found that the child studying spelling independently does not follow the prescribed steps. His failure to follow these steps may be attributed to the complexity of the steps or perhaps to sheer boredom with a less than exciting routine.

Motivating student interest

The most important task of the spelling instructor is to develop student interest and concern for spelling. What are the reasons for learning to spell words? The discussion of this topic proves beneficial at the beginning of a school year as a means for motivating student interest in learning this skill. The listing of student-contributed reasons often is more influential in affecting student opinion than is a teacher-prepared list, although both lists might include the same point:

1. People can understand what you have written.
2. You make a better impression on those reading your work.
3. You make better grades in school on written work.
4. There is personal satisfaction in doing something well.

Why do we need standardized spelling? Why not permit everyone to spell as he chooses? This sentence written on the board will bring laughter, but should make your point:

Noo Girzee lize ahn thu koste.

The next problem in motivating interest is to select techniques which are stimulating rather than routine. Moving from the usual method of test-study-test-study-test, the perceptive teacher will find varied ways for teaching spelling, methods which will have more lasting effects on ability to spell. In selecting stimulating activities the teacher must be discriminating, for many Spelling Games are of little real value in teaching children to spell or even in motivating interest. The Spelling Bee is one example of an activity which has little benefit, for its emphasis on oral spelling is of questionable value in teaching the written skill of spelling and too few children are actively involved at one time.

● BEWARE of the SILENT LETTER is the caption of a display featuring words (contributed by students) that contain silent letters which are printed in contrasting colors, for example:

gnat knob debt cupboard column slide

- ARE YOU TEED OFF? asks the caption of a display which features words containing the sound TEE with emphasis again on student discoveries:

  teeny   teepee   eternity   teasing   society   teaspoon

- Student prepared word quizzes can feature interesting pairs of words that will prove intriguing to others:

  quiver, quaver   stunt, stint   boner, banner

- TWENTY-SIX SCADOO! has all students racing to write a word for each letter. Specify rules according to the ability level: each word must be at least six letters; each word must contain three syllables, etc.

- BEAT THE CLOCK requires each student to write 10 (set the number according to the group) words beginning with any given sound before the second hand goes all around the clock. As the second hand approaches 12, write the letters *tr*, for example, on the board. Each student immediately begins writing: *Treat, Trust, Truth*, etc.

- SELF-DIAGNOSIS is an excellent means for interesting the student in bettering his spelling. At the beginning of the year give the students a test (never too long at any one time) of words which all should know how to spell—*said, what, who, and, that, which, them, she, can, like*, and so forth. If you don't have a list compiled, ask several students (poor spellers will be motivated by assuming this responsibility) to prepare a list of words they think all should know. Repeat the test several times during the year as each tries to master the group of words. Refer to these words incidentally also to keep them in everyone's mind.

- CATTY WORDS is the caption which accompanies a group of words which contain the syllable CAT. Encourage students to discover words with a similar relationship to introduce to the class: THESE WORDS ARE DOGS! (*doggerel, dogged, dogma*), HAVE YOU PAID YOUR FEES? (*fealty, coffee, phenomenon*), CAN YOU SEE? (*season, deceive, seep*).

- Each student develops a CHAIN REACTION as he creates a new word by changing one letter at a time, thus: *tear, dear, deaf, leaf, loaf, loan, loon, noon*.

- As each child leaves the room, he spells a difficult word before being allowed to PASS! The word in one room might be *Mediterranean* (if the group is studying that area in social studies); in another it might be *eighth* (a word that has caused repeated difficulty).

Orthographic Rules. Many teachers spend much time teaching spelling rules and frequently teach students mnemonic devices to aid spelling. Many rules, however, have so many exceptions that they cause more confusion than aid. Mnemonic devices are also of questionable value because the same memory aid will not work for every person. Aids to remembering tricky spellings, therefore, should not be taught unless they are highly consistent, as in the following:

1. Use I before E except after C
   Or when sounded like A as in *neighbor* and *weigh*.

2. In English a Q is followed by U; the combination is pronounced KW. Conversely, the sound KW is spelled QU.

3. The silent E at the end of a word is dropped before adding a *suffix beginning with a vowel*.
   slide-sliding   hope-hopeful-hoping   state-statehood-stating

4. When a root ends in Y, the Y is usually changed to I before adding a suffix.
   baby-babied-babies   happy-happiest-happily

   If a vowel precedes the Y, the Y may remain unchanged.
   monkey-monkeys   money-moneys (monies)   play-played-playful

5. Many one-syllable words ending in a consonant double the final consonant before a suffix is added.
   pin-pinning   net-netting   dot-dotted   pat-patted

   It is interesting to compare words like these:
   pin-pinning   tub-tubbing   hop-hopped   can-canned
   pine-pining   tube-tubing   hope-hoped   cane-caned

Creative ways with spelling

Can the teaching of spelling actually be creative? Let's exercise our rusty imaginations as we have a brief "brainstorming" session to consider methods of heightening the creativity of our own methods. A creative method will be one that attacks the problem from a different direction or views the problem differently. Here are a few suggested ideas, but we hope that you will carry the ball from here as you explore creative ways for focusing attention on spelling.

- HOW MANY WAYS can you spell? Students will be intrigued by attempts to spell words differently by using correct phonic principles. Say a word and write the standard spelling for this word on the board as you challenge students with producing additional "correct" spellings. Given, LITER, for example, enterprising students might suggest:

  LITER: leeter, leater, leetar, leiter, leator, etc.

  What generalizations might be made about this group of spellings? Why did the L and T never change? What type of information does this activity teach?

- Practice spelling words which are not known. Even the longest word can be spelled readily if it follows regular phonic patterns. Familiarity with common prefixes and suffixes is also helpful. Pronounce words carefully as children write them and build confidence through success. Aren't these words easy?

plantation	equitable	surrounding
fantastic	explanatory	blameless
convention	discovery	alliteration
insistent	reputation	equation

How would this exercise assist children in composition skill? Would you grade these words? What would you say if a child left out one L in alliteration?

● Unusual characteristics of words lend interest to the study of spelling as they do the study of words (See Chapter 3). This poem can be read aloud, although each person should be looking at a copy, as an introduction to a study of Homonyms:

A TAIL OF WHOA

Iris M. Tiedt

(Two bee red allowed)

Eye stood before the window pain
To stair out on the stormy seen.
    The wind it blue
    With grown and mown
As rein pored threw the lain.

Eye razed my head to view the cite
And new my hart wood brake
    Four rested from hour would
    Were awl the furs sew tall and grate
Know more too waive the see.

Aisle ne'er forget that dreadful knight—
A quire of desolation maid
    Buy hale and creek of bows—
    Yet still no paws or lesson.
The whether it was fowl!

Then shown at last the mourning son.
The heir now boar the fare suite cent
    Of rows and hair belle whet.
    At piece the wind; knot sew my sole,
Fore their the land lei waist.

● WHAT WORD IS THIS? might be the title of these riddles which focus attention on the spelling of specific words as in this example:

I like green but I don't like purple.   (G)
I like house but not mouse.   (H)
I like autos but not cars.   (O)
I like sheet but not blanket.   (S)
I like night but not nigh.   (T)

    (GHOST: 1 letter indicated by each line. Each letter is within the first word but not the second.)

HOW DO YOU SPELL IT? Why, i,t, of course!

Books to Investigate

Allred, Ruel, *Application of Spelling Research*. Eugene, Ore.: Oregon School Study Council, 1965.

Emery, Donald W., *Variant Spellings in Modern American Dictionaries*. Champaign, Ill.: National Council of Teachers of English, 1958. Pamphlet reporting an interesting research study.

Fergus, Patricia M., *Spelling Improvement: A Program for Self-Instruction*. New York: McGraw-Hill, 1963.

Hall, Robert A., Jr., *Sound and Spelling in English*. New York: Chilton, 1961.

Hanna, Paul, and Jean Hanna. "The Teaching of Spelling," in *Readings on Contemporary English in the Elementary School*, Iris M. Tiedt and Sidney W. Tiedt, eds. Englewood Cliffs, N.J.: Prentice-Hall, 1967.

Horn, Ernest, "Spelling," in *Encyclopedia of Educational Research*, Chester W. Harris, ed. New York: Macmillan, 1960, pp. 1337-54. An invaluable reporting of research in spelling.

Parker, Don H., and Frederic R. Walker, *Teacher's Handbook for Spelling Laboratory IIIa*. Chicago: Science Research Associates, 1960.

Webster's Third International Dictionary, "Spelling." Springfield, Mass.: Merriam, 1961, pp. 23a-28a. Outline of spelling generalizations. See also "Capitalization."

Williams, Ralph M., *Phonetic Spelling for College Students*. New York: Oxford University Press, 1960.

The desire for writing grows with writing.

Erasmus

9

Writing Creatively

Some of the most rewarding activities in the elementary school classroom center around various types of creative writing. Given the necessary motivation and an atmosphere conducive to writing, children produce delightfully creative imagery as they express their ideas on widely varied topics.

What do we mean when we say "creative writing?" How does it differ from other writing? Of what value is creative writing? These are questions raised frequently by teachers. It is our purpose in this chapter to introduce the various facets of creative writing as part of the English program in the elementary school. We shall explore the following areas of concern as we investigate the possibilities for encouraging creativity through writing:

How can we define creative writing?
Why should we teach creative writing?
How can we best plan for writing experiences?
How is creative writing motivated?

Defining Creative Writing

The term *creative writing* has long been used by teachers and writers. Substitutions have been suggested by those who shy away from the *creative* terminology, for example, personal writing, writing for fun, expressive writing, free writing. It is our feeling, however, that these phrases remain mere substitutes which are not quite as descriptive as the original term.

What are the elements of creative writing which make it different from other writing? As we begin listing these characteristics, you will soon note that they are similar in nature to attributes of creativity, for creative writing is usually characterized by original, individual expression writing and imaginative, experimental thinking that is guided but not confined by direction.

Types of creative writing

There are many types of creative writing which are appropriate to the classroom; indeed, almost any kind of writing is appropriate for exploration.

> Sentence stories, descriptive paragraphs
> Jokes and riddles
> Diaries and letters
> Skits, plays
> Fables and myths
> Short stories, books
> Poetry

Creative writing, you will note, includes both poetry and prose. We feel, however, that since poetry is so very important and since the techniques used differ sufficiently from those of prose that this type of creative writing should be discussed in a separate chapter, with the present chapter focusing on the writing of prose.

Why Teach Creative Writing?

> Children are creative persons, not scholiasts; they use language as the artist the world over and in all ages has used his medium, not as an end in itself but as a means for the expression of thought and feeling. Language in itself, they sense, is comparatively unimportant; if the vision is steady and the feeling is true these will find their proper vehicle. The attention is never on the word but upon the force that creates the word.[1]

So writes the imaginative and sensitive teacher Hughes Mearns in a charming and enlightening book, as he describes his attempts to stimulate creativity.

Writing is only one area of the elementary school curriculum in which we can stimulate creativity. It is, however, an area which requires very little in the way of equipment and materials, and therefore, perhaps, is an area in which many teachers find themselves more at ease, more prepared to encourage creativity. It is also, as stated by McCarthy, an area of a

---

[1] Hughes Mearns, *Creative Power: The Education of Youth in the Creative Arts* (New York: Dover, 1958).

child's development in which more striking degrees of individual variation can be observed than in almost any other phase of growth.[2]

"Language is the dress of thought," wrote Samuel Johnson, and it is
this concept we wish to stress in encouraging the young writer. When he
views language as a means for achieving a desired end, that is, the recording of his ideas and the communication of these ideas to others, then
he will become concerned with the learning of the skills of writing. He
will have a reason for learning these skills, but emphasis should remain
on the stimulation of creative thought.

The objectives of creative writing

We need to examine the objectives of teaching creative writing to
help us direct these learning activities toward the achievement of the
greatest good for each student, and therein lies the primary objective of
all teaching—to assist each child in developing to the greatest extent of
his abilities. More specifically, however, the objectives of teaching creative writing might be stated thus:

1. Stimulation of the creative expression of ideas
2. Development of a sense of potency and personal worth for each child
   and his contributions
3. Establishment of rapport among children and teachers to encourage
   freedom of expression
4. Development of writing skills and vocabulary to facilitate writing as
   a form of communication

These objectives are focused on the child and his personal development, for we are not overly concerned with the product of this process.
We have not stated, therefore, as an objective: "The production of a
short story with full development of characters, plot, and setting," for it
is not our purpose through teaching creative writing to discover child
prodigies or to encourage students to produce work which compares
favorably with that of adult writers. We would hope rather that at the
end of any year each child would be writing more sentences, using new
words, and expressing ideas more freely than was true at the beginning
of the school year.

Planning Writing Experiences

Planning for writing experiences is essential if this part of the English
program is to be effectively carried out. Without careful attention to
planning it is easy to lose sight of long-range goals. There is also the

[2] Dorothea McCarthy, "Language Development in Children," in *Manual of Child
Psychology*, L. Carmichael, ed. (New York: Wiley, 1954), pp. 492-630.

danger that writing experiences will never materialize, lost in the multitude of other areas which demand time in the busy elementary school classroom. We shall examine three aspects of planning for writing which frequently perplex the teacher: (1) time for writing, (2) sources of new ideas, and (3) lesson plans.

Time for writing

One of the aims of the creative writing program is frequent opportunity to write, but classroom teachers sometimes complain that they just do not have this time for creative writing. Admittedly the elementary school schedule is a crowded one, but writing can be included without excluding other subjects. There are a number of ways for finding more time for writing as we begin to think about this problem:

1. Scheduled writing periods

   Example: Several 30-45 minute periods are scheduled each week for introducing new writing tasks. This amount of time is usually allotted by the course of study.

2. Relating writing to other subjects

   Example: Writing an adventure set in Brazil which utilizes knowledge of the geography of that country

3. Writing before school

   Example: Designate the five or ten minutes before the bell rings as the WRITERS' WORKSHOP when each writes a daily entry in his personal Idea Book.

4. Writing at home

   Example: Encourage able students to continue writing activities at home. Writing done at home is also placed in the Writing Folder and can be the subject of an individual conference.

5. Writing clubs meeting after school

   Example: Those students who are especially interested in writing can form a club called PEN POINTERS or WRITERS, INC. They can meet once or twice a week using the time to write, to discuss their writing, or to learn about writing. With a chairman, the club can be student-managed.

6. Writing when other work is completed

   Example: Writing is an excellent individualized activity which can be pursued independently by a student who has completed assigned work in social studies, and so on. He is free to get his Writing Folder at any time; he might, for example, be publishing a collection of his poems at the Publishing Center at the back of the room.

Sources of new ideas

To sustain continued interest in writing the teacher must have varied ideas for motivating student writing. The regularly scheduled writing period should usually be designated for beginning new writing tasks although at times these periods will be needed for completion of longer writing projects. Several new ideas will be required each week, which at first may appear to be too much to expect of a teacher. Let us consider, therefore, ways of finding new ideas or of making *old* ideas appear *new*.

1. *Alternating the writing of prose, poetry, and word study.* A class may work on poetry for a week or two, then concentrate on forms of prose for a period of time. As different forms of prose and poetry are introduced, students will have a wider range of ideas for independent writing. The study of words adds to interest in writing both prose and poetry.

2. *Adapting ideas so that they appear new* the next time they are presented. If the technique of drawing several lines on a blank sheet of paper has been used to intrigue student imagination as he completes the drawing and writes about it, several weeks later interesting shapes can be cut from colored paper which the student is to arrange in any fashion on a larger sheet adding lines as he wishes to complete a drawing about which he writes.

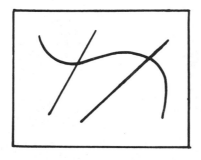
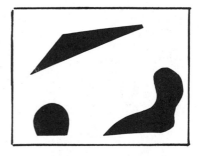

lines   shapes

3. *Repeating the same idea after a period of time* has elapsed. A good idea is worth repeating if it is not worn out. If one day the students based their writing on three unrelated nouns which were written on the board, the same technique can be used several weeks later; they will welcome the assignment as something familiar but still challenging especially if three different words are used. Instead of three nouns, three adjectives, three verbs, or a combination of noun, verb, and adjective can be suggested. The students can also select the words to be used, for another slight change.

4. *Alternating the type of motivating devices used.* One day a device is used which appeals visually, such as a picture about which the children

write. The next day a record is played or the sense of touch is the stimulus through the use of an unknown object concealed in a paper bag which all have a chance to feel.

5. *Inventing ideas for motivating student writing.* A writing period can be allocated for "brainstorming" exciting first lines about which to write. These lines are then used to motivate writing.

It was sinking, but there was nothing I could do.
"One, two, three. Go!" he shouted.
He looked and looked but it was nowhere to be seen.

6. *Collecting new ideas from varied sources.* The teacher must always remain alert to new ideas which are described in journal articles about creative writing. Check copies (even older issues) of *Elementary English, Instructor, Grade Teacher.* Often ideas are gathered from fellow teachers who describe techniques they have tried. It is an excellent practice to jot each new idea on a file card so these ideas are readily available when needed. We use this form in recording ideas briefly on file cards:

Title of Activity: *Jigsaw Story*
Area of Study: *Creative Writing*
Description of Technique:

Cut a square of construction paper in four irregular pieces on which are written:
2 characters, 1 setting, 1 noun
Each student gets an envelope containing a Jigsaw Story which he assembles; he then writes a story relating the four parts.

Lesson plans for creative writing

Each writing experience should be carefully planned, for the lesson is sure to be more effective if the teacher is certain of the motivational device to be used, the method for its introduction, and follow-up activities. It is also helpful if suggestions are noted after the activity has been completed, for the teacher is continuously learning as she teaches. We find that a simple lesson plan form like the one illustrated provides the necessary guidelines for a successful writing activity. This form aids the teacher in thinking through the activity from start to finish, clarifying the development of the teaching technique.

LESSON PLAN FOR CREATIVE WRITING

Title: *Traveling Tales*

Time: *45 minutes*

Technique:

Questions:
  "*Have you ever traveled?*"
  "*Have you ever heard of a Traveling Tale?*"
  "*What does this kind of <u>tale</u> mean?*" *(write on board)*
  "*What would a traveling tale be?*"

Directions:
  Today we are going to write Traveling Tales, stories that move from place to place. Each one of us is going to begin a story. When I say TRAVEL TIME, you will pass your story to the person behind you. Then each of you will read what is on the paper and add what you think would happen next. We'll have our stories travel several times so that each of you will work on several different stories. Then we'll read the stories to see how they grew as they traveled.

Tips:
  Stop writing soon enough so a number of students can read their tales.
  At each passing allow enough time for passing as well as for writing.
  Each child can finish one of the stories next day.
  Compile stories in a book: Traveling Tales

Notice that the activity has been given a *Title*. Students respond more readily to an activity which bears an intriguing name so that, if possible, an imaginative name should be used rather than Writing Activity Number Twenty-Seven. Students may apply an apt name to the activity which can be adopted for future use.

The amount of *Time* required for this activity may appear to be too long. Experience will prove, however, that an effective warm-up period requires perhaps 10 minutes, that students need about 20 minutes to write using this technique, and that 15 minutes is not too long a time to allow for reading some of the results. Other activities may not require as long a period of time; certainly 45 minutes will usually be the longest writing period needed. The second day of this activity, for example, does not require as much motivation because students do not have to read new material as it is passed to them. Thirty minutes would suffice. As experience is gained in teaching, the teacher is better able to judge the amount of time required for varied activities.

Under the heading *Technique* should be included the exact words that will be said to the class as the writing project is introduced. The teacher may begin with a question, by showing the class an object of interest, by writing something on the board, or by pinning words or a picture on the bulletin board. The objective of the opening procedure is to arouse the interest of the class immediately.

In the example described, the teacher has chosen to begin by asking the question, "Have you ever traveled?" which she is sure will elicit a positive response to involve the entire class. She follows that question with another, "Have you ever heard of a Traveling Tale?" which she assumes will mystify the class of third graders. She may then write the word *tale* on the board, asking someone to identify the homonym *tale* as a story, leading them further to identify a traveling tale as a "story which moves around or goes from place to place." The teacher can then proceed by saying:

> "Today we are going to write Traveling Tales, stories that move from place to place. Each one of us is going to begin a story. When I say, TRAVEL TIME, you will pass your story to the person behind you. Then each of you will read what is on the paper and add what you think would happen next. We'll have our stories travel several times so that each of you will work on several different stories. Then we'll read the stories to see how they grew as they traveled."

If the children have not written much before this experience, they may be assisted in getting started by the supplying of one or two first lines which can be used by anyone who needs help:

> I ran happily down the beach, but stopped suddenly when I saw . . .
> It was eleven o'clock one evening when the telephone rang.

Sufficient time is allowed for the children to write a few sentences before calling "Travel Time." If the teacher walks around the room during the writing period, she can easily ascertain when most students have written enough. The time allowed must be progressively longer, for the growing story requires more time to read. Time must be allotted, too, for some of the stories to be read aloud before the writing project is put aside for the day. The reading of these efforts shows the class the wide variety of possibilities for developing stories. It also points up the value placed on their work as all enjoy it together. (Tip: If one child from each row is called to read, probably something written by almost every child will be read.)

On the following day each child may be given one of the partially completed stories with the instructions to read the story, make any changes desired, and complete the story. Again some stories can be read. The entire group of stories can be compiled (by one or two students) in a book entitled TRAVELING TALES. Other students can illustrate the volume.

Motivating Creative Writing

Perhaps the most important single aspect leading to successful creative writing experiences is the motivation of the student. The child who lacks motivation may find the writing period a chore and a bore, and there will be little that is creative about his writing.

There is a great need for research regarding the techniques of motivating creative writing. Many people question, for instance, whether this type of writing can be motivated effectively. Through questionnaire, interview, and observation in 40 elementary schools, Smith compiled a list of 10 factors useful in motivating creative writing: [3]

1. Providing attractive classrooms rich in materials
2. Encouraging pupils to write from their own interests and needs
3. Providing rich experiences about which a child can express himself
4. Developing sensitivity to good writing which in turn helps a child improve his own writing
5. Using real needs of children or helping them to develop new ones
6. Providing freedom from fear and helping pupils gain confidence in their ability to create
7. Providing abundant time and opportunity for writing in many areas and in many forms
8. Developing skill in mechanics without sacrificing spontaneity
9. Sharing the end products of writing
10. Evaluating the writing in terms of the total growth of the child

[3] Ethel Smith, *Procedures for Encouraging Creative Writing in the Elementary School* (Doctoral dissertation, Northwestern University, 1944).

How can the teacher best implement the findings of research about the motivation of creative writing? How can effective motivation be achieved in the classroom? We have found that the teacher of language arts best stimulates creative writing through (1) creating a climate for writing, (2) providing a warming-up period before writing, and (3) using varied techniques for motivation.

Creating a climate for writing

If we wish students to write creatively, we must provide an atmosphere in the classroom which is conducive to writing freely without fear or concern for criticism, an atmosphere which clearly communicates the feeling that whatever each child writes has value. What do we mean by "an atmosphere conducive to writing?" This concept is so vital to successful writing in the classroom that we need to examine the components of this atmosphere—teacher attitude and student attitude.

If we truly value writing as a means to learning and self-expression, we must operate on the theory that there is *worth in the writing of every child,* some small item that rates a favorable comment, something for which to praise the child, which will in turn encourage his efforts.

As a teacher, what would be your comment after reading the following short composition written by a second-grade girl?

Judy

My dog is blak.
He is a good dog.
We play ball after skool.

Judy was eager to share this story with "Teacher," who would surely like it. Her teacher might have made any number of remarks:

1. "Your story is not very long. Why not add more to it?"
2. "I see two words that are misspelled. See if you can find them."
3. "Why, Judy, I didn't know you had a dog. I'd like to hear more about him."

The first two statements are certainly justifiable and are not unkind, but the third would be made by a teacher who understood, a teacher who was concerned for the development of a child. The focus remains on the child and her ideas, not on her mistakes, and carries a warmth and interest in the child as well as the writing. The use of the student's name is also an excellent device for adding to her security in the classroom situation. The teacher's desire to know more about Judy's dog suggests obliquely that Judy write more while at the same time approving subject matter which is familiar to the child. It is this type of teacher enthusiasm and understanding which stimulates the child to write freely.

In order for the child to write effectively, creatively, he must feel *a sense of freedom*. By freedom we do not, however, mean license. We would borrow the words of Robert Frost who defined this type of freedom: "Freedom is feeling easy in your harness."

The child functions well in the harness which in this case is the controlled situation of the classroom, but he needs this feeling of being at ease, of being free to experiment with language, of daring to disagree or to try something different from that which others are doing. To feel free to be original he must know that originality or difference will not be condemned or ridiculed by his peers.

The young writer, too, must be reassured that intimate emotional revelations will not be tacked on the bulletin board for all to read. There must be some way of protecting his privacy or he will never risk putting these words on paper; certainly he will never ask his teacher to share them. Some teachers have employed the practice of telling students early in the year that anything they write which is not for reading aloud may be marked NOT TO BE READ or PERSONAL. A child's Writing Folder can also be clearly designated as his personal property with the understanding that no writing *has* to be shown to anyone else, even to the teacher.

Anyone entering a classroom will know that *writing is important* if there is evidence that children are writing. Writing is displayed around the room—on bulletin boards, compiled in booklets, on the classroom reading table. The Writing Center also serves to add to the importance of writing. The purpose of this activity center is to encourage writing and to provide a place where students can work undisturbed and undisturbing. This helpful addition to the classroom requires few materials which are not readily available. Suggested here are types of equipment and materials which add to the Writing Center:

> Table and chairs to accommodate about six students
> Paper supplies, pencils, erasers
> Dictionaries suitable to grade level
> File of individual writing folders
> Typewriter (a motivating addition if available)

Sometimes the Writing Center is designated as a Publishing Center with the emphasis still on writing. The student is encouraged, however, not only to write but to publish his work in simple form with an attractive cover. His publication may consist of a leaflet with appropriate illustrations by the author. The more ambitious, prolific author may produce a book which can be properly stitched and bound. Publishing lends an additional note of value to the writing of each child. Published works of individual children make excellent gifts for parents and provide a good way to let the public know what the school is doing.

Writing must be *an integral part of the child's learning* activities. A regularly scheduled daily writing period provides time for the development of language abilities. When a student completes assigned writing tasks, he is then free to develop any writing project in his writing folder which may include the following:

1. An assignment he wishes to develop from a previous writing period
2. A topic which he has noted for exploring
3. A long story or book which he is writing independently
4. Checking definitions for words accumulated in his WORD BOOK
5. Preparing a copy of the selection he plans to discuss during his individual conference
6. Preparing a final draft of writing to be published or displayed

An interesting technique for providing daily writing practice is that which we call Timed Writing. This technique is especially suitable to the classroom in that it can fit into any small amount of time you may have available—before school, the last five minutes before recess or lunch. These regular writing periods add to the student's fluency, his ability to get words on paper. The object of the exercise is to write for five or ten minutes without ceasing no matter what is written. It is usually most effective to direct students to write about something of personal interest— what they do at home, something they saw on the way to school, something they would like to do. These writings can be done on single sheets of paper which are filed in the Writing Folder or they can be written in a spiral notebook in the form of a journal, diary, or log.

Warming-up before writing

There is little likelihood that students will be stimulated to write interesting, creative stories if the teacher passes each student a clean sheet of composition paper and says, "Now I want each of you to write an interesting story." The situation will be little remedied even if she states, "I want each of you to write an interesting story about a cat."

The writing experience can, however, be rescued if the teacher allots just a few minutes for a warming-up period before the students have a sheet of paper before them. Suppose, for example, we use the suggested topic of cats. The teacher might begin something like this:

"How many of you have a cat at your house? What kind of cat do you have, John?" (Students name the species, color, size of their house pets.)

> "Are there other types of cats than those which have already been described?" (She elicits the naming of wild animals in the cat family—tiger, lion, jaguar—which are listed on the board as named.)
>
> "Where would you see cats like these?" (Jungle, circus, zoo—pictures can be shown.)

By beginning the writing period with this type of discussion, students become involved with the topic. Each one has begun to think of some sort of cat in a specific situation. A wide variety of possibilities have been opened up by the discussion. Each child is ready when the teacher continues:

> "Today I want each of you to write a story about a cat, any kind of cat that interests you. While I pass paper to you, you can begin thinking of the cat you will describe. Where is this cat? What does he look like? What is his name? What is he doing? Is he with a human being or another animal?"

Some of the resulting stories will be about the common feline. but others will describe leopards, panthers, or Bengal tigers. Some will be based on real experiences whereas other young authors may stretch their imaginations as they track the jungles of Kenya or sail down the Ganges. At any rate each student will produce a story, long or short, which can be included in a class book of CAT TALES.

Another important aspect of preparing for writing is the *development of the student's self-image as a writer*. It is infrequent that the home environment provides the student with the image of himself as a writer, for parents usually regard any type of writing as an undesirable task. To develop the student's interest in writing it is helpful if he can visualize himself as a writer, secure in the knowledge that his writing has value. Although it is true that an objective in teaching students to write is not that they produce writing of commercial quality, yet we wish to promote the concept that writing, like reading, is a desirable occupation whether one earns his living through writing or merely writes for personal enjoyment.

One good method for strengthening the desirability of writing is the knowledge that the teacher writes. Students are greatly impressed by this fact. If the teacher can share personal writing experiences of any nature with the class, they will respect her not only as a teacher but as a writer who really knows what writing is all about.

Another effective device for developing student interest in writing is to acquaint them with published authors in a variety of ways. At times there will be a local author who can be invited to visit the school to talk with the class about writing. In lieu of the real person, books can be found which tell about an author's views of writing. Portions of *Writers at Work*, edited by Malcolm Cowley (Viking), which is a collection of interviews of famous authors—Joyce Cary, Dorothy Parker, James

Thurber, William Faulkner, and many others—can be read. Each author describes his writing experiences and his feelings toward writing.

A page of biographical information as well as a picture is included for each writer, which further humanizes the members of this profession. Revealing also is the sample sheet of each author's manuscript which is shown with corrections and changes as made by the writer. Even the young child will be interested in hearing some of the comments about writing such as those of Frank O'Connor who recommends, "Get black on white ... I don't give a hoot what the writing's like. I write any sort of rubbish which will cover the main outlines of the story, then I can begin to see it." In conjunction with this same author's comments it would be interesting to play his recording of one of his best stories, "My Oedipus Complex" (Caedmon, TC 1036) which appeals to both child and adult. His pleasant Irish voice reads the humorous story of five-year-old Larry who resents the return of his father from war.

Using varied techniques for motivation

One of the surest methods of maintaining a high level of interest in writing is the use of widely varied approaches in stimulating student thinking. Devices used may appeal to different senses—auditory, visual, olfactory, tactile—or they may involve the use of varied materials—pictures, records, books, films, words. The writing of prose can also be alternated with word study or the composing of poetry to achieve greater variety. We shall examine here types of motivational devices (with examples of each) which have been used successfully in the elementary school classroom.

Words—A single word or a group of words can provide stimulus for writing.

● The teacher writes the word HAPPINESS on the board. She asks the class to identify the word and questions the meaning of this word for them. Each class member then writes a brief essay on the meaning of happiness for him. This idea originated with the publication of *Happiness Is a Warm Puppy* by Charles Schulz (San Francisco: Determined Press, 1963), which can be used to stimulate discussion. Other abstract nouns can also be explored in this manner—LIBERTY, LONELINESS, LOVE.

● A group of words can be written on the chalkboard or printed on cards around a picture displayed on the bulletin board. The words focus on one theme—*ship, ocean, suitcases, vacation, porthole, exploration, engine trouble*—to motivate student thinking about a possible story.

Titles—The title (or several titles) can be provided by the teacher or written by the class.

● The teacher asks each student to write two titles at the top of his paper. Each student then passes his paper to the person behind him or the papers are collected and redistributed. As students receive a paper, they select one of the two titles and write a story based on that title.

- Three provocative titles can be written on the chalkboard (it is best to use a limited number). Each student may then select one title about which to write. Titles should allow for many possibilities:

Do You Know What I Saw?	What I Like to Do Best
Early in the Morning	It Happened at Six O'Clock
I Couldn't Believe My Eyes!	Was I Embarrassed!

Sentences or Phrases—Either first or last lines can be suggested by the teachers or students.

- A sentence is written on the board. After a discussion about the possibilities for story material based on that beginning sentence, each student is directed to write the sentence on his paper and to create a story situation. A comparison of results is especially effective when all begin with the same line, for it demonstrates the many approaches to one topic and also the differences in individual thinking.

When I heard the door open, I turned around quickly.
What could be the meaning of the words I had just heard?
"Tell me where it is," he begged.

- The last line for the story can be supplied in the same manner. Each student writes his story so the given line will be an appropriate ending.

Was I ever relieved to see Mom and Dad!
I had no desire to enter that house again.
That was the last time I ever saw the big dog.

Paragraphs—A short paragraph can be the stimulus for the development of a story.

- A descriptive setting can be typed for duplication. Each student then writes a story using that paragraph to set the action.

It was dark in the woods at eight even though it was July. We walked slowly along the path guided by the light of Jim's flashlight. The tall trees grew thick along the narrow stream, but the path was wide. As we approached a familiar outcropping of rock we knew we were almost to our camping spot.

- A short letter is an effective way of motivating writing. Again the letter can be duplicated so that each student has a copy or it can be written on the board.

Dear Bruce,

I must see you soon to discuss our plans for the big event. I hope you've been thinking of ways for selling them on our idea. Call me to arrange a meeting.

Paul

Stories—Stories that are read by students often supply ideas which motivate writing.

● A story that is unfamiliar to the class is read to the students. The reader stops at a crucial point in the story, asking, "What happened next?" Each student writes a conclusion for that particular story. Student endings can be read and later that of the original author, not to set the author's work as a model, but again to demonstrate differences in thinking. Try:

> Lindgren, Astrid, *Pippi Longstocking*. (Viking.)
> McCloskey, Robert, *Centerburg Tales*. (Viking.)

● Often students express the desire for a story to continue. After reading a story together the class may write stories based on the same characters telling of further adventures. These adventure stories can be compiled as a class book.

Books—We read books to children; children read books to themselves. Often the ideas and illustrations of these books are highly provocative. Described here are several books which have been found especially effective in motivating student writing.

● Young children are fascinated by *The Hole* by Cliff Roberts (Watts), which explores the many possibilities of a single shape, the crescent. A large crescent-shaped hole is cut from cover to cover in this book forming part of each illustration—a piece of watermelon, the body of a crane, and so on. Children can expand this idea by drawing pictures based on other given shapes—cone, triangle, cylinder. After the drawings have been completed each child can write a story to accompany his picture.

● Another charming book is *Here comes the WHOOSH!* by Vincent Fago (Golden Press). "Here it comes . . . WHOOSH . . . there it goes and in such a hurry, no one could see it . . ." and the reader never does see the mysterious creature, whatever it is. He is introduced, however, to many other interesting animals—the pigadoon, the snakearoo, and a whole family of be-whiskers. This book can lead to the invention of many unusual animals as children describe their habitats, appearances, and behavior.

● Both of the above books are picture books, but they are used successfully with older children who appreciate the imaginative humor of these modern authors. Others which we recommend for use in similar fashion include:

Younger Ideas:
> Borten, Helen, *Do You See What I See?* (Abelard-Schuman).
> Borten, Helen, *Do You Hear What I Hear?* (Abelard-Schuman).
> Joslin, Sesyle, *What Do You Say, Dear?* (Harcourt).
> Krauss, Ruth, *A Hole Is to Dig* (Harper).
> Munari, Bruno, *Who's There? Open the Door* (World).

More Mature Ideas:

Piatti, Celestino, *The Happy Owls* (Atheneum).

Rand, Ann, *Umbrellas, Hats and Wheels* (Harcourt).

Reid, Alastair, *Supposing* (Little, Brown).

Straight, Dorothy, *How the World Began* (Pantheon).

Wolff, J., and B. Owett, *Let's Imagine Thinking Up Things* (Dutton).

Pictures—Pictures and drawings represent one of the most often used techniques in motivating creative writing. Pictures, both large and small, should be collected by the teacher and students so that a good collection is always available. Parents will contribute magazines for classroom use.

● One large picture can be displayed before the class, which discusses the action depicted, suggesting names for characters, possibilities for the setting, and so forth. The use of a large picture is a good beginning activity in writing as it provides excellent stimulation of ideas and an opportunity for the teacher to observe with the class the author's right to name the characters as he pleases, to have events develop as he chooses, that is, the possibilities for original, divergent thinking.

● Smaller pictures can be distributed to students for use as illustrations for stories. Each student writes about one picture, mounting his story and picture on one large sheet. The next writing is based on another picture which again is mounted on a large sheet together with a story. After this activity has been repeated several times the sheets can be stapled together with an attractive cover to form individual story collections.

● A more advanced type of motivation is the incomplete drawing which requires the student to complete a picture based on several given lines or shapes. He then writes about the completed drawing. Inkblots are used in this manner also, with the student interpreting what he sees in the blot or what the shape brings to mind.

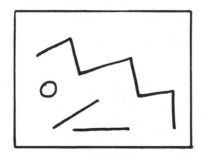

incomplete drawing   inkblot

Objects—Both familiar and unfamiliar objects lend themselves to use as stimuli in writing.

- A delightful type of motivation is achieved through hiding an object in a large paper bag. Each child in turn feels the unfamiliar object without seeing it and then writes about it. It is interesting to compare results and then to display the object for all to see—a coconut in the hull, an eggplant, an empty plastic bottle, a wooden animal, pumpkin seeds, and so on.

- Another somewhat unusual device which elicits a good response from students is the use of an old bottle which has a cork or cap. Inside this bottle the teacher places a note. The bottle containing the note is shown to the class as the teacher excitedly explains that the bottle was found on a local beach (or sent by a friend). The class speculates on the contents of the note, its origin, etc. in writing. That night the teacher "breaks" the bottle and the next day reads the note to the class.

- An inanimate object can be given life with each student playing the role of a chair, a pencil, a book, or, to be more imaginative, a picture frame, a traffic light, a crown. The student imagines the feelings of the chosen object, describing the activities of the day, reactions to the behavior of people, and so on.

Recorded Materials—Both recorded music and recorded sound add real variety to the writing experience. Tapes can be prepared by students or the teacher to fit specific needs of the class.

- The playing of recorded music for the class is often used as a stimulus to writing. The mood of the music may suggest settings for stories or the music may actually suggest action. Several effective musical selections are:

  Danse Macabre, Saint-Saëns
  The Moldau, Smetana
  Flight of the Bumblebee, Rimsky-Korsakov
  Capriccio Italien, Tchaikovsky

- There are excellent recordings of stories which can also be utilized in stimulating writing. Rudyard Kipling's *Just So Stories* (Caedmon) will interest young writers in producing original stories which explain how animals came to be made as they are in similar fashion to Kipling's explanation of "How the Camel Got His Hump." This writer's wonderful imagination and his way of playing with words serve to inspire students.

- The tape recorder, too, offers the teacher a way of motivating. Taping "sound situations" is an interesting experience for the teacher or students. The sound situation consists of the combination of several intriguing sounds—a clock ticking, footsteps, a door slamming—which suggests a situation, the basis for a story.

Films—Slides, filmstrips, and movies challenge the imagination in a visual manner and serve to vary the more routine approach.

● Movies have been prepared specifically for the purpose of motivating creative writing. A series of short films, entitled "Finish the Story" (Rocky Mt. Films, 1956), has been developed to introduce characters and action opening up a story situation which the student completes.

● Two other films which combine music, color, and imagination most effectively have been found useful as writing motivators. They have appeal for both child and adult.

   Begone Dull Care. (International Film Bureau, 1958)
   Adventures of an Asterisk. (Guggenheim Museum, 1958)

● Filmstrips of stories such as *Alice in Wonderland* and *Bambi* (Encyclopaedia Britannica Films) are used also as introductory material for imaginative writing. Students can write more adventures about the same characters or they can imagine changes in the action—"What would have happened if . . . ?"

● The teacher's personal collection of colored slides will also offer pictures to inspire writing. A group of pictures on varied topics can be shown while students rapidly suggest titles for each picture. Two or three related pictures can be shown to furnish material for a class discussion which leads to writing. The picture of an old house will lead students to imagining the past of this house, the people it has known, and so on.

Publicizing student writing

One of the most effective methods for guiding and evaluating student writing in a concrete fashion is through the publicizing of that work which is considered well done. Care must, of course, be taken that each student receives some measure of publicity for his endeavors. The publicizing of good writing can be accomplished in a number of ways.

1. Displays on classroom bulletin boards can feature writing. A display might, for example, be focused on a large picture mounted in the center of the board around which are pinned paragraphs by each student based on this picture.

2. Collections of writings can be made containing a selection by each child. If the class is writing tall tales, have each student submit his best one for a book entitled WHOPPERS!

3. A student publication can be produced periodically bearing an appropriate title such as REFLECTIONS, IMPRESSIONS, SHOWCASE, SPICE, VENTURES. Different types of writing can be featured, from interesting phrases to short stories, so that all have a chance to contribute. The entire group can take part in the tasks of publishing.

Through the stimulation of creative writing in the elementary school classroom we are attempting to apply the theories of research in creativity to practices in the teaching of the language arts. Although there remains some doubt about the possibility of teaching creativity itself, it is accurate to state that we can teach *for* creativity, making every effort to encourage creative endeavors, and above all, avoiding the stifling of these germs of creativity. Creative writing offers an effective means for stimulating creative thinking and the creative use of language. To encourage creative writing the teacher should:

1. Provide many opportunities for writing
2. Establish a relaxed atmosphere conducive to free expression
3. Encourage students to experiment with forms and subjects for writing
4. Use varied approaches to motivate writing
5. Use evaluative techniques which encourage rather than discourage

Books to Investigate

Applegate, Mauree, *Easy in English*. Evanston, Ill.: Row, Peterson, & Co., 1960.

Burrows, Alvina T., *et al.*, *They All Want to Write*. New York: Holt, 1964.

Cowley, Malcolm, ed., *Writers at Work*. New York: Viking, 1957. Two volumes; paperback.

Manners, William, *Wake Up and Write*. New York: Arc Editions, 1962.

Mearns, Hughes, *Creative Power: The Education of Youth in the Creative Arts*. New York: Dover, 1958.

Myers, R. E., and E. Paul Torrance, *Just Imagine*. Boston, Ginn, 1961. One of a series of workbooks designed to stimulate creativity.

Radlauer, Ruth S., *Good Times with Words*. Chicago: Melmont, 1963. A book about writing for intermediate grades.

Reid, Alastair, *Supposing*. Boston: Little, Brown, 1960. An imaginative book with ideas that will stimulate writing.

Tiedt, Sidney W., and Iris M. Tiedt, *Creative Writing Ideas*. San Jose, Calif.: Contemporary Press, 1964.

Yates, Elizabeth, *Someday You'll Write*. New York: Dutton, 1962. An experienced writer talks to young people about writing skills.

10

The World of Poetry

How does poetry fit into the classroom? How do you find time for poetry? What does poetry teach a child? Does poetry have to rhyme? What is poetry anyway?

These are the questions we hear which represent the teacher's dubious approach to the use of poetry in the classroom. We must admit that poetry does present problems, for the very definition of poetry is nebulous as is indicated by the following quotations from poets who are acknowledged masters of the art:

"Poetry is the journal of a sea animal living on land, wanting to fly the air," said Carl Sandburg.

"Poetry has two things, meter and rhythm. Meter is a set thing, like a tennis court or a checkerboard, and on it you perform with rhythm. Neither of these is the poem. It is the stress of one on the other that lifts a sound from it, a tone from it, that is the poem . . ." commented Robert Frost.

"A poet's autobiography is his poetry . . . The work of a true poet is not only a moving, breathing, sound-filled portrait of his time— it is also a self-portrait, just as vivid and just as comprehensive . . ." wrote the Russian, Yevgeny Yevtushenko.

If poetry escapes definition, if poetry is that elusive, how can we present it to children? How can we tell them what it is? Our response is to surround them with poetry—read poetry, listen to poetry, write poetry. Go to poetry to find out what poetry is. We would not confine poetry by a stereotyped definition, but would attempt instead to develop a feeling for poetry like that expressed by Eleanor Farjeon:

> What is poetry? Who knows?
> Not the rose, but the scent of the rose;
> Not the sky, but the light of the sky;
> Not the fly, but the gleam of the fly;
> Not the sea, but the sound of the sea;
> Not myself, but something that makes me
> See, hear and feel something that prose
> Cannot; what is it? Who knows?

Discovering Poetry

"Children remember poetry," writes May Hill Arbuthnot in her introduction to *Time for Poetry* (Scott, Foresman, 1951), and she comments further:

> The child finds in verse what the adult finds—an exhilaration that comes from the compatibility between ideas and manner of expression, from the melody and the movement of the lines, and from the little shiver of delight that these qualities induce. More than any other type of literature, poetry trains the child's ears to the cadence of words and develops his sensitivity to the power and music of the English language.

Poetry has something to say and it says this something in a way not usually possible in prose. The rhythm and music of poetry have an appeal and power that causes the mind to attend. The inherent brevity of the poetic form requires a greater polish to each word and places greater responsibility on each word. Consider this long-time favorite with both children and teacher, "The Squirrel," written by an unknown author:

> Whisky, frisky,
> Hippity hop,
> Up he goes
> To the tree top!
>
> Whirly, twirly,
> Round and round,
> Down he scampers
> To the ground.
>
> Furly, curly
> What a tail!
> Tall as a feather,
> Broad as a sail!
>
> Where's his supper?
> In the shell.
> Snappity, crackity,
> Out it fell!

Only 46 words, and what do they say? A little squirrel is running up a tree to find a nut for his supper. He then runs down the tree and cracks open the nut. There is no comparison between this prosaic translation and the gay lilt of the lines in verse form. Children will find themselves repeating the poem, but the prose statement of the same ideas would barely catch their attention.

"A performance in words," is another of Robert Frost's succinct descriptions of poetry. It is perhaps this approach which can be used in bringing children and poetry together, for in poetry we see a poet performing with words and we admire his performance. His delight in words brings delight to us. His thoughtful contemplation of the sky, the earth, or humanity creates a responsive thoughtfulness in us. Poetry speaks to the emotions in a way that most prose does not.

What understandings are we trying to impart to children as we present poetry in the classroom? It is important that we examine these understandings ourselves in order that our presentations will work toward furthering these understandings in students. There are a number of attitudes or values which we are attempting to nurture a few of which we shall examine here:

1. Poetry is personal.
2. Poetry is related to music.
3. Poetry is communication.
4. Poetry can discuss any subject.
5. Poetry takes many forms.
6. Poetry contains imagery.

Poetry is personal

Poetry is written by widely differing poets and it is read by widely differing readers. It is inevitable, therefore, that some readers will not care for some poetry. What appeals to 10-year-old Jim, whose mind is usually traveling far from the classroom, may ring a discordant note for the teacher, whose interests are obviously not those of the boy.

As teachers, we must constantly remember the varied backgrounds of age, sex, knowledge, and experience which we and the students bring to the same poem. It is important that we present poetry that appeals to varied segments of the membership of the class. It is our responsibility, furthermore, to refrain consciously from inflicting our own preferences on the students with whom we work. Certainly it is natural that a teacher shares a favorite poem with the class, for teacher enthusiasm and participation adds to that of the students, but a wide variety of poetry must also be presented directed toward capturing the interest of all.

Divergent interpretations of a single poem should also be stressed as each student is encouraged to form his own individual opinion of a selection, to react to it freely. We must refrain from tagging a poem as *good* or another one as *bad* so that students learn to determine for themselves whether a poem has something to offer them.

Poetry is related to music

Poetry is the music of language. Its meters are related to the measures of the musical score, and many terms are common to both music and poetry; for example, *composing.* We also stress the rhythm and the music of the words as we arrange them to achieve effects similar to those of music—figures of speech, repetition, themes, patterns, rhythm.

Onomatopoeia, a Greek word that has a certain enchantment of its own, adds to the music of poetry. "Imitative words," words that imitate natural sounds, add to the effect of writing in both poetry and prose. Vowels and consonants produced toward the back of the mouth may combine to produce a sound effect that is broad, low-pitched, and rough as in these words: *rumble, growl, gong, howl, croak, chug, snarl.* By contrast, vowels and consonants produced toward the front of the oral cavity are often higher in pitch, giving sharper onomatopoetic effects as in: *ouch, hiss, click, bounce, whistle, jingle, rasp.* The short *U* sound combines with *l* and *m* to form soft words; for example, *lull* and *hum.*

● A committee of students can prepare a bulletin board display featuring onomatopoetic or "echoic," words. Using the caption, ECHOES, this committee can display examples contributed by class members.

tinkle	creek	splash
blare	bark	purr
whoosh	buzz	murmur
whisper	snore	patter
mutter	whine	shriek

● Encourage students to invent new words which imitate sounds. They should provide a definition for each invented word, thus:

CLONK: the sound of a hammer on wood

SWIZZLE: the sound of water spurting from a sprinkler

What, for example, would you call the sound made when your soda is almost gone?

● Find examples of onomatopoeia used in poetry as in these examples:

"The slippery slush
As it slooshes and sloshes,
And splishes and sploshes . . ."
"Galoshes" by Rhoda W. Bacmeister

"He bumps
And he jumps
And he thumps
And he stumps . . ."
"The Goblin" by Rose Fyleman

Alliteration is another poetic device which adds to the melodious effects of poetry. "The repetition of the initial sound of a word in one or more closely following words" is a provocative technique if it is not overworked. Remember that alliteration is based on *sound*, not just on the repeated use of a letter—*sticks and stones, phonics fun, chic shape* (Don't slip on the French *ch*).

● Have students experiment with writing descriptive alliterative phrases as in these examples:

> Slippery, slithery sleuth
> Proud princess Prudence
> Gloomy glowering glance
> Shining, shimmering shells

● Set out on an EXPLORING TRIP to discover uses of alliteration in poetry. Each student will need a book of poetry unless small groups work on this project at different times. This type of exploratory browsing introduces students to much poetry as they search for examples like these:

> "ribbon roads"
>> in: "The Rock" by T. S. Eliot
>
> "camel caravan" "mosque and minaret"
>> in: "Travel" by Robert Louis Stevenson
>
> "Slowly, silently, now the moon
> Walks the night in her silver shoon."
>> in: "Silver" by Walter de la Mare
>
> "Sing a song of seasons!"
>> in: "Autumn Fires" by Robert Louis Stevenson

Poets have long been considered "makers of music" with language as their medium. Wrote A. W. E. O'Shaughnessy:

> "We are the music-makers,
> And we are the dreamers of dreams . . ."

● Print the above lines on a large piece of construction paper for use with a display of children's poetry. The words MUSIC MAKERS or DREAMERS OF DREAMS supply excellent captions for displays or titles for collections of student writing.

● Play the recording of Dylan Thomas reading his beautiful poetic prose selection, "A Child's Christmas in Wales," (Caedmon TC 1002) that has become a classic tale which more mature students will enjoy.

Poetry is communication

Poetry is "Man speaking to men," wrote the English poet, William Wordsworth. What is the poet trying to say? It may be a feeling or an experience. In some poetry he may try to teach a lesson. The main point is that poets differ in the type of "speaking" each one does, and the message varies as does the poet and his intent.

● Examine poetry together to decide what the poet's message is, what he is trying to communicate. Point out the interesting fact that poems continue to communicate the thoughts of their originators even after the poet has died.

What, for example, is Carl Sandburg telling us in "Phizzog"? *

This face you got,
This here phizzog you carry around,
You never picked it out for yourself, at all, at all—did you?
This here phizzog—somebody handed it to you—am I right?
Somebody said, "Here's yours, now go see what you can do with it."
Somebody slipped it to you and it was like a package marked:
"No goods exchanged after being taken away"—
This face you got.

● As a way of interpreting a poem, each student can prepare a booklet with one line of the poem written on each page. An appropriate illustration is drawn or mounted with each line. These booklets can then be shared as a way of exchanging ideas about favorite poems.

Poetry can discuss any subject

"The poet gathers fruit from every tree,," observed poet Sir William Watson, and this statement can quickly be substantiated as we read poetry about widely varied topics, for example, "The Drugstore" by Karl Shapiro and "The Knob" by John Updike.

● Stress the variety of subject matter particularly to dispel the mistaken impression that poetry is "feminine, associated with flowers, love, and other womanly topics." Read a variety of poems with the class; for example, the following: [1]

"Wind-Wolves" by William D. Sargent
"Trains" by James S. Tippett
"Cargoes" by John Masefield
"Bejamin Franklin" by Rosemary Carr and Stephen V. Benét
"Godfrey Gordon Gustavus Gore" by William B. Rands
"Indian Children" by Annette Wynne
"Macavity: The Mystery Cat" by T. S. Eliot
"The Escalator" by Phyllis McGinley

● Introduce students to Robert Burns, who has written delightful poetry about homely topics as in "To a Mouse" or "To a Louse." The Scottish words when read aloud often resemble our modern English closely so that students will have little difficulty with these two stanzas from "To a

* From *Good Morning, America,* copyright 1928, 1956, by Carl Sandburg. Reprinted by permission of Harcourt, Brace & World, Inc.
[1] All of the poems listed here are included in: May Hill Arbuthnot, *Time for Poetry* (Scott, Foresman, 1951).

Louse" which was written as the poet supposedly watched the small bug crawl on a lady's bonnet in church:

> Ha! Whare ye gaun, ye crawlin' ferlie?
> Your impudence protects you sairly:
> I canna say but ye strunt rarely
>   Owre gauze an' lace;
> Though, faith! I fear ye dine but sparely
>   On sic a place.
>
> Ye ugly, creepin', blastit wonner,
> Detested, shunned by saunt an' sinner,
> How dare you set your fit upon her,
>   Sae fine a lady?
> Gae somewhere else, and seek your dinner
>   On some poor body . . .

After reading from Burns' work students may try to write poems addressing some lowly creature, for the humor of this approach has great appeal.

Poetry takes many forms

The variety of form is closely related to the variety of subject, and we endeavor again to expose children to many different types of poetic forms so that their view of poetry is in no way limited. Forms of poetry will be discussed in more detail as we progress to the writing of original poems, but here are suggestions for furthering the concept that forms of poetry vary widely:

- Read poems that represent varied forms—long, short, rhymed, unrhymed —as in these examples: [2]

  "Automobile Mechanics" by Dorothy Baruch
  Unrhymed free verse

  "Newspaper" by Aileen Fisher
  Couplets

  "How Doth the Little Crocodile" by Lewis Carroll
  Quatrains (*abab* rhyming)

  "A Fairy Went A-Marketing" by Rose Fyleman
  Octaves (2 quatrains, *abcb* rhyming)

  "The Jumblies" by Edward Lear
  Use of a refrain

  "The Old Pond" by Bashō
  Haiku

- Have each student collect his favorite poems to produce his own personal anthology of poetry. Each student-editor can try to include a variety of forms which may be listed by the class before the editors set to work.

[2] The poems listed here appear in Mary C. Austin and Queenie B. Mills, *The Sound of Poetry* (Allyn & Bacon, 1963).

● Encourage students to experiment with highly individualized forms for their poems as in this example:

PICTURES ON THE FLYING AIR [3]

Scott Alexander

A
poem
can play
with the wind
and dart and dance
and fly about in the mind
like a kite in the cloudy white
sky at so dizzy a height it
seems out of reach but
is waiting to be
very gently
pulled
down
to
the
page
below
by a
string
of
musical
words.

Poetry contains imagery

The imagery—the pictures, the petite vignettes of poetry—is the most important element distinguishing poetry from prose. Prose that is rich in imagery comes close to being poetry whatever the form, as in "A Child's Christmas in Wales" by Dylan Thomas. The image may be achieved through the use of simile, metaphor, or an extension of the latter. As poetry is read aloud or silently, it is most rewarding to encourage the sharing of imagery that is discovered.

● Prepare a bulletin board with the caption, POETIC IMAGES, where students can mount copied words, phrases, or whole poems which contain particularly effective imagery. The title of the poem and the poet's name should appear with each example, thus:

"... a road with a mountain tied to its end,
Blue-humped against the sky...."

From: "Roads" by Rachel Field

[3] Reprinted by permission. Copyright 1966, *The Instructor,* F. A. Owen Publishing Company.

". . . He is a conscious black and white
Little symphony of night."
>   From: "The Skunk" by Robert P. Tristram Coffin

". . . the big, big wheels of thunder roll . . ."
>   From: "The Woodpecker" by Elizabeth Madox Roberts

● Have students illustrate images that have been found in the above activity. Fold 9 x 12 sheets of drawing paper in half to form folders on the front of which can appear the illustration while the poem or a portion of the poem is written inside.

● Read Emily Dickinson's poem, "I Like to See It Lap the Miles," as an example of excellent imagery and the use of intriguing words:

>   I like to see it lap the miles,
>   And lick the valleys up,
>   And stop to feed itself at tanks;
>   And then, prodigious, step

>   Around a pile of mountains,
>   And, supercilious, peer
>   In shanties by the sides of roads;
>   And then a quarry pare

>   To fit its sides, and crawl between,
>   Complaining all the while
>   In horrid, hooting stanza;
>   Then chase itself down hill

>   And neigh like Boanerges;
>   Then, punctual as a star,
>   Stop—docile and omnipotent—
>   At its own stable door.

After reading this poem aloud, ask questions to stimulate the students' thinking:

>   What is Emily Dickinson describing in this poem?
>   How do you know she is writing about a train?
>   Does the word ever appear in the poem?
>   To what is the poet comparing a train?
>   What words make you think of a horse?

Draw attention to the provocative words: *supercilious, prodigious, omnipotent*. Have the students try guessing their meanings from the context of the poem before checking with the dictionary.

Introduced here, too, is a reference to mythology, a technique which is not often found in children's poetry. Have one child investigate Boanerges, the Sons of Thunder.

● Compare Emily Dickinson's poem about a train with poems about trains by other poets. Other poets have compared the train differently. Rowena Bennett, for example, wrote: "A train is a dragon that roars through the dark . . ." in "A Modern Dragon." Frances Frost gives the trains human characteristics as she describes trains that ". . . whistle softly and stop to tuck each sleepy blinking town in bed!" in "Trains at Night."

Problems in Poetry

Why is poetry not present in all classrooms? Why do some teachers have much greater success with poetry experiences than do others? There are a number of problems related to the use of poetry in the classroom, and a discussion of these may in part answer some of the questions which arise and may assist the beginning teacher in developing a successful approach to poetry with young people. The problems, as we see them, revolve around the following:

1. Teacher knowledge of poetry
2. Attitudes toward poetry
3. Methods of presenting poetry

Teacher knowledge of poetry

The teacher who knows poetry and enjoys it finds time for poetry in the classroom. It emerges in the classroom in many subtle, unexpected ways, for this teacher is prepared to open the door when poetry knocks.

How can you, as a prospective teacher, develop a knowledge of poetry that will lead to this type of *poetry readiness?* An introductory course to poetry in a college English department may develop the requisite attitudes toward poetry as adult poetry is explored, but it is not likely that you will come to know Eleanor Farjeon, Walter de la Mare, or the many other wonderful poets who have written poetry especially for children. A course in Children's Literature will probably introduce some of the poetry for children, but not in the quantity necessary for the challenging opportunities of the elementary school classroom.

In order to become really familiar with the marvelous poetry available to you and to the young people whom you will teach, you should *explore* independently in order literally to steep yourself in poetry for children. This is not a laborious chore, for you will find that children's poetry is not only charming, delightful, and thoroughly enjoyable but it also offers a pleasant variety ranging from the nursery rhyme to poems by John Ciardi or T. S. Eliot.

Every teacher should have at least one good anthology of poetry for personal use so that it can be underlined and marked with marginal suggestions for using poems that have been particularly successful or ideas about presenting a poem. Listed here are a number of collections which are recommended for your perusal and possible purchase:

Arbuthnot, May Hill, *Time for Poetry.* Scott, Foresman, 1951.

Association for Childhood Education, International Literature Committee, comp. *Sung under the Silver Umbrella.* Macmillan, 1935.

Austin, Mary C., and Queenie B. Mills, *The Sound of Poetry.* Allyn & Bacon, 1963.

Brewton, John E., comp., *Under the Tent of the Sky*. Macmillan, 1937
———, *Gaily We Parade*. Macmillan, 1940.
———, *Bridled with Rainbows*. Macmillan, 1949.
Ferris, Helen J., ed., *Favorite Poems, Old and New*. Doubleday, 1957.
Huffard, Grace T., *et al.*, *My Poetry Book*. Winston, 1956.
Sheldon, William D., *et al.*, *The Reading of Poetry*. Allyn & Bacon, 1963.
Untermeyer, Louis, ed., *Rainbow in the Sky*. Harcourt, 1935.
———, *This Singing World*. Harcourt, 1923.

Attitudes

How do you feel about poetry? Do you conceive of poetry as language which is somewhat frilly, frothy, and feminine? Do you think every student ought to memorize poetry? Would you assign the memorization of a poem as a type of punishment? Do you feel that you know which poetry is "good" contrasted to that which is "bad"? The attitudes of both teacher and student are based on past experiences with poetry. They may represent the attitudes expressed by parents and peers.

The attitude, for example, that *poetry is feminine* has led to the feeling, particularly among boys, that poetry is not something which should rightfully interest a man. Is poetry "sissy stuff"? It is if you present only poems about the blue sky, lovely flowers, pretty girls, and LOVE. To snag the boys' interest we must clearly demonstrate that poetry is for boys; poetry is for men.

● Point out that the majority of poets have been men. Conduct a small research study by having several boys examine 6 to 10 anthologies of poetry, first counting the number of poets listed in the index. Then they can count the number of these names which are masculine to determine the percentage of male poets. Conducting this study themselves will impress some students who would scarcely believe your own statement of the same fact.

● Read a variety of poetry written by men: Carl Sandburg, Robert Frost, Walt Whitman, Walter de la Mare, John Masefield, James Whitcomb Riley, James Tippett, Robert Louis Stevenson, Lewis Carroll, Edward Lear, to mention only a few of the many.

● Display pictures of men who write poetry. Record albums, magazine covers, articles will provide pictures which can be mounted on a bulletin board with samples of poetry as well as quotations from these men:

Robert Frost: "Poetry is my kind of fooling."
Paul Laurence Dunbar: "What's so fine as being a boy?"

The *memorization of poetry* as an end in itself has long been discarded as a method of enjoying poetry and certainly as a means of punishment. Many students voluntarily choose to memorize a poem which has particular meaning for them. Poetry is also memorized incidentally through repetition as it is recited in chorus or read frequently by individuals as a result of its appeal. Often, too, students will learn first lines or lines which are repeated in poems although the whole poem has not been memorized. Examples of lines which many children come to know include:

"The fog comes on little cat feet . . ."
  Carl Sandburg: "Fog"

"You can't go to court in pajamas, you know."
Beatrice C. Brown: "Jonathan Bing"

"If I had a hundred dollars to spend
Or maybe a little bit more . . ."
  Rachel Field: "The Animal Store"

"Some one came knocking
At my wee, small door . . ."
  Walter de la Mare: "Some One"

"The Owl and the Pussy-Cat went to sea
In a beautiful pea-green boat . . ."
  Edward Lear: "The Owl and the Pussy-Cat"

"I'm hiding, I'm hiding,
And no one knows where . . ."
  Dorothy Aldis: "Hiding"

The *analysis and evaluation of poetry* should not be heavily stressed with the child, for our stress is on the enjoyment of poetry. There is little doubt that the poem loses something as it is pulled apart line by line. This is not to say, on the other hand, that students should not discuss the meaning of unusual words used by the poet or that effective imagery should not be pointed out as an object of admiration. Certainly, if the class shows particular interest in the subject treated by the poem, discussion will logically develop, but we then return to the poet's "performance" as a whole.

Methods of presenting poetry

How do you introduce a poem to the elementary school child? There are numerous ways, but all of them revolve around the technique of "setting the stage" or creating a "receptive mood." How is this mood created by the teacher? It can be developed subtly by first introducing a familiar incident related to the poem or presenting an object or picture which will then suggest the poem. Sometimes we begin by writing several provocative words on the board which will lead us into the poem or we may ask several questions to stimulate a discussion.

"Now I am going to read a poem about colors," states the teacher, and the children immediately squirm. You will be more certain of a positive reaction to the poem if you provide a brief "warm-up" session. To present

Christina Rossetti's lovely poem, "What Is Pink?" the teacher might effectively begin with a discussion about colors which would arouse interest thus:

"What color is Jill's dress?" (pink)
"And what color is this flower?" (pink)
"What other things come to mind when you think of pink?
    What is pink?"
(powder, ice cream, a kitten's tongue, chilly cheeks)

From this point the discussion could easily move to several other colors and the objects they recall. Participation in the discussion has started minds working and the reading of the poem is a natural consequence.[4]

WHAT IS PINK?

Christina Rossetti

What is pink? a rose is pink
By a fountain's brink.
What is red? a poppy's red
In its barley bed.
What is blue? the sky is blue
Where the clouds float thro'.
What is white? a swan is white
Sailing in the light.
What is yellow? Pears are yellow
Rich and ripe and mellow.
What is green? the grass is green
With small flowers between.
What is violet? clouds are violet
In the summer twilight.
What is orange? Why, an orange,
Just an orange!

A natural setting for poetry is often provided by the weather. Children who have just come in with snow still on their mittens and in their minds will be quite ready to tell the teacher excitedly of their feelings about snow. "What words can you use to describe snow?" queries the teacher. Soft, white, fluffy, cold, light, sparkling. "Let me read you a poem that talks about snow; we'll see how this poet describes snow."

Rain, wind, and sunshine can each provide an effective mood for poetry. A holiday, the season, the blooming of flowers suggest poems on varied topics. Subjects studied in the classroom will provide opportunity to relate appropriate poetry. The teacher who knows poetry, who

4 Also use Mary O'Neill, *Hailstones and Halibut Bones* (Garden City, N.Y.: Doubleday, 1961). An excellent film is available which combines artful designs and color with the reading of the poems from this book.

has "the right poem at the right time" will be able to take advantage of these times for poetry, and she will also be able to plan the right setting for an exciting experience with poetry.

Experiences in Writing Poetry

Perhaps one of the most rewarding outcomes of a child's familiarity with poetry will be the writing of his own original verse. The creation of his own poetry augments the child's interest in the poetry of others while at the same time knowledge of poetry written by others increases the student's desire and ability to write poetry. As he sees that poetry comes in a wide variety of sizes and shapes, and that poets "talk" about any topic that appeals to them, the young person will feel at home with poetry and will be able to conceive of himself as a poet. The development of this image of himself as a poet is the key to the stimulation of student composed poetry.

As teachers, we must be ready to take advantage of natural opportunities that arise. When a child expresses a thought or an apt bit of imagery, we must be alert to say, "I like the way you said that, Phil. Let's write it on the board so everybody can enjoy it." Some teachers keep strips of manila paper on which phrases or sentences can be lettered quickly with a felt pen so that the children's words can be recorded for display on a bulletin board. Displayed with the caption POETRY PLEASES in one first grade room were these examples:

quiet as a flea at work

SALLY

soft, secret sound

PHIL

Our earth is round,
All water and ground

STAN

walking and talking

MARGIE

The bear clumped and humped,
thumped and bumped.

BOB

Poetry is a word, two words, and more. The teacher must be aware of the possibilities for poetry as it occurs in natural form. When Dave brings his frog to school, for example, and calls it "my funny, funny frog," the mere repetition of Dave's phrase leads children to add other lines to produce a spontaneous class composition. " 'My funny, funny frog'

—that sounds like a poem. Who can add another line?" As the first words are written on the board, someone suggests, "Hippety, hippety, hop," and another child cries excitedly, "Will he ever stop?" and there is a poem!

> My funny, funny frog.
> Hippety, hippety, hop.
> Will he ever stop?

The teacher cannot, of course, wait patiently for the unplanned experience in writing poetry to come. We must plan experiences which seem as natural and desirable and those which are initiated in the manner just described, but we must provide the stimulus. A sequence of experiences in the writing of poetry can be readily developed, beginning with the least complicated types of poetry for primary grades and progressing in difficulty through the grades. The emphasis in the *writing* of poetry remains on enjoyment, as was true in the *reading* of poetry. The elementary school child who is steeped in poetry will find writing original poetry a natural means for expressing his own thoughts.

What forms of poetry are suitable for the elementary school student? There really is no limit, for able students will reach out to try almost any form of poetry which they meet and they will even create original forms. Although the simplest forms can continue to be used in upper grades, more mature students will be challenged by exploring further if they have had a background of experience in writing poetry. Listed here is a sequence of poetry forms which seem appropriate to ability levels:

1. Words and phrases
2. Free verse
3. Haiku
4. Couplets
5. Triplets
6. Limericks
7. Quatrains
8. Additional forms

Words and phrases

Experimenting with words and the writing of phrases will encourage a feeling of freedom in the use of written language. It will also stimulate the student's thinking as he concentrates on producing inventive imagery. Experiments in using alliteration and onomatopoeia have already been discussed and many activities presented in the chapter on words will be appropriate to stimulate the use of words and phrases in poetry. Presented at this point are ideas specifically directed toward the first steps in poetry:

● Have students list words which fit a certain mood or theme. To stimulate thinking you may show a picture; for example, a dark, stormy scene, a little child crying, a family picnic (to mention only a few possibilities). Questions asked by the teacher will assist the flow of thought.

"Is this picture of something happy or sad?"

"Would you use *dark* or *light* words to describe this scene?"

"How does this picture make you feel?"

● Introduce children to the idea of the simile (an expressed relationship between objects of different classes). A good way to begin is to write a trite simile on the board—as black as night, as quiet as a mouse, as happy as a lark. Students can think of *fresh* comparisons as in these samples:

as happy as . . . a hot boy running toward the pool.

. . . a rabbit that has eluded the hounds.

. . . three ladies trying on hats in April.

● Simile Formulae can be developed by relating two objects through the action of a single catalyst, thus:

Given: BOY, DOG
     Catalyst: Happiness

BOY   =   DOG

Elated   =   Dog with a bone

The elated boy was as happy as a dog with a bone.

Given: BOY, DOG
     Catalyst: Unhappiness

Dejected boy   =   Dog with no master

The dejected boy was as unhappy as a dog with no master.

Free verse

The type of poetry which many teachers have found highly successful with children who have had little experience with the writing of poetry is *free verse*. Beginning poets may write only one line, whereas the more able or experienced child will soon write two, three, and more lines. Why is free verse especially suited to inexperienced writers? The key word is *freedom*, for in free verse there is:

1. No rhyming to lend artificiality.
2. No set pattern of rhythm or meter.
3. Free variation in length of lines, form, and content.
4. Emphasis on the thought expressed.

The fact, too, that free verse may consist of one or many lines provides a built-in accommodation for individual abilities. The child for whom writing is laborious finds success in composing one line whereas the child for whom writing comes with greater ease may extend his ideas into ten lines. For this reason the following suggestions for motivating the writing of free verse may be used at any level of ability.

● Write these words on the board: "Rain is . . ." (Use this idea on a rainy day for best results. As appropriate, try "Snow is . . ." or "Sunshine is. . . .") Then ask the class what rain means to them. Have them write their ideas on paper beginning each new idea on a fresh line (the poetry form). When completed, each child will have a poem of varied length about rain.

Type each poem on a large raindrop shape for display encouraging children to read the differing ideas about rain.

> Rain is . . . patter on the roof.
> . . . a day for hiding behind furniture.
> . . . the flower maker.
> . . . the producer of umbrellas.
> . . . the washer of leaves.

● Display a large picture of a boy and girl. Ask some provocative questions: "What are these children doing? What are they thinking? Can you imagine that you are the boy or girl in the picture?" Pretending that he or she is one of the figures in the picture, each student writes the thoughts that are in his mind. Again, suggest that each thought begin on a new line, thus:

> I wish I could get a new bike.
> Then I'd go like the wind—
> Down Madison Street,
> Across the Highway—
> No place would be too far for me
> If I had a bright shiny new bike.

● Use the senses to motivate the writing of poetry by providing an object that is concealed within a box or a large paper bag. To feature the concept of SOFTNESS, for example, use a piece of soft fur or velvet. After students have felt the concealed article, ask them how it felt.

When someone mentions the adjective *soft*, ask the question, "What is soft? How would you tell someone what you mean by softness?" Have each one write his ideas on paper as he tries to think not of how many thoughts he can write, but of *how interesting or unusual* each thought is.

> What is Soft?
> Softness is a feeling.
> Softness is velvety fur.
> Softness is a small kitten's paw.
> Softness is my mother's cheek.

● Show the class a series of slides or a group of pictures about one theme— the ocean, mountains, the city. Ask each one to write any thoughts he has about the group of pictures shown. A series of ocean scenes resulted in the following effective response from a sixth grade student:

> Break waves,
> Fruitlessly challenging flexible shores.

● Read poems to children which do not require rhyme. Poems by Hilda Conkling, Carl Sandburg, E. E. Cummings, and Walt Whitman provide excellent examples. This passage from Whitman's *Song of Myself* describes a handsome stallion which could inspire students to write poems about an animal they know.

A gigantic beauty of a stallion, fresh and responsive to my caresses,
Head high in the forehead, wide between the ears,
Limbs glossy and supple, tail dusting the ground,
Eyes full of sparkling wickedness, ears finely cut, flexibly moving.
His nostrils dilate as my heels embrace him,
His well-built limbs tremble with pleasure as we race around and return.

Haiku

Perhaps one of the most delightful unrhymed poetry forms used in the elementary school classroom is that of the ancient Japanese poets, Haiku. Discovered by America as a result of translations, this poetic form has become very popular.

Haiku is a three-line verse form which originated in thirteenth-century Japan. Early masters of the form include Buson, Boncho, Moritake, Bashō, Sōkan, and many others.[5] Authentic Haiku has several distinct characteristics which have been followed rather consistently by Japanese writers and those who have translated their work:

1. The poem consists of only three lines totaling 17 syllables.
   Line 1:   5 syllables
   Line 2:   7 syllables
   Line 3:   5 syllables
2. The season, location, and references to nature are included.
3. There is no rhyme and few articles or pronouns are used.
4. The poem contrasts diverse ideas, is subtle, symbolic.

Here are two examples of Haiku translated from the original Japanese:

BASHŌ

First cold showers fall.
Even little monkey wants
A wee coat of straw.

HASHIN

All sky disappears
The earth's land has gone away;
Still the snowflakes fall.

In popular use today many poets have taken liberties with this versatile verse form. American Haiku have been written about a wide variety of topics and lines have not always remained the prescribed length, as may be seen in current publications.[6]

[5] For more information about the history of Haiku, see the very readable: Harold G. Henderson, *An Introduction to Haiku* (Garden City, N.Y.: Doubleday, 1958).

[6] An interesting publication is: *American Haiku,* a small booklet issued twice yearly (Box 73, Platteville, Wis.).

Children are most successful with this brief verse form if emphasis is rightly placed on the thoughts they are expressing rather than on the confining form. The beauty of Haiku for children is that they do succeed in producing charming examples which compare well with those created by adult writers. The following examples corroborate this point: [7]

> The sun shines brightly.
> With its glowing flames shooting
> It goes down at night.
>
> RICKY

> The old cypress tree,
> So beautiful by the rocks,
> Has been there for years.
>
> MARJORIE

> The snowflakes fell hard.
> The ground was covered with them;
> Not one flake the same.
>
> MARTHA

> The trees above me
> Swaying across the blue sky
> Make a lovely sound.
>
> STEVE

After first thinking about an idea he wishes to express, the student is encouraged to write it on paper. He can then examine his written thought to determine how it can be divided into three parts. Experimentation with word arrangement, imagery, changing the order of the lines and choice of words used should be encouraged as the poem is developed, for the deceptively simple form requires more delicate handling than does free verse. Here are ideas for working with Haiku in the classroom:

● One way of introducing a class to Haiku is through the reading of a number of examples such as those found in the artistic little volume *Cricket Songs* by Harry Behn (Harcourt). After reading a number of these short poems, provide each student with a duplicated sheet (or write on the board) containing several examples of Haiku. Let them discover the Haiku pattern, the subject treated, and other characteristics by rereading the poems, thus:

Count the number of syllables in each line. How many syllables does each line contain?

1_____ 2_____ 3_____

Is this true of each poem?_____

What season of the year is indicated in each Haiku?

_____

[7] Fourth-grade children at the Van Meter School, Los Gatos, Calif. Teacher, Doris Schade.

● Japanese poetry makes us think of cherry blossoms or other spring blossoms. Use a twig of any flowering fruit tree to prepare an attractive display to motivate the writing of Haiku. The flowers may be combined with pictures mounted on a bulletin board or music may be played to assist the development of a mood for Haiku.

● Type Haiku written by a class on a duplicating master using two long columns so that the folded sheets will produce two long, slim pages. Cut the duplicated sheets to form pages of an attractive booklet which can be encased in a decorative cover.

● Motifs for booklet covers should be appropriate to the poetry. Students can experiment with brush stroking to produce Japanese writing or the reeds, bamboo, flowers, and so on, associated with their art.

The word HAIKU can be printed using letters that have an oriental appearance, thus:

HAIKU

One student teacher experimented with producing a cover consisting only of lines made on the master carbon as shown on page 228.

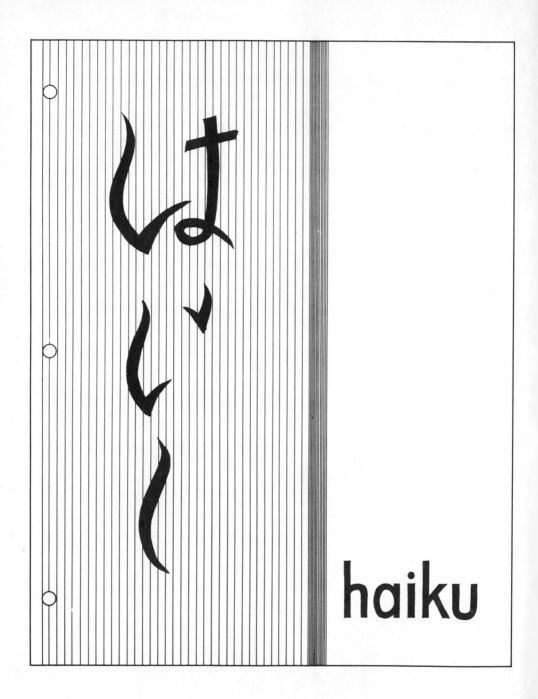

はいく

haiku

● A most rewarding art experience which correlates well with the writing of Haiku is the blowing of ink with a straw. Washable black ink is applied in a swath near the bottom of an unlined file card (or any non-absorbent paper). The wet ink is then blown with a straw to direct the ink in the desired direction. Blowing across the ink causes it to branch attractively. When the ink is dry, tiny dabs of bright tempera may be applied with a toothpick to add spring blossoms to the bare branch. The student then writes his Haiku on the card below the flowering branch, and the card is used for display or as a gift for parents.

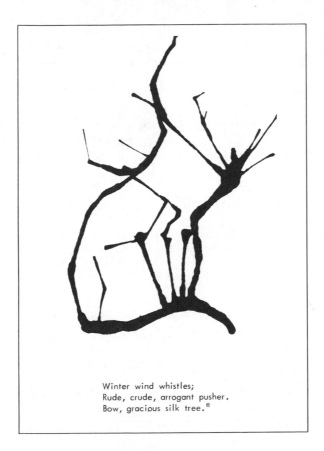

Winter wind whistles;
Rude, crude, arrogant pusher.
Bow, gracious silk tree.[8]

● For an authentic presentation of Haiku use rice paper (or thin onion skin or tissue paper) mounted inside colored paper. The poem is written (a felt pen will write on thin paper) together with an oriental motif—reeds, moon over water, flowering branch—and the author's name. The cover is folded so that the front flaps overlap slightly as in the sketch. A ribbon is then tied around the folder which is ready for presentation as a gift.

[8] Unless otherwise indicated, illustrative poetry is by Iris M. Tiedt.

Folded slightly overlapping...
...tied with ribbon

Couplets

The couplet is the simplest type of rhymed verse, and therefore offers possibilities for introducing rhyme to young writers. Many couplets are produced incidentally as children experiment with language—"Jean, Jean, your hair is green," or "Pink, pink, she drank some ink"—the jingles and rhymes of childhood. An excellent way to begin composing couplets is through group composition.

- To introduce students to the couplet and the techniques of writing rhymed poetry first discuss rhyming if the class members are not already familiar with the making of rhymes. Oral activities will quickly familiarize the class with the skill of rhyming as lists of rhymes are developed. Stress the following understandings:

  1. Rhymes are based on the sound, not the appearance of a word.

     day, neigh, lei, prey
     theme, dream, seem
     sane, gain, reign, rein
     rhyme, climb, time, I'm

  2. Not all words have rhymes. (Silver)

  3. You must pronounce a word correctly and listen carefully to determine whether words really rhyme:

     sand–tan   few–too   kind–fine

- After a class has learned to rhyme easily the teacher can select an appropriate theme—the month, season, weather, state, event, person—about which the class will compose a poem together. For a beginning experience lines can be provided as in this example of a poem about Halloween.

  The subject of Halloween is introduced through a discussion or the singing of Halloween songs, after which the teacher says, "Let's write a poem about Halloween. Will you help me?" She then writes a first line on the board being sure that the line ends with an easily rhymed word: "Ghosts and goblins are all around." Class members then suggest possible second lines as indicated here:

Ghosts and goblins are all around. (Teacher)
An owl is hooting with mournful sound. (A child)

There are devils and demons and cats of black (Teacher)
And each one carries a great big sack. (A child)

Aren't you afraid to be out this night, (Teacher)
For devils are fearsome and cats might bite? (A child)

Oh, no, not I, for don't you know, (Teacher)
The cat is Susan, and that devil is Joe! (A child)

● Hints about group composition:

1. Have several lines suggested each time before selecting a best one to be written on the board.

2. Select lines by different people each time so that as many as possible have contributed to the finished product. You may also choose to have two poems produced at the same time so more than one line can be used; simply work on two boards inserting a different student line after the given first line each time.

3. Children can learn to tap out the rhythm of the given line as they try to produce similar rhythm in the second line—the beginnings of meter.

● After a class has composed couplets together orally, the teacher can supply a variety of beginning lines as each student writes one or more ending for each line supplied. For the line, "Flowers now are growing," these examples were written:

> Flowers now are growing.
> And the grass is showing.

> Flowers now are growing.
> Gentle winds are blowing.

> Flowers now are growing,
> And the grass needs mowing.

> Flowers now are growing;
> Baseballs we are throwing.

Triplets

The triplet, an intriguing verse form which is not widely used, offers interesting possibilities as a form of rhymed poetry which young writers can create effectively. These three-line poems tell a brief story and are often humorous. As with the couplet, the initial experience can be a group composition. Teachers who have used this verse form have found that students are more successful if each first produces a rhyme list.

● Each child selects a word that interests him. The word selected must be one that rhymes easily, so you may choose to provide a list from which each person selects his word; for example, PLANE, JET, TRAIN, CAR,

SWIM, FISH, PLAY, BOOK, SKY, RIDE, GAME, SING, BOX, FORT, EAT, DOG, CAT, BALL, SEA. The word chosen is then written at the top of a sheet of paper and a column of rhyming words is developed. Three related words are used to compose a triplet.

From a list of words rhyming with GAY one person produced the following triplet:

> Our cat likes to play;
> His antics are gay.
> "See me?" his eyes say.

Another poet used the word SEA to inspire this triplet:

> Standing silent before the sea
> I thought the water talked to me
> Then laughed aloud with sudden glee.[9]

● An interesting variation which we developed to add to the enjoyment of writing triplets as a verse form is the TRIANGULAR TRIPLET.[10] As in the example, the reader may begin reading at any point of the triangle. The poem must be composed so the lines may be in any order.

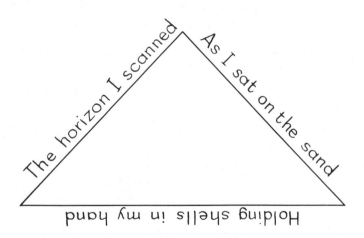

Limericks

"Did you know there is a city in Ireland named Limerick through which flows the River Shannon?" The limerick, which actually consists of a triplet and a couplet, is a form of verse which students usually enjoy. The form has consistently been used for humorous, nonsense verse

[9] Tiedt, Sidney, and Iris M. Tiedt, *The Elementary Teacher's Complete Ideas Handbook* (Englewood Cliffs, N.J.: Prentice-Hall, 1965), p. 93.
[10] Tiedt, Sidney and Iris M. Tiedt, *Creative Writing Ideas* (San Jose, Calif.: Contemporary Press, 1964, p. 19.

which perhaps explains its appeal for young people. A number of examples can be read from the verse of Edward Lear and others. Write one example like the following on the board so that the form can be examined together:

> There once was a boy from Rome
> Who never used a comb.
>   His hair was a sight;
>   It never looked right!
> A boy like that should stay home!

The triplet consists of lines 1, 2, and 5, whereas lines 3 and 4 form a couplet. Students will soon observe, too, that limericks often begin with the words, "There once was ...," which is helpful to the beginner, but the use of these words is not mandatory. Remind students to arrange the wording so that easily rhymed words end each line.

● Limericks can be written about characters from familiar literature—Tom Sawyer, Jack Horner, Charlotte, Henry Huggins, Homer Price, Ellen Tibbets—to relate interest in reading to that of writing verse.

> Tom Sawyer was a barefoot lad;
> Far from good, not really bad.
>   Aunt Polly he teased,
>   Sid and Mary displeased.
> His story will make your heart glad.

● Have students invent the strangest animal they can imagine. They can draw or paint pictures of the animals as well as write a limerick to accompany their art.

> There once was a kangeroogo,
> Who would only go where you go.
>   He ate jam and bread
>   And could stand on his head.
> He constantly read Victor Hugo.

Quatrain

The quatrain is the most commonly used verse form, perhaps because of its versatility. You can readily find examples of varied rhyme schemes —*aabb, abab, abcb,* and others. An effective method of introducing the quatrain to a class is to write several on the board with the class commenting on the similarities and the differences:

1. Quatrains contain four lines.
2. The lines are of uniform length.
3. There is rhyme.
4. The rhyme pattern varies.

Students who have had experience in writing poetry will not find the quatrain particularly difficult. One rhyme pattern develops naturally from the couplet as the quatrain is composed of two couplets. The other patterns are not unlike the couplet as the rhyming is still in paired lines although lines may intervene.

● Biographical sketches of authors, historical figures, or other famous people can be depicted through the quatrain with one or more stanzas being written as in this example:

> A silversmith I was by trade,
> But that does not explain my fame.
> By lighting a lantern I warned of a raid
> Have you guessed? What is my name?

● The quatrain can be arranged in varied forms for added interest. Have students create QUADRANGLES which, like Triangular Triplets, can be read from any starting point.

● Encourage students to combine forms of poetry which they know. A completed poem, for example, may consist of three quatrains and a couplet (a sonnet) or a series of quatrains may be used to form a poem of any length.

Additional poetry forms

In addition to the more common varieties of poetry forms already discussed, additional forms have been developed which can be introduced to the more able student or to a class which shows unusual interest and ability. Familiar forms include:

1. Octave: Eight-line stanza (varied rhyme pattern)
2. Sonnet: An octave plus a sestet (6 lines)—Italian
                Three quatrains plus a couplet—English
3. Blank verse: Unrhymed iambic pentameter

To further the more talented student's interest in poetry there are a number of other intriguing forms of poetry which can prove most challenging. Try some of the following:

● Acrostic poems are poems of varied length and rhyme scheme. The unusual aspect of such poems is that the first letter of each line is part of a word which can be read vertically. Poems have occasionally been written in this fashion to spell the name of a famous person who is being honored by the poet, and in at least one case the name of the poet himself is spelled. Following is a short example which spells the subject of the poem—SPRING. (Note the rhyme scheme in this poem.)

> Silent the winds come a'bringing,
> Primroses, dogwood and heather.
> Rapidly winter has vanished;
> Into the past it is banished.
> Now in bright Aprilly weather,
> Go we to work lightly singing.

● Cinquains are, as the name reveals, poems of five lines. Although there are many varieties possible for five-line poetry (the limerick is one), the cinquain is an invented form [11] more akin to Haiku. The stress should still remain on the thought to be expressed, but the unrhymed lines of the cinquain are supposed to fit these specifications:

Line 1:   One word (which may be the title)
Line 2:   Two words (describing the title)
Line 3:   Three words (an action)
Line 4:   Four words (a feeling)
Line 5:   One word (referring to the title)

Here are examples written by college students who, like you, were venturing into poetry:

> RAINBOW—
> Sky's umbrella
> Turned upside down
> Lovely splash of color
> Aftermath.
> KAYE HAWLEY

[11] This form has been attributed to Adelaide Crapsey, a minor American poet and author of *Verse* (Rochester, N.Y.: Manas Press, 1914).

WEEKEND—
Carefree days
Sleeping-in on Saturday
Relaxed, warm, cheery
Contentment.

FRANCES CLEARY

● Tanka are five-lined Japanese poems which contain a Haiku (the first three lines). Like the Haiku, they are unrhymed and follow a well-defined syllabic pattern with a total of 31 syllables for entire poem:

Line 1:   5 syllables
Line 2:   7 syllables
Line 3:   5 syllables
Line 4:   7 syllables
Line 5:   7 syllables

Following is an example of the Tanka:

Silver raindrops fall:
A puddle of water stands.
Ocean before me,
All the world is reflected.
Look hard and you see black mud.

IRENE TABATA

● The Diamante [12] (dee ah mahn' tay) is a seven-line contrast poem which forms a diamond, thus:

1 word :   subject noun
2 words: adjectives
3 words: participles (-ing, -ed)
4 words: nouns related to subject
3 words: participles
2 words: adjectives
1 word :   noun (opposite of subject)

Air
Balmy, soft
Floating, wafting, soothing
Typhoon, wind, gale, cyclone
Twisting, howling
Bitter, cold
Blast.

VERA HARRYMAN

● The Septolet consists of 7 lines (14 words) followed this pattern; note the break between the two parts:

[12] This form and those which follow were invented by Iris M. Tiedt.

———————

—————————

———————————

—————————————

—————

———————

—————————————

Kitten
Padding stealthily
Amongst green grasses
Most intent.

Bird
Ascends rapidly
Causing great disappointment

BEVERLEY OLDFIELD

● The Quinzaine (kăn zĕn′) consists of 15 syllables in 3 lines (7, 5, 3) which make a statement followed by a question as in this example by a teacher-student:

Boys screaming in the distance—
When will they drop to stillness
On this dusk?

IRMA JOHNSON

● A Quintain (kwĭn ten′) is a syllabic progression: 2, 4, 6, 8, 10, thus:

Poems
Read for pleasure
Before the bright firelight
Words meant for all those who enjoy
Delightful, soothing, lovable music.

L. WILLE

Ways with Poetry

Poetry can become an integral part of the elementary school classroom in many different ways. Why, then, is poetry not evident in many rooms? The reasons given are numerous:

"I don't read well."

"The children aren't interested."

"We don't have time for poetry."

These excuses are far from valid, however, for the teacher or prospective teacher can learn to read poetry. The children will be interested in poetry if the teacher is interested and if stimulating experiences are planned. And time for poetry can be found by the resourceful teacher who introduces poetry in varied ways.

Reading poetry aloud

The teacher is the logical person to introduce the reading of poetry to the class, selecting poems which have proved popular with children for many years. Good poems for reading aloud can be about almost any topic, but they must have appeal—rhythm, humor, narrative. Some poems which we have enjoyed reading aloud in the classroom include:

The Elf and the Dormouse	Oliver Herford
The Clown	Dorothy Aldis
Whisky Frisky	Anonymous
There Once Was a Puffin	Florence P. Jaques
The Woodpecker	Elizabeth M. Roberts
Trains	James S. Tippett
Who Has Seen the Wind?	Christina Rossetti
Sneezles	A. A. Milne
Sea Fever	John Masefield
Eletelephony	Laura E. Richards
Daffodils	William Wordsworth
Antonio	Laura E. Richards
My Shadow	Robert Louis Stevenson
I Think Mice Are Nice	Rose Fyleman
The Road Not Taken	Robert Frost

Children are very much impressed by poetry which their own teacher has written. Have you tried any of the suggestions for writing poetry discussed in this chapter? If you do, you will be more familiar with the technique described and you will also have samples of your own poetry to share with the class you teach. Following our own sagacious advice, here are several poems which we have written as we experimented with varied techniques—it's fun!

Cherry blossoms white
Adorn aseptic classroom—
Touch of rare beauty.

SWT

(Written after college class
learned to write Haiku.)

FREE

One day I walked
Beside the sea.
  I looked for shells;
  I looked for stones;
And all' of them were free!

IT

WHAT CAN YOU DO?

A dog can bark;
A horse can trot;
A hen can lay an egg.

A cat can mew;
A bird can sing;
A stork stands on one leg.

What can you do?

I can walk, and
I can talk, and
I can print my name.

I can hop, and
I can stop, and
I can play a game.

I can sing, and
I can swing, and
I can color, too.

I can ride, and
I can slide, and
I can play with you!

IT

After children become familiar with a variety of poetry, they, too, can choose favorites to read to the class. Discuss the qualities of effective reading of poetry, pointing out the fact that sentences appear in poetry just as in prose, and that punctuation must be observed so that the poem "makes sense."

● A class can practice reading poems orally together after hearing the teacher read. Stress the reading of sentences rather than lines to avoid a sing-song effect which is often associated with poetry. Try these with middle graders:

Theme in Yellow	Carl Sandburg
A Story in the Snow	Pearl R. Crouch
Brooms	Dorothy Aldis

● Children can prepare a tape recording of their reading of poetry. Each child reads one poem, either original or by known poets, which may be grouped on one theme—the season, a holiday, favorite things, vehicles, traveling. Music can be played softly to produce a pleasant background for the recording.

The poetry chorus

The reading of poetry has much the same attributes as the singing of songs in a group. The values of the poetry chorus include:

1. Participation by even shy children
2. Sharing of enjoyable language experience
3. Group empathy developed
4. Improvement of pronunciation
5. Vocabulary development
6. Enjoyment and appreciation of poetry

The poetry chorus does not have to be an extremely complicated matter. Almost any poem offers potential for group enjoyment. Students will become interested in experimenting with different effects with spoken poetry. Encourage suggestions of possible effects to be achieved through varied grouping of voices, different ways of interpreting lines, or even the use of sound effects when appropriate. Poetry interpretations can be varied through these techniques:

1. Use of one solo voice for a few lines
2. Division of the class into two to four groups that alternate lines or stanzas
3. Boy and girl groups (light and dark voices) speak lines to vary tonal quality
4. Varied speed of lines
5. Experiment with varying pitch for unusual effect

Treat the group as a chorus, using some of the same techniques which you might use in singing. Some poems can be read in unison, but others lend themselves to part work—many verses, repetitive lines or refrains, conversation, contrasted stanzas. Students have fun saying poetry together just as they do singing songs together; they soon build up an excellent repertoire.

● A poem which is effective with older elementary school students is Lewis Carroll's "Father William," which consists of a conversation between a father and his son. The girls, with their higher voices, can speak the young man's part with sprightly rhythm while the boys, use their lower voices to portray the part of Father William, speaking slowly and impressively until the final verse.

FATHER WILLIAM

Lewis Carroll

"You are old, Father William," the young man said,
    "And your hair has become very white;
And yet you incessantly stand on your head—
    Do you think, at your age, it is right?"

"In my youth," Father William replied to his son,
    "I feared it might injure the brain;
But, now that I'm perfectly sure I have none,
    Why, I do it again and again."

"You are old," said the youth, "as I mentioned before,
    And have grown most uncommonly fat;
Yet you turn a back-somersault in at the door—
    Pray, what is the reason of that?"

"In my youth," said the sage, as he shook his gray locks,
    "I kept all my limbs very supple
By the use of this ointment—one shilling a box—
    Allow me to sell you a couple?"

"You are old," said the youth, "and your jaws are too weak
    For anything tougher than suet;
Yet you finished the goose, with the bones and the beak—
    Pray, how did you manage to do it?"

"In my youth," said his father, "I took to the law,
    And argued each case with my wife;
And the muscular strength which it gave to my jaw
    Has lasted the rest of my life."

"You are old," said the youth, "one would hardly suppose
    That your eye was as steady as ever;
Yet you balanced an eel on the end of your nose—
    What made you so awfully clever?"

"I have answered three questions, and that is enough,"
    Said his father. "Don't give yourself airs!
Do you think I can listen all day to such stuff?
    Be off, or I'll kick you down-stairs!"

● Even the youngest of children enjoy repeating the lines of poetry if the poem has rhythm, repetition, and some humor. Other poems which are especially suitable for speaking in a group are:

Puppy and I: A. A. Milne   (Conversation)
Poor Old Woman: Anonymous   (Refrain and Repetition)
The Mysterious Cat: Vachel Lindsay   (Repetition)
The Owl and the Pussy-Cat: Edward Lear   (Repetition)
The Monkeys and the Crocodile: Laura E. Richards   (Repetition,
                Conversation)

Music and poetry

Many familiar poems have been set to music; for example, some of the nursery rhymes, "Grandfather's Clock," Christmas carols, "Twinkle, Twinkle, Little Star," "The Star-Spangled Banner," "Home, Home, Sweet Home," and many others. Children are intrigued by seeing the verses of the songs in the form of a poem.

Interest in singing poems that someone else has set to music can lead to the selection of a poem by each child for which a melody can be written. A piano, small xylophone, or tonette will assist the students in producing the music they feel is appropriate to the poem selected. They will want to learn something about musical notation in order to write their songs with the words placed below the notes, thus:

The original poetry of children can also be set to a melody which they can sing for the class or teach to other members of the class. This technique lends further importance to the poetry produced by the child. His own poem set to music can be mounted inside a decorated "song-sheet" to be used as a gift for his parents.

Music can also be used to assist the development of an experience in either reading or writing poetry.

● Play appropriate music before reading a poem. Before reading the poem "Sea Fever," for example, play music which suggests the surf. Oriental music can set the stage for the writing of Haiku.

● Music can also be played while poetry is being read. A soft musical background serves to provide a theme and unites a group of poems. Play Christmas music softly while Christmas poetry is read.

Art and poetry

Art techniques offer varied, challenging ways to enhance the pleasure of poetry.

● Each student can select a poem to portray in a poetry broadside (poster). The poem can be typed or printed on a card or sheet of paper which is mounted on the broadside in some appropriate place. One youngster chose to print his poem, "The Balloon Man," on a bright yellow balloon which floated through the air above a town.

Another concealed several poems about clouds beneath cloud shapes which were lifted to reveal the poems, "White Sheep," "The Cloud," and "Clouds."

● The collage, an abstract presentation of an idea or theme, is another excellent medium for presenting a poem. In order to construct a collage the student must first examine the poem selected for elements which can be portrayed. Some poems, for example, "The Owl and the Pussy-cat," contain many concrete references which can be included in a collage. Other poems which convey a mood will require a thoughtful use of color, texture, and shapes to help convey that mood.

● Crayons can be used to tell the story of a poem read. "See if you can draw a picture which will make the class know which poem you have in mind." Each picture can then be presented to the class to see if anyone can guess which poem is pictured. The artist can read the poem he selected.

Poetry and the social sciences

Much good poetry treats topics related to the areas of history and geography. One immediately thinks of Stephen Vincent Benét and his wife, Rosemary Carr Benét, who have written many fine poems depicting the figures of American history. A collection of these poems is entitled: *Book of Americans* (Rinehart, 1933). Poems can be read aloud by either the teacher or a child to add interest to a study of history. "Abraham Lincoln" and "Nancy Hanks" are two titles which could be featured during a study of the Civil War. Other ideas relating poetry to social studies include:

● An exciting way to present background material for a study of foreign countries is through the reading of poetry by poets from these countries. Good translations of many poets are available, and it is interesting, too, to use short passages in the original language.

Here is the refrain of a poem by Spanish poet Jose de Espronceda, "Canción del Pirata."

> Que es mi barco mi tesoro;
> Que es mi Dios la libertad;
> Mi ley la fuerza y el viento;
> Mi única patria la mar.

SONG OF THE PIRATE

> My boat is my treasure;
> Liberty is my god;
> My law the force and the wind;
> My only homeland the sea.

● Other poets can be explored as different countries are featured in a truly humanistic approach to the social studies. Suggested here are poets whose work is available in translation from a variety of countries:

France: Victor Hugo.
Scandinavia: Dag Hammarskjold, *Markings.* (Knopf, 1964).
Russia: Yevgeny Yevtushenko.
Japan: Haiku, Tanka (See earlier discussion).
England: Wordsworth, Shelley

Poetry on display

Poetry can be brought into the classroom also as part of an attractive display—bulletin board, poster, mobile, table exhibit. Poetry is a suitable addition to a display on almost any topic. A poem or two can be typed or printed (let students help select and prepare) to be mounted on a bulletin board which features Mexico, England, The West, Exploring; even mathematics topics can include a poem such as Carl Sandburg's "Arithmetic." Here are a few suggestions for incorporating poetry in displays:

● For a seasonal display print a short poem on light colored paper or poster board. Around this poem can be scattered appropriate motifs on which are printed words related to the season, thus:

In October use the poem, "Autumn Woods" by James S. Tippett or "Fall" by Aileen L. Fisher.

Around the printed poem scatter large leaves cut from colored construction paper on which are printed words and phrases which connote autumn.

falling leaves	Columbus Day	frosty grass
Halloween	chilly nights	fall flowers
football	pumpkins	shorter days
crisp air	colored leaves	Indian summer

● Lines of poetry, phrases from poems, or titles of poems often provide excellent captions for a display. The whole poem may then be included as part of the display. Try these suggestions:

THE FLAG IS PASSING BY!

A patriotic display about citizenship might feature this poem, "The Flag Goes By," by Henry H. Bennett.

SING ME A SONG

This phrase, which appears in "Sea Shell" by Amy Lowell, can be used to feature the poetry written by the class.

SEA FEVER

The title of John Masefield's familiar poem makes an effective caption for pictures or writings about the sea.

A WORLD OF WONDERS

This caption comes from a line of Walter de la Mare's "Dream-Song" which could be used with children's writing about their own dreamings.

● Frequently display the poetry written by the class even though individual contributions may be very short.

> The three-line Haiku can be printed on small paper fans or colored butterflies which are scattered over a board.
>
> Triangular Triplets can be written on bright construction paper triangles of varied size. Glue two of the same size on a triangle of cardboard so that poems appear on both sides of the triangle. Suspend these triangles mobile fashion.
>
> Cut a large tree shape from black or brown paper and fasten to a bulletin board. Short poems can be written on flower shapes which are placed on the branches of the tree.
>
> Use a large paper map as the background for a display of poetry about travel or exploration. Each poem can be written on a ship or plane shape (let each student design his own).

● Collections of student compositions can be exhibited on a table. Each child may compile an individual booklet of his best poetry written over a period of time or the class may combine efforts to produce one or more books of poetry. Have students prepare an attractive design for the cover with a title, for example:

> POETRY PLEASES
>
> THE POETRY OF GREG WESTON (the child's name)
>
> OUR POETRY
>
> OCTOBER VERSES
>
> ARE YOU WELL-VERSED?

Books to Investigate

Arnstein, Flora J., *Poetry in the Elementary Classroom*. Champaign, Ill.: National Council of Teachers of English, 1962.

Behn, Harry, *Cricket Songs*. New York: Harcourt, 1964. A delightful collection of Haiku.

Ciardi, John, *How Does a Poem Mean?* Boston: Houghton Mifflin, 1959. A provocative invitation to explore poetry.

Henderson, Harold G., *An Introduction to Haiku*. Garden City, N.Y.: Doubleday, 1958.

Oakland School District, *Find Time for Poetry*. Hayward, California: Alameda County School Dept., 1964. A creative guide to poetry in the primary grades.

O'Neill, Mary, *Hailstones and Halibut Bones: Adventures in Color*. Garden City, N.Y.: Doubleday, 1961. Imaginative poetry about colors; film available also.

Walsh, Chad, *Doors into Poetry*. Englewood Cliffs, N.J.: Prentice-Hall, 1962. An excellent introduction to poetry.

Walter, Nina, *Let Them Write Poetry*. New York: Holt, 1962.

Ward, Herman M. ed., *Poems for Pleasure*. New York: Hill and Wang, 1963. A paperback collection of favorite poems recommended for you.

> ...Words are things, and a small drop of ink
> Falling, like dew upon a thought, produces
> That which makes thousands, perhaps millions,
> think.
>
> *Lord Byron*

11

Reading as a Language Skill

What is reading? We cannot return one glib definition, for reading is a many-faceted act viewed from many perspectives. It has been pointed out, for example, that reading involves skill development, a visual act, a type of perception, a reflection of cultural background, and an act of higher mental processes which has a continued relationship to a child's social and personal development.[1] Kress defines reading as "thinking that is stimulated by written symbols." [2] The definition of reading by the reader himself might focus on adventure, entertainment, and information, for the voracious reader knows that "Reading," as Charles de Montesquieu observed, "enables a man to exchange the wearisome hours of life which come to everyone for hours of delight."

However we define reading, one generalization which we can safely make is that reading is more than the physical visual act of recognizing words on a printed page, and it is a highly important aspect of learning about which there is yet much to be learned. As Heilman points out:

> Learning to read is probably one of the most important accomplishments that the child will achieve during his formal schooling. This is not to imply that learning to read will be his most difficult or dramatic academic achievement, for if he gets off to a good

[1] George D. Spache, *Reading in the Elementary School* (Boston: Allyn & Bacon, 1964), p. 26.
[2] Roy A. Kress, "That All May Learn to Read," First Annual Reading Conference at Syracuse University (June, 1959).

start the whole process may be so uneventful that he will not recall how this particular learning took place. On the other hand, if he fails in reading, the frustrations and defeats which can beset him in the future are so numerous and varied that they have never been tabulated in one source.[3]

Teaching Reading

Our schools have typically been reading-centered, and this tendency continues to be true of the elementary school. Reading is only one facet of language development; like the skill of listening, reading is a receptive skill and can be accomplished at a higher rate of speed then can speaking or composing, both of which require the human mechanism to "do something" physical. Although usually taught last, therefore, reading soon overtakes other language skills, particularly that of writing.

With the knowledge explosion comes an ever greater need to read, for the number of books and periodicals produced each year is overwhelming. Because it is literally impossible to read everything printed, emphasis must be placed on selection of that which is to be read. We become more aware, too, of our purposes in reading as we vary the type of reading to the purpose. The limited nature of time, that priceless commodity, also leads us to attempt to speed up the reading process. Concern for reading is universal as individual educational aspirations and social goals rise. As college attendance increases, a greater number of persons will require advanced skills of reading to accomplish the educational task.

Progress in reading instruction

Criticism there is, and critics there will always be, but when we survey the history of reading instruction in the United States, we cannot deny that reading has progressed. Analyzing trends in reading as they have appeared historically, we can develop the following outline: [4, 5]

Prior to 1900	Spelling and alphabet approach to reading Moralistic reading materials; the *Bible* *The New England Primer,* 1683 *The American Spelling Book,* 1790 *McGuffey Readers,* 1836
1900-1910	Reading-focused curriculum Emphasis on oral reading

[3] Arthur Heilman, *Principles and Practices of Teaching Reading* (Columbus, Ohio: Merrill, 1961), p. 33.

[4] Nila B. Smith, "What Have We Accomplished in Reading?—A Review of the Past Fifty Years," *Elementary English* (March, 1961), pp. 141-50.

[5] Charles C. Fries, *Linguistics and Reading* (New York: Holt, 1962), pp. 1-34.

1910-1920	Scientific analysis applied to reading achievement Standardized tests of reading Beginnings of silent reading
1920-1930	Many research studies Concept of individual differences Remediation in reading
1930-1940	Reading as part of the Activity Program Reading Readiness concept
1940-1950	Focus on adult literacy Mass media influence Interrelationships of language arts
1950-1960	Public criticism of reading instruction Influence of television Individualized instruction
1960-1970	Innovation in beginning reading instruction Concern for education of disadvantaged child Influence of linguistics on study of reading Technology in reading instruction Stress on literature in reading and English programs

As we consider current trends in teaching reading, we note that improvement of reading instruction is still a major concern in education. As Lewis noted in 1966, the following areas still merit research:

1. How to reduce the learning difficulties inherent in the very complex process called reading
2. How to individualize instruction for children with a wide range of background and abilities [6]

It is interesting to speculate about future developments in reading instruction. Will reading be de-emphasized as other methods of assimilating knowledge are perfected? Experiments are now being conducted, for example, with instruction during sleep. Researchers note also the possibilities for listening as a way of learning, citing the high rate of speed at which we can listen compared to the slower rate of reading. We have only begun to explore, too, the potentials of audio-visual aids as means for imparting knowledge. Is it possible that we, who have focused attention in education almost exclusively on reading, will eventually depend on other methods of learning and transmitting knowledge?

Contemporary objectives of teaching reading

What ends are we trying to achieve as we plan a reading program? Usually, lists of objectives are stated in terms of what we adults would

[6] Edward R. Lewis, *The First R: A Survey of Selected Current Practices in Reading Instruction*, Monograph 18 (Burlingame, Calif.: California Elementary School Administrators Assn., 1966), p. 1.

have children do, but what are the aims of a reading program for the student himself? Might they not be stated somewhat like this?

A STUDENT'S READING AIMS

I want to read easily and with relative speed,

> To learn new words and to increase my vocabulary,
> To increase my rate of speed in reading,
> To read interesting books for fun.

I want to explore all kinds of books,

> To browse freely in the library,
> To get help in choosing books sometimes,
> To hear about new books.

I want to find out things through reading,

> To learn about different lands,
> To discover new ideas,
> To find out how other people live.

I want to read good stories,

> To compare different kinds of stories,
> To admire an author's performance with words,
> To enjoy the story he tells,
> To try to write stories myself.

I want to tell others about the ideas I have,

> To talk about ideas with other students,
> To compare points of view about one book,
> To be able to read aloud.

If we subscribe to these objectives for the reading program we must seriously consider patterning the reading program to meet these needs. We shall explore the possibilities for incorporating these objectives in the reading curriculum as we describe an effective reading program for contemporary elementary school students.

Innovation in Reading

It is impossible in one chapter to discuss all approaches to reading instruction with sufficient depth to be able to analyze their strengths and shortcomings. For that reason we will discuss only a few selected approaches which are both innovative in nature and appear to have unusual promise. New methods in reading include the Initial Teaching Alphabet, Programmed Instruction, Language-Experience Instruction, the Phonemic Approach, and Individualized Reading. Before studying innovative programs we should briefly examine the reading program as it typically exists at present.

The basal reader approach

The method of instruction most widely used in reading at the present time is the "basal reader," or "controlled vocabulary," approach. Almost every textbook company has a series of reading books for grades one through eight, usually with two or more titles prepared for each grade level. This highly structured method of teaching reading is based on student texts, workbooks, and teacher's editions which provide detailed guidance for the teacher. Use of the basal reader series has the following attributes:

1. It represents an early attempt to provide for the sequential development of reading instruction.
2. It assists the beginning teacher who is uncertain about the teaching of reading.
3. It provides the poorly trained teacher with an approach to reading which is acceptable.

As new approaches to reading have been explored, the basal reader approach has received much critical attention. Slavish adherence to the "system" has sometimes resulted in attitudes like that of the principal who stated: "I don't care how well Ann reads. She is to go through the basic reader as any other fourth grader. And I don't want to find her in the library again doing special work." [7] The following questions have been raised:

1. Can any *one* system provide for individual needs of students?
2. Is the material read in this reading program of highest literary quality?
3. Is the basal reader program monopolizing the reading program to the exclusion of the teaching of literature in the elementary school?
4. Are teachers using the program to its fullest potential or is it used as a "crutch"?
5. Are teachers, especially at upper grade levels, really *teaching* reading?
6. Are children motivated to read each story or are reading experiences assigned routinely, with workbook pages used as *busy work*?
7. Has the basal reader program been successful in producing a citizenry that reads?

Initial teaching alphabet

Consisting of an augmented Roman alphabet of 44 letters, the Initial Teaching Alphabet, commonly known by the acronym ITA, represents an attempt to provide a one-to-one correspondence between the sounds of English and the letters which we used to signal each sound. To avoid confusion, no special upper case letters are used. This alphabet is reproduced on the opposite page.

[7] Cynthia Parsons, Education Editor, *The Christian Science Monitor* (January 22, 1965).

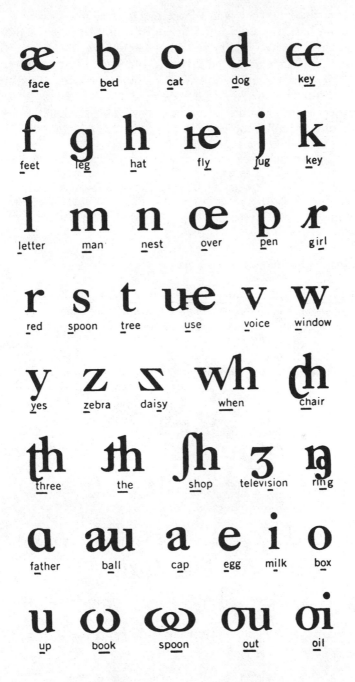

æ face b bed c cat d dog cc key

f feet g leg h hat ie fly j jug k key

l letter m man n nest œ over p pen ɹ girl

r red s spoon t tree ue use v voice w window

y yes z zebra ƨ daisy wh when ch chair

th three th the ſh shop ʒ television ŋ ring

ɑ father au ball a cap e egg i milk o box

u up ω book ѡ spoon ou out oi oil

The contribution of Sir James Pitman, ITA was introduced in England in 1959 and has been used in both England and the United States. The Early to Read Series consists of seven books using the Initial Teaching Alphabet; the last book of the series is aimed at assisting the transition to traditional orthography. Both the reading texts and titles from children's literature are available.

An experimental program in the Fremont Unified School District, California, found the following advantages in the use of ITA:

1. First-grade children learned to write creatively at the middle of the year.
2. Interest level of ITA materials was considered higher, with less repetition and with vocabulary similar to that used by the child.
3. With the sound symbols, the child could attack any word.
4. Parents were favorably impressed.

Disadvantages noted were:

1. Difficulties when children transferred to other schools.
2. Expense of the program (texts were not state-adopted).
3. Substitute teachers were unable to teach this alphabet.[8]

One creative teacher who teaches in the above school district produces materials like this to use with her class:

the beetls
bie j. oe'neell

the beetls ar a swinging grœp,
thae reelly ar the fad.
but when ie plae thaer records loud,
it maeks mie paerents mad.

[8] James T. Howden, "Exploring the Initial Teaching Alphabet," *The First R* (Burlingame, Calif.: California Elementary School Administrators Assn., 1966), pp. 21-2.

She has also found it relatively easy to adapt familiar songs for use with children who are reading with the Initial Teaching Alphabet as in this "translation" of the folksong, "Go Tell Aunt Rhody."

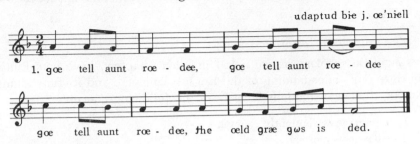

udaptud bie j. œ'niell

1. goe tell aunt roe - dee, goe tell aunt roe - dee

goe tell aunt roe - dee, the œld græ gws is ded.

Words adapted by Janie O'Neill. Used by permission.

Programmed instruction

Books have been prepared by Sullivan Associates which guide the beginning reader step by step through the acquisition of reading skills. Programmed materials can be especially helpful at varied levels of reading development ranging from visual discrimination to the study of affixes to exploration of literature concepts. Programmed materials include not only books and workbooks but also "machines" which immediately indicate whether the student's answer is correct. An interesting study is being made of instruction in reading with a computer-assisted instructional system at Stanford University where first grade children are being taught to read.[9]

The advantages of programmed instruction are several:

1. Programs can be used individually with little aid from the teacher, and each student works at his own rate of speed.
2. The response is immediately checked against the right answer; there is no waiting period for correction of papers.
3. A carefully designed sequence will cover all points in a developmental program.
4. Programs are planned in such small learning units that children are able to succeed.
5. The teacher is freed for *teaching;* drill type tasks, for example, spelling, identification of letters, can be programmed.

Disadvantages of the programmed approach lie in the following:

1. Teacher resistance to the idea of a "teaching machine."
2. Limitation to use with factual knowledge, fixed learnings.
3. Slow students are less motivated to work independently.

[9] Richard C. Atkinson, Project Director. *Progress Report: A Reading Curriculum for a Computer-Assisted Instructional System: The Stanford Project.* Stanford, Calif.: Stanford University, 1966.

Realizing the limitations of the programmed approach, elementary school teachers and reading experts are discovering the possibilities of programmed materials used in conjunction with other approaches to reading.

The phonemic approach

Linguistic scholars, as we noted in other chapters, have contributed much to our understanding of the English language and its functioning. Among their contributions have been the following concepts:

1. Language is constantly changing.
2. Change is normal.
3. English sentences follow specific patterns.
4. Word order conveys meaning.
5. There are specific phonemes and graphemes for the English language.
6. The grammar of a language is its structure.
7. Usage is not rigid but relative.

The application of these concepts of language has revolutionized the teaching of language and approaches to composition. It is not surprising that linguists have also attempted to apply linguistic concepts to reading instruction. Thus far, however, the results are disappointing, for the linguistic approach, almost solely a phonemic-graphemic presentation, has produced material like this:

had	can	cat	bag
lad	Dan	fat	nag
pad	man	hat	rag
sad	pan	rat	tag

Dan had a bat.
Has Ann a bag?
Ann had a bag.
Nat had a nag.
A fat cat had a rat.
A man had a hat.
Fat had a nap.[10]

The linguist's approach to reading is essentially based on the presentation of words by phonemic and graphemic groups. As in the linguistic approaches to spelling, the child is introduced to a family of words, for example, *look, book, cook, took, hook.* Those advocating this linguistic approach to beginning reading point out that children can learn groups of words rather than single words. While learning *eat,* the child might

---

[10] Leonard Bloomfield and Clarence L. Barnhart, *Let's Read, A Linguistic Approach* (Detroit: Wayne State University, 1961), p. 2.

just as well learn *beat, heat, meat, neat, seat,* and so on. It is a simple step also to branch out to related phonograms as in this Linguistic Relationship Diagram.

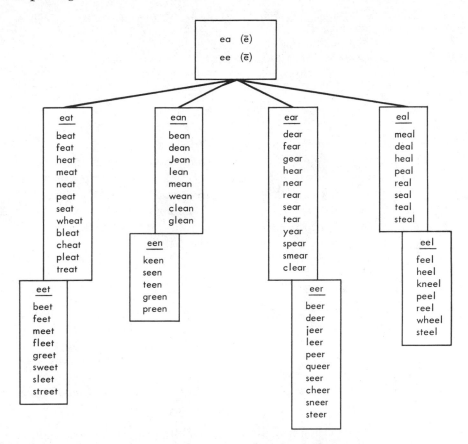

Although this approach has validity for the teaching of spelling, as an answer to beginning reading instruction it leaves much to be desired. What is it that linguists are ignoring in approaching reading?—children's interests, their previously acquired large vocabulary, their knowledge of language patterns. Critics of the "basal reader" approach to reading instruction have long decried the "Dick and Jane" content of basal readers which relied on sight recognition of words which were repeated *ad nauseam* to enable the child to learn the words.

Are the linguists offering a more stimulating content when they suggest reading matter like that advocated by Fries //Pat a fat cat// //Pat a fat rat// [11] It is audacious, perhaps, but enlightening, to compare this

[11] Charles C. Fries, *Linguistics and Reading* (New York: Holt, 1962), p. 203.

material with that produced by Theodore Geisel, hardly a linguistic scholar, in *The Cat in the Hat* (Random House).

As one critic of the linguistic approach notes:

> One danger of phonemic reading programs is that their scientific base will give them great respectability and they will gain wide use before they have been sufficiently tried. There are two other dangers. One is that fuller application of linguistics to reading will be delayed. The other is that educators will reject linguistics while rejecting phonemic reading programs.[12]

We must be cognizant of the "faddish" tendency to tack the magic "linguistic" label on all English and reading programs. It is important to probe further to determine how linguistic findings have been brought to bear on content presented, how linguistics has improved effectiveness of instruction. We must not hesitate to criticize because we are intimidated by the reputation of those who are, sometimes for the first time, delving into the field of reading instruction. Linguistics has made a tremendous contribution to the study of English, but much rethinking and study of applied linguistics must take place before its fullest potential is realized, particularly in the teaching of reading.

Language-experience

Associated with the work of teachers in San Diego County, California, the language-experience approach to reading considers reading as part of the total language development of the child. Beginning experiences in reading evolve from experiences with oral and written language. Child-dictated experiences, child-composed sentences and stories, furnish the material for reading as described by Van Allen and Lee.[13] The steps followed are these:

1. An experience common to the group—field trip, story read, an experiment, film, classroom incident, topic introduced by the teacher, a picture
2. Class discussion with sentences recorded by the teacher, aide, or students
3. Reading the composed story aloud, discussion of words
4. Duplicated copy of story is used in individual and group reading experiences
5. Follow-up activities—varied reading opportunities, dictation of individual sentences according to ability, small group work to extend abilities, language study, listening to literature, extension of vocabularies

[12] Kenneth S. Goodman, "The Linguistics of Reading," *The Elementary School Journal* (April, 1964), pp. 357-8.
[13] R. Van Allen and Doris M. Lee, *Learning to Read through Experience* (New York: Appleton, 1963).

This approach to reading is distinctly different from others described, for it moves away from the prepared reading text. It appears to have the following advantages:

1. Reading material has high interest value; the child is able to read what he has composed. He knows the vocabulary.
2. The approach develops according to individual needs, interests, abilities; the child reads because he *wants* to read.
3. Repetition of skill instruction in separate areas of language study, for example, phonology, is eliminated through a total approach to language study.
4. Reading material reflects the child's knowledge of English grammar—sentence patterns, word order, intonation.

The chief disadvantage of the language-experience approach from the view of a teacher is that it is less highly structured. Each group of children, each child, having varied experiential backgrounds, will produce different reading material. The teacher is required to be more flexible, and for that reason, may feel less secure in working with this type of approach which she must guide as it evolves. This is the same difficulty the teacher encounters in any oral language program. Another disadvantage which is noted is that content is limited by the child's knowledge; there is no provision for vocabulary development. New concepts and vocabulary must be introduced through planned experiences, through wide reading of literature, and through incidental instruction.

In spite of this demand on teacher ingenuity and skill in working with the group as it learns and develops its own materials (which makes for a more creative approach to teaching), this approach warrants careful consideration, for is it not a truly "linguistic" approach? Recognizing its limitations, it appears to the authors that the total language approach to language, composition, and reading (evolving quickly into literature) potentially incorporates all the concepts of linguistics with our knowledge of the needs of children and the best of learning theory, and therefore has much to commend it as a beginning approach to reading instruction.

Individualized reading

The individualized approach to reading is scarcely a new concept, for it was an essential part of the Progressive Movement in the 1930's. The Winnetka Plan (Illinois) is one example of these earlier attempts to individualize learning. Children read silently at their individual rates of speed, answered prepared questions on the material read, and read aloud individually to the teacher.

Another plan for individualized learning was the Dalton Plan (Massachusetts) which used a laboratory approach to encourage students to achieve self-determined contracts for units of work to be accomplished.

This plan granted the student much freedom and experience in planning and in budgeting his time.

Both of these plans were rigid in content, however, and goals were in terms of adult needs rather than those of the child. Contemporary attempts at individualizing reading instruction stress not only quantity of reading but also the child's motivation to read more extensively. Great varieties of reading materials are needed for a successful individualized reading program.

The advantages of the individualized approach to reading include:

1. Wide use of library materials, free selection.
2. Broader range of reading subjects.
3. Learning experiences are extended.
4. Reading skills are taught through small group approaches.
5. Evaluation includes personal conferences.
6. Stress on individual development to fullest potential.
7. Stimulates the gifted student.

There is no set prescription for individualized program in reading. As Leland Jacobs observes:

> In the first place, "individualized reading" is not a single method with predetermined steps in procedures to be followed. It is not possible to say that every teacher who would individualize guidance in reading must do this or that. It is not feasible or desirable to present a simple, single methodological formulation of what is right in "individualized reading" which every teacher shall follow.[14]

The individualized approach to reading has had excellent results with average and superior readers. The one disadvantage noted is the inability of slow students to cope with the individualized method of working. Better readers enjoy the opportunity to read widely and to share their reading experiences with other students. They also respond to the stimulus of the individual conference.[15] We shall explore individualized reading as a means for bringing literature into the elementary school reading program in the next chapter.

A Forward-Looking Reading Program

Which of these reading programs shall we choose? None of them? All of them? Can we wait until the perfect program is developed? No single approach to reading appears to have all the answers. It is interesting to note that research findings are inconclusive. Studies of individualized

[14] Leland Jacobs, "Individualized Reading Is Not a Thing," in *Individualizing Reading Practices,* Alice Miel, ed. (New York: Teachers College, 1958).
[15] Harry Sartain, "The Roseville Experiment with Individualized Reading," *The Reading Teacher* (April, 1960), p. 277.

instruction, for example, provide findings which favor group instruction as well as findings which show the individualized approach to be best.[16] This discrepancy in research findings points up the fact that the reader must beware of research which is not carefully structured. Also, one must note the nature of the specific programs being compared. At this stage we have no research evidence which conclusively recommends one approach to reading over another. There is a need for well-organized longitudinal studies in reading instruction.

Our only recourse, then, is to be eclectic, selecting those approaches which best serve the needs of a superior reading program, for we must assume the responsibility for providing students of the Space Age with a forward-looking reading program. Our students demand a program that:

1. Begins where the student is and permits progress at individual rates of speed
2. Guarantees success from the initial experiences
3. Stresses development of oral language skills and continues to be closely coordinated with the English program to avoid repetition, as in a well-planned phonological sequence
4. Teaches reading skills using reading material of interest to the child
5. Does not belabor the teaching of skills but moves quickly into a program of wide reading of literature with instruction in literary concepts
6. Uses multimedia to present information and to motivate reading
7. Extends abilities to think—analysis, comparison, criticism, comprehension
8. Experiments with varied approaches to meet individual needs incorporating the best of each approach to reading
9. Stimulates real interest in reading for pleasure and information; develops habits which will extend into adulthood
10. Develops research techniques and familiarity with library tools

As we turn our efforts toward development of an excellent reading program, we might note Stauffer's advice:

> ... one must, first, drop the notion that a basic reader program in and of itself is final and sacred. It is not. Second, one must drop the notion that time can be equated with equality. Not every group must be met every day for the same length of time. Third, the idea that a basic book recommended for a grade level must be "finished" by all pupils in a grade before they can be promoted must be discarded. Fourth, teaching reading as a *memoriter* process by presenting new words in advance of the reading and then having pupils tell back the story must be stopped. If reading is taught as a thinking process, even short basic-reader stories will be read with enthusiasm. . . . Sixth, effective skills of word attack must be

16 Nila B. Smith, *Reading Instruction for Today's Children* (Englewood Cliffs, N.J.,: Prentice-Hall, 1963), pp. 154-9.

taught. Basic reading books do not provide for such skill training; neither do trade books.[17]

How can we best meet the criteria we have established? Let us consider the various approaches to reading in terms of these criteria. It is our observation that the language-experience approach most nearly meets the first four requirements, for the students are highly motivated to read the stories which they have composed, and the stories can be successfully read because the vocabulary is known to the child. Included are interesting words as well as the commonly used vocabulary, the basic sight words which the child needs to know. This reading program is closely coordinated with the English program, for children develop skills of composition and reading as a direct result of spoken language, and children have repeated opportunities to use sentence patterns and varied classes of words before formal grammar study is initiated. Emphasis is placed on the development of listening skills as well as speaking skills as the teacher introduces literature through reading aloud and as many opportunities are provided for dramatization and sharing of experiences.

Linguistic approaches to the teaching of phonology and structure of words can be taught in a well-organized sequence of development which benefits the whole language program (including reading) and avoids the repetition of instruction. The coordination of spelling with reading and composition following the linguistics approach which presents linguistic families—*came, game, tame, lame, same, fame*—is a sound method which makes the spelling task more efficient. These aspects of language are taught in conjunction with the language-experience instruction in beginning reading rather than as three distinct "subjects"—reading, spelling, English.

As soon as the child develops a basic reading vocabulary—and this stage may be reached in first or second grade, depending on the background and ability of the child—he is able to begin reading selections from literature. A core of titles can be assigned to each reading level so that children progress through the wonderful world of children's literature. Titles at the first level might include: [18]

Maurice Sendak, *Where the Wild Things Are.* Monsters can be captivating.
Wanda Gág, *Millions of Cats.* The refrain has appeal.
Dr. Seuss, *The Cat in the Hat.* Simple vocabulary, but fun!
Else H. Minarik, *Little Bear.* Four stories; illustrated by Maurice Sendak.
Syd Hoff, *Danny and the Dinosaur.* Adventures with a museum dinosaur!

[17] Russell G. Stauffer, "Individualized and Group Directed Reading Instruction," *Elementary English* (October, 1960), p. 381.
[18] Elizabeth Guilfoile, *Books for Beginning Readers* (Champaign, Ill.: National Council of Teachers of English, 1962).

What about vocabulary level? What about wordlists? We have too long been hampered by these scientific approaches to a child's vocabulary. The child who comes to school chattering about space flights and other adult information that he grasps with amazing enthusiasm and eagerness should not be hemmed in by that mythical 200 words which supposedly is all he can manage.

We must credit ideas and intriguing words with some motivating power in themselves. Children are fascinated by monsters, so the "wild things" portrayed by Maurice Sendak lead them to read the story which includes interesting words, for example, "rumpus," which children love. We are missing an opportunity to make *readers* of these children.

We should supply, furthermore, the "grown-up" words for concepts, objects, ideas, for children hear them; in many cases they use them; they will delight in reading them, too. As Nancy Larrick points out:

> The practice of teaching children wrong names for things that have relatively simple names is certainly open to question. Indeed, if one purpose of reading is to help the child reach out and grow, why not use the exact word he will hear in school conversation and TV news reports instead of a baby-talk substitute? At first he may miss the more grown-up word in print, but the chances are that he knows it by ear. His pride in learning to read such a word may add to his self-respect and do a great deal to increase his interest in reading.[19]

The child continues to progress by reading literature of increasing difficulty. The coordination of reading and composition continues as the student reads his own compositions, the writing of other students, and the writing of known authors, literature. Both individual and small group approaches to the reading of literature are used, with students being encouraged to discuss literary concepts both as a composer and as one who appreciates the skill of others. This type of discussion is facilitated through individual conferences and student seminars. Varied reading skills are stressed as students work in other subject areas and engage in individual research.

Programmed materials can be drawn into the reading program for the teaching of word attack skills, development of vocabulary, and comprehension. The Initial Teaching Alphabet appears to offer excellent possibilities in reading remediation in that the "new alphabet" has appeal for the reader who has not been successful with other approaches.

We will discard "grade level" limitations which restrict progress and tend to routinize the teaching of reading in favor of an exploratory attitude toward reading which involves three stages: (1) preparation for reading, (2) introduction to reading, and (3) independent reading. Stage

---

[19] Nancy Larrick, *A Teacher's Guide to Children's Books* (Columbus, Ohio: Merrill, 1963), p. 26.

1 occurs during preschool and kindergarten years; Stage 2 may begin in the kindergarten year and extend through first, second, and third grades; Stage 3 may begin in third grade and will continue throughout life.

Preparation for Reading

Encourages positive attitudes toward learning
Develops oral abilities
Provides many listening experiences
Works toward linguistic fluency and sentence expansion
Develops vocabulary—speaking and listening
Orients the child to words and books
Develops auditory and visual perception
Provides experiential backgrounds
Enjoys literature through dramatization and listening

Introduction to Reading

Coordinates writing and reading activities
Develops a program in phonology for reading and spelling
Continues to extend vocabularies—oral, written, read
Introduces poetry appreciation and composition
Continues varied listening activities, increasing attention span
Encourages creativity in all language activities
Uses small group and individual approaches
Diagnoses individual needs through conferencing
Provides a broad background in literature

Independent Reading

Encourages wide reading of literature
Introduces literary concepts in poetry and prose
Uses individual and seminar approaches
Employs discovery techniques and individual research
Teaches library skills and basic library tools
Coordinates literature and language learnings
Stimulates the sharing of books and book reviewing
Extends learnings through reading
Assists the student in book selection
Develops the habit of reading for pleasure and information

Preparation for Reading

Perhaps the chief purpose for many parents in sending their child to school is to have him learn to read. It is with great expectancy on the part of both parent and child that he enters first grade "ready to read." But is he really "ready"?

What is readiness?

Our first problem in determining readiness for reading is to clarify the meaning of this term. *Readiness* is no clearly defined time in a child's development, for we can talk about readiness to learn almost any new skill which may be taught at varied periods of a student's life. Readiness, we see, is not a term associated exclusively with reading. Readiness is a state of being prepared, sufficiently mature and mentally able, to undertake a task, and being interested in attacking the learning job. We are always ready to learn something.

When is a child ready to read? We cannot state with any certainty that he will be ready, for example, to read at the age of six, if he has an IQ of 100, for readiness varies with each individual. The child is ready to read when he shows that he is ready, when he notices letters, asks what they are, and begins trying to read words. This state of readiness depends on a complex multiplicity of abilities which in many cases are acquired incidentally but which in other cases require formal instruction. We can develop readiness for reading as well as for other learning by stressing activities which develop (1) positive attitudes toward school, (2) oral language abilities, (3) experiential backgrounds, (4) visual and auditory discrimination, and (5) word and book orientation.

Positive attitudes toward school

An important aspect of preparing a child for learning is the development of a positive attitude toward learning, which for the child is usually concretely exemplified by the teacher and the school building. First experiences in the school situation must leave the child with a feeling of satisfaction, a sense of having succeeded in the adventure of moving out in the world. He must also retain an assurance that the teacher likes him and respects him as a worthwhile individual. In order to produce positive feelings in the discerning child the teacher must project warmth and enthusiasm which is conveyed through many small acts during the day:

1. Eye contact with the students, as during a story hour
2. Physical contact—in a game, a friendly pat of encouragement, a hand on the shoulder while helping
3. Direct address by name when requesting assistance, greeting, saying good-bye, calling on students to respond
4. Smiling, a touch of humor, show of enthusiasm
5. PRAISE for the individual and the group to promote feelings of success

Oral language

With the emphasis of linguistic studies on the oral language has come renewed awareness of the importance of oral language development as a firm basis for beginning reading experiences. The interrelationship of oral language development and success in reading has been pointed out by the Task Force Report published by the National Council of Teachers of English, which recommends greater stress on oral language, for:

Only as progress is made in the use of oral language will there be substantial improvement in reading and writing. The interdependence of these language skills has been demonstrated both in research and in practice.[20]

Walter Loban states: "Schools are beginning to be aware that research shows a powerful linkage between oral language and writing or reading—one much greater than has previously been realized."[21] The neglect of oral language instruction he attributes to the lack of clear-cut evaluation methods. It is obvious that teachers have shied away from oral instruction in favor of reading and writing possibly because oral activites are less structured.

The chapters on speaking and listening both supply numerous suggestions for developing oral language abilities, as does that on language for the disadvantaged. Let us note, however, the wide range of classroom activities which contribute directly to oral language abilities which in turn contribute to reading success:

Listening

> Attention span
> Auditory discrimination
> Following directions
> Understanding the other person
> Listening for a purpose

Individual speaking to the group

> "Sharing" or "Show and Tell"
> Impromptu talks
> Storytelling
> Reporting
> Telling a joke or riddle

Speaking simultaneously

> Choral approaches to poetry
> Sentence pattern practice
> Finger plays

Discussions

> Preparation of experience charts
> Planned discussion about a picture, object, etc.
> Exploring other subjects—science, social science, health
> Planning together
> Committee participation

[20] NCTE Task Force on Teaching English to the Disadvantaged, *Language Programs for the Disadvantaged* (Champaign, Ill.: National Council of Teachers of English, 1965), pp. 272-3.
[21] Walter Loban, "Oral Language Proficiency Affects Reading and Writing," *Instructor* (March, 1966), p. 97.

Singing

Repetitive songs
Familiar choruses
Folk music
Games and dances

Conversation

Role playing
Dialogue in dramatizations
Telephone
Interview
Progressive pattern practice
Introductions

Dramatization

Puppetry
Creative play
Humorous skits by students
Pantomime
Retelling a story

How does the development of oral language prepare a child to read with greater success? One of the major contributions is in the enjoyment of language and the many ways we use language; the reading of language thus becomes a natural progression for the child who is prepared to be receptive to this new way of working with language. A second important aspect of oral language is the development of the child's vocabulary, for beginning readers will progress more surely if they are familiar with many words so that language to be read is understandable in meaning if not in form. The sounds of English are introduced orally, for aural discrimination between sounds is important to later identification of differences between words.

Experiential backgrounds

In the elementary school, experiential backgrounds typically vary widely in a single classroom. The horizons of some children may be very narrow compared to the broad horizons of those who have had many opportunities to explore. The experiential background of the child is the total product of his way of living, his environment, his family origins, and will be influenced by all of the following factors and more:

Education of parents
Encouragement of child's development
Socioeconomic status of the family
Number of books and periodicals in the home
Opportunities to travel, to explore the community
Encouragement of self-expression

The child who lacks the background which provides him with a wide variety of concepts must be assisted in developing a background of experiences to supplement his meager knowledge, for experiences stimulate thinking. They provide referents for the reading of new words. The classroom teacher can expand horizons through:

Educational trips—zoo, post office, fire station, library, airport, parks, nearby cities, train and bus rides

Classroom adventures—a pet, interesting person, new games, unusual objects, different foods

Multimedia—films, records, filmstrips, pictures

Reading aloud—science information, stories, new items

Visual and auditory discrimination

Before beginning the formal reading program the child needs practice in making discriminations, in noting differences and likenesses. In this way he is prepared to make the more minute discriminations necessary when two similar words are encountered in reading. Experiences which help the child notice similarities and differences can be visual as in these examples:

Put an X on the two shapes which are the same. (Directions are oral.)

Draw a circle around the star which is biggest.

Which two letters are exactly alike?

B   b   T   B

Underline the two words which look exactly alike.

book   man   go   man

Auditory discrimination involves listening and the ability to hear differences and similarities of sound. A variety of activities will assist the child in making these discriminatons:

Which word begins like FALL?

pan   fence   hello

Which two words begin alike?

happy   bed   horse

Which word does *not* begin like the others?

carrot   help   candy   coffee

Can you name another word that begins like *chair?*

Many will be suggested; some will be wrong so the teacher will need to repeat *CHAIR* to help the child see the difference.

shell—The child is confusing the *SH* sound with *CH*.
mare—The child is rhyming the ending sound rather than comparing the beginning sound.

Which word begins like SHEEP? (Closer discrimination.)

slip   shoe   stay

Word and book orientation

As a part of readiness for learning, the child is introduced to the word as a symbol which conveys meaning long before he is actually taught to read. Orientation to words is easily achieved by the use of words as identifying labels around the room: *chalkboard, Tom Turtle, Helpers, October, Mrs. Walton.* . . . These words are introduced casually with no effort to move into reading. Children will gradually show more interest, however, in knowing words, and certainly their questions along these lines should be answered, for there is little to be gained by saying, "Wait," to an eager child.

In this same way the child is introduced to books as something to read, and he learns to hold a book right side up, to open the cover toward the left. He learns that the printed symbols are words which will tell him a story, that we read from left to right, and that we begin reading at the top of the page. (Later, students will be fascinated to learn that these habits are not the same for all countries or languages.) Book orientation is best achieved through the handling of books, and most children have already acquired much of this knowledge before entering school. The teacher can informally present these concepts as she reads aloud from a book. The left to right concept is reinforced as experience stories are printed on the chalkboard.

Introduction to Reading

We have already discussed in some detail various methods of teaching children to read. In this section, therefore, we shall concentrate on the development of a reading vocabulary. The recognition of words, the ability to associate the printed symbol with meaning, depends on a variety of skills: (1) knowledge of phonology, (2) structural analysis skills, (3) sight recognition, and (4) the use of other clues. Let us explore instruction along these lines.

Sight words

There are many small words that are used frequently and that do not usually lend themselves to analysis—*a, the, who, were* . . . These words are the ones which children must learn to recognize without hesitation if skill in reading is to be attained. Many lists have been compiled, for example, that by Edward Dolch [22] which consists of 220 words (no nouns).

There is some question whether a sight vocabulary need really be that large, however, for the newer trend of teaching words in linguistic groups would teach *all, call, fall, small* (included in the Dolch list) as part of the *all* family along with *ball, hall, tall,* and *wall.* In the same manner, *an, can,* and *ran* (from the Dolch list) would be taught with *Dan, fan, man, tan.* These words are regular in pronunciation and are readily learned on the basis of the phonogram represented.

Certainly there is a core of words which must be learned by sight, for they are not related to a linguistic family or are irregular in pronunciation —*are, been, does, from, of, one, said, very, was, what.* These words should be taught in context as much as possible rather than through drill on isolated words. Many words become "sight" words for the able reader who no longer needs to analyze every word he meets. We need chiefly to provide many opportunities for the child to read and to reinforce his knowledge of words through use.

> Labels used around the room can develop into phrases and sentences which include words that trouble children.
>
> the chalkboard
> Many Helpers
> What does Tom Turtle eat?
> One fish is black. Two fish are gold.
>
> Introduce children to Reversals, which we sometimes call PUSH-ME-PULL-ME words because they can go either direction. Interest in this study of word oddities will assist children in identifying *WAS* and *SAW* which are just like other pairs they will discover:
>
> NOT—TON   SPEED—DEEPS   DRAW—WARD

A sequential phonics program

The study of English phonology is essential not only to the reading program but also to speaking and to spelling as a part of composition.

---

[22] Edward W. Dolch, *Methods in Reading* (Champaign, Ill.: Garrard, 1955), pp. 373-4.

This study of the sounds of English begins orally at the kindergarten level. It is important that a well-organized sequence be presented to children in the primary reading levels with appropriate reinforcement as reading ability progresses. It is *equally important, however, that undue repetition be avoided*. Because there is often great confusion and inaccuracy in the teaching of phonology and also because few college students and teachers appear to *know* generalizations of English phonology, we shall include here a developmental sequence based on linguistic findings. More than 40 sounds have been identified for English, and we begin with the least complicated.

STEP I: Initial Consonant Phonemes

/b/, /d/, /f/, /h/, /j/, /k/, /l/, /m/, /n/, /p/, /r/, /t/, /v/, /w/, /y/, /z/

> Bird begins with the letter *b, bird.* (Print on board.)
> Can you tell me other words that begin like *bird?*
>
> (Later) Who can tell me what letter we hear at the beginning of ball?
>
> Can you tell me other words that begin with *b?*
>
> Which word in this group does not begin with *b?*
>
> boy   barn   cow

CAUTION: Do not introduce too many sounds at one time. Begin as shown with only one sound. Review this sound the next day, and introduce one new sound, and so on. Call attention to the known sounds as they occur in other activities for excellent reinforcement.

Never present a consonant sound isolated from a word, for children may later have difficulty blending the beginning consonant and the following phonogram. The child who has been taught to say *buh* for the sound of *b* may pronounce the word *bent* as *buh ent*.

After children know a number of consonants, a valuable practice requires them to substitute consonants to make new words:

> With which letter sound does ball begin? (*b*)
>
> Who can make a new word by changing *b*'s sound to *t*'s sound? Substitute other known sounds: /f/, /h/, /w/
>
> What letter sound do we hear at the beginning of *hold?* (*h*)
>
> Can you make a new word that begins with *t*'s sound?
>
> Let's see if we can put *b*'s sound in front of these little words.
>
> and   eat   ad   in   at
>
> Can anyone put *b*'s sound in front of *ring?* in front of *right? link? low? lame?*

Repeated oral practice with sounds will later aid a linguistically sound approach to independent writing of words as the child learns to print in first grade.

> STEP II: Uncomplicated vowel sounds
> "Short vowels": /e/, /æ/, /i/, /ə/, /a/,
>   as in: hen, sat, pit, nut, got
>
> The short u, /ə/, is called the schwa. It is also made by other vowels in *un*accented syllables as the *i* in family.
>
> "Long vowels" /iy/, /ey/, /ay/, /ow/, /yuw/ [23]
>   as in: he, hay, ice, go, use

The linguist's designation of diphthongs (commonly called "long vowels") is confusing for the student unfamiliar with Romance languages. The first sound above for example, is *ē;* because the *i* has that sound in Romance languages. (The letter *e* sounds like *ā;* the letter *a* sounds like *ah;* the *u* is pronounced *ŏŏ*). The *y* and *w* which follow each sound indicate a gliding sound which we make faintly after the first sound. Try saying words containing these vowel sounds to notice this effect.

Although the vowel sounds are presented orally in kindergarten and first grade, their real study waits until writing and reading experiences. Again we can make use of substitution.

> What vowel sound do we hear in *hat?* Can you put another *short* vowel sound in place of the *a?* What words can you make?
>
>   hit, hot, hut Does *het* make a word?
>
> If you know how to spell the word *luck* (write on the board), how would you spell *lock? lick? lack?*
>
> Can you read this word? (Print *miss.*)
>
> If we change the vowel (*moss*), what word do we have?
> If we change the vowel (*muss*), what word do we have?
> If we change the vowel (*mass*), what word do we have?

Use inductive or discovery methods to introduce concepts of phonology also. Ask the children, for example, to begin naming words which contain *long* vowels. List 20 to 30 on the board for examination:

name	boat	hope	slide	many
see	heel	use	seed	might
leaf	speedy	diet	write	sadly
right	kite	light	late	speech

---

[23] Linguists do not include the sound /yuw/ as a separate phoneme because it is actually two sounds, /y/ and /uw/, but we find it helpful to teach *ū* with the other vowels because in practice they really do "say their own names."

Use a large number of samples so the class will note variations in spelling of long vowel sounds. They can make generalizations like the following derived from their observations:

1. A double *ee* is pronounced *ē*.
2. When a silent *e* is on the end of a word, the vowel before the *e* is long.
3. The letters *ight* produce a long *i* sound.
4. When two vowels are together, the first is long and the second is silent. (The group will find exceptions to this "rule" later, for example, *diet* does not fit this statement.)
5. The *y* on the end of a word is usually pronounced *ē*. (This statement may later be amended to "a word of two or more syllables" and even that generalization has exceptions. Also see the note on page 171.)

This kind of discovery activity causes the student to think as he observes language. The teacher must permit students to make their own discoveries (and their own mistakes) although the "correctness of a recorded statement previously made by the class may be questioned when new cases are discovered. Students should be encouraged to share and to record any LINGUISTIC DISCOVERIES made as the study progresses.

STEP III: Initial Consonant Blends

Blends: *bl, cl, fl, gl, pl, sl*
br, cr, dr, fr, gr, pr, tr
sc, sk, sm, sn, sp, st, sw, tw
scr, shr, spr, str, spl, sch, thr

The blends are introduced in the same way as the initial consonants and are expanded through substitution and induction or discovery techniques.

Give students difficult words they could scarcely know how to spell. What blend do you hear at the beginning of FLUCTUATE? SMITH-EREENS? STRIPLING? PRIMROSE? GROUSE? STIPEND? This is an effective way to encourage students to try spelling unknown words as well as to introduce them to some interesting words which can be explained or used in a sentence by the teacher as seems appropriate.

STEP IV: Irregular Consonants

Letters that have no sound of their own: *c, x, q*

C sounds like S in *cent* and K in *cow;* there really is no C sound.
X sounds like KS in *fox* and *excuse* and Z in *xylophone.*
Q is always followed by U and always sounds like KW as in *quit.*

Letters that have two or more sounds: G and S (C and X borrow two sounds)

G has a "hard" sound as in *gave* and borrows the "soft" sound of J as in *age.*

S has several sounds as in *sit, rose* (Z), *measure* (Fr.j), and *sure* (SH).

A WORTHWHILE RULE: C is *soft* before I and E (and Y when Y substitutes for *I* and *E*), but *hard* before other letters—*cake, coat, creek, cure, clean.*

STEP V: Consonant Digraphs

CH as in *chest, chorus* (Greek), *champagne* (French)

SH as in *short*

TH as in *the, thing*

WH as in *where, who*

GH as in *ghost, laugh*

PH as in *phone*

PS as in *psalm*

NG (an ending sound) as in *hang*

NK (an ending sound) as in *think*

What is the difference between a blend and a digraph? In a blend you can hear the letter sounds which blend, but in the digraph the identity of individual sounds is lost and a new sound is produced.

STEP VI: Silent Letters

W as in *wrist*

K as in *knot*

B as in *comb*

C as in *sick, scene*

L as in *walk*

G as in *gnaw*

H as in *honest*

T as in *witch, often*

U as in *guide* (The *u* serves to keep the g hard.)

GH as in *light*

STEP VII: Vowels Followed by R

AR as in *car*

ER as in *her*

IR as in *sir, mirror*

OR as in *for, favor*

UR as in *nurse*

The R causes the vowel to produce a sound that is neither long nor short, yet is relatively common; for example, *er*.

An *e* following the Vowel + R causes the Vowel to be long, thus:

car = care   fir = fire   her = here

STEP VIII: Vowel Digraphs

A	E	I	O
ai gain	ee wee	y by	oa goat
ay may	ea meat	uy buy	ow own
ei neigh	ei receive	ei height	
ey they	ie believe	igh high	

STEP IX: Vowel Diphthongs

> The diphthong is a single blending sound produced by two vowels usually ending in a gliding sound (*y* or *w*).

OW as *now, slow*
OU as *house, rough, slough, dough, could*
EW as *few, knew*
OO as *food, good*
AU as *caught*
AW as *saw*
OI as *oil*
OY as *boy*

STEP X: Phonograms

at	ed	it	ot	un
ate	et	in	ote	ung
ail	eat	ip	oat	ub
ain	ean	id	oar	ug
ait	eed	ing	ore	unt
an	eet	ind	on	ule
ang	end	ine	one	up
ap	ent	int	ong	ull
ag	eam	ick	ort	um
ab	en	iss	oon	uss
ad	eg	ite	ool	ut
ack	ell	ice	oom	ute

The list of phonograms is almost inexhaustible. These ending sounds may be used in conjunction with learning of initial consonants and blends. How many of the above phonograms will form a word if the letter *s* is placed before them: *sat, sail, sang, sap,* and so on?

A WORD WHEEL is useful in the primary classroom as students try to combine initial consonant sounds with varied phonograms. Simple wheels can be made, as in the diagram, or commercial varieties are available.

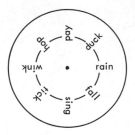

More advanced work in phonology can introduce students to examples of foreign language in English which affects our pronunciation and causes supposed irregularities in English pronunciation. Why, for example, do we look at the word *cello* which might be pronounced *sello* and say *chello?* It's an Italian word, of course, which requires the *ch* sound according to Italian linguistics. We can observe many *loan* words: *plaza, prima donna, tempo, séance, requiem, mirage, per capita, piñata, boudoir, cuisine.* Often we have retained the original pronunciation, but sometimes we anglicize the borrowed words as in *detour, bonbons, ensemble, adroit.*

Fallacies in Phonics Instruction. Most teachers are not familiar with phonics generalizations, although they are the ones who teach this information to the elementary school child. One study found that when 293 teachers and teacher trainees were tested, they scored only 57% right on a test of phonics generalizations.[24] We say it is surprising, but the reason for this lack of knowledge is obvious. These people were never taught this type of information. Only in the past few years has it become common to at least encourage elementary school teachers to take a course in modern grammar or an introduction to linguistics which might teach this information. In what other course would it be presented?

We have noted many examples of fallacious thinking on the part of students and teachers, for whom we have just provided an excuse, on the part of professors writing textbooks, who should be better informed, and even on the part of linguists, who are supposed to be expert. Let us observe the following:

1. Very few "rules" are consistent enough to warrant teaching. Several which are consistent we have inserted within the phonics sequence. As soon as there are many exceptions, rules have little value and serve only to confuse the beginning reader.

---

[24] I. E. Aaron, "What Teachers and Prospective Teachers Know About Phonics Generalizations," *Journal of Education Research* (May, 1960), pp. 323-30.

2. Sounds of single letters or combinations of letters should be pronounced in the context of a word. A consonant cannot make a sound at all unless a vowel sound follows it, which explains the presence of a vowel in every syllable. The *number of vowel sounds heard* indicates the number of syllables in the word.

3. There is much confusion about the vowel sounds of Y. As we note in more detail on pages 171-172, Y can substitute for long *i* as in *cry,* short *i* as in *crypt,* or long *e* as in *happy.* It is the latter case which has caused much uncertainty as it has been the practice to label the *y* in *baby* as short *i* when in reality it is commonly pronounced as a long *e,* as is noted in *Webster's Third International Unabridged Dictionary.*

4. We must be certain of our linguistic knowledge and our ear for the sounds of English before introducing questionable concepts to students. We must remember, too, that regional variations in pronunciation exist; the fact that they differ does not make them *wrong.*

Structural analysis

Awareness of the structure of words is another aspect of word recognition which can begin in the first years of school as an oral approach to language. As with phonics, these understandings are introduced and then continually reinforced through usage. We can explore the following types of word analysis with the child.

Compound Words. The compound word is composed of two smaller words which have been united to form one nonhyphenated word; for example, *workshop, highway, railroad, storefront, spillway, sidewalk.* Once students are acquainted with the idea of the compound word they will "spot" the pair of words, each of which is usually relatively short and often familiar, so that the *long* word is broken down into manageable parts.

> Begin a collection of compound words as students bring examples clipped from newspapers and magazines. Notice the difference between the compound word and that which contains an affix, which may confuse the beginning reader.

Phonograms. We have already discussed the use of phonograms in a phonics sequence, but these groups of letters also can be thought of as part of the word's structure. Neither root word nor affix, the phonogram is a unit of sound which reoccurs frequently, as *ell* in *fell, bell, sell,* and so on. Although the phonogram is at times a small word, we are not teaching it as a word, but as a part of many words. The phonogram, *ail,* for instance, is a small word, but the meaning of this word has nothing to do with its appearance in *bail, fail, hail, jail.* . . . Structurally, *ail* could have significance as a root in *ailment* or *ailing.*

Affixes. Affixes are used so frequently as either a prefix (*un, ex*) or a suffix (*ing, ed*) that students should be introduced to an increasing knowledge of common affixes and their meanings. Here is a list of common affixes to be taught gradually as they occur in written work and material being read. Those marked with an * are more frequently used and would, therefore, be taught first.

Prefixes		Suffixes
a	meta	able, ible
ad	neo	ant, ent
an	ob	*ed
ante	omni	*er
anti	para	*es
auto	per	*est
bi	post	ic
*con	*pre	*ing
contra	pro	ism
cum	*re	ite
*de	*sub	ive
deca	super	*le
dia	*trans	*ly
*dis	tri	ous
*ex	*un	*sion, tion
hemi		*y
homo		
*in		
inter		
intra		
intro		

Roots. The study of roots which are used in forming many words proves fascinating for more advanced students as an approach to word analysis. We can introduce a variety of Latin and Greek roots, thus: [25]

capio: (hold, seize)—capture, captivate, capacity
curro: (run)—course, current, cursive, occur
malus: (bad)—Maleficent (the witch in *Sleeping Beauty,*) malady, malice, malpractice
onyma: (name)—synonym, homonym, pseudonym, antonym
phone (sound)—telephone, megaphone, microphone, phonics

Syllabication. Ability to break a polysyllabic word into its component parts has some degree of value as a word attack skill although, if the child has to struggle beyond recognition of affixes and root words, he may completely lose interest in reading the story before him. A complete list of rules for syllabication (which are helpful in dividing words at the

[25] For more information see Wilfred Funk, *Word Origins,* Chapter 22 (New York: Grosset, 1950).

end of lines in writing) is included on page 177. The following are considered helpful in beginning word attack.

1. Recognition of prefixes and suffixes as syllables:
    speedily   control   helpful   hurriedly

2. Division of the word between double consonants:
    horrible   sputter   puddle   stammer

3. Knowledge of the pronunciation of *le* on the end of a word as it combines with the preceding consonant.
    stable   giggle   mumble   trouble

Practice in Analyzing Words. Once the child has been taught phonology and the skills of structural analysis, he requires much practice in using these skills as he meets words in context and attempts to "crack the shell" of the unknown word. The teacher can assist word analysis by asking guiding questions as in these examples:

1. Tim ran *quickly* down the street.
    Do you see *ly* on the end of the word, Bob? What does it say?
    Let's cover up *ly* now so you can see the rest of the word better.
    What is the beginning sound of this word?

2. The black dog was *enormous.*
    The first syllable of this word is *ē* all by itself, Jan.
    Now can you see a second syllable?

A child should never be left to struggle too long with a word. It is better to tell him the word after assisting with some parts of it. After identifying the known parts of a word, the child is also encouraged to try words which make sense in the context of the sentence or story and also fit the known sounds. In the sentence, "Mother bought a bright red *blanket."* the child knows the underlined word must be something Mother might buy according to the sense of the story and that it must start with the blend *bl* which is known. Here we have demonstrated also the importance of a vocabulary sufficiently large to provide words to try.

Developing Reading Independence

"The more we read the better we read," is an excellent motto for the elementary school classroom. Once the child develops skill with basic vocabulary, he begins reading independently with assistance from the teacher or a "buddy" only as needed. Good literature tends to provide its own motivation, but the wise teacher will continue to stimulate student reading. She will also aid students in evaluating their own progress in reading. Some children may need individual or small group guidance to assist development in specific skills of word attack, extending vocabulary, and comprehension.

The teacher will plan classroom reading instructional activities, too, which will encourage interaction among students who are working independently. The following "guide to good reading" provides a humorous recipe for reading success which may be used to inspire students:

1. Read.
2. Read.
3. Read some more.
4. Read anything.
5. Read about everything.
6. Read enjoyable things.
7. Read things you yourself enjoy.
8. Read, and talk about it.
9. Read very carefully some things.
10. Read on the run, most things.
11. Don't think about reading, but
12. Just read.[26]

Stimulating student reading

The best stimulus to wide reading is a large collection of varied titles in a well-organized central library. We can motivate student reading through a variety of strategies, thus:

● *Creative Art Techniques.* Students delight in creating favorite animal characters from newspaper glued in several layers (4-6) over a two-pound coffee can or a large bottle which has been rubbed with oil. After the paper shape has dried, legs, antennae, tails and other needed accouterments can be added as Charlotte, Wilbur, the goose, and other barnyard friends appear. The Musicians of Bremen provide other characters for this medium.

Paper strips glued around an armature of rolled paper or wire permits the creation of upright figures. There's skinny, rollicking Ribsy and coming along behind is Henry with a rolled newspaper in his hand. A group of students who like to work in miniature could produce the Borrowers—Pod, Homily, and Arrietty.

● *Bulletin Board Displays.* Let children take turns decorating a small bulletin board with the caption GUESS WHO? Displayed are pictures, drawings, small realia that suggest one book or one character. The creator then tells about his display explaining why he included various items.

● *Stimulating Innovation.* Encourage students to utilize innovative approaches to sharing their reading. After the teacher has demonstrated

26 Irving H. Anderson and Walter F. Dearborn, *The Psychology of Teaching Reading* (New York: Ronald, 1952), pp. 165-6.

more exciting ways of presenting a book to the class, students will vie
to produce the more unusual presentation. Suggestion might include:

Mobile	Scroll Theater
Diorama	Book Jackets
Peekbox	Bookmarks
Collage	Mural
Puppetry	Literature map
Creative Dramatics	Storytelling
Broadcasting	Displays
Interviewing an author	Advertisement
Poster	

● *Seminars.* Students will appreciate a mature approach to reading which
permits them to gather to discuss a book which a number of the group
have read. The group can later unite their efforts to present the book
to the class through dramatization or puppetry.

● *The Round Robin Book Club.* An interesting way of encouraging reading is the exchange of student-owned books through a Round Robin Book
Club arrangement. On a specified day each child brings one book to
school, and the exchange begins. To ensure each child's receiving every
book, a list is made of the children's names, and each child passes his
book to the person whose name follows his own name, that is, he always
passes a book to the same child. The passing of books should be regularly
scheduled, perhaps once a week, for instance, every Friday. If this
proves too short a time, books can be exchanged every other Friday.

● *Teacher Aids.* Included here are a variety of books suggesting activities
that assist the teacher in stimulating reading.

Darrow, Helen F. and R. Van Allen, *Independent Activities for Creative Learning.* New York: Teachers College, 1961.

Games and Self-Testing Activities for the Classroom. Washington;
D.C.: U.S. Government Printing Office, 1961.

Kingsley, Bernard. *Reading Skills.* San Francisco: Fearon, 1958.

Russell, David H. and Etta Karp. *Reading Aids through the Grades.*
New York: Teachers College, 1951.

Tiedt, Sidney W. and Iris M. Tiedt. *Exploring Words.* San Jose (Box
1524), California: Contemporary Press, 1964.

● *Periodicals for Young People.* There is an increasing interest in both
magazines and newspapers for young people. These publications have
the advantage of coming throughout the year, and for that reason
tend to encourage the continuation of reading beyond the classroom.
They also feature current information about interesting topics and can
be used to stimulate both speaking and writing experiences. Magazines
recommended for young people include:

American Forests. 919 17th St., N.W., Washington 6, D.C.

American Girl. 830 Third Ave., New York 22. N.Y.

Analog. Conde Nast Publications, 420 Lexington Ave., New York 17,
N.Y.

Boy's Life. New Brunswick, N.J.

Child Life. O. H. Rodman, 136 Federal St., Boston, Mass.

Children's Digest. Bergenfield, N.J.

Highlights for Children, Homedale, Penn.

Humpty Dumpty's Magazine. Bergenfield, N.J.

Jack and Jill. Curtis Publishing Co., Independence Sq., Philadelphia, Pa.

Junior Natural History. 79th St. and Central Park West, New York 24, N.Y.

My Weekly Reader. 1250 Fairwood Ave., Columbus 16, Ohio.

National Geographic and *National Geographic School Bulletin*. 16th and M Sts., N. W., Washington 6, D.C.

Scholastic Magazines. Varied Titles. 902 Sylvan Ave., Englewood Cliffs, N.J.

Science Digest. 200 E. Ontario St., Chicago 11, Ill.

Sky and Telescope. Sky Publishing Co., Harvard College Observatory, Cambridge 38, Mass.

Story Parade. 200 Fifth Ave., New York, N.Y.

Wee Wisdom. Lee's Summit, Mo.

Young American. Eton Publishing Corp., New York, N.Y.

Young Miss. Bergenfield, N.J.

Commercial Book Clubs. There are a number of commercial book clubs which are popular with children and serve to encourage reading and the exchange of books, as well as the acquisition of a personal library for the child. Several are offering inexpensive hardback editions while others specialize in paperback editions at very low prices. You can obtain information about these clubs to make available to children and parents.

Catholic Children's Book Club. 262 E. 4th Street, St. Paul 1, Minn.

Junior Literary Guild. Garden City, N.Y.

Parents' Magazine's Book Clubs. Bergenfield, N.J.

Scholastic Book Clubs, 904 Sylvan Ave., Englewood Cliffs, N.J.

For other suggestions about motivating children's interests in reading review the following chapter on Literature.

Continuing vocabulary growth

The avid reader usually has no difficulty in acquiring an extensive vocabulary, but even he may require assistance with pronunciation and connotations, if not denotations, of words that he encounters. The study of words adds much to intellectual development at any stage, and it certainly is not limited to the reading period alone, for much effective learning about words takes place in other subject areas.

As noted frequently throughout this book, teacher interest and enthusiasm for words will be contagious. The teacher who leads the way in making discoveries and talking to children about words will produce students who are aware of words and their meanings and who often observe intriguing features of words. Through writing and speaking experiences they come to delight in using new, less common words, in searching for synonyms, and in "trying out" discoveries on classmates as well as the teacher. Our daughter, for example, is currently referring to the rumblings of her stomach as "borborygmi" which mystified us all until she shared her discovery. And remember how delighted you were when you first heard of words like "expectorate" and "osculate"?

Use interesting words as you speak to children (not the above examples, perhaps); they will absorb them as their own. "You're an example of *sartorial* splendor, Mike! Do you know what that means?" Write it on the board, but let him do his own investigating. "I see Vicky has a new *coiffeur* today." "The king *abdicated* his throne." "Let's *speculate* about what might have happened if we had not entered the war." The only requirement for this approach to word study is knowledge on the part of the teacher; you may need to "grow a vocabulary" ahead of or with your students, and if you work with a group of able fifth or sixth graders, they may lead the way. Even in the primary grades we can eliminate "baby talk," avoid "talking down," and help them reach out to grasp new words to express new ideas. It's a pleasant, creative way of learning, and it's effective.

Walking Words—Introduce young children to varied ways of walking through creative dramatics. As they begin walking around a circle or "following the leader" in a line, ask them if they can *sneak* as if they didn't want anyone to see them. Suggest that they *march* like soldiers, *tramp* like noisy boys, *scamper* like puppies playing, *stride* like tall men, *waddle* like fat bears, *strut* like peacocks. Then discuss the words and ask if they can suggest different "ways of walking." Other synonym groups can be explored also.

Favorite Words—Share a group of your favorite words with the class— *scintillating, effervescent, exquisite, bombastic*—the choice is up to you! Write one of the words on the board as you say it. Ask them what they think it means. Use it in a sentence. Then invite them to share their favorite words they have discovered which they think are especially appealing. Display words which have been shared.

Word Attack Skills. Although skills in phonics and structural analysis are introduced in the early grades, they may require reinforcement and even reteaching with small groups of students. We should take care, however, to avoid the practice of forcing all students to study and restudy the same information, which in many cases is unnecessarily repetitious.

The able reader who is reading independently, often at adult levels, is usually intrigued by language and should be encouraged to extend his knowledge at more advanced levels by reading from books listed in the

Linguistic Library on pp. 38-40. Seminars of able students can focus attention on more mature vocabulary development through discussion of fascinating, but useful, words. A programmed approach to word study may be useful for this type of independent study.

To assist students who have not fully grasped phonics concepts and skills of structural analysis, small groups can work together orally. Sheets torn from workbooks can also be used for practice as appropriate to the needs of each child. A card should be kept for each student to note his skill development, for the teacher working with 30 children (particularly in an individualized approach to reading) will find it impossible to remember the needs of every child. Small group work can be planned to assist children with specific knowledge; only those children who need a particular skill will be called to study at one time.

Word Play. Words, words, wonderful words! Students should be inspired with a positive attitude toward words as they learn to use them and to enjoy them. They should be introduced to "serendipity" and be prepared to make discoveries. Word play provides an excellent motivation toward learning more about words (See Chapter 3) as in these examples:

> May I Sew You to a Sheet?—Here is an example of the Spoonerism, an inversion of beginning sounds attributed to Rev. William Spooner. Other examples of word play which can be researched by able students include Malapropisms and Wellerisms.

> CHAIN REACTION—An excellent way to practice knowledge of phonics is to begin a word chain. By changing only one letter to make a new word each time, see how long the chain can be made. A chain (or more than one) can be started with children adding to it in their free time, thus:

TAME	FORT	SPOUT
tale	sort	sport
sale	port	short
pale	part	shirt
page	cart	shirk
wage	dart	shark
wade	dark	spark
wide	darn	spare
hide	dare	spire
side	care	spine

> TREASURE HUNT—Begin a search for words of a specific nature as everyone adds to a list mounted on the bulletin board or the wordlist begun on the chalkboard. For example, begin a search for words which end in *tion, ong,* or *able* to provide practice with specific suffixes or phonograms. Lend interest to syllable practice by listing words of four, five, or six syllables. For younger children ask for words with 3 syllables or words with 8 letters.

Evaluating reading success

In evaluating progress the child must be compared with himself, for this method permits the teacher to analyze exactly which reading skills he has acquired and which he has not, and he determines the course of instruction for that particular child. Many teachers rely on simple vocabulary tests alone to discover the amount of growth in reading. Evaluation should encompass attitudes toward reading, the amount of reading the child actually does, and his willingness and ability to use knowledge of phonology in attacking new words. The following strategies are useful in analyzing individual status in reading and in conferring with students' parents.

Diagnosing Difficulties. The teacher can readily note student reading deficiencies during any classroom activities, but the individual conference is an excellent way of studying individual progress. A large file card can be kept for each child to facilitate the teacher's prescribing for the needs of that child. A simple checklist will aid in noting specific skills which require review. Those who need the same type of information or practice can be brought together at a table for reteaching. One side of the card might be arranged like this:

Phonics:

    Initial consonants
    Blends
    Digraphs
    Vowels—short
           long
    Digraphs
    Diphthongs

Structural Analysis:

    Prefixes
    Suffixes
    Roots
    Syllables

Comprehension:

    Context Clues
    Vocabulary Development

Oral Fluency:

Others:

On the front of this card will appear the student's name, a record of test scores, books read, notes about attitude toward reading, and any other pertinent information.

Educational Prescriptions. We must do more, however, than diagnose student difficulties and needs. As educational specialists, we must prescribe remedies. Unfortunately there is no magic pill which will produce a successful reader, so prescriptions must be made in terms of "practice with groups on sounds: *ch* and *sh*" or "read individually with me to develop positive attitude toward reading."

Are prescriptions only for remedial cases? No, the gifted students should be checked as well, for too often we ignore their need for vitamin pills and assume that the busy reader who devours books is progressing nicely. We have a responsibility to assist these able students in extending their learning also although it is easy to be deceived into thinking that we owe more to those who are farther behind in the reading task. For the able student we might prescribe an experience in "storytelling with the first or second grade," "developing a bibliography of books about China," or pursuing some individual interest through independent study.

The process of evaluation must be continuous, and it is a process in which the child should be directly involved. The child is interested in his own progress, not necessarily compared with that of others. It is encouraging to share with the teacher, if you are Steve, the mutual project of improving Steve's reading ability, to watch it grow together. "Now what are we going to work on today, Steve?" The individual conference approach to assistance gives a personal touch and demonstrates the real interest of the teacher in a child and his individual problems. This in itself is encouraging to the child.

Books to Investigate

Barbe, Walter B., *Teaching Reading: Selected Materials.* New York: Oxford University Press, 1965. A book of readings covering the broad field.

California Elementary School Administrators Assn, *The First R: A Survey of Selected Current Practices in Reading Instruction.* Burlingame, Calif.: The Association, 1966. A booklet exploring new strategies in reading.

Carner, Richard L., and William D. Sheldon, *Teaching Reading through Closed Circuit Television in the Elementary School.* Albany, N.Y.: State Dept. of Education, 1959.

Darrow, Helen F., and Virgil M. Howes, *Approaches to Individualized Reading.* New York: Appleton, 1960. Pamphlet which describes evaluating growth and recording it.

Downing, John, *Experiments with an Augmented Alphabet for Beginning Readers.* New York: Educational Records Bureau, 1962.

Evertt, Richard M., Jr., *Comparison between Conventional Basic Reading Programs and the Language for Learning Program.* New York: Washington Square Press, 1960. The Richards-Gibson approach.

Fries, Charles C., *Linguistics and Reading.* New York: Holt, 1963. A short, much-quoted work by a known linguist.

Margulies, Stuart, and Lewis D. Ellgen, *Applied Programmed Instruction.* New York: Wiley, 1962.

Rambausch, Nancy M., *Learning How to Learn; An American Approach to Montessori.* Baltimore: Helicon Press, 1962.

Van Allen, R., and Gladys C. Halversen, *The Language-Experience Approach.* Boston, Ginn, 1961.

Van Allen, R., and Doris M. Lee, *Learning to Read through Experience.* New York: Appleton, 1963.

The function of literature is to turn events into ideas.

George Santayana

12

Literature and Language

What is literature? Does literature for young people differ from adult literature? How much emphasis should be placed on reading the classics? What is the place of literature in the school? These questions directly concern the teacher of English in the elementary school as much as they do English teachers at other levels.

Many attempts have been made to define literature varying from the broad definition which includes everything written to the narrow interpretation which excludes all but the "classics." Perhaps we can best define literature in terms of what we expect "good" literature to do. One author lists objectives of good literature which may serve to identify that which we can properly label as literature. Does the work—

—meet individual needs?
—encourage creative expression?
—transmit the cultural heritage?
—promote social understandings?
—increase understanding of self?
—present quality writing? [1]

Are there other qualities you might include in this list?

Literature speaks to us. What it transmits may not be tangible.

[1] Edith V. Walker, "What Is the Role of Children's Literature in the Elementary School?" in *Children's Literature—Old and New* (Champaign, Ill.: National Council of Teachers of English, 1964), p. 3.

It may not even be recognized at the time of reading. But the writer communicates in his own individualistic manner of thinking and writing, and we respond as individuals representing widely varied backgrounds of experience, mentality, and personality. As Charles Kingsley wrote:

> Except a living man there is nothing more wonderful than a book! a message to us from human souls we never saw. And yet these arouse us, terrify us, teach us, comfort us, open their hearts to us as brothers.

Through the early introduction of children to challenging literature we are endeavoring to ensure that each child has this opportunity to engage in conversation with many skilled authors. As Fred pores over a book absorbing a tale well told by a master storyteller, he is also absorbing the wisdom of living, for E. B. White not only whispers the story of Charlotte and Wilbur but also conveys mature concepts of friendship, loneliness, and even death.

Literature communicates ideas, attitudes, values, and information. The elementary school must assume its share of the responsibility for bringing literature and children together, for the school is the only institution which reaches all children. It alone is in a position to present an organized sequence of literature experiences that will make certain that most children will know the literature of their age. From the slowest child, the culturally deprived, to the brightest student, and the culturally advantaged each will gain from having known Winnie-the-Pooh, Toad, and Peter Pan.

Teaching Literature

In the junior high school, in the high school, in the college, literature has always been an integral part of the English program. Yet, literature appears in the elementary school English program only incidentally; it is clearly regarded as an "extra" to be included after other work is completed.

Need for planned programs

A place must be made for literature in the elementary school curriculum so that it is no longer a "frill" but is drawn firmly into the main core of essential content to be taught. Comments Charlotte Huck, co-author of *Children's Literature in the Elementary School:*

> We have no literature program in the elementary school when we compare it with carefully planned developmental programs in reading, spelling and arthmetic. All our efforts are directed towards teaching children to read—no one seems to be concerned that they *do* read or *what* they read. The means have become the end.[2]

[2] Charlotte S. Huck, "Planning the Literature Program for the Elementary School," *Elementary English* (April, 1962), p. 307.

How can we best incorporate literature in the elementary school program? The obvious place for literature in the busy curriculum is in the reading program. There is a need for a carefully conceived developmental sequence for presenting various literature titles to avoid repetition and to ensure all children's knowing a major portion of this rich inheritance. Guidelines will assist articulation without unduly hampering the teacher's individual planning.

Will the study of literature, that is, analysis, destroy the child's enjoyment of a story as many purists fear? On the contrary, it has been our observation that exploring beyond the superficial story value of an author's work actually leads to greater interest in reading and aids in the development of critical thinking. Emphasis still remains on reading for enjoyment, but this enjoyment is enhanced through the addition of appreciation of the writer's skilled performance.

Literature in the reading program

Literature has seldom been part of the reading program in the elementary school, for reading has been dominated by the basal reader series. What are the advantages of a literature-reading program over the traditional controlled-vocabulary anthology? The use of literature in a reading program for elementary school students offers quality content to a course of study which has concentrated solely on the teaching of skills. It is time that we acknowledge the value of provocative material in exciting the student about reading. Until we have this excitement present in the reading lesson, we will not develop a nation of readers.

Many titles from children's literature can be, and are being, used as reading text material. The advantages of *Pippi Longstocking, A Wrinkle in Time,* and *Johnny Tremain* over the familiar basal reader are overwhelming:

1. Excellent writing—imagery, use of words, storytelling ability.
2. Continuity of a longer story—plot development, characterization.
3. Greater interest value—intrigue, atmosphere, entertainment.
4. Integration of literature, language, and composition studies.

The only advantage undeniably present in the basal reader is controlled vocabulary. In light of our singular lack of success in producing adults who read widely, however, one wonders if the controlled vocabulary may not literally drain the vitality from the fare served our enthusiastic beginning readers. As Phyllis McGinley observes in *Sixpence in Her Shoe:*

> Whose invention was this vocabulary restriction I cannot say. Librarians deplore the trend, publishers disclaim responsibility, authors declare themselves stifled by it, children detest it. But the fact remains that somebody has set up as gospel the rule that odd words, long words, interesting

words, grown-up words must be as precisely sifted out from a book for, say, five-year-olds as chaff from wheat or profanity from a television program. . . .

Are children never to climb? Must they be saved from all the healthy bumps and bruises of exploration? . . . The genuine reading child . . . wants, even at six or seven or eight, gourmet fare. . . .

The study of literature offers infinite possibilities for a stimulating approach to the language arts which coordinates the areas of language and composition with that of literature. Skills of reading, writing, speaking, and listening are utilized as the child attacks intellectually challenging material.

The Nebraska Curriculum Development Center is developing an elementary school English curriculum which does focus attention on core literature texts. The aims of this language, literature, and composition program are stated to be:

1. To teach students to comprehend the more frequent grammatical conventions;

2. To teach students to comprehend the more frequent conventions of literature composed for young children—formal or generic conventions and simple rhetorical conventions;

3. To teach students to control these linguistic and literary conventions in their own writing.[3]

Individualized Reading Programs. The teaching of literature lends itself well to the trend toward individualizing reading. Many teachers are experimenting with the use of trade titles, having each student read a different book selected from a group of specific titles. The completely individualized approach to reading literature has the advantages of (1) individual selection of books (within limits), (2) progress at varied rates of speed, (3) usually greater quantity of reading, and (4) no child without something to do.

To operate with maximum effectiveness this approach requires that the teacher guide individual development through extensive student conferencing. Activities for extending learning must be planned (until they are commercially available) for each book so that students are doing more than just reading title after title. The standard book report form hastily completed by the disinterested student is a waste of time and paper and may actually cause children to dislike reading.

Small Group Seminars. Other teachers are finding that the purchase of multiple copies of several titles provides excellent material for small group approaches to literature study. This approach to literature study

[3] Nebraska Curriculum Development Center, *A Curriculum for English; Introduction to the Elementary School Program: K-6.* Mimeographed report. (Lincoln, Neb.: The University of Nebraska, 1965), p. 2.

limits student selection, but offers certain advantages for the teaching of literature: (1) use of seminar techniques in discussing a common body of reading, (2) concentration of teacher and student efforts on fewer books to be examined in depth, (3) individualized responses to independent open-ended activities for extending learning, and (4) experiences in group dynamics.

Whether each child is reading a different title or a small group is reading the same title, the use of literature offers stimulating reading which should lead to greater enjoyment of reading and actually to *more reading*. Perhaps the best method of presentation will prove to be a combination of the individualized and the small group approaches described. Neither approach, we should add, actually teaches literature, however, for the success of these techniques of teaching lies essentially with the teacher. Teacher enthusiasm, knowledge of literature, ability to guide without domination, and wisdom in planning will, as in all of teaching, play a significant role.

Planning literature experiences

What procedures shall we follow in presenting a title? The techniques used will vary according to the particular books under discussion, but each literature experience will be based on the reading of a sizeable portion of the book. Books that are divided into chapters are particularly adaptable for study with the chapter providing a natural division. A very short book might be treated as a whole. Steps in presenting the literature lesson will, however, usually follow a sequence like this:

1. *Reading a portion of the book.* Children may read silently or they may take turns reading aloud. It is highly desirable that the teacher frequently read aloud to a group as this technique adds to the pleasure of the experience and prepares the group for immediate follow-up activities.

2. *Discussion or study of portion read.* Focus can be on any aspect of the literature being examined.
    a. vocabulary (talk about the words used, not just a list to study)
    b. theme (author's message, ideas behind the action)
    c. specific examples of imagery (similes, picturesque use of words)
    d. meaning of specific phrases or references (idioms, clichés)
    e. reaction to provocative statements
    f. discussion of action, characters, setting

3. *Extending Experiences.* A variety of ideas should be suggested with each student completing several; some may be group activities.
    a. Composition
       Write a reaction to points made by the author.
       Write a story suggested by the content.
       Write poetry based on an idea presented.

   b. Language

Discuss unusual uses of words.
Observe description of sounds, colors, etc.
Study a specific sentence structure.
Enact a portion of dialogue.

   c. Art

Paint an imagined portrait of a character from the word picture.
Draw a pictorial map of the setting of the story.
Develop a mural depicting the action of the story.
Paint one vivid scene from the action.

   d. Literature

Read another book similar in content and compare the two.
Read another title by the same author and compare.
Find out about the author who wrote the story.

   e. Social Studies

Locate the setting of this story.
At what period of history does it take place?
Compare the life of the characters with your life—school, housing,
family, clothing.

If students are reading individually, these experiences will usually be explored independently. Suggested activity sheets can be prepared so that the student can select several as he progresses with the book being read. Activities should be specific and should be directly related to the title read as in the sample Plans of Operation for three literature studies which are described on the following pages.

We recommend the keeping of a Reading Log by each individual student in grades three through six as he reads any title. The Log is a highly individualized approach offering a challenge to the gifted student and permitting growth of the slower student. The term *log* is introduced through the explanation of its use by a ship's captain to record events during a trip. (This analogy can be extended.) Each student keeps a log in a small notebook in which he records:

1. Interesting new words
2. Colorful imagery
3. Written reactions to the story
4. Written answers to questions for Extending Learning
5. Special pages suggested—collections of synonyms, homonyms, other categories of words
6. Poetry and prose motivated by guided activities

These logs provide the teacher with a clear picture of what any student is doing (without routine book report forms, test questions, etc.)

and the progress he is making. They can be used as the basis of individual conferences or a few at a time can be read by the teacher.

Plan of operation: grade 1

And To Think That I Saw It on Mulberry Street
by Dr. Seuss (Vanguard, 1937)

This early work by Theodore Geisel tells the story of Marco, who usually diverts himself by imagining interesting things as he walks home from school. When he tells his father, however, his father does not appreciate the fanciful tales. The father's attitude forces Marco to face reality as he admits there was nothing but a "plain horse and wagon on Mulberry Street."

Extending Learning Activities. This short book could be read aloud to the class if used at the beginning of the year. During the last half of the year small groups of students could read the book together after which it could be discussed along the lines suggested.

1. Why did Marco enjoy imagining things?
2. Which of his imaginary things did you like most?
3. Do you ever imagine things? What is your favorite imagining?
4. What did Marco's father think about imagining? Did he perhaps think Marco was lying?
5. Is imagining things the same as lying? How are they different?
6. What words do you remember from the story? Why do you remember those particular words?

Follow-up and culminating activities can be a combination of individual and group activities. Many times these actvities will be suggested by the questions and interests of the children involved.

- Name all the different things Marco imagined, printing them on the board for word orientation and for experience in reading. Plan a parade down Mulberry Street to be painted cooperatively as a mural. Encourage use of the imagination; the illustrations of the book should not confine production.

- Write sentence stories about individual imaginings. Give help as needed so that each child has a story about something he imagines. Crayon resist pictures of these imaginings can be produced (thin tempera wash over completed crayon picture). The picture is then shown as the story is read by each child.

- Write a group-composed letter to Marco to extend sympathy, to tell reasons for enjoying his ideas, and to share original ideas.

- Talk about color words used in the story. Have the class name other known color words. Add a few useful, but less common, examples to extend vocabularies—*scarlet, crimson, lime, olive.*

Plan of operation: grade 3

The Children of Green Knowe
by Lucy Boston (Harcourt, 1954)

This imaginative story of Tolly, a young boy who goes to live with his grandmother at Green Knowe, is set in Great Britain. It is rich in imagery and offers an opportunity to compare British English with American English. Although this book is not divided into chapters, it does fall easily into parts suitable for use as learning experiences. The following activities are based on the first section of the book (pp. 9-23).

1. Tolly thinks of the train as an Ark floating on flood waters, and he imagines all the noises of the animals.

    What a noise there would be, with the lions roaring, elephants trumpeting, pigs squealing, donkeys braying, horses whinnying, bulls bellowing . . .

    How many additions can you make to Tolly's list? Try to think of ideas no one else will include:

    dogs *yapping*

    cats

    bears

    (Each example in this exercise uses the present participle form of a verb. Explore the varied forms of verbs as: *go, went, going, gone.*)

2. This story is set in Great Britain. Although Britishers speak the same language we do, we find that they have different ways of saying some things. On page 14, for instance, the cab driver asks Tolly whether he has any "gum boots." What are "gum boots?"

    Begin a list of examples like this one. Give an explanation in American English. Keep adding to this list:

    p. 14. gum boots   rubber boots
    p. 11. cheerio   goodby
    p. 12. windscreen   _____

3. How do you know that Tolly is used to being lonely? After reading this much of the book, what do you know about Tolly? Write a description of this boy.

4. Heavy rains are falling on the flooded countryside. On the first page of this book the author describes the rain as it appears to Tolly, "splashing against the windows and blotching downward in an ugly, dirty way." On another page she talks of the women getting off the train "into the hissing rain."

What is your impression of rain? What does it sound like to you? Is it pleasant or unpleasant? How does it make you feel? Write your ideas about rain like this:

RAIN is . . .

> the sprouter of bright umbrellas,
> a cozy, snugged-in feeling,
>
> *a day for hiding games*

RAIN is . . .

_____ ,

_____ ,

_____ .

Write as many ideas about rain as you wish. Your ideas will form a poem. Paint a picture of one of your ideas to go with your poem.

Plan of operation: grade 5

The Cat and Mrs. Cary
by Doris Gates (Viking, 1962)

The story of twelve-year-old Brad's adventures as he visits his aunt, Mrs. Cary, has both a boy and a girl as leading characters. The chief character, however, is THE CAT, who condescends to live with Mrs. Cary and even to eat her food. An independent tomcat, he talks to Mrs. Cary although no one else ever hears his words. Mrs. Cary not only hears him, but replies aloud much to the amazement of those who just happen to be listening. Activities for extending learning are based on Chapter I of this book.

1. On page 12 notice the description of THE CAT. Describe an animal which you have observed. Can you make this animal seem real? Does your animal have personality?

2. Why does THE CAT say, "When it comes to catching fish, you've never seen anything to match my equal"? (p. 15.) How would you have said the same thing? Why do you think he said it in this unusual way?

3. Read the description of the Major on page 17. Can you draw a picture of this gentleman from the word picture painted by Doris Gates? Do you like the Major? Why or why not?

4. Usually when a person speaks, we use the word "said" followed by the speaker's name to make the identity of the speaker clear to the reader as in this sentence:

   John said, "What are you doing?"

Notice the use of dialogue on page 14. Has the author always used the word "said" to identify the speaker? In your log begin a page listed SYNONYMS FOR SAID. On this page list the words used by Doris Gates and add others that you can think of.

What words might you substitute for "said" in these sentences? Can you suggest more than one each time?

1. Susan *said,* "I need help."   *shouted*
2. Mother *said,* "I have a secret." *whispered*
3. "Who will help?" *said* Paul.   *questioned*
4. "Wait for me," I *said.*   *called*
5. "You will see," Mr. Day *said.*   *promised*

Encouraging Reading Addiction

Most students who enroll in the first grade learn to read to a greater or lesser degree, yet it is surprising how many students in the sixth grade are not avid readers. It is obvious that the child needs more than the mere recognition of words to spark his own sense of involvement with reading. He has to acquire a real feeling for books, the knowledge that books have something which he *needs,* that they have something that he *wants.*

It has been pointed out that the mechanical, drill-focused approach to reading may kill interest in reading at a time when enthusiasm for learning is high, and even more significant, that this readiness for learning will not be easily achieved again. Discussing this problem in reading, an expert in child psychoanalysis observes:

> The long years spent by our children in mastery of the mechanics of reading rob them of pleasure and discoveries in literature, and also rob them of the possibility of *addiction,* which is one of the characteristics of the good reader. The addiction to reading is acquired at an early age —usually, I believe, under eight or nine.[4]

How do we ensure this addiction to reading? How do students acquire this sense of involvement with reading? How do we teachers motivate youngsters to read so widely that they will never lose the habit? There is no *one* answer and there is no *right* answer, but there are many possibilities which are well worth exploring:

1. Use of exciting, quality literature in the reading program
2. Stress on stimulating coordinated reading and composition activities
3. Special attention to the reading interests of boys
4. Decrease in drill-type approaches to learning to read

[4] Selma Fraiberg, "The American Reading Problem," *Commentary* (June, 1965).

5. Exposure to many, varied experiences with literature—storytelling, dramatization, discussions of books, choric speaking

6. Many opportunities to share the excitement of reading; new approaches to book reviewing

7. Teacher enthusiasm and knowledge of literature and ways of presenting literature in the classroom

Focusing attention on books

Open books for students in varied ways, for few can resist the tempting illustrations, and the reading of a few intriguing words on a page is often enough to snag the interest of one who stops to look at a book propped open on the windowsill or a classroom table. Bookholders can be purchased or they can be made from two identical shapes cut from heavy cardboard taped together as illustrated.

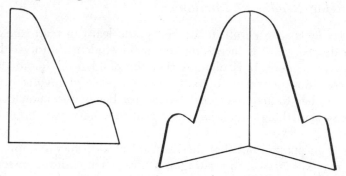

Another obvious way to open books is to *read aloud to a class*. After the last page of Mary Norton's *The Borrowers* (Harcourt) has just been completed, there will be many requests for that title and others by the same author. Showing the illustrations as the story is read is particularly important in the primary grades. The excellent illustrations by Maurice Sendak in Janice Udry's book, *Moon Jumpers* (Harper), for example, add much to the spell and deserve special attention.

Students can open books for each other by simply talking about a book that they have enjoyed and personally showing the book to the class or to an individual student. Writes the Director of the Junior Book Awards for Boys' Clubs of America:

> There is nothing like a child for word-of-mouth advertising among his peers. The librarian may recommend a book and the youngster will read it to please her because he likes her, but if he does not like the book, wild horses can not get him to recommend it to a Clubmate. But just let one of the boys say, "you ought to read such-and-such"—and the line can form on the right for those eager to read it.[5]

[5] Iris Vinton,, "What Children Like to Read," *Junior Libraries* (January, 1959), p. 5.

Displays of books also serve to whet the reading appetites of students. A display of colorful book jackets on a bulletin board is always eye-catching. Captions can be used, for example, THE BOOK BAG (with books spilling from a real bag) or IT'S BOOK TIME (a clock face with jackets at the number spaces). Another display might consist of scattered book jackets under the caption HAVE YOU READ? As children read these books, each one adds his name tag to the cover of that book. Comparisons of total books read should definitely be avoided, with stress remaining on individual development and enjoyment of books read.

Provocative methods of presenting stories to other members of a class can be explored as the children themselves strive to "sell" others on reading a book they have enjoyed. The *preparation of a collage* about a favorite title is an excellent way of interesting others in reading the book. Imagine, for instance, what a fascinating collage could be prepared featuring *The Twenty-One Balloons* by William Pène Du Bois (Viking), depicting the professor's misadventures on Krakatoa; the pictorial qualities of such a book are numerous.

Better book reviewing

The book review or "book report" as it is more commonly called is in many cases a dull, routine task which adds little to student enthusiasm for reading. What is the purpose of the book report? Its use is usually justified on the grounds of (1) checking on student reading, (2) keeping a record of books read, and (3) stimulating student interest in reading. The questionnaire that is completed repeatedly as books are read throughout the year does not serve to meet any of these requirements, for the questions asked can frequently be answered by anyone who holds the book in hand, students read far more than is recorded under duress, and this practice is far from stimulating.

We should like to suggest, therefore, as a first step toward developing this aspect of literature with children that the term *book reporting* be discarded in favor of *reviewing* or *sharing* of reading. The term *review* connotes thought, analysis, and reaction, while *sharing* connotes encouragement, enjoyment, and pleasure in telling the peer group about what has been discovered. Both sharing and reviewing approaches have validity and should be used during the year in varied ways. Variety is essential, for any technique repeated *ad nauseam* becomes dull and stultifying.

What are the possibilities of the book review? Encourage students to read and discuss book reviews which appear in the *Horn Book Magazine, Elementary English*, and magazines for children. More mature readers can examine commentaries in *Time* and *Saturday Review*. The book reviews read will demonstrate to the young reader a type of reacting to a book which is probably not familiar to him. It will suggest reactions other than "The book was interesting."

The book review can also supply provocative statements with which a student might disagree or arguments which a student might wish to amplify as he cites examples justifying critical comments about a work. The professional book review also suggests varied style and format for a book review, and examination of reviews should lead to a broader concept of the term *criticism*.

The primary objective of reviewing or sharing books should not be merely to "check on" student reading. Rather we should aim at multiple goals which are actually directed toward eliminating the need to check, for reviewing should ideally: (1) stress the enjoyment of reading, (2) lead to further reading, and (3) develop critical thinking.

If these goals are met, children will want to read because they find reading stimulating, entertaining, and informative. Our focus then is directly on the motivation of reading so that children will read, find it a pleasure, and wish to share their experiences with others. Sharing and book reviewing can more properly be regarded as means for motivation. In planning book review activities we must bear these points in mind:

1. Not all reading needs to be reviewed; students should be encouraged to read widely without the penalty of reviewing the quantity they read.

2. Varied review techniques must be used to provide for stimulating experiences.

In what ways can we vary the sharing of books? Once we move away from the rigid concept of the Book Report Form, the possibilities for sharing books are numerous, provocative, and enriching. These approaches to book sharing can be oral or written. They can be related to other areas of the curriculum—history, geography, art, music, science, mathematics. They can take forms which branch out into more creative media. We can challenge our students to discover a different, more exciting way to share a book. Ideas will grow out of experimentation.

● The *diorama* is an excellent medium for depicting a scene from a story. Homer Price (cardboard or papier mâché figure) could be shown with Aroma, his pet skunk, as they creep up on the robbers who are camping in the woods. The diorama also can be used to portray a scene from historical fiction or from the life of a figure in American history.

● A *mobile* can present a book by displaying the characters as well as objects or ideas essential to the story. *The 500 Hats of Bartholomew Cubbins* might, for instance, be interpreted through a mobile which features many unusual hats created in three dimensions.

● *Music* can be related to book sharing as a student or a small group of students composes a ballad about Charlotte, Wilbur, and their friends. Older students might write a calypso or a folk song about the adventures of Huckleberry Finn or a real person about whom they have read.

● A *collage* is an intriguing method of combining art with literature. *Chitty-Chitty-Bang-Bang*, for example, might be depicted on a large poster which includes a cut-out drawing of this distinctive green car, the faces of Man-Mountain Fink, Joe, the Monster, and the twins. Portions of a map of England, the English Channel, and northern France might be worked into the background as would be other motifs taken from the story. Words can also be incorporated in the collage—*Paris, transmogrifications, Paragon Panther, Ian Fleming,* etc.

Book-centered activities can be listed with each child selecting one which is appropriate for exchanging information about the particular book he has read. Other activities not only share information about a book but also extend the learning of the individual reader. Activities included might be some of the following:

● *Dramatize a story* with several children who have read the same book participating in a short skit. One adventure from *Mary Poppins* or tales from such folklore as *Pecos Bill* will provide exciting material for creative drama.

● *Compile a bibliography* for the library about topics of interest to many people—Horses, Dogs, Cats, Girls, Boys, Mystery, Science Fiction, China, The Civil War. Each listing can contain fiction as well as nonfiction titles which are in the school library collection. A team of students can work together.

● *Keep a list of interesting words* and phrases which the author used. This project can be a continuing activity related to both reading and writing.

● *Read several books by the same author.* Compare the books by subject, year written, point of view, ideas expressed. What similarities are noted? Do the books seem to be written by the same person?

● *Find out as much as possible about your favorite author* as you write a short biography including magazine and newspaper clippings, drawings made, and any other related information about the person and his writing.

● *Make a miniature billboard* advertising the book read. What feature will be advertised to make others interested in reading this book?

● *Write a letter to a favorite character.* Describe what might be included in another adventure or offer advice for solving his problems.

● *Read several books on the same topic* in order to compare the treatment of the topic by different authors. Compare the points of view, author style, the coverage of the topic.

The Teacher and Literature

As has been pointed out, the teacher's own enthusiasm for good stories and her knowledge of children's literature will determine the success of any classroom literature program. Are books present in the classroom? Do children know authors? Are they developing a taste for good literature? Do they voluntarily share a book experience with the teacher?

In addition to establishing a classroom atmosphere that encourages the reading of literature the teacher also has other responsibilities. It is the teacher who must (1) find time for literature in the program, (2) provide for all levels of ability, and (3) select books to be presented to the class and those to be purchased for school libraries.

Time for literature

Literature can appear in the elementary school classroom in many ways. Literature can, of course, be the material through which reading is taught. In this form literature becomes a text which is read, discussed, studied, as reading skills are practiced.

Literature is also an excellent starting point for many creative writing activities. Tall tales of Paul Bunyan, the adventures of Robin Hood, Aesop's fables serve to suggest short stories which children can write. The Moffat books by Eleanor Estes demonstrate the adventurous possibilities which are present in everyday happenings familiar to all children.

Literature is recreation as the teacher reads aloud. There are few children who do not hurry to their desks after recess as they notice the teacher seated with book in hand ready to read the third chapter of *The Lion, The Witch, and the Wardrobe* by C. S. Lewis (Macmillan). Other titles recommended for reading aloud include:

Mr. Popper's Penguins (Little) by Richard and Florence Atwater.
Rabbit Hill (Viking) by Robert Lawson.
The Children of Odin (Macmillan) by Padraic Colum.
Story of King Arthur and His Knights (Scribner) by Howard Pyle.
The Wind in the Willows (Scribner) by Kenneth Grahame.
Henry Huggins (Morrow) by Beverly Cleary.
The Long Winter (Harper) by Laura I. Wilder.
The Witch of Blackbird Pond (Houghton) by Elizabeth G. Speare.
Peterkin Papers (Houghton) by Lucretia P. Hale.
It's Perfectly True and Other Stories (Harcourt) by H. C. Andersen.

Although it is true that the teacher will often read a book aloud which a child could read himself, a technique that motivates reading, another purpose of reading aloud is to present material that stretches, that makes the child's mind reach. The child can understand ideas and vocabulary far beyond his reading ability so that the first grade child will chuckle delightedly over the antics of Pippi Longstocking although not able to read this book independently. He will later enjoy reading the same book himself as he rediscovers Astrid Lindgren's humorous tale.

From *Pippi Longstocking* by Astrid Lindgren. Copyright 1950 by The Viking Press, Inc. Reprinted by permission of The Viking Press, Inc.

Literature for all children

One of the very real assets of children's literature is its infinite variety. Almost every subject matter is covered by titles prepared for both beginning and advanced readers.

Young readers

Perhaps some of the most intriguing, thought-provoking story material is appearing in books for the very youngest reader. Enhanced by artful, vivid illustrations, these books have instant appeal, first as books read to the child, and later as books to read independently.

The teacher will find a receptive audience, for the child who enters first grade today has usually had a wide background of experiences. His listening vocabulary is estimated at 20,000 words, and he can fully comprehend a surprising number of rather complex concepts. Through television, parental reading aloud, and talking with other children and adults, children today are exposed to varied topics which little concerned the child of a generation ago.

What do children of this age enjoy most in literature? Individual interests are varied, but in general they thrive on humor, repetition, action, and stories about real people. Young boys who follow the astronauts through space and back again will search for books about space. Favorite books for this age group are the Dr. Seuss stories—*McElligott's Pool, Horton Hatches the Egg;* Anderson's horse stories—*Blaze and the Gypsies, Billy and Blaze;* Jerrold Beim's stories of real children—*Andy and the School Bus, Twelve O'Clock Whistle;* Marjorie Flack's animal tales—*Story about Ping, New Pet;* Margaret Johnson's *Joey and Patches, Snowshoe Paws, Stablemates;* Lois Lenski's *Cowboy Small, Little Fire Engine, Surprise for Davy;* and Hans Rey's amusing tales of *Curious George.* There are, of course, numerous other titles which could and should be named, but we shall leave that to your own exploration.

The able student

Most gifted children have little difficulty with reading and already enjoy this pursuit often to the exclusion of other tasks. The reading period for these students should not degenerate into a period of "free time" which offers little stimulus. Less time will be spent on learning word attack skills and phonics while the able student extends his thinking beyond the superficial enjoyment of the story content of a book.

No child should be pushed beyond his ability, but on the other hand the teacher should not place artificial ceilings on the reading of alert children. Grade level categorization of books has little meaning for the good reader, for he will almost certainly be reading several levels ahead of the school grade. Many children will, indeed, be reading titles from adult literature—*Cheaper by the Dozen, Life with Father, Born Free,* and many others. One need not fear that any child will "run out of things" to read, for it is presently impossible to read all of literature in one lifetime, and the storehouse of literature increases each day.

The growth of these individuals can be encouraged through the formation of a BOOK CLUB whose objectives will be established by its members. The group might choose to discuss one specific book each week with all members reading that title and preparing questions, observations, ideas to discuss. Each member can serve as discussion leader or deliver a short prepared book review. The group may decide to present a book to the class by preparing a display, dramatization, or a book talk. Members of the Book Club could gain much experience in book selection and oral language skills by planning presentations for younger students as the school initiates a CAMPAIGN FOR BETTER READERS.

Book selection

How do we choose books to read to a class? How do we select books for purchase by the school library? On what basis do we recommend books to students? It is obvious that the teacher needs to become acquainted with children's literature. A course in children's literature is a must for any elementary school teacher, but even that will not serve to keep the teacher's knowledge current. Frequent visits to the children's department of the library, reading of book reviews, noting publisher's advertisements, talking to others who enjoy children's books—these are some of the ways to inform yourself about news in the children's book world.

Personal examination of each title is fun and rewarding, but there is no denying that it is also time-consuming. The teacher must, therefore, often rely on the judgments of others in selecting books that cannot be personally examined. Following is a list of book selection aids which should be in the school's professional library or in the school library:

The Booklist and Subscription Books Bulletin, A Guide to Current Books, American Library Association. 60 E. Huron St., Chicago, Illinois.

Children's Books Too Good to Miss, May Hill Arbuthnot, comp., Cleveland, Ohio: Western Reserve University Press, 1963.

Children's Catalog, New York: H. W. Wilson Company. With regular supplements. The most complete, annotated listing.

Fare for the Reluctant Reader, 3rd ed., Anita E. Dunn, comp. Capital Area School Development Assn., State University of New York. Albany, N.Y.

Gateways to Readable Books, 3rd ed., Ruth Strang, *et. al.,* eds. New York: Wilson.

The Horn Book Magazine, The Horn Book, Inc., 585 Boylston St., Boston, Mass. 02116.

Reading Ladders for Human Relations, Muriel Crosby, ed. American Council on Education, 1963. Primary to adult books.

A Teacher's Guide to Children's Books, Nancy Larrick. Columbus, Ohio: Merrill, 1960.

Let students take an active part in the selection of books whether it is the individual selection of a book to read or the purchase of a group of titles for the school library. As adults we sometimes have far different values than do the children we teach. Have a stock of 3 x 5 file cards on which students (and you, too) can throughout the year note books for purchase. If title, author, and publishing information are included, the compilation of a purchase list can then be done efficiently when the list is required.

One fifth-grade class studied books published in 1964 using a list published by the Library of Congress [6] as a basis for their exploration. Their task was to select one title to be purchased with PTA funds for each of 12 classroom libraries. Their teacher, as school library coordinator, wisely placed this selection job in the hands of three committees. The twelve books selected were:

Group 1:

De Regniers, Beatrice Schenk, *May I Bring a Friend?* Illus. by Beni Montresor. Atheneum. Clever story of small boy who brings unusual friends to visit his royal acquaintances who invite him to tea.

Lionni, Leo, *Tico and the Golden Wings.* Pantheon Books. Lionni's beautiful illustrations help to tell the story of the bird that was born without wings.

Piatti, Celestino, *The Happy Owls.* Atheneum. A fable of two owls who observe the poultry yard squabbles.

Surany, Anico, *Ride the Cold Wind.* Illus. by Leonard E. Fisher. Putnam. Adventures of a Peruvian shepherd boy who disobeys his father.

Group 2:

Cretan, Gladys Y., *A Gift from the Bride.* Illus. by Rita Fegiz. Little, Brown. Mari wants to learn to read, but there is no school in her village.

Haywood, Carolyn, *Eddie's Green Thumb.* Illus. by author. Morrow. Third graders have a mix-up with garden seeds.

Hodges, Margaret, *The Wave.* Illus. by Blair Lent. Houghton Mifflin. Story of a Japanese grandfather whose wisdom saves the village.

Holman, Felice, *Elisabeth the Treasure Hunter.* Illus. by Erik Blegvad. Macmillan. Elisabeth and Charles practice treasure hunting on the beach.

---

[6] Virginia Haviland and Lois B. Watt, comps., *Children's Books: 1964. A List of 200 Books for Preschool through Junior High School Age* (Washington, D.C.: Library of Congress, U.S. Government Printing Office, 1965). (15¢.)

Group 3:

Alger, LeClaire, *Gaelic Ghosts*. Illus, by Nonny Hogrogian. Holt. A collection of humorous ghost stories.

Clarke, Pauline, *The Return of the Twelves*. Illus. by Bernarda Bryson. Coward-McCann. The lost soldiers of the Brontë children find their adventurous way home.

Fitzhugh, Louise, *Harriet, the Spy*. Illus. by author. Harper & Row. Harriet's written observations of her "friends" are exposed.

Rodman, Maia (Wojciechowska), *Shadow of a Bull*. Illus. by Alvin Smith. Atheneum. Because Manolo's father is a bullfighter, he is expected to become a bullfighter, too.

Book Awards. Each year selected titles in children's literature are awarded honors. Two of the most famous awards are the Newbery and Caldecott medals which were established by a publisher, Frederic G. Melcher.

The Newbery award was first given in 1922 to Hendrik Van Loon's *The Story of Mankind.* Named in honor of John Newbery, an early English publisher who is credited with "discovering" children's literature, this award is given for "distinguished literature." The award list includes many familiar titles:

*1922 Van Loon, Hendrik W., *The Story of Mankind*. Liveright. (7-9).

1923 Lofting, Hugh, *The Voyages of Dr. Dolittle*. Stokes. (4-6).

1924 Hawes, Charles B., *The Dark Frigate*. Little. (7-9).

1925 Finger, Charles J., *Tales from Silver Lands*. Doubleday. (5-7).

1926 Chrisman, Arthur Bowie, *Shen of the Sea*. Dutton. (5-8).

1927 James, Will, *Smoky: The Cowhorse*. Scribner. (6-9).

1928 Mukerji, Dhan G., *Gay-Neck, The Story of a Pigeon*. Dutton. (5-9).

1929 Kelly, Eric, *The Trumpeter of Krakow*. Macmillan. (7-8).

1930 Field, Rachel, *Hitty: Her First Hundred Years*. Macmillan. (4-7).

1931 Coatsworth, Elizabeth, *The Cat Who Went to Heaven*. Macmillan. (5-7).

1932 Armer, Laura, *Waterless Mountain*. Longmans. (5-8).

1933 Lewis, Elizabeth F., *Young Fu of the Upper Yangtze*. Winston. (7-9).

1934 Meigs, Cornelia, *Invincible Louisa*. Little, (7-9).

1935 Shannon, Monica, *Dobry*. Viking. (5-8).

1936 Brink, Carol R., *Caddie Woodlawn*. Macmillan. (6-8).

1937 Sawyer, Ruth, *Roller Skates*. Viking. (7-8).

1938 Seredy, Kate, *White Stag*. Viking. (6-9).

1939 Enright, Elizabeth, *Thimble Summer*. Farrar. (5-7).

* Dates given are the years of the award. Each book was published in the year immediately preceding.

1940 Daugherty, James, *Daniel Boone.* Viking. (5-9).

1941 Sperry, Armstrong, *Call It Courage.* Macmillan. (5-8).

1942 Edmonds, Walter, *The Matchlock Gun.* Dodd. (4-6).

1943 Gray, Elizabeth J., *Adam of the Road.* Viking. (6-9).

1944 Forbes, Esther, *Johnny Tremain.* Houghton. (7-9).

1945 Lawson, Robert, *Rabbit Hill.* Viking. (3-6).

1946 Lenski, Lois, *Strawberry Girl.* Lippincott. (4-6).

1947 Bailey, Carolyn S., *Miss Hickory.* Viking. (4-6).

1948 DuBois, William Pène, *The 21 Balloons.* Viking. (5-9).

1949 Henry, Marguerite, *King of the Wind.* Rand. (5-8).

1950 De Angeli, Marguerite, *Door in the Wall.* Doubleday. (4-6).

1951 Yates, Elizabeth, *Amos Fortune, Free Man.* Aladdin. (7-9).

1952 Estes, Eleanor, *Ginger Pye.* Harcourt. (4-7).

1953 Clark, Ann N., *Secret of the Andes.* Viking. (6-8).

1954 Krumgold, Joseph, *. . . And Now Miguel.* Crowell. (5-8).

1955 De Jong, Meindert, *Wheel on the School.* Harper. (4-7).

1956 Latham, Jean L., *Carry On, Mr. Bowditch.* Houghton. (6-8).

1957 Sorensen, Virginia, *Miracles on Maple Hill.* Harcourt. (4-7).

1958 Keith, Harold, *Rifles for Watie.* Crowell. (6-9).

1959 Speare, Elizabeth, *Witch of Blackbird Pond.* Houghton. (6-9).

1960 Krumgold, Joseph, *Onion John.* Crowell. (5-8).

1961 O'Dell, Scott, *Island of the Blue Dolphins.* Houghton. (5-9).

1962 Speare, Elizabeth G., *The Bronze Bow.* Houghton. (5-9).

1963 L'Engle, Madeline, *A Wrinkle in Time.* Farrar. (5-8).

1964 Neville, Emily, *It's Like This, Cat.* Harper. (4-7).

1965 Wojciechowska, Maia, *Shadow of a Bull.* Atheneum. (5-8).

1966 De Treviño, Elizabeth B., *I, Juan de Pareja.* Farrar. (5-9).

1967 Hunt, Irene, *Up a Road Slowly.* Follett. (6-9).

The Caldecott Medal is awarded to the best picture-book of the year. Named in honor of Randolph Caldecott (1846–1886), an English illustrator of children's books, the first Caldecott Medal was awarded in 1938 to Dorothy Lathrop for illustrating *Animals of the Bible.* Note in the following list that the first name given is that of the illustrator, who in some cases is also the author.

1938 Lathrop, Dorothy P. (illus.), *Animals of the Bible.* Text edited by Helen D. Fish. Stokes. (1-4).

1939 Handforth, Thomas (author-illus.), *Mei Li.* Doubleday. (1-3).

1940 Aulaire, Ingri and Edgar d', (author-illus.), *Abraham Lincoln.* Doubleday. (3-4).

1941 Lawson, Robert (author-illus.), *They Were Strong and Good.* Viking. (4-6).

1942 McCloskey, Robert (author-illus.), *Make Way for Ducklings.* Viking. (1-3).

1943 Burton, Virginia Lee (author-illus.), *The Little House*. Houghton. (1-4).

1944 Slobodkin, Louis (illus.), *Many Moons*. Text by James Thurber. Harcourt. (4-5).

1945 Jones, Elizabeth Orton (illus.), *Prayer for a Child*. Text by Rachel Field. Macmillan. (1-3).

1946 Petersham, Maud and Miska (author-illus.), *The Rooster Crows*, Macmillan. (1-3).

1947 Weisgard, Leonard (illus.), *Little Island*. Text by Margaret W. Brown. Doubleday. (1-3).

1948 Duvoisin, Roger (illus.), *White Snow, Bright Snow*. Text by Alvin Tresselt. Lothrop. (1-3).

1949 Hader, Berta and Elmer (author-illus.), *The Big Snow*. Macmillan. (1-3).

1950 Politi, Leo (author-illus.), *Song of the Swallows*. Scribner. (1-3).

1951 Milhous, Katherine (author-illus.), *The Egg Tree*. Scribner. (1-3).

1952 Mordvinoff, Nicholas (illus.), *Finders Keepers*. Text by William Lipkind. Harcourt. (1-3).

1953 Ward, Lynd (author-illus.), *Biggest Bear*. Houghton. (2-3).

1954 Bemelmans, Ludwig (author-illus.), *Madeline's Rescue*. Viking. (1-3).

1955 Brown, Marcia J. (illus.), *Cinderella*. Text by Charles Perrault. Scribner. (1-5).

1956 Rojankovsky, Feodor (illus.), *Frog Went a-Courtin'*. Text by John Langstaff. (1-4).

1957 Simont, Marc (illus.), *A Tree Is Nice*. Text by Janice Udry. Harper. (1-2).

1958 McCloskey, Robert (author-illus.), *Time of Wonder*. Viking. (2-4).

1959 Cooney, Barbara (illus.), *Chanticleer and the Fox*. Text by Chaucer. Crowell. (1-5).

1960 Ets, Marie Hall (co-author and illus.), *Nine Days to Christmas*. Co-author of text, Aurora Labastida. Viking. (2-4).

1961 Sidjakov, Nicholas (author-illus.), *Baboushka and the Three Kings*. Parnassus. (1-5).

1962 Brown, Marcia (author-illus.), *Once a Mouse*. Scribner. (1-3).

1963 Keats, Ezra J. (author-illus.), *The Snowy Day*. Viking. (1-2).

1964 Sendak, Maurice. (author-illus.), *Where the Wild Things Are*. Harper, (1-3).

1965 De Regniers, Bernice (author-illus.), *May I Bring a Friend?* Harcourt. (1-2).

1966 Hogrogian, Nonny (illus.), *Always Room for One More*. Text by Sorche Nic Leodhas. Holt. (2-5).

1967 Ness, Evaline (author-illus.), *Sam, Bangs and Moonshine*. Holt. (K-3).

Should these lists be used as purchase lists for a beginning library? A well-established elementary school library will contain all these titles, but one must remember that books are selected for varied reasons. In examining these lists, for example, one immediately notices that the

Caldecott award list is composed of books for the primary grades judged on the value of their illustrations. The list of titles for the Newbery award focuses largely on books for grades four through nine with a heavy concentration of books for the junior high school level. Too, it must be remembered that much excellent nonficition is required for the school library. These titles must be evaluated, therefore, in terms of the needs of the school library as a whole.

It must be remembered, too, in examining award lists that many of these books were selected 20, even 30, years ago. Some of these titles do not prove as tempting today as they may have been then, as new interests and tastes develop. One wonders also whether there is not a tinge of "what adults think children should like" about awards of this nature. An interesting study could be conducted by classes to determine which books are favorites with class members. Which titles from these lists are named as favorites? Which are not, and why? Here is an opportunity to develop critical thinking as children realize that a printed list proves nothing in itself.

Literature Enriches Learning

Literature pervades the curriculum. How much more exciting is the history lesson that talks of real people who live through their biographies, the science lesson that opens books that explain why, where, and how? The textbook can introduce, but beyond that introduction must come books, books, and more books to satisfy that "satiable curtiosity," which is not typical of the elephant's child alone.

What do we require of the literature of learning? "Integrity, however achieved, is the quality we look for in children's books. This includes integrity with regard both to writing and to subject matter . . ." writes Alice Dalgliesh,[8] author of many fine titles for young people. In the classroom we are especially concerned with integrity, and we are concerned with accuracy of information provided and the qualifications of those who provide it.

Social studies

There is a growing collection of excellent books for young people in the areas of history, geography, government, and citizenship. Both fiction and nonfiction offer many titles to augment understandings, to supply factual knowledge, and to extend interests.

> Enlarge a United States (or world) map which can be mounted on a bulletin board. As students read books, have each pin a small pennant on the

[8] Alice Dalgliesh, "A Matter of Integrity," *Saturday Review.* (November 13, 1965), p. 51.

map bearing the title of the book with the location revealing the setting of the story. Figures of the main characters can also be used to mark the setting, with Tom Sawyer marching beside the Mississippi and Paul Bunyan in the North Woods.

Examine the names of children in the class. Are there Irish names, French, Italian? Were any children born abroad? How many are native to the state? Questions like these can lead to an interesting study of the origins of the settlers of the United States. Biographies of Americans who came from other lands will add much to the understanding of these people; for example, *William Penn* by Hildegard Dolson (Holt, 1962). Many fine history books describe these pioneers and their lives in the new country.

Jamestown: First English Colony, by Marshall W. Fishwick (Harper & Row, 1965). Jamestown revisted; many photographs.

Gateway to America: Miss Liberty's First Hundred Years, by Hertha Pauli (McKay, 1965). Includes contributions of the immigrant.

America Is Born (1959), *America Grows Up* (1960), *America Moves Forward* (1960), by Gerald Johnson (Morrow). An excellent series for grades 5-8.

Understanding of the lives of people in different countries or regions of the United States can be gained through the reading of fiction. Kate Seredy's *The Good Master* is an excellent example of an exciting story which also describes, in this case, the Hungarian legends and holiday celebrations as well as the everyday life of the people. Other titles include:

Banner in the Sky, by James R. Ullman (Switzerland)
Call It Courage, by Armstrong Sperry (Polynesia)
Crow Boy, by Taro Yashima (Japan)
The Family Conspiracy, by Joan Phipson (Australia)
Lotte's Locket, by Virginia Sorensen (Denmark)
Spiro of the Sponge Fleet, by Henry Chapin (Greece)
The Wheel on the School, by Meindert DeJong (Holland)
Young Fu of the Upper Yangtze, by Elizabeth Lewis (China)

"Where in the World?" asks the title of Philip Egan's provocative, answer-filled book (Rand McNally, 1964) that is certain to appeal to children from grade four through six. "What was Columbus doing in Iceland?" "Where in the world are diamonds found?" "Where in the world can today become yesterday?"—these questions arouse curiosity and immediately satisfy it.

Don't miss Miroslav Sasek's beautiful guidebooks which are for young and old a true delight. The latest is *This Is Greece* (Macmillan, 1966), but others include *This Is San Francisco, This Is London, This Is Paris.*

Folk tales are receiving well-deserved attention in titles such as *The Valiant Chattee-Maker; A Folk Tale of India Retold,* by Christine Price (Warne, 1965), and *The Sea of Gold and Other Tales from Japan,* adapted by Yoshiko Uchida (Scribners, 1965). The folklore of a nation develops insight into the ways of its people.

Any topic or subject in the social studies can be enriched through the use of these stimulating titles. Use book selection aids; for example, the *Children's Catalog,* to suggest titles for units of study.

Science

Contemporary focus on science has led to the publication of many exciting books in the various fields of science. One of the leading writers in science for youth has been Isaac Asimov, who writes for the more advanced student. He is author of *Building Blocks of the Universe* (Abelard, 1957) and *The Clock We Live On* (Abelard, 1959), as well as *Words of Science* (Houghton Mifflin, 1959) and adult science fiction.

Another familiar name is Herbert Zim, whose small handbooks on Mammals, Insects, Stars, Trees, Birds, and so on are inexpensive and reliable reference books. Now available in paperback editions, these books are popular purchases for the young scientist himself as he collects rocks, butterflies, or studies the stars.

Activities which relate science and literature might include the following:

Read the very fine description of the life of a hermit crab told by Holling C. Holling in *Pagoo* (Houghton Mifflin, 1957). This adventure story is accompanied by superb illustrations in both black and white and color. Follow the reading of this book by showing the unique film *The Story of a Book* (Churchill Films) which describes the work of Mr. and Mrs. Holling in developing this idea for a book—the origin of the idea, observation of the hermit crab, preparation of illustrations, writing of the text.

Use fishnet as an attractive background for a display of books about the sea. Include some of these titles:

Brindze, Ruth, *The Rise and Fall of the Seas; the Story of the Tides* (Harcourt, 1964).

Buck, Margaret W., *Along the Seashore* (Abingdon, 1964).

Clarke, Arthur C., *The Challenge of the Sea* (Holt, 1960).

Kenyon, Ley, *Discovering the Under Sea World* (Sterling, 1961).

Books of experiments are intriguing to the boys, as are books about space. Encourage the publicizing of new *finds* of this type which interest students.

Encourage students to read biographies of Men of Science. Gifted students will be especially interested in learning more about inventors, discoverers, scientists. Information gained can be shared by the preparation of a display which depicts the contributions of the individual.

Bigland, Eileen, *Madame Curie* (Criterion).

Dickinson, Alice, *Charles Darwin and Natural Selection* (Watts).

Freeman, Mae B., *The Story of Albert Einstein* (Random). Jewett,

Frances L., and Claire L. McCausland, *Wilderness Treasure* (Houghton Mifflin). Eight brief biographies of botanists.

Kamm, Josephine, *Malaria Ross* (Criterion).

Manton, Jo, *The Story of Albert Schweitzer* (Abelard).

Sullivan, Navin, *Pioneer Astronomers* (Atheneum).

Tannenbaum, Beulah, and Myra Stillman, *Isaac Newton, Pioneer of Space Mathematics* (Whittlesey).

Thomas, Henry, *Charles Steinmetz* (Putnam).

Weir, Ruth C., *Thomas Alva Edison, Inventor* (Abingdon).

White, Anne Terry, *George Washington Carver, The Story of A Great American* (Random).

Books to Investigate

Adams, Bess P., *About Books and Children*. New York: Holt, 1953.

American Library Association, *Basic Collection for Elementary Grades*. Chicago: Scott, Foresman, 1960.

Arbuthnot, May Hill, *Children and Books*. Chicago: Scott, Foresman, 1957.

Baker, Augusta, *Books about Negro Life for Children*. New York: New York Public Library, 1957.

Crosby, Muriel, ed., *Reading Ladders for Human Relations*, 4th ed. Washington, D.C.: American Council on Education, 1963.

Fenner, Phyllis, *The Proof of the Pudding*. New York: Day, 1957. A delightful book about reading for enjoyment.

Hazard, Paul, *Books, Children and Men*. Boston: Horn Book, 1960.

Huck, Charlotte, and Doris A. Young, *Children's Literature in the Elementary School*. New York: Holt, 1961. A book of readings covering the broad field.

Larrick, Nancy, *A Teacher's Guide to Children's Books*. Columbus, Ohio: Merrill, 1960. Information about books and about using them in the classroom.

Moore, Anne C., *My Roads to Childhood*. Boston: Horn Book, 1961.

Robinson, Evelyn R., *Readings about Children's Literature*. New York: McKay, 1966.

Smith, Lillian H., *The Unreluctant Years: A Critical Approach to Children's Literature*. Chicago: American Library Association, 1953.

Wofford, Azile, *Book Selection for School Libraries*. New York: Wilson, 1962.

Is there anything sadder in the world than poverty of words?

John Haggerty

13

English for the Disadvantaged Child

Who is the disadvantaged child? How are his needs different from those of other children? How can the school help meet his needs? These are questions which are involved in attacking the problem of economic disadvantage, a problem that is the concern not only of those in education but also of the sociologist, anthropologist, psychologist, and linguist.

Nor is this a small problem to be treated lightly, for the numbers involved are impressive. James Olsen points out in "Children of the Ghetto," for example, that "More than one-third of the total enrollment in the 14 largest school systems in the U.S. are children from the slums." [1] Former U.S. Commissioner of Education, Francis Keppel, noted, furthermore:

> Clearly the primary and secondary schools have been doing their worst job for the children who need it most, namely, the children of the poor, roughly five million of them with a heavy concentration in the South and in the slums of the great cities of the North. [2]

President Johnson's emphasis on War on Poverty has focused attention on the disadvantaged American and a massive effort has been instigated to remove the disadvantage through compensatory education beginning with preschool Head Start programs and including programs for adults.

[1] James Olsen, "Children of the Ghetto," *High Point*, (March, 1964), p. 26.
[2] Francis Keppel, "Who Is to Speak for English?" An address given at the Modern Language Association meeting in Chicago, December 29, 1963.

The problem of compensatory education for the disadvantaged focuses on the alleviation of language impoverishment, and it is for that reason that we are devoting a chapter in this book to English for the disadvantaged child.

Understanding the Disadvantaged

What is deprivation? Is it synonymous with poverty? Is it always found in slums? Deprivation, or disadvantage, whichever term you prefer, connotes more than poverty alone, and it entails more than mere residence in a slum. The disadvantaged person, equated with no single ethnic or racial group, has been bypassed by the benefits which the average American has come to assume as his right, his way of living, and this disadvantage usually has been accorded through no fault of his own. Born in an economically depressed locality, a worker whose job disappears through automation, a migrant worker dependent on the vagaries of the crops, a small farmer striving to exist on exhausted land—these are disadvantaged members of our society who exist on substandard incomes. What chance do children born into these families have to obtain what for most of us are the necessities of life?

Factors focusing attention on the problem

Poor people have always existed in our society. The slums have not sprung up overnight nor is deprivation a condition that is completely new to us (although the term may be). Why then are we suddenly concerned about deprivation and the needs of the disadvantaged child? A number of factors account for our unprecedented national concern for assisting disadvantaged Americans: (1) the unconscionable contrast between affluence and poverty, (2) civil rights activities, (3) high cost to the nation, (4) increasing numbers of unemployables, and (5) our national prestige.

The contrast between the impressive affluence of the majority of American citizens and the poverty-stricken, hopeless condition which is the present lot of others is difficult to justify. Americans are typically pictured as affluent individuals who might be described thus:

> They drive one or more cars, watch one or more television sets, own one or more telephones. They have added freezers to their refrigerators, automatic dryers to their automatic washers, swimming pools to their backyards, air conditioners to their homes and cars; and they have more time than ever to switch off the appliances and get away from it all.[3]

[3] *The War on Poverty*. A Congressional Presentation under the direction of Sargent Shriver, March 17, 1964.

But is this image the picture for all Americans? No, for in the midst of apparent national wealth there still exist "pockets of poverty" whose depth is appalling when contrasted to the lives of middle class Americans. The Bureau of the Census report in 1962 included the following depressing statistics:

9.3 million families had incomes below $3,000.

These 9.3 million families contained more than 30 million people, of whom 11 million were children.

More than 1.1 million of these families contained 4 or more children.

5.4 million families (more than 17 million people) had incomes below $2,000.

More than 1 million children were being raised in families with 6 or more children and incomes of less than $3,000.

It is estimated that approximately one-fifth of the United States' population was living in poverty in 1962. "These," states the Shriver Report, "are the people behind the American looking glass. Being poor is not a choice for them; it is a rigid way of life. It has been handed down from generation to generation in a cycle of inadequate education, inadequate homes, inadequate jobs and stunted ambitions."

A second influential factor, the civil rights movement, has focused national attention on the plight of the Negro. Studies find that the Negro has been hardest hit by poverty, for the long history of racial discrimination, segregated educational facilities, and limited political representation has made the Negro truly a "second-class citizen" who has traditionally been "hired last, paid less, and fired first." One study reports that in 1963 nearly one-half of the American Negro population (8 million individuals) lived in families with less than $3,000 annual income.[4] It is small wonder that Negro Americans have at last revolted on a large scale. The increasingly responsive federal government has assumed a leading role in bettering educational facilities, assuring voting rights, and generally upgrading the status of this racial group as well as that of other submerged segments of society.

A third, highly practical, factor which has led to national concern for alleviating deprivation is the extremely high cost to the nation as a whole. The Department of Labor provides statistics relevant to the cost of unemployment to the nation. To maintain only one unemployed person through his lifetime, for example, can cost the nation a minimum of $40,-000. Our annual bill for public assistance in 1963 (excluding costs of side effects leading to crime and delinquency) was $6 billion. It is pointed

[4] Vivian W. Henderson, *The Economic Status of the Negroes in the South* (Atlanta, Ga.: Southern Regional Council of Churches, 1963).

out, on the other hand, that full employment of the Negro portion of the labor force alone would add potentially $13 to $17 billion annually to the Gross National Product.

A fourth factor is that many of those who are unemployed are actually "unemployable." What is the high school drop-out prepared to do to earn a living? When our society permits the sixteen-year-old to leave school, untrained, unprepared to lead a useful life, we must immediately assume financial responsibility for maintaining this person. We can easily recognize the dollar and cents value of reaching each child long before he approaches the drop-out age. This need is further dramatized by the large number of draftees who are rejected on a literacy basis. It is incredible that illiteracy should exist in our society with its highly developed system of education.

Another factor which has placed the spotlight on the deprived fifth of the nation is our struggle for prestige in the eyes of the world. We are highly conscious, for example, of the disapproval of other nations as they view our treatment of the Negro. Extreme poverty contrasted to general affluence is also difficult to justify to a critical world. Even more pressing, however, is the undeniable need in our complex industrialized society for a national labor force that is highly literate and capable of learning continuously so that we can continue to progress at top-level efficiency. It is imperative that all resources be explored and developed to the fullest potential.

Who is the disadvantaged child?

The disadvantaged child may be a Mexican-American boy living in California, an American Indian on a Utah reservation, a poor white from Appalachia, a Puerto Rican girl living in New York City or a Negro living along South State Street in Chicago. The point is that economic disadvantage is limited to no particular racial or ethnic group nor to any special locality; it is spread literally across our nation, for it is present in every city, in most small towns, and in many rural areas.

As Richard Corbin states in the excellent report published by the National Council of Teachers of English:

> Whatever the racial or ethnic background of these disadvantaged, their circumstances are much the same. They come from families that exist on annual incomes which fall below the established national minimum subsistence level, that have known little or no schooling, that have no job security. More than half have only one parent (generally the mother), and many have never known either parent. They come from families who seldom aspire, or when they do, aspire unrealistically, who are often idle because few jobs are open to them. They are the people who exist—one can hardly say "live"—on the wretched rim of an otherwise affluent world.

And they number not fewer than one quarter of our total national population.[5]

Studies have identified certain characteristics which are typical of children of all ages who are classified as deprived or disadvantaged. The typical disadvantaged child can be described thus:

1. He lacks self-confidence. His insecurity may cause unruly behavior in the classroom or juvenile delinquency. His attitude toward his own ability and his possibilities for success in life is negative, and he feels that others view him as "a worthless individual." Racial discrimination has accentuated the poor self-image for the Negro child. The disadvantaged child is afraid, ill at ease in the school situation. He lacks the security of a stable home, for he frequently moves and has little opportunity to develop friendships.

2. The home he lives in does not provide educational stimulus. The family is economically poor as well as educationally impoverished. Money is not available for books and magazines or the daily newspaper, and even were money available, there is little desire for spending it in this way; it would more likely be used to buy entertainment, food, or clothing. Paper, pencils, and crayons are not available in the home nor are varied toys to stimulate play. There is no precedent for obtaining an education, as parents and grandparents have had little formal schooling. A college degree or even a high school diploma is beyond the aspirations of this child. There may be hostility toward teachers and the school with the latter viewed as a jail and the teacher as jailer. The child may enter school already looking forward to the time he can drop out. The experiential background of this child is limited, for he has had little opportunity to travel, to be read to, to visit museums, and to explore the world in general.

3. He is not physically well-cared-for, and in many cases is undernourished. He shows evidence of neglected illness and may have physical handicaps which need attention. He has not made regular visits to the dentist or had his eyes checked. Lack of parental supervision and adequate sleeping facilities may mean this child will come to school tired, and he may arrive hungry, having had no breakfast.

4. His language skills are impoverished. The speech heard at home is meager with little elaboration. Mother directs the child's activities by single-word commands, saying "Here," to the young girl to whom she hands the baby. She does not elaborate as a more educated person tends to, "Here. Hold Manny while I start peeling the potatoes for dinner. He keeps crawling under my feet, and I'm afraid I'll step on him." The working mother, who herself may not be physically well, is tired and is preoccupied by providing the essentials—food, beds, clothes, a roof overhead. Although there may be many people living in the same apartment, the extent of the vocabulary to which the child is exposed is actually small, and no one has time to sit talking to a

---

[5] Richard Corbin, "Literacy, Literature, and the Disadvantaged," in *Language Programs for the Disadvantaged* (Champaign, Ill.: National Council of Teachers of English, 1965), p. 6.

child about his games or to tell him stories nor is he particularly encouraged to talk. The child is left largely to his own devices, often having little contact with the English language, especially in its standard dialects. Mexican-American or Puerto Rican children may have the further disadvantage of not speaking English at all or of living in a home where English is not usually spoken. The English that this child learns is only that heard on the street. He is proficient in neither language. Entrance in elementary school requires the learning of English, therefore, as a foreign language for these children, who must become bilingual.

The Deprived Child in School

Our focus as teachers is not on the broad social problem of deprivation, however, but on helping the child who is the victim of deprivation; even more specifically, our concern in this book is for instruction in English as one part of the elementary school curriculum. In order to plan a program designed to aid the child in developing language skills it is first necessary to determine his needs.

Needs of the deprived child

The needs of the deprived child are varied, and they include more than academic knowledge, for this child comes to school psychologically handicapped, a factor which impedes learning. The objectives of any program for compensatory education must be cognizant of the child's need to develop:

1. Language skills: thinking, listening, speaking, writing, reading (in the order named)
2. Feeling of personal worth; confidence in his ability to succeed
3. Recognition of school as pleasant and learning as pleasurable
4. Enthusiasm and interest in environment; wide experimental background
5. Interest in others and respect for them; ability to work and play with others

These skills, attitudes, and abilities are largely assumed to be part of a child's preschool development, and in a home in which the parents are concerned about the needs of the child and make a concerted effort to provide stimulating experiences for the child, it is probable that a foundation will have been built before entrance in school. The child usually enters school eagerly, confident about learning to read and about liking his teacher. We commonly take these factors for granted, proceeding immediately with readiness programs based on a preparation of five years directed toward helping the child grow and develop abilities. The disadvantaged child, however, requires a program directed toward providing experiences which will develop these attitudes and abilities which have not been developed in the home as well as concentration on compensating for language deficiencies.

The important role of the teacher

Is "disadvantaged" synonymous with "uncultured?" Are disadvantaged children to be regarded as potential delinquents? Must all teaching time be spent disciplining? Must creativity, discovery methods, and enrichment activities be discarded in favor of a rigidly teacher-controlled classroom? These are only a few examples of the fallacious thinking which teachers openly or unconsciously reveal.

A most influential factor in the deprived child's chances for success in school is his attitude toward school, the teacher, and toward learning, and the three are encompassed in one complex feeling of uncertainty, hostility, and predestined failure. The burden for dispelling the child's fears lies on the classroom teacher, and he quickly senses her attitude toward him. Authoritative tone of voice, aloofness, coldness of manner, the obvious view of the child as an inferior being—all serve to substantiate the child's preconceived idea of school; they do nothing to make him feel welcome, wanted, warm.

Why should young Chuck wish to communicate with a teacher who talks to him only when she points out his mistakes? Why should he try to read when he knows before he tries that he will fail as he has always failed? Isn't it natural that this child much prefers the familiar street on which he leads a relatively happy existence with others like himself who "speak his language" in an environment which accepts him for what he is? On what grounds can we meet these children, these "nonstandard" students?

We teachers must make a concerted effort to understand these children. We must realize that the culturally different child doesn't understand us or our middle class culture any more than we understand his. And we must overcome our own prejudices. As one young teacher of urban children describes it in 1964:

> I feel a part of the children; I know them, their spontaneity, enthusiasm, freedom, humor, innocence—all the childlike qualities that make them children. In these qualities, they are not deprived or disadvantaged. They are still children and can be reached as children. More important, they want to be reached and cared about and taught.[6]

The standard English which we speak is as foreign to the child as his dialect may be to us. The poem written by gifted Langston Hughes may provide insight for the teacher as well as the student:

[6] Dorothy McGeoch, *Learning to Teach in Urban Schools* (New York: Teachers College, 1965), p. 4.

> I play it cool and dig all jive.
> That's the reason I stay alive.
> My motto, as I live and learn,
> Is: "Dig and Be Dug in Return."

What personal objectives should the teacher (as well as courses for the teacher) of the deprived child consider when preparing to teach? We would direct the prospective teacher toward:

1. Understanding the lives and the learning styles of children in depressed areas
2. Understanding the psychological and sociological roots of prejudice and the problems within and between ethnic groups
3. Developing a positive attitude toward serving in programs for disadvantaged students
4. Developing, through study and supervised experience, teaching skills and patterns appropriate for working with culturally different children
5. Developing new curriculum guides and original teaching materials reflecting awareness of the needs and the special disabilities of disadvantaged children, but also capitalizing on interests and abilities of these children.[7]

One approach to understanding the child is through reading not only the nonfiction listed at the end of this chapter but also fiction and biography which present a type of case study of disadvantaged children in the context of their environments. Written by skilled authors, these works make no attempt to synthesize deprivation, but tell the reader about one specific human being, describing his behavior, his feelings, his motives. Let us examine a number of books which can lend us insight into the problems of the disadvantaged child: [8]

Agee, James, *Let Us Now Praise Famous Men* (Houghton). Intimate study of lives of the southern cotton picker and his family.

Bakker, Piet, *Ciske the Rat* (Doubleday). Story of a young delinquent who needs love, but cannot always accept the overtures of his teacher.

Burgess, Anthony, *The Clockwork Orange* (Norton). Teenagers speak a different language.

Fast, Howard, *The Children* (Duell). Children in New York's slums.

Godden, Rumer, *An Episode of Sparrows* (Viking). Children of the London streets.

Lewis, Oscar, *Children of Sanchez* (Random). An authentic recording of life in the slums of Mexico City.

[7] NCTE Task Force Report, *Language Programs for the Disadvantaged* (Champaign, Ill. National Council of Teachers of English, 1965), p. 171.

[8] For a more complete listing see: Iris Tiedt and Sidney Tiedt, *Unrequired Reading*, rev. ed. (Corvallis, Ore.: Oregon State University Press, 1967).

Miller, Warren, *Cool World* (Little). An excellent portrayal of a Negro boy's life with his gang.

Parks, Gordon, *The Learning Tree* (Harper). Newt, a Negro boy, is helped toward an education.

Thomas, Mac, *Gumbo* (Grove). Young Toby is the son of textile mill workers.

Stories of teaching in depressed areas also supply enlightening descriptions of the problems of teaching disadvantaged children and the approaches used by specific teachers in specific situations. Explore some of the following: [9]

Ashton-Warner, Sylvia, *Teacher* (Simon and Schuster). Teaching primary grades in a Maori school in New Zealand.

Braithwaite, E. R., *To Sir, With Love* (Prentice-Hall). Teaching in London's slum schools.

Giles, Janice H., *Miss Willie* (Westminster). Teaching in the small rural school.

Hunter, Evan, *The Blackboard Jungle* (Simon and Schuster). The problems of teaching urban deprived students.

Perkins, Virginia C., *The End of the Week* (Macmillan). The big city elementary school.

Saint, Dora J., *Village School* (Houghton). Experiences in a two-teacher grade school in England.

Interesting film series: *Teaching the Disadvantaged Child* (McGraw-Hill), 3 black-and-white films.

1. *Portrait of a Disadvantaged Child: Tommy Knight.* (16 min.)
2. *Portrait of the Inner City.* (17 min.)
3. *Portrait of the Inner City School: A Place to Learn* (17 min.)

Planning for the Disadvantaged Child

The program we plan for the disadvantaged child must consider the needs of the child, both psychological and curricular, and we will find that curricular needs may have to wait while more pressing psychological needs are met. Our aim, however, will be at all times to provide compensatory education for this child, and because the child has much "catching up" to do, the program we plan will be directed toward very specific goals. The course we decide to follow must represent the shortest and most effective route between the child and his present abilities and the goals to be reached. Methods and content must be carefully evaluated to determine efficiency, effectiveness, and value to the child.

[9] For additional selections, see: "Understanding the Teacher" in Iris and Sidney Tiedt, *Unrequired Reading*.

Considering our purposes, would 30 minutes of classroom time, for example, be more effectively spent in unstructured play at keeping house which involves some language usage or should we decide to spend that 30 minutes working with a language record which combines listening to English sentences and responding orally as directed? Both activities have value, but we must decide which has *more* value, for time is a commodity which we cannot afford to waste. The needs of each child must be diagnosed and an educational prescription prepared which will remedy his ills in the quickest possible manner.

Objectives of the English program

It has been pointed out that language deficiencies are so pronounced for the deprived child that it is on oral language that primary stress must be placed. Beginning activities can be planned to work toward the dual objectives of developing security in the school situation and of developing language fluency. Our objectives are listed in sequential order based on the child's needs. The final objectives will not, therefore, be met until those listed first have been at least partially achieved.

1. Development of a positive attitude toward the school, the teacher, and learning
2. Development of a self-image that includes ability to succeed and a feeling of personal worth
3. Extension of experiential background involving all the senses and including many experiences with literature as well as field trips and classroom experiences
4. Development of oral linguistic fluency and listening abilities; enjoyment of language; beginning study of English phonology
5. Development of abilities in composing through creative methods; enjoyment of language
6. Developing skills of reading which have already been introduced; sequential development of reading abilities; appreciation of literature through listening, viewing, reading

It is felt that achievement of the first four goals must begin immediately, for a positive attitude toward the school situation, a positive self-image, experiential backgrounds, and some degree of fluency in language are necessary before the skills of writing and reading will find adequate response. It is obvious, of course, that the third and fourth objectives are building foundations for both writing and reading, and that skills of composition and reading will continue to be introduced gradually as the group is ready to proceed.

It should be noted, too, that the objectives listed here are not particularly different for the disadvantaged child than they are for any child. How then is this program different from that planned for other children?

It is largely a matter of degree or emphasis. For the child of a middle class family the first three objectives would not require much special attention, for the child is prepared to like school and his teacher, and he has no reason to doubt his ability to learn to read and write. He is prepared to succeed in school. The disadvantaged child, on the other hand, lacking this assurance, must be shown that he can succeed. He needs repeated experiences which demonstrate to him and to his peers that he is able to cope wtih the school situation. He also needs, as we have pointed out, to acquire language skills as tools to assist him in succeeding with these beginning steps and with increasingly more complex learning.

Where do we begin?

We begin with the child as he exists at any grade level and at any stage of language development. We accept his abilities and inabilities, one of which is his language, which we may consider an ability although it may at the same time represent a disability in that it is probably a dialect other than standard English. Whatever the dialect, however, the teacher accepts the language of the child as a means of communicating which has been successful in the eyes of the child. Branding the child's language as being "wrong" or "unacceptable" accomplishes only adverse results—resentment, self-consciousness, fear, unhappiness, a sense of failure.

At the same time, aware of our long-term goals for improving the impoverished language abilities of each child, we direct activities and learning experiences toward achievement of the stated objectives. We provide a new environment for the elementary school student. Although initial activities may actually be directly focused on building up self-confidence and a positive attitude toward school, the child is immediately exposed to standard English as spoken by the teacher-model and her aides. The child is encouraged to begin talking about varied experiences. Instruction in composition and reading wait, for efforts to instruct are inefficient and ineffective until the child is psychologically ready. Attempts to teach the student to read, while he still resents school and the teacher, has only meager ability with the English language, and has no personal motivation for reading will surely produce definite antagonism toward reading.

The Task Force Report conducted by the National Council of Teachers of English stresses the necessity for developing abilities in oral language as the first step in helping the disadvantaged child: "Everything known about language suggests that the improvement of writing and reading must be built upon instruction in oral English. Even more obvious is the fact that if children are to develop skill in using English dialects other than their own, they need oral instruction." [10] The first school ex-

[10] NCTE Task Force Report, *Language Programs for the Disadvantaged* (Champaign, Ill.: National Council of Teachers of English, 1965).

periences for the child will be directed, therefore, toward developing oral language abilities and to meeting the psychological needs—confidence, positive attitude toward school, and an image of himself as a successful learner and a worthwhile person.

Developing positive attitudes

Both the first and second objectives involve the development of positive attitudes for the child toward (1) school and (2) himself. Just providing "more of the same" will not reach the disadvantaged child nor will it solve his problems. We need to open new doors, and the entrance may not be through the front door. We will not limit ourselves, therefore, to the formal front door entrance which is more familiar to the beginning teacher. We will go around the house trying all the doors and even peering in windows. We may unexpectedly discover an opening through art, music, or science, for the child who once begins to smile, to ask questions, to answer "Yes," is responding, and in the beginning stages it matters not to *what* he is responding, for the initial steps toward communication have been taken.

As noted, one of the most important needs of the child is the experience of success in the classroom situation. He needs (whether a five-year-old in kindergarten or a ten-year-old in third grade) to participate in many simple activities or games which are easily handled and prove enjoyable in order to develop a feeling of self-confidence, a willingness to attack more difficult tasks. What activities are particularly suitable for this stage of development? Keeping in mind our dual aims, we stress enjoyable activities that involve language abilities, too.

Playing group games which include singing or chanting of simple familiar refrains:

Young children—"A Tisket-A-Tasket"
"Farmer in the Dell"

Older children—"What's Your Trade? Lemonade!"
Jumping rope

Oral activities which stress auditory discrimination:

Which words begin alike? Which one does not?

bird   baby   teacher

Which word begins like *horse?*
hospital   apartment   spoon

Enjoying a good story together.
The teacher reads aloud, showing the illustrations as she proceeds.

Favorites with younger children include:

May I Bring a Friend?, Beatrice De Regniers
White Snow, Bright Snow, Alvin Tresselt
The 500 Hats of Bartholomew Cubbins, Dr. Seuss
Millions of Cats, Wanda Gág
Curious George, H. A. Rey
The Five Chinese Brothers, Claire Bishop

Older children will enjoy:

Charlotte's Web, E. B. White
Little Eddie, Carolyn Haywood
Henry Huggins, Beverly Cleary
We Live in the South, Lois Lenski

Films and records can also introduce excellent stories which provide topics for discussion and add to the child's experiences.

Weston Woods (Weston, Conn.) has produced films of familiar stories from children's literature, for example, "The Doughnuts" from *Homer Price* by Robert McCloskey and *Millions of Cats* by Wanda Gág. Of special interest is *A Snowy Day*, the film of a young Negro boy's adventures in the snow.

Positive reinforcement is essential to the disadvantaged child's success in school. As we teach varied content, therefore, our methods will reflect awareness of this need of the child for reassurance. It is especially important that the teacher display positive attitudes toward the child and his abilities, for he soon senses the true feelings of the adult. Specifically, we can:

1. Praise liberally and sincerely, avoiding negative criticism
2. Avoid punishment by redirecting activities
3. Maintain contact with the child
4. Modify evaluation techniques

Praise liberally and sincerely. Children respond to praise; doesn't everyone? The teacher's approval is actively sought by many children, and although it is not openly sought by those who are more reticent, it is an effective catalyst in the classroom which produces warmth and response. True praise must be dispensed in a natural, sincere manner without artificiality, but there are many opportunities in the day for the teacher to *appreciate* the students and their performances.

"Thank you for listening so attentively when Mrs. James read *Madeline*. "Would you like to have Mrs. James read you another story tomorrow?" (The whole class is happy and so is the new aide.)

"My goodness, Bill, what a nice straight back you have!" (As you pass him in a line for recess.)

"Lindy, that is the funniest clown I have seen in a long time. You must have enjoyed painting him."

"What a pretty dress, Anne. It must be your birthday."

Praise takes both direct and indirect approaches, and it can be addressed to the group or to individuals. However it is used, it adds a real feeling of warmth and congeniality to the classroom atmosphere which will lead to the concept that school is a good place to be.

Avoid punishment by redirecting activities. The teacher must be unusually perceptive to spot trouble before it really gets started. Disciplinary action is seldom necessary in the classroom, however, if the children are (1) busy with varied activities, (2) stimulated to attack the task at hand, and (3) working at a task within their capabilities.

Varied activities must be planned, for excessively long periods of doing the same thing will naturally cause fidgeting and provide time for mischief. If the group has been listening to a recorded story, don't follow this experience with another listening activity, but select an activity which permits the child to move about. Remember, too, that attention spans vary and that that of the deprived child may be especially limited.

Are the children really interested in doing the task at hand? This may be influenced by the motivating techniques used by the teacher or by the abilities of the children to do the task. The disadvantaged child may show little interest in talking about life on the farm until he has seen pictures, viewed a film, or visited a nearby dairy farm. Before he will be motivated to talk, in other words, he needs something to talk about, experiences to relate, some reason to try expressing himself. The child who is not equipped to partake will be uninterested in the discussion and may cause disturbance in order to get his measure of attention. Remember, too, the background of the disadvantaged child has not prepared him to accomplish many tasks which we would usually expect children at a specified grade level to perform.

Maintain contact with the child. The child needs to feel that the teacher as an adult really likes him and that she will take time for him as an individual. The child may need actually to touch the teacher physically and to be touched by this adult who smiles at him and seems to be interested in what he says and what he does.

A practice which we have recommended repeatedly for teachers at all levels is that of assessing daily personal contact with students with whom they are working. Is there some child to whom you did not directly speak during the day? During the last half hour of class make certain that you get to those children in some way so that for them the day spent in the classroom will have more personal meaning.

Call José to your desk to help you sort a pile of papers.

Walk past Sally's chair as you smilingly say, "You really worked hard today, Sally. Don't forget to take your story home to read to your mother."

The personal conference is a good device which also aids in maintaining direct individual contact with each child. The number of conferences per week with each child will depend on the size of the class and the number of assistants available to the teacher. The conference period (10 minutes) may be focused on needs specific to each child. When sitting with Buck at a small table, the teacher may say, for instance, "I want you to play a game with me, Buck. It's called Echo. Do you know what an echo is?" After introducing Buck to the idea of repeating what she says, the teacher may say words or phrases which contain sounds with which this child has trouble. She will not use the entire conference period for the instructional game, however, but will ask Buck questions about his activities, members of his family, and so forth as a means toward knowing the boy better, demonstrating interest in him as an individual, and perhaps most important, persuading him to talk. Conferences, designated less formally as Talking Time, may be rotated among the teacher and her aides or each adult working with the group may serve as personal consultant for a small number of students for a certain period of time, perhaps one month.

Modify evaluation techniques. Evaluation must also exemplify positive reinforcement if it is to be helpful. The familiar techniques of redpenciling a child's composition have no place in this classroom, for the disadvantaged child already has a defeated air and a certainty of failure. If it is to be effective, evaluation must be positive in nature. The child must be praised for what he *has* accomplished, not criticized for what he *did not* do. As Joubert wrote, "Children have more need of models than critics."

Nor can we measure the achievements of this child against nationally established norms provided with a commercial achievement test. His achievement must be measured for him as an individual. Where was he before he began this program? How far has he progressed during a given period of time? We need new tests more appropriate for the child who is not verbally skillful. A checklist prepared by the teacher for the specific class she is teaching may be more informative if completed at the beginning of the year and again at the end of the year's work. This checklist will reflect the skills the teacher is trying to teach, and her evaluation of each child's abilities at the end of the year will indicate the extent toward which these abilities have been taught to each child. It will also indicate the work that remains to be done so that the next teacher who works with Sam will know more clearly how to plan for him. This type of checklist does not necessarily reflect on the individual teacher's teaching ability, for there are many factors which, as we have noted, impede learning for the disadvantaged child.

The checklist in this case has been completed for a young American-Mexican girl who is cooperative, but very quiet, shy, and lacking in linguistic fluency. Completed at the beginning of the school year, this form

CHECKLIST FOR EVALUATING
STUDENT PROGRESS

Child *Marcie Garcia*

Teacher *West*

Date *9/20/6 —*

Psychological and Social Adjustment	Low 1	2	3	4	5	6	High 7
1. Ability to get along with other children			3				
2. Willingness to try new tasks			3				
3. Positive attitude toward school				4			
4. Responsiveness to teacher				4			
5. Self-discipline							7

Language Abilities

1. Interest in listening to a story			3				
2. Ability to understand story content		2					
3. Ability to distinguish sounds (auditory)		2					
4. Participation in discussion	/						
5. Ability to pronounce specific sounds		2					
6. Ability to speak sentences			3				
7. Attention span			3				
8. Interest in writing words							
9. Ability to write sentences				*not applicable*			
10. Interest in learning to read							
11. Approximate reading level							
12. Independent reading							

Specific problems:

indicates Marcie's weaknesses and at the same time the direction which instruction for this child must take. Specific information about weaknesses, for example, specific sounds which cause this child difficulty, can be noted on the back of the checklist sheet. Note also that for this child entering first grade (or the first level of an ungraded primary) the composition and reading skills have been marked "Not applicable."

Developing oral language abilities

The aim of the language program for the economically deprived child is linguistic fluency, a tool through which he can attack more complex studies. Fluency in English can be achieved through (1) developing the child's desire to talk, (2) supplying topics for discussion, and (3) providing many opportunities for speaking. During the first stages of language development we are not concerned about direct instruction in the use of standard English. The teacher, other adults in the classroom, and recordings heard by the children will present standard English which will serve as models. As new vocabulary is presented through new experiences, the child will learn through imitation to pronounce words more nearly as these models do.

How do we stimulate the child to talk? There are many techniques which may prove successful, and we shall experiment by using a variety of methods, for different children respond to different types of stimuli.

1. Humor tends to lend warmth to the classroom atmosphere. The teacher who laughs with the class will certainly break down barriers of reserve as children respond.

    ● Humorous poetry:
    Have children paint pictures of strange animals they might imagine after thinking of "The Purple Cow."

    > I never saw a purple cow;
    > I never hope to see one:
    > But I can tell you anyhow
    > I'd rather see than be one.
    >
    > GELETT BURGESS

    Use a flannel board to present figures from the anonymous repetitive poem, "There Was An Old Woman." Keep it simple at first with only a few animals, but add others as the class becomes familiar with speaking together.

    > There was an old woman who swallowed a fly.
    >
    > Class: Oh, my! Swallowed a fly?
    > Poor old woman, I think she'll die!
    >
    > There was an old woman who swallowed a bird;
    > That's what I heard; she swallowed a bird!

Class: She swallowed the bird to kill the fly;
 Oh, my! Swallowed a fly?
 Poor old woman, I think she'll die!

There was an old woman who swallowed a cat;
Think of that, she swallowed a cat!

Class: She swallowed the cat to kill the bird;
 She swallowed the bird to kill the fly;
 Oh, my! Swallowed a fly?
 Poor old woman, I think she'll die!

There was an old woman who swallowed a dog;
Jiggety, jog, she swallowed a dog!

Class: She swallowed the dog to kill the cat;
 She swallowed the cat to kill the bird;
 She swallowed the bird to kill the fly;
 Oh, my! Swallowed a fly?
 Poor old woman, I think she'll die!

(*Other verses may be invented.*)

There was an old woman who swallowed a horse!

Class (quickly): She died, of course!

● Stories that are read aloud.

Read stories aloud, showing the illustrations, explaining a word casually so children can understand, talking about the story and its characters.

> *The Fast Sooner Hound*, by Arna Bontemps and Jack Conroy.
> *Slappy Hooper, the Wonderful Sign Painter*, by Arna Bontemps and Jack Conroy.
> *Mr. Popper's Penguins*, by Richard and Florence Atwater.
> *Freddy the Detective*, by Walter Brooks.

Use finger puppets to encourage children to retell the stories heard, allowing free translation of the content. While several children manipulate puppets, the others supply guides to the development of the dialogue. What happened next? What do you think Mr. Popper might have said? In this way the whole of a small group participates. Audience and puppeteer roles rotate frequently.

● Jokes and Riddles.

Tell simple jokes and riddles. Encourage children to tell riddles that they know, and print some on the board, for children are intrigued by seeing something they told in print and will be interested in reading it, for example:

What did the wallpaper say to the wall?

"I've got you covered!"

> See: *Book of Laughs*, by Bennett Cerf
> *Riddles, Riddles, Riddles*, by Joseph Leeming.

2. Curiosity is natural to the child and can be useful in motivating speech.

CAN YOU GUESS? The teacher holds a familiar object (or a picture of one) behind her as she tells the children, "I have something you can't see. Can you guess? It starts with B."

Is it a book? No, it is not a book.
Is it a ball? No, it is not a ball.
Is it a basket? Yes, it is a basket.

This activity can be varied to stress different learning experiences which require both listening and speaking, thus:

I have something that sounds like BALL. (doll)
I have something your mother uses in the kitchen. (Pan)

Children can be guided to supply patterned responses, thus:

Is it a book? (All children will use this form for practice.)
Do you have a book? Do you have a pencil? Do you have. . . .
I think it is a book. I think it is a pencil. I think it is a. . . .

WHAT HAPPENED NEXT? Read a simple short story, stopping before the denouement to ask, "What do you think happened next?" "Did Jack get caught by the giant, Bill?" "How did he get away, Mary?" Elicit many responses before reading the ending of the story.

THE TAPE RECORDER is a fascinating machine which arouses the curiosity of all children, particularly the boys. A boy who is usually reluctant about speaking will pay for the privilege of running the machine by asking the children questions or simply calling each child to come record his story. Again, the teacher can supply patterns, thus:

It's your turn now, Jane.
Please, come tell your story now, Jane.

What color is this book, Jane?
What color is this table, Nick?
What color is this paper, Susan?

3. Emphasize the game-like qualities of any learning experience.

WHO HAS A SENTENCE? Display a large picture before the group as you ask, "Who has a sentence about this picture?" A picture of a boy and his dog might elicit this type of response:

The dog is big.
The boy likes the dog.
The boy and his dog are running.

The teacher can print each sentence on an experience chart to lend importance to the composed sentences and to provide orientation to words and reading.

SINGING GAMES AND SONGS add to the enjoyment of speaking as words are repeated with relative ease. After hearing this song a few times, children will be able to supply first the rhymed words and soon they can sing the whole song:

Quickly   Alabama Folk Song

Hush,   little___ ba - by,   Don't   say   a   word;

Ma-ma's gon-na buy   you   a mock - ing   bird;   And...

(continue)

Hush little baby, don't say a word;
Mama's gonna buy you a _____ (mocking bird).

And if that mocking bird won't sing,
Mama's gonna buy you a _____ (diamond ring).

And if that diamond ring turns brass,
Mama's gonna buy you a _____ (looking glass).

And if that looking glass gets broke,
Mama's gonna buy you a _____ (Billy goat).

And if that Billy goat won't pull,
Mama's gonna buy you a _____ (cart and bull).

And if that cart and bull turns over,
Mama's gonna buy you a dog named _____ (Rover).

And if that dog named Rover won't bark,
Mama's gonna buy you a _____ (horse and cart).

And if that horse and cart breaks down,
You'll still be the nicest boy (class) in town.

Other songs which offer excellent language practice include:

"Old MacDonald Had a Farm"
"The Farmer in the Dell"
"Go Tell Aunt Rhody"
"Are You Sleeping?"

An enjoyable record which combines words and motions is "The Hokey Pokey" which emphasizes Right and Left concepts and the parts of the body (Methodist Publishing House, 810 Broadway, Nashville 2, Tenn.).

Another interesting record is *Call and Response; Rhythmic Group Singing* by Ella Jenkins with children and instruments (Folkways/ Scholastic Records, 906 Sylvan Ave., Englewood Cliffs, N.J. 07632).

The problem of providing topics about which the child can talk is important, for the disadvantaged child's background is limited. Varied experiences lead to vocabulary development, too, as the child seeks out the needed words to talk about something he has seen or done. Experiences which are common to the whole group stimulate conversation both in and out of the classroom. What can we talk about?

1. *Pictures* are excellent, easily-obtained sources of Speech Stimulators which can be used in a variety of ways:

   Give each child a picture about which he says a few sentences as he shows the picture to the other children. These pictures can be smaller than others.

   Fasten one large picture on the bulletin board so that one small group can talk about it. They can ask questions about the pictured activity or answer questions asked by the teacher. The group can compose a story which the teacher records on tape or prints on a chart.

   A listening activity can require the child to point to something in the picture as the teacher says:

   "Can you find something yellow, Anabel?"
   "Where is the big German Shepherd, Joey?"
   "Is there a kitten in the picture, Bill?"

2. *Classroom experiences* can be planned to stimulate talking, for example:

   An animal brought to the classroom can stimulate talking, and the children can dictate a story to the teacher.

   Tommy, the hamster, is visiting our classroom.
   He will go home tomorrow.
   He likes to run and play.
   He eats seeds and carrots.

   Eating an interesting food is exciting. Try fortune cookies, crisp Chinese noodles, or pretzels.

   Recorded stories provide food for conversation, for instance, Kenneth Grahame's *The Reluctant Dragon* read by Boris Karloff or Carl Sandburg's reading of his *Rootabaga Stories* (both from Caedmon, distributed by Houghton Mifflin Co., 53 W. 43rd St., New York 10036).

3. *Field experiences* take the children out of the classroom to visit or observe things farther afield. Change in environment helps provide talking topics. Experiences might include:

   Nature walks in a nearby park or around the neighborhood to make DISCOVERIES. Children might be directed to see how many different animals they can see on this Discovery Walk or they could notice specifically all the different SOUNDS heard.

   A trip to the library serves to acquaint the children with the location of the library and to give them a chance to go inside for a Book Talk with the Children's Librarian.

Trips can be planned to varied facilities available in most areas:

Post Office
Fire Station
A museum or zoo
Airports, bus or train stations
A beach, the wharf

4. *Filmed materials* can present many interesting topics in the classroom. The short film or filmstrip, as well as slides, is useful in working with small groups who are encouraged to react to the pictures presented.

An interesting film is the wordless story, *The Hunter in the Forest* (Encyclopaedia Britannica Film Co.) which uses fine camera work to portray a sensitive story which can be discussed. The story can be told by the children.

The teacher who is aiming at developing linguistic fluency must plan a program that provides many opportunities for the *child* to talk, for our elementary school classrooms are more typically dominated by teacher talking. We can emphasize the use of oral language by:

1. Forgetting the desire for a quiet classroom
2. Encouraging children to ask questions and to react to classroom experiences
3. Using language laboratory equipment that involves listening and speaking activities
4. Working with small groups so that proportionately more children can speak at any one time
5. Planning for a high percentage of classroom time to be devoted to oral language

Beginning composition experiences

In conjunction with listening and speaking activities the teacher has consistently introduced the children to printed words as they have dictated stories, listed things seen, heard words in stories, and so forth. As their interest in classroom experiences gradually develops, many children will be ready to learn to print and to begin writing words and sentences independently. The advantage of working with small groups is again apparent, for one group may be moving much more quickly than are others; they will begin composing sentences and short stories which may form the basis of their first reading experiences.

Early experiences in composition will not emphasize grammar or spelling, but will focus on the thrill of recording an idea so that others can also share it. Beginning experiments will continue to stress the development of positive attitudes toward learning and feelings of success as a young writer. The chapters on Creativity and Creative Writing contain many suggestions which would work well with the deprived child, but here are a few we have selected as being especially suitable for these children.

Writing grows from talking. After a discussion about a picture that the group is viewing, everyone will have many ideas that can be recorded. Let each write a word, a phrase, or a sentence or two which can be mounted on strips beside the picture. Each child can "read" his own contribution.

Children enjoy rhymes. Again, begin orally with rhyming experiences as you give a word and the child says one that sounds alike. Then you can give a word (choose one which has many rhymes) and print it on the board. Ask who could print a rhyming word—a real challenge! Ignore misspellings at this stage.

After children are familiar with the making of rhymes, you can supply a short line, "Today the sun is hot," while they venture to supply a rhyming line, "Hunt for a shady spot." The poems produced should be printed on cards (by the teacher if necessary) for display and later taken home to share with parents.

Children can write their own experience stories. Instead of dictating experiences to the teacher these children will be able to write sentences to contribute to a group composition and gradually will write a story of several sentences independently. A group BOOK OF STORIES can be compiled.

Imaginative literature inspires writing. Children often like to write their responses to a story they have enjoyed hearing or seeing on film. Again, these commentaries will grow from one sentence to a paragraph or more as abilities develop.

Children can write free verse and cinquains. As children respond more freely to new experiences, they can be guided toward the writing of simple poetry. Group compositions are effective first steps toward individual writings. The month or season provides a topic familiar to all, for example, WINTER. The group talks about winter, the things they do, how it differs from other seasons; pictures may be shown. Then ideas are recorded by the teacher who prints them in poetry form, thus:

WINTER . . .
Snow falls on the street.
Children throw snowballs.
There is ice on the puddles.

The Cinquain (*Sánken*), a five-line, unrhymed poem, is a poetry form which primary children find easy to follow as the emphasis is on words or syllables: Here is an example written on the same topic:

WINTER—	(One word; the subject)
Snow falling;	(Two words about subject)
Slipping, sliding, tumbling.	(Three words describing action)
Snowball fights and sleds—	(Four words; a feeling)
DECEMBER	(One word refers to subject)

Reading and literature for the disadvantaged

As Loban notes, "Schools are beginning to be aware that research shows a powerful linkage between oral language and writing or reading —one much greater than has previously been realized." [11] Although the above strategies do not involve direct instruction in reading, therefore, we have scarcely been ignoring reading skills, for emphasis on the development of fluency in English, vocabulary growth, listening for auditory discrimination, and awareness of words are all preparing the child to read. Efforts to develop positive attitudes toward school and learning will serve to ensure the child's willingnesss to "try reading."

As with composition, reading is introduced as part of the total language experience. There is no traumatic moment when we suddenly begin to read, for experiences with language have enticed the child to begin reading as he wrote. The teacher simply takes more time to talk about words, to see that more words are placed before his eyes, and that he has opportunity to use them. Word cards become part of oral and written language experiences, and the child is encouraged to voice his ideas, to write them, and to read them. Small group work continues to facilitate assistance of individual growth as children begin to read selections from literature that they, in many cases, will have already heard or viewed, for example, Ezra Jack Keats' *Snowy Day*.

The Listening Center is extended to include books as the child reads while he listens to the sentences read by an adult voice. He can "listen-read" the same story several times, and he can try to read the story himself with assistance as needed. When he feels confident about his ability to read that story, the book goes home to be read to anybody who will listen. Thus, through the experience-literature method the child has learned to read with confidence and enjoyment. All he requires now is the availability of more good books and guidance and assistance from the teacher or aide.

Another aspect of literature for the disadvantaged child is literature as a means of understanding himself. Gradually, children's literature is reflecting concepts which society is beginning to acknowledge—all children are not white, not all families live in lovely suburban settings, few people speak standard English *all* the time. (Don't you sometimes say, "Yeah," "Whacha doin'?" "What got inta him?" and so on?) A great effort is being made toward further understanding of minority groups (even for members of the groups themselves) by the inclusion of titles which

[11] Walter Loban, "Oral Language Proficiency Affects Reading and Writing," *Instructor* (March, 1966), p. 97.

depict characters who are Negro, Mexican-American, etc. Included here is a portion of one reading list of books about American Negroes: [12]

Kindergarten through Second Grade

Beim, Lorraine, and Jerrold Beim, *Two Is A Team;* illus. by Ernest Crichlow. New York: Harcourt, 1945. $2.75. 61 pp. A simple story of friendship and cooperation between two boys which can be read independently by younger children. Only the illustrations convey the fact that one of the boys is Negro.

Keats, Ezra Jack, *Snowy Day;* illus. by author. New York: Viking, 1962. $3.00. 32 pp. Preschool and kindergarten age children will enjoy the adventures of a little Negro boy as he plays in the snow. Distinguished, colorful illustrations add to the beauty of this simple story. (Film available from Weston Woods, Weston, Conn.)

Keats, Ezra Jack, *Whistle for Willie;* illus. by author. New York: Viking, 1964. $3.50. 33 pp. Another book about the hero of *A Snowy Day.* A young child who has tried to whistle will thoroughly enjoy this beautifullly illustrated picture book.

Showers, Paul, *Look at Your Eyes;* illus. by Paul Galdone. New York: Crowell, 1962. $2.75. Through easy text and attractive illustrations, children discover, along with a young Negro boy, some of the basic facts about the function of the eyes. A beginning science book of general interest to young children.

Third through Sixth Grade

Bontemps, Arna, *Frederick Douglass: Slave, Fighter, Freeman;* illus. by Harper Johnson. New York: Knopf, 1959. $3.00. 177 pp. A vivid, dramatic account of the life of an ex-slave whose philosophy and actions continue to have great meaning in today's society.

Brooks, Gwendolyn, *Bronzeville Boys and Girls* (poems); illus. by Ronni Solbert. New York: Harper, 1956. $2.50. 40 pp. A delightful collection of poems about city children by a noted Negro poet and Pulitzer Prize winner. Delicate illustrations, especially of Negro children, capture the mood of the poetry.

Evans, Eva, *People Are Important;* illus. by Vana Earle. New York: Golden Press, 1951. $3.95. 86 pp. A factual appraisal of the world's peoples and their habits presented with a sparkling, often humorous approach.

Fritz, Jean, *Brady;* illus. by Lynd Ward. New York: Coward, 1960. $3.50. 223 pp. Excellent characterizations and a well-developed story of the underground railroad. Good supplementary reading for the study of the Civil War period.

Hughes, Langston, and Meltzer, Milton, eds., *Pictorial History of the Negro in America,* rev. ed. New York: Crown, 1963. $5.95. 337 pp. The broad panorama of the history of the American Negro, presented through excellent text and numerous photographs. Useful both for students, teachers, and many classroom libraries.

[12] Council on Interracial Books for Children, Inc. 9 E. 40th St., New York, N.Y. 10016.

McGovern, Ann, *Runaway Slave;* illus. by R. M. Powers. New York: Scholastic Book Service, 1965. 212 pp. Simple, lyric prose and sensitive illustrations capture the dignity and strength of Harriet Tubman. Although primarily for third and fourth grades, it can also be handled comfortably by the "slow" or reluctant readers.

Shotwell, Louisa R., *Roosevelt Grady;* illus. by Peter Burchard. Cleveland, Ohio: World, 1963. $2.95. 151 pp. Although some events in the lives of this Negro migrant family may not be familiar, children in both urban and suburban communities will understand and sympathize with their hopes and dreams for a permanent home.

Sterling, Dorothy, *Mary Jane;* illus. by Ernest Crichlow. Garden City, N.J.: Doubleday, 1959. $2.95. 214 pp. A sensitive portrayal of a young girl's lonely experience as one of a small group of Negroes in a junior high school that provides token integration. A realistic yet optimistic presentation which will have significance for both white and Negro children today.

An interesting class project is the development of an annotated list like the one just presented. Here is the nucleus of a bibliography on Mexican-American children which could be prepared first on cards by each individual explorer and later compiled in a useful list:

Bailey, Bernadine, *Famous Latin American Liberators.* New York: Dodd, 1960. 158 pp.

———, *Picture Book of New Mexico.* New York: Albert Whitman, 1960. 26 pp.

Blecker, Sonia, *The Aztec: Indians of Mexico.* New York: Morrow, 1963. 160 pp.

———, *The Maya: Indians of Central America.* New York: Morrow, 1961. 160 pp.

Flack, Marjorie, and Karl Larsson, *Pedro.* New York: Macmillan, 1940. 96 pp.

Goetz, Delia, *Neighbors to the South,* rev. ed. Harcourt, 1959. 179 pp.

Good, Loren, *Panchito.* New York: Coward-McCann, 1955. 160 pp.

Hogner, Dorothy C., *Children of Mexico.* Boston: Heath, 1942. 64 pp.

Kidwell, Carl, *Arrow in the Sun.* New York: Viking, 1961. 254 pp.

Lay, Marion, *Wooden Saddles: The Adventures of a Mexican Boy in His Own Land.* New York: Morrow, 1939. 175 pp.

MacDonald, Etta B. and Julia Dalrymple, *Manuel in Mexico.* Boston: Little, Brown, 1909. 118 pp.

Moon, Grace, *Tita of Mexico.* New York: Frederick A. Stokes, 1934. 213 pp.

Politi, Leo, *The Mission Bell.* New York: Scribners, 1953. 30 pp.

Rhoads, Dorothy, *The Story of Chan Yuc.* Garden City, N.J.: Doubleday, 1941. 43 pp.

Rose, Patricia, *Let's Read about Mexico.* Grand Rapids Mich.: Fideler, 1955. 160 pp.

Sawyer, Ruth, *The Least One*. New York: Viking, 1941. 89 pp.

Schweitzer, Byrd B., *Amigo*. New York: Macmillan, 1963. 41 pp.

Thomas, Margaret L., *Carlos: Our Mexican Neighbor*. Indianapolis, Ind.: Bobbs-Merrill, 1938. 189 pp.

Wilson, Barbara K., *Fairy Tales of Mexico*. New York: Dutton, 1960. 39 pp.

Witton, Dorothy, *Crossroads for Chela*. New York: Messner, 1956. 192 pp.

Organizing for an effective program

Examination of the various elements that comprise an effective program for the disadvantaged child will assist us in organizing for efficient and effective instruction which will reach our stated goals most directly.

The Teacher. Certainly the basic requisite for instructing the deprived child is a well-qualified teacher who should possess the majority of these characteristics:

1. Warm, outgoing personality
2. Sincere interest in helping the disadvantaged
3. Knowledge of child psychology
4. Knowledge of linguistics and language development
5. Ability to teach toward specific goals

Small Class. In order to facilitate the type of instruction required by the disadvantaged child it is imperative that the pupil-instructor ratios not exceed ten children per adult, for only through work in small groups will the child have adequate opportunities to speak and to develop desirable feelings of success and personal worth. Even in the storytelling situation there are distinct advantages (considering our objectives) in talking to a small group of children rather than a class of 30, for the adult is able to maintain eye contact with all the children, discuss story content with the children, and to maintain a higher degree of attention from each child.

The Ungraded Primary. The ungraded primary (and upper levels, too) provides an ideal organization for the deprived child who needs to work according to his ability and may need an extra year or more to reach the level of work usually attained by the completion of the primary years. Within the ungraded class framework, he is placed with others of similar abilities, and in some cases he even remains with the same teacher for longer than the usual one-year period.

Aides. One excellent teacher can operate to better advantage with the assistance of aides or paraprofessionals who have received some training in techniques of assisting the teacher. The trained teacher who supervises the work of several aides can provide for more children than can a single teacher operating alone. In what specific ways can the aide help the trained teacher?

1. Read aloud to a small group of children
2. Supervise play periods
3. Conduct oral language activities
4. Supervise the Listening Center
5. Give more adult attention to children
6. Serve as additional model of standard English

Who are these aides? Where can this type of help be found? An excellent source of semiprofessional help is the college student who is interested in working with disadvantaged children. The experience of working in the classroom with a superior teacher proves invaluable while at the same time the college student can really help the teacher work with the children. Another type of aide is the interested community member who might be the parent of a child in the program. The parent aide serves a unique function in promoting public relations and in interesting other parents in the purpose of the program.

Scheduling. The teacher, working with aides, must plan a flexible rotating schedule. It is usually effective if each member of the instructional staff develops a specialty and small groups of children are assigned to meet with each person at least once during the day. One aide, for example, can be familiar with the Listening Center and the equipment available so that she is responsible for that portion of the child's daily program.

An effective language program can be developed for any level, with approximately half the student school day devoted to language-centered activities. Special classrooms, Language Centers, can be developed to service two groups of students, each using the Center only half a day. Here is a sample schedule for a class of 32 children taught by a teacher and two aides. This teacher may be a language specialist who teaches two classes of students, half a day each, with the same two aides working with her. A second teacher would then work with both classes on mathematics, social science, science, art, music, and health. The 32 students work in groups of eight designated on the schedule as A, B, C, and D. Each child works at four different stations in the classroom (see the classroom design which follows) during the time spent in the Language Center.

FLEXIBLE ROTATION SCHEDULE

4 groups: 32 children in all
1 teacher, 2 aides

9:00   Large group in Laboratory

9:15   Small group sessions (8 each)

        Group A   Listening Center   Aide I
        Group B   Library   Aide I
        Group C   Language Learning   Teacher
        Group D   Oral Language   Aide II
               in Activities Room

9:40   Small group sessions 2

        C   Listening
        D   Library
        A   Language
        B   Oral Activities

10:05   Language-Play (Supervised by aides)

10:30   Large group—Language Learning (Teacher)

11:00   Small group work

        B   Listening
        A   Library
        D   Language
        C   Oral Activities

11:25   Small group work

        D   Listening
        C   Library
        B   Language
        A   Oral Activities

11:50   Lunch

The Classroom. If the emphasis of the program for the disadvantaged child is to remain on language activities, the classroom must reflect this aim. It must, for example, include areas which permit groups to speak aloud without disturbing the work of others. A Language Center like the following plan contains two soundproofed areas which can be used for reading and speaking aloud. Planned to accommodate 32 children instructed by a teacher working with two aides, this Language Center can be used by two different teachers (one in the morning; the other in the afternoon) or, as mentioned under Scheduling, one specialist who works with two classes in turn. Two aides are assigned to the Language Center full-time or these positions could be half-time, employing four different persons. The class which is not in the Language Center works in a regular classroom as they study other areas of the curriculum.

Thirty-two stations are provided equipped with both sending and receiving devices permitting the use of recorded instructional materials which include oral responses made individually. The teacher can monitor any individual child as well as address an individual or the whole group. When not in use this equipment disappears out of sight beneath the desk

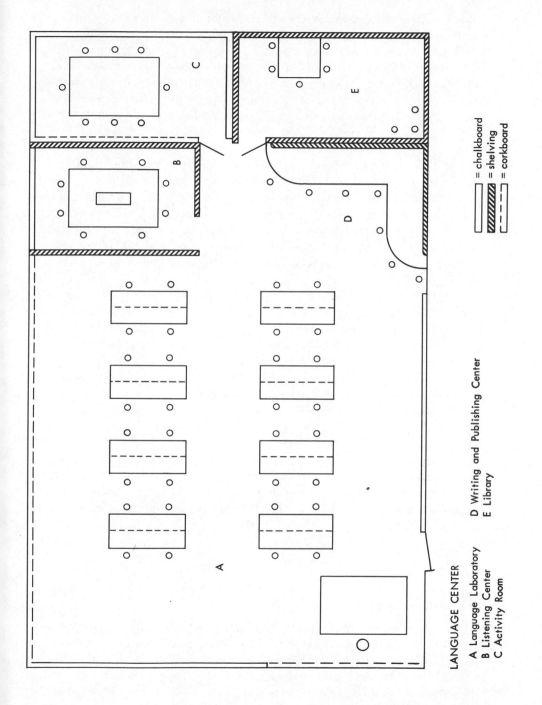

LANGUAGE CENTER

A Language Laboratory
B Listening Center
C Activity Room

D Writing and Publishing Center
E Library

= chalkboard
= shelving
= corkboard

top. The main portion of the room is, therefore, flexible in use as children write, speak, meet for group presentations (a speaker, film, a panel).

The Listening Center is designed for the use of small groups which use earphones to listen to taped stories for which books are also available. The aim of listening experiences is to provide opportunities to hear standard English by varied voices as well as to add to the child's experiential background. Teacher-taped materials can also be used for listening experiences. This center is divided from the main room by a three-foot divider which eliminates visual distractions.

The Activity Room focuses on providing additional speaking and listening experiences which develop the child's experiential background. The aide working with children in this room might, for example, use filmstrips, short films, or the flannel board to motivate speaking by children. Activities can develop into composition and reading experiences. At one end of the room is a chalkboard with a mounted screen above. This room is glassed above three feet on the classroom side with shelves and bulletin board surfaces on the other wall spaces.

The Library, which is essential to any good elementary school program, offers many titles of varied difficulty to encourage individual exploration as interest and ability develop. Children's magazines, viewing devices, and newspapers will also be included to motivate reading.

With this classroom design the teacher can work with the language laboratory equipment with both large and small groups. One aide is able to supervise the Listening Center and the Library while a second aide works in the Activity Room. This Language Center is clearly focused on the development of language abilities in their broadest ramifications— listening, speaking, writing, and reading. The best of equipment and materials will lead to an effective program which will reach our goals as rapidly as possible for each child. Although presented in a chapter directed toward working with the disadvantaged child, we realize that a Language Center would be an excellent approach for any elementary school child.

Books to Investigate

Bloom, Benjamin S., Allison Davis, and Robert Hess, *Compensatory Education for Cultural Deprivation*. New York: Holt, 1965.

Clark, Kenneth B., *Dark Ghetto*. New York: Harper, 1965.

Crosby, Muriel, *An Adventure in Human Relations*. Chicago: Follett, 1965.

The Disadvantaged Child: A Program for Action. Trenton, New Jersey: New Jersey Education Assn., 1964.

Educational Policies Commission, *Education and the Disadvantaged American*. Washington, D.C.: National Education Assn., 1962.

Harrington, Michael, *The Other America*. Baltimore: Penguin, 1962.

McGeoch, Dorothy, *et al.*, *Learning to Teach in Urban Schools*. New York: Teachers College, 1965. The experiences of beginning teachers.

NCTE Task Force Report on Teaching English to the Disadvantaged, *Language Programs for the Disadvantaged*. Champaign, Ill.: National Council of Teachers of English, 1965. Exceptionally fine resumé of programs in action.

Passow, A. Harry, ed., *Education in Depressed Areas*. New York: Teachers College, 1963.

Riessman, Frank, *The Culturally Deprived Child*. New York: Harper, 1964.

Tiedt, Sidney W., ed. *Teaching the Disadvantaged Child*. New York: Oxford, 1967. See chapters: "Developing Language Abilities," "Reading Instruction," and "Literature Learnings."

14

Innovation in English

A subject of study remains alive and stimulating only in proportion to the innovation and creative effort which is an integral part of the study. We can point out many promising practices and examples of innovation in English today which are making this subject area an exciting study.

Innovation in English occurs within the context of our American society. The trends in this society have direct influences on instruction in English as do trends in the broad field of education. Let us examine a number of these societal trends which are of a general nature yet have direct influence on the teaching of English: (1) increased population, (2) urbanization of society, and (3) rising aspiration level. Permeating these aspects of society, of course, is the all-encompassing trend of change itself, for the distinguishing characteristic of the twentieth century is CHANGE.

The population of the United States has steadily increased throughout history. In 1800, for example, the national census counted less than 5½ million people in continental United States; compared to 76 million in 1900. This is a gain of more than 70 million people. Between 1900 and 1950, only half a century, the population doubled to reach a total of 151 million, and in the following decade there was a growth of more than 25 million people as the 1960 census showed the population to be more than 178 million in coterminous United States.

As the population has increased so has the density of population, which was only 26 persons per square mile in 1900 compared to 60 in 1960. The tremendous growth in population and the resulting concentration of population in urban areas have had significant effects on all of education. Within this population explosion we note certain demographic characteristics of interest; for example, it is estimated that in 1968 the average age of Americans will be twenty-five. The heavy proportion of the population on the "young" end of the continuum exerts tremendous pressure on the schools of the nation, and it promises to have unforeseeable implications for the values of our society.

With the increase in population and centralization of population has developed a complex industrialized society. This type of society makes great demands on the educational system, for it requires an advanced type of literacy and increases the necessity to communicate in abstract ways. There is no longer "room at the bottom" in our society.

The technological revolution, automation, cybernation, and other advances will result in increased leisure for many persons as well as in a higher degree of affluence than has ever been known. Automation in education itself has just begun. Already we see the mergers of publishing companies with large firms involved in the multimedia systems to education. We notice the hardware of the technological revolution moving into the classroom: teaching machines, classroom computers, retrieval systems, television, films and filmstrips, recording devices.

The present society is also witness to a revolution in the social sphere; namely, the revolution of the downtrodden, the poverty-stricken, the minority groups. We have witnessed the civil rights movement and the War on Poverty. This rising level of aspiration has spread throughout the world and we have the Peace Corps and other forms of aid to underdeveloped or disadvantaged countries. The drive for freedom and greater opportunity is a worldwide trend with tremendous implication for education.

Another trend, almost a revolution, is the fight to alleviate poverty which exists in our wealthy nation and to compensate for its effects through education. The whole nation has become involved in assisting the educationally disadvantaged, a movement that began with the long legal battle to ensure desegregation of southern schools ending, or perhaps we should say "beginning," with the Brown Case in 1954 which concluded that segregated schools are inherently unequal. This landmark decision moved the nation to begin programs of compensatory education to remedy the years of educational neglect not only of the Negro but of other submerged segments of society as well. This movement has such significance for the teaching of English that we have devoted a chapter to "English for the Disadvantaged Child."

With the rise in group and individual aspiration has come the increased responsiveness of the federal government to the needs and demands of the citizenry. This trend is reflected in the federal government's concern for education, evidenced in the passage of massive education legislation. "The Great Society" concept led to the passage of the Economic Opportunity Act of 1964, for example, which initiated the Head Start program, an attempt to provide compensatory education before the child enters school in first grade. The passage of such education acts as the Elementary and Secondary Education Act of 1965 gave the 89th Congress the well-deserved name of the Education Congress.

Trends in Education

Woodring states that most recent reforms in education have been due to social and political pressures and to discontent with the present education system.[1] Since the launching of Sputnik in 1957, the trend nationwide has been one of questioning and questing as we have asked whether what we are accomplishing educationally is sufficient and whether there might not be better ways. This concern has led to many innovations in education, for education mirrors the culture. Reflecting the trend toward change, Shaw notes, "School curricula have changed more in the past ten years than in any other decade of our national history." [2] Let us examine a selected number of the more important changes that have been taking place in education:

1. Raising of standards
2. Involvement of academicians in curriculum
3. Trickle down of content
4. Flexibility of organization
5. Centralization of effort

We might note that no trend develops in a vacuum. Broad societal trends affect educational trends and these trends affect emergent practices in all fields of study, including English. It is for this reason that we must be cognizant of the context of society and the field of education within which English operates.

Raising of standards

The raising of educational standards has the effect of raising standards throughout the schools as well as of extending education both upward to college and downward into preschool programs such as Head Start.

[1] Woodring, Paul, "Reform Movements from the Point of View of Psychological Theory," *Theories of Learning and Instruction,* Sixty-third Yearbook, National Study Society for the Study of Education (Chicago: University of Chicago Press, 1964), pp. 286-305.
[2] Frederick Shaw, "The Changing Curriculum," *Review of Education Research* (June, 1966), p. 343.

In 1966, for example, the Educational Policies Commission recommended that schools begin educating children at the age of four. This influential group feels that an early beginning, which was initially used for compensatory education, is beneficial for all children.

Our concern for the quality of education has led to a longer school day, in some cases an extended week, and a lengthened school year. Raising standards also has the effect of increasing the years required for teacher preparation. To assist in the improvement of teacher education the federal government established an institute program under the National Defense Education Act (Title IX) which now covers almost all fields of the elementary school program. Title III of this act allows districts to buy supplies and equipment and to be reimbursed at the rate of $.50 per dollar. This plan has made possible the purchase of language laboratory equipment as well as films, records, and reference books which can be of direct assistance to the teacher of English. The government's aid to the purchase of library resources and other instructional materials was further extended under the Elementary and Secondary Education Act of 1965, Title II.

Involvement of academicians in curriculum

Academic specialists have increasingly become involved in the development of elementary school curriculum. Their involvement has been in terms of the writing of texts and the preparation of materials as well as work with teachers and school districts. In general this involvement has proved beneficial, resulting in better quality text materials and new methods of instruction.

The inquiry method, for example, stems from the idea of Jerome Bruner that future scientists should learn science by doing the work that scientists do. This discovery method has been utilized in all fields of study including English. In English we find linguistic scholars concerned with teaching linguistics to children, and we find linguists involved in preparing texts which present modern concepts of grammar and usage, for example, that by Paul Roberts (Harcourt) which begins with grade three.

Trickle down of content

One of the most pervasive trends in American education is the movement of content from higher levels to lower levels. In each of the content areas there is a tendency to introduce ideas and concepts earlier. This movement has been most pronounced in mathematics, as first graders talk of sets and equivalence. Economics and sociology, which were formerly reserved for college instruction, are now being taught in many high schools. Foreign languages, formerly allocated to the high school and college, moved into the junior high school and currently are being taught in most elementary schools.

Within the elementary school itself we find concepts introduced at earlier levels in all subject areas. The concept of readiness has come under attack as we find that students can handle more complex abstract thought than we had conceived. Primary level children are absorbing concepts of space science. Children of all ages are delving into research and independent study as they reach out for information to satisfy their desire to know.

Flexibility of organization

We see many examples of flexibility in educational organization and scheduling—team teaching, classrooms which can be changed in size, arrangements for individual study, and materials for individualized learning. The individual student is being given more freedom and more opportunity for self-education and self-exploration through tutorial programs and through the use of programmed instruction. In some cases individual students are encouraged to develop their own creative efforts through exploring a topic or idea individually.

"Providing for individual differences" has become almost a cliché in educational circles, but at this juncture we are trying to do just that in terms of methods, materials, and administrative arrangements. The teacher is spending less time in front of the class while the student takes the initiative in learning.

All learning does not take place in the classroom, therefore, for the library is providing study corrals and listening corners for student use as they conduct research and engage in creative efforts.

Centralization of effort

Like society, education has moved toward fewer, but larger districts and schools. The only number in education that has been going down has been the number of school districts, which represents a consolidation of districts.

Another example of this tendency toward centralization is the educational plaza or park, a plan whereby all the school buildings of a community (elementary, junior high, high school, vocational, adult education, junior college) are located on one central campus. In a large city several campuses are developed. This challenging idea offers many possibilities for combining efforts toward effective education. Staff members can be exchanged among the schools for the more efficient use of specialists. An audio-visual center eliminates expensive duplication of equipment as does a central library used by all schools.

Trends in the Teaching of English

What trends can be noted in English instruction at the elementary school level? In what direction is English moving? What efforts are being made to upgrade the teaching of English? In selecting the more important trends to be included here several criteria were used, for so many changes have been taking place in education that it is difficult, perhaps impossible, to assess all the many movements in one field.

The intent, therefore, of this chapter is to examine some of the newer, more significant, and more promising innovations in the field of English as it relates to the elementary school. To be included, a trend must have some geographic spread and must have appeared in the literature, for these ideas are not just newly created by fertile brains but represent movements that have made substantial contribution to the field of elementary education.

Linguistics

Certainly the most far reaching and important of all the influences in the field of contemporary English is that of linguistics. It is so important that we have devoted a chapter to exploring "Linguistics and The Study of Language," which probes the implications of this field of study for elementary school education.

Linguistics developed as a science through the efforts of such men as Leonard Bloomfield, whose book, *Language,* was published in 1933. The science developed as a method of noting and recording languages, some of which had existed only in spoken form and often had a structure that was different from the languages traditionally studied by philologists. Many linguists, for example, studied the language of the American Indian and sought to discover and record as accurately as possible the spoken language of the group. Linguistics, then, is not a new science although its application to English and its introduction into the elementary school classroom is a trend of the sixties.

What does this study of language have to do with the teaching of English? First of all it subsumes a different attitude toward language, particularly toward English grammar. It attempts to eradicate that self-righteous approach to grammar which Hans Guth notes: "Traditionally, the teacher had treated the schoolroom grammar as if it had been created on the eighth day." Traditional grammar, based on that of Latin and Greek, has been criticized on at least two counts. (1) it forced English into a Latin mold and (2) it tended to define terms on a "notational" or "meaning based" system; for example, a verb was defined as a word that expresses action, but so do words that are clearly not verbs, as *action* itself or *movement*. The linguist moved away from this grammar and examined the English language itself, basing the new grammar on English word forms and word order.

The linguist approaches usage with a more liberal and liberating attitude. Since linguists conceive of the spoken language as the primary language, the spoken word is given increased importance. Another contribution of linguistics has been the conception of language as constantly changing, with the understanding that change does not represent deterioration. The linguists have contributed a breath of fresh air to the study of English with their stress on appropriateness as a criterion of acceptable usage rather than rigid concepts of "rightness" and "wrongness."

The promises of linguistics are many although instruction in modern grammar is only recently influencing elementary school curricula, and it will be some time before all teachers accept these "radical" departures from traditional procedure. New approaches to the study of English as a living language promise to make language study exciting and challenging to modern students, not just a required subject they "have to take."

Media

Second in order of importance only to the influence of linguistics would be that of new media. The English curriculum has made less use of technological advances than have other fields, but it remains only for English teachers and educators to see the possibilities of new media for English.

Computers can grade papers, keep records, translate languages, and they can program learning.

Tape recorders are all-purpose machines which will record lessons for presentation, assist with oral pattern practice, replay a speech, permit evaluation of oral language, teach listening.

Videotape machines will capture a school performance so that it can be reviewed or replay a television program at a more convenient time.

Television permits large group instruction (even across the country) and makes full use of an expert who can speak to many students at one time; it helps the teacher teach subjects by presenting information visually and orally to supplement text presentations.

Records of books, stories, and poetry add to the study and enjoyment of literature; specially prepared records aid the study of dialectology and vocabulary development.

Transparencies used with overhead projectors assist the presentation of information about language, poetry, any subject; transparencies of student themes can quickly be made for purposes of group evaluation; overlays permit the supplying of answers to a test or a word game or aid in showing students how to expand a basic sentence pattern.

Programmed instruction can be in booklet form or a machine which will "wash the dirty dishes" for the English teacher by teaching spelling, usage, punctuation, and vocabulary. It helps individualize instruction.

Tele-lectures bring any person in the United States into your classroom at a prearranged time; students can question the expert.

Duplicating facilities have been improved to permit the preparation of a ditto master and a transparency at the same time.

Wireless listening techniques provide each student with a receiver (usually mounted on his head) through which he receives messages from a coil which encircles the room.

A Listening Center combines listening with reading as children use earphones to hear a story while they follow the book in their hand.

Films can present a book, information about authors, background information for literature, or motivation for poetry writing experiences. New loop films can be operated by any child and can be viewed individually or projected on a screen for group viewing.

Filmstrips and slides can be animated and used to present any concepts about language, poetry, literature. Used in combination with records or tape they present possibilities for use by individuals or groups.

If you include books in the category of media, one of the most interesting trends is that of the paperback edition. Paper editions have been used for many years on the college level, and for several years they have pre-empted the high school literature anthology. Now we find the paperback book moving into the elementary school as teachers, administrators, and parents recognize the advantages of these inexpensive editions of good literature. Children are encouraged to purchase books for personal libraries through the establishment of bookstores in the school itself.

Paraprofessionals

The use of teacher aides, lay readers, or paraprofessionals represents a trend toward utilizing a type of semiskilled person with perhaps junior college education who is able to handle some of the more routine matters of the instructional program. The following are tasks which can be performed by the paraprofessional:

grading tests
reading student writing
preparing duplicated material
working with reading groups
telling or reading stories
giving individual help during writing
operating varied media

School districts are utilizing paraprofessionals to assist in the education of the disadvantaged child. Here they are employed to help youngsters with language deficiencies by talking to and with them or listening as children work with oral pattern practice. The aide facilitates work with smaller groups than would be possible with a teacher working alone.

In his book *Careers for the Poor,* David Reissman advocates hiring persons from the disadvantaged community as aides, which not only provides a job that is needed but also helps develop good public relations for the educational program in the community which may show some resistance.

The addition of a semiskilled person in the classroom to work with a trained teacher may change the role of the teacher. The classroom teacher must develop administrative abilities to coordinate the learning experiences and must learn to delegate part of the classroom work to another person. He becomes a type of internist who diagnoses educational ills and prescribes a remedy or refers the patient to a specialist. We can see this role of the teacher extending so that specialized functions are developed requiring different levels of ability—paraprofessional, assistant teacher, classroom teacher, supervising teacher.

Earlier introduction of content in English

More and more, faster and faster, seems to be the trend in all areas of the curriculum, and English is no exception. This movement has come about for three reasons. One, we have become increasingly aware of the vast amounts of knowledge that have been created in the last few years, so we feel pressured to get started as soon as possible on the teaching of this content. Primary level children will be learning the concepts of linguistics through sentence pattern practice and expansion of basic patterns.

Secondly, we have found through research, for example, the study of children's language by Ruth Strickland at Indiana University,[3] that students are more aware of the world they live in and have a greater vocabulary than had been assumed by previous authorities. How can we explain this increased background? The greater affluence in our society accounts for cultural activities and travel. More books are available, and that much maligned medium, television, deserves much credit for improving the modern child's vocabulary.

Third, involvement of subject matter specialists in curriculum making has provided a fresh point of view on what students can learn. Bruner's contention that we can teach any subject to a child has been followed by many. These scholars have not been inhibited in their thinking by what "can be done" and what "can't be done" or what "has always been done." Many scholars working with children have expressed the opinion, furthermore, that young people are the most intellectually curious element

[3] Ruth Strickland, "The Language of Elementary School Children: Its Relationship to the Language of Reading Textbooks and the Quality of Reading of Selected Children," *Bulletin of the School of Education,* Indiana University, Vol. XXXVIII, No. 4 (July, 1962), 1-131.

in our population, and they stress the importance of stimulating this curiosity.

Fourth, new media have been developed to make it physically possible for very young students to learn. The most intriguing use of media is that of pioneering Omar Khayyam (O.K.) Moore who is working on the premise that youngsters two and three years old can read and write. His approach to this problem has been the "talking typewriter," which consists of a regular typewriter with a standard (nonjamming) keyboard, colored keys, a speaker, and a frame on which printed material can be shown complete with a pointer, a projector, and a dictation machine. This set-up is called a Responsive Environments Laboratory. When the child strikes a key, the letter appears on the frame and the letter is pronounced. The child, through exploration, discovers letter patterns and words.

The effect of this trend is already clear: (1) to introduce reading at an earlier age, (2) to expect more of students at each level, and (3) to present more advanced content at each level of the elementary school. One area of content which has recently been introduced in the elementary school is foreign language instruction, which we shall discuss in the next section.

Instruction in foreign languages

Foreign language instruction in the elementary school resulted from our national "interest" and our concern that we were perpetrating a "language gap" that could prove almost as disastrous as the "space gap." The original National Defense Education Act of 1958 included foreign languages as an area to be stressed together with mathematics and science.

A theory that strengthened this movement to include foreign language in the elementary school curriculum is that children are natural imitators and thus are able to learn a foreign language easily and early. Their lack of inhibition and their flexibility are also elements that help them learn languages.

The inclusion of this new subject in the elementary school curriculum raises some vital questions. If foreign language comes in, what goes out? What effect will this early instruction have on the upper levels? Are provisions being made for scope, sequence, and articulation? Where will well-qualified teachers be found?

The teaching of foreign language in the elementary school represents a trend in methodology and materials as well as content. The audio-lingual or aural-oral approach follows the theory that we learn the spoken form of language first and that we learn through listening and speaking. The sequence in learning follows that theory: hear the word, say it, read it, and write it. In the audio-lingual approach the student is learning the structure of the language without really knowing that he is learning structure just as we learn the grammar of our native language. The traditional method of teaching grammar deductively with rote memorization of rules, conjugation of verbs, and emphasis on reading and writing has been replaced by a more realistic approach to language which teaches the child to communicate in the language.

To demonstrate the extent to which this trend has permeated the elementary curriculum we note that in 1965-1966 an estimated 4 million students in elementary school were studying a second language, usually Spanish or French. By contrast, in 1953 only 145,600 pupils were studying a second language.

Inquiry or discovery method

One of the most exciting ideas to come on the English horizon is the inquiry, or discovery, method. Briefly, the inquiry methods is an approach which encourages student generation of theories or generalizations from data which they collect or which is presented to them. The steps of the approach involve:

1. Observation of data
2. Discovery of elements
3. Generalization
4. Testing of generalization
5. Possible modification of the generalization

This process is similar to John Dewey's five steps to problem solving.

An example of the inductive method in English might teach children about Haiku poetry in this manner. The students are first presented with a duplicated sheet of examples of Haiku. After studying these examples, students observe the characteristics of this poetry form, for example:

> Each poem contains three lines.
> The lines do not rhyme.
> Each poem refers to nature.
> The lines follow the same pattern.

These and any other observations are written on the board for future reference as students perhaps explore other examples to check their generalizations. They can be led to discover the specific syllabic pattern also.

The deductive method, a more commonly used teaching strategy, would teach students about this poetry form through a presentation by the teacher. The students would be told rather than guided to "discover." The advantages of the inquiry method are the following:

1. The student is involved in learning through questioning, researching.
2. It develops the questioning attitude and the ability to probe, to investigate, to ask intelligent questions.

3. Emphasis is on the process of acquiring knowledge rather than on storage of knowledge.

4. Focus remains on thinking rather than on rote memorization.

5. The student has a chance to develop his own potency; he develops confidence in his ability.

6. The student finds that there is still much to discover and much to create.

7. Intuitive thinking abilities are developed and encouraged.

New alphabets

There have been repeated attempts to produce simplified alphabets which would eliminate the confusing elements of the English language. These efforts have been aimed at simplifying spelling by providing a one-to-one correspondence between sound and letter by increasing the alphabet symbols to around 40 which include some of the present symbols plus others which are assigned to specific sounds. With spelling difficulty removed, it is pointed out, children can then write any word they know (and even those they hear, but do not know). They can both encode and decode the language with less effort.

The most recent of the new alphabets is the "Augmented Roman" or, as it has been more recently called, the Initial Teaching Alphabet. ITA consists of 44 symbols which represent the common phonemes of the English language. In some cases the symbols are the same as in the traditional alphabet, but others have been invented. Note that an effort has been made to use symbols which resemble the grapheme in traditional orthography (T.O.).

Although these alphabets have not been widely used, they do show some promise. The Initial Teaching Alphabet is currently beginning to be accepted by a number of districts which are looking for an answer to problems of reading instruction. The hope in these approaches is that the correspondence between phoneme and grapheme will free the child to write without fear of misspelling words. It also permits the use of a more extensive and more interesting vocabulary than is used with most beginning reading material. The Initial Teaching Alphabet is discussed in greater detail as a reading method in Chapter 11.

English for the disadvantaged

As much a concern as a trend is the problem of improving the teaching of English to the disadvantage child. Action on the part of the federal government through the War on Poverty program and more specifically through the Elementary and Secondary Education Act, Titles I, II, and III have given this problem area financial muscle.

One of the most successful efforts of the Office of Economic Opportunity has been the Head Start program, which is basically an attempt to compensate for the impoverished language and lack of experiential background or as Deutsch terms it, "stimulus deprivation," in the home of the disadvantaged child. There are, of course, other aims, such as providing the child with a positive image toward himself and toward school.

In the 1964 extension of the National Defense Education Act teachers in disadvantaged areas were included in the NDEA Institute program. Thus they were provided with a special type of training for their work. The needs of these youngsters are primarily and desperately in the field of English—speaking, writing, reading. As noted in the *Review of Educational Research:* "Language instruction has been commonly accepted as an area of curriculum to be given priority in dealing with the culturally disadvantaged." [4] The National Council of Teachers of English in its Task Force Report on *Teaching English to the Disadvantaged* has performed a real service by reporting some of the more important and successful programs in English.

Another problem for many, if not most, disadvantaged youngsters is their dialect. This is not necessarily a problem unless the teacher sees the correction of the child's dialect as her prime function. Dr. Loban and others have advocated allowing the child to use his own dialect when he enters school making no effort to "convert" him to standard English until he has already had much successful school experience and is ready to be taught standard English as another dialect of English, one which society accepts as the educated form of English.

Out of our great, genuine concern for the disadvantaged child and related experimentation are coming some exciting methods and approaches for the teaching of English. Inadvertently, work in compensatory education has focused attention on the importance of methodology in instruction. Teaching the disadvantaged child requires superior teaching skills to reach the child who is unable to meet the teacher's expectations. All the skills of the teacher are called upon to *teach*—to motivate, to explain, to challenge, to modify attitudes, to encourage.

Techniques of the audio-lingual approach in foreign language, for example, pattern practice, are being used to help youngsters learn the standard English dialect. Some of the approaches used to teach English as a second language are aiding the bilingual children, for emphasis is on oral methods as in the teaching of other foreign languages.

Creativity and English

Recent research in the field of creativity has had an important influence on the English curriculum and methods of instruction, specifically in composition. Teachers have found that, like children's art, children's

---

[4] Margaret B. Parke, "Teaching Materials and Their Implementation," *Review of Educational Research* (June, 1966), p. 383.

writing represents a fresh view of the world, and there has continued to be much interest in motivating "creative writing" which has proved pleasurable and successful.

Torrance, a leading researcher in creativity, points out that:

> Everyone possesses to some degree the ability involved in being creative, that these abilities can be increased or decreased by the way children are treated, and that it is a legitimate function of the home and the school to provide the experiences and guidance which will free them to develop and function fully.[5]

Writers in the field of creativity, for example, Torrance, Taylor, and Guilford, have been influential in changing attitudes toward evaluation of student writing. They have tended to liberate the teacher from concentration on detailed marking of all procedural mistakes made by the student in favor of appreciating the ideas expressed. This approach leads to stress of positive reinforcement rather than the negative carping which has been characteristic of so much of our grading of student effort.

Trends for the future?

We have devoted the major section of this chapter to a description of the most influential innovations in contemporary English. Now we would like to list a few emergent practices which we would like to see become trends to be reported when this book is revised five years from now.

- *Better coordination and articulation of the various parts of the English program.* There is, for example, generally no pattern or sequence to the poetry program in the elementary school, and there is little articulation in the teaching of English from the elementary school to the college.

- *Changed attitude toward the elementary English program.* We need more research, more institutes, more money spent on English in the elementary school. The field, including the professional organizations, is dominated by college and high school interests. One concrete example is the scarcity of NDEA institutes designed for the elementary school teacher of English. There has been a tendency instead to include the elementary teacher under a program oriented toward secondary and college methods and materials.

- *A better job of teaching the less able student in English.* James Squire's study of high school English departments [6] found a discrepancy in the teaching of honors groups contrasted to groups of poorer students. Even when the same teacher was involved this discrepancy was found. There is a tendency, too, for the better teacher to want to teach the top groups rather than those which contain reluctant learners.

[5] E. Paul Torrance, *Guiding Creative Talent* (Englewood Cliffs, N.J.: Prentice-Hall, 1962).

[6] James Squire, Speech before the National Council of Teachers of English at the ASCD Conference, March, 1966.

● *An improvement in elementary school libraries.* As Commissioner of Education, the first education law we would recommend would require every elementary school to have a library with personnel and books as recommended by the American Library Association. We cannot have superior elementary school programs without well-developed libraries to permit individual study and research.

● *Unity in the elementary school English program.* Whether we ascribe to a trichotomy—Language, Literature, Composition—or a number of different subjects or a language-centered program, there is a need for development of contemporary programs of English which consider scope, sequence, and articulation.

● *More time spent on teaching literature.* Both poetry and prose should be taught as an integral part of the curriculum, with elementary children coming to know the qualities of good literature through reading and examining it. Literature study and composition can be closely coordinated as children develop vocabularies, encounter provocative ideas, and enjoy the work of the skilled author. They can be introduced to mature concepts of genres, symbolism, imagery, and poetic devices which will be studied in greater depth later.

● *Efficient use of time.* The amount of time we have to spend on teaching has limits. For this reason we must constantly evaluate instruction to determine if we are teaching the most important content and if we are using the most effective methods. We must be critical of our own efforts on behalf of the children we teach, for the demands of our society make it imperative that we not waste time.

● *An improved image for English.* Too often English is thought of as a feminine area of study, too precise and precious for masculine manipulation. We must strive to dispel this "old-maidish" image by drawing more men into the field of teaching English and by pointing out that poets, writers, linguists, and many professors of English are men. We must strive, too, to make English something boys can enjoy. Stress on ideas, use of new teaching technology, and teaching of linguistic approaches to English should help to emphasize the exciting content of English and to remove emphasis from comma correcting and picayune points of "wrong" usage.

● *Alleviation of the English lag.* We must work to close the gap between English and other curriculum areas. English has lagged far behind science and mathematics in producing new methods and materials and in leading the way in elementary school education. To corroborate the existence of this lag we can cite Goodlad's *School Curriculum Reform* (1964) which describes recent curriculum research projects. A crude, but meaningful, index of activity in each of the curricular areas is the number of pages devoted to each in this report and the proportionate number of studies:

	Total pages	Number of studies
Science	19	10
Mathematics	10	8
Social Science	5	5
English	2	2
Foreign Languages	½	1

● *Effective research of English education.* There are many areas of English instruction about which we still know relatively little. We need more research of composition, the teaching of modern grammar, practices in teaching reading, and in developing oral English skills. We must also disseminate this knowledge and assist the elementary teacher in putting theory into practice.

Books to Investigate

De Grazia, Alfred, and David Sohn, eds., *Revolution in Teaching.* New York: Bantam, 1964.

Drucker, Peter F., *Landmarks of Tomorrow.* New York: Harper, 1957.

Jewett, Arno, and Charles E. Bish, eds., *Improving English Composition.* NEA-Dean Langmuir Project. Washington, D.C.: National Education Assn., 1965. Informative reports by those who participated in this study.

Miles, Matthew B., ed., *Innovation in Education.* New York: Bureau of Publications, Teachers College, 1964.

McLuhan, Marshall, *Understanding Media.* New York: McGraw-Hill, 1964. A new conception of media in our society.

Shugrue, Michael F., and George Hillocks, Jr., eds., *Classroom Practices in Teaching English.* Champaign, Ill.: National Council of Teachers of English, 1965. Third of a series of articles about classroom experiences—promising Practices Committee.

Tiedt, Sidney W., *The Role of the Federal Government in Education.* New York: Oxford University Press, 1966. An analysis of the government's influence in education.

Index